Problems of Chronology in Gandhāran Art

Proceedings of the First International Workshop of the Gandhāra Connections Project, University of Oxford, 23rd-24th March, 2017

Edited by
Wannaporn Rienjang
Peter Stewart

ARCHAEOPRESS ARCHAEOLOGY

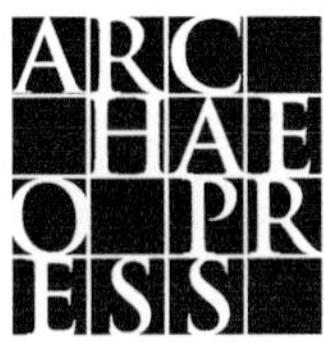

Archaeopress Publishing Ltd
Summertown Pavilion
18-24 Middle Way
Summertown
Oxford OX2 7LG

www.archaeopress.com

ISBN 978 1 78491 855 2
ISBN 978 1 78491 856 9 (e-Pdf)

Printed in England by Holywell Press, Oxford

This book is available direct from Archaeopress or from our website www.archaeopress.com

Contents

Acknowledgements

The editors would like to thank all of the participants in the Gandhāra Connections workshop of March 2017, including members of the audience and those who took part in the discussions without contributing papers to this volume.

Our intention to make the published proceedings of the workshop available as quickly as possible – within a year – and to the widest possible audience, has been facilitated by the kind cooperation of the authors involved, in the face of heavy, competing commitments. We are especially grateful to David Davison of Archaeopress for his flexibility and *sang-froid* in respect to simultaneous physical and online publication within such a tight schedule, and to Vanda Stachan for voluntarily taking on the task of additional proof-reading and corrections.

Above all we wish to express our sincere gratitude to the Bagri Foundation and to Neil Kreitman, whose generous and warm support has made the Gandhāra Connections project possible.

Note on orthography

The editors have aimed for consistency in orthography and use of diacritics, as well as some other conventions, throughout this book. We have endeavoured to apply a reasonable compromise between widely varying practices, but have permitted exceptions in certain cases, where an individual author has particular reasons for applying variant spellings.

Contributors

Stefan Baums is lead researcher of the Buddhist Manuscripts from Gandhāra project at the Bavarian Academy of Sciences and Humanities, and teaches Sanskrit, Pali, and Prakrit language and literature at the University of Munich. His research focuses on early Buddhist manuscripts and inscriptions, and on the linguistic description of Gāndhārī. His recent publications include a new corpus and translation of Gandhāran relic inscriptions, and the ongoing *Dictionary of Gāndhārī*.

Kurt Behrendt is an associate curator of South Asia at the Metropolitan Museum of Art. He has done more than half dozen exhibitions including *Buddhism along the Silk Road* (2012) and on topics related to the Himalayas and Indian painting. He has published widely on Gandhāra including *The Buddhist Architecture of Gandhāra* (2004) and *The Art of Gandhara in the Metropolitan Museum of Art* (2007).

Robert Bracey is responsible for South and Central Asian coins at the British Museum. His main interests include the history of the Kushan period and numismatic theory. He currently works with the ERC-funded Beyond Boundaries project (609823).

Joe Cribb is former Keeper of Coins and Medals at the British Museum, where he worked for forty years (1970–2010). He is also an Honorary Research Associate of the Ashmolean Museum. He is a specialist in the monetary history of Asia and has published catalogues on Chinese ingots and Javanese coin charms in the British Museum and Kushan coins in the American Numismatic Society, New York. His current research is focused on the ancient coinages of Pakistan, Afghanistan, and northern India.

Anna Filigenzi is a lecturer at the University of Naples 'L'Orientale'. Since 1984 she has been a member of the ISMEO Italian Archaeological Mission in Pakistan and since 2003 the director of the Italian Archaeological Mission in Afghanistan. She has published and taught extensively on Indian and Central Asian archaeology and art history.

Ciro Lo Muzio is Associate Professor of Indian and Central Asian Archaeology and Art History at the Sapienza University of Rome. From 1995 to 2009 he was a member of the Italian-Uzbek archaeological mission in the Bukhara oasis, Uzbekistan. Much of his work has been devoted to the iconography of pre-Islamic Central Asia and Gandhāra, especially the origins of wall-painting in this region and the diffusion of imagery into Central Asia from the classical world, Iran, and India.

Luca M. Olivieri is director of the ISMEO Italian Archaeological Mission in Pakistan. He has been working in Swat for more than thirty years. His main long-lasting project is the ongoing excavations at the urban site of Bazira/Barikot. His principal interests include excavation and heritage management methodologies. In 2017 he was awarded with the *Sitara-i-Imtiaz* of Pakistan for his three decades of archaeological work in Swat.

Juhyung Rhi is Professor of Buddhist Art History at Seoul National University. He specializes in Buddhist art, mainly focusing on early South Asia and Korea. He has written extensively on diverse aspects of Gandhāran Buddhist art and also worked on the relationship between South Asia and East Asia with a particular attention to East Asian pilgrims to India.

Wannaporn Kay Rienjang is Project Assistant of the Gandhāra Connections Project at the Classical Art Research Centre, Oxford. She completed her doctoral degree in Archaeology at the University of Cambridge on Buddhist relic cult in Afghanistan and Pakistan. Before starting her PhD, she worked as a research assistant for the Masson Project at the Department of Coins and Medals, the British Museum. Her research interests include the art and archaeology of Greater Gandhāra, Buddhist studies, and working technologies of stone containers and beads.

Peter Stewart is Director of the Classical Art Research Centre and Associate Professor of Classical Art and Archaeology at the University of Oxford. He has worked widely in the field of ancient sculpture. His publications include *Statues in Roman Society: Representation and Response* (2003) and *The Social History of Roman Art* (2008). Much of his research concerns the relationship between Gandhāran art and Roman sculpture.

Monika Zin studied art history, Indology, and drama at Krakow and Munich and taught Indology at LMU Munich's Institute for Indology and Tibetology until 2016. Her numerous books and articles have dealt with a wide range of subjects, from the paintings of Ajanta to narrative art in ancient south India and Indian drama. Since 2016 she has been leading the team of the Research Centre 'Buddhist Murals of Kucha on the Northern Silk Road' at the Saxon Academy of Sciences in Leipzig.

Introduction

Wannaporn Rienjang and Peter Stewart

In 2016 the Classical Art Research Centre at the University of Oxford launched a three-year project entitled 'Gandhāra Connections', which has been generously supported by the Bagri Foundation and the Neil Kreitman Foundation.[1] Its aim is to stimulate and support fresh research and discussion on unresolved problems in the study of Gandhāran art, and in particular the long debated question of the links between Gandhāran and Graeco-Roman artistic traditions. During the consultation process that laid the foundation for the project, a variety of scholars with interests in Gandhāra made the same observation: that several fundamental topics needed renewed attention in the light of recent research, as a precondition for understanding classical connections with Gandhāran art and many other matters besides. At the forefront of their minds was the problem of the chronology of Gandhāran art and archaeology. Chronology therefore provided the focus of the first international workshop of the Gandhāra Connections project, hosted in Oxford on 23rd and 24th March 2017, on which this volume is based.

Chronology is far from being a new concern in Gandhāran studies. Indeed it has been one of the most consistent obstacles to the understanding of Gandhāran art since its rediscovery in the nineteenth century. But intense study in recent years has led to important new insights, which deserve to be tested against a continually expanding body of published archaeological evidence. This volume presents and builds upon modern hypotheses in the context of archaeological discoveries in the region.

Two problematic aspects of its chronology are addressed here. The first is the paucity of absolute dates in the history and archaeology of Gandhāra as compared even with other ancient societies that have to be explored through fragmentary evidence. A consequence of this lack of fixed points for art history is that the dating of individual artefacts is usually only provisional. Proposed, or feasible, dates can commonly differ by two centuries or encompass wide spans (for example, '*c*. second-third century AD'). It has been hard to win from such temporally mobile material a secure sense of the artistic development of sculptures – to construct the sort of chronological framework that is so fundamental in many other fields of ancient art and archaeology.

The art history of the classical world – to use a closely relevant example – is not without such latitude in dates, and the highly conservative and retrospective character of the Roman artistic tradition – a character which we also encounter in certain categories of Gandhāran art – can undermine attempts at dating on the basis of style. Yet here the apparatus available for trying to place individual works chronologically is much more extensive. It is built on a much greater wealth of material from systematic and well recorded excavations that include datable evidence; many more inscriptions on works of art or relevant to them; abundant literary evidence (including annalistic histories); historical knowledge about the circumstances in which some monuments were made, used, or destroyed; and a comparatively tightly dated numismatic corpus. All of these types of evidence also exist for the Gandhāran region, but they are much sparser. A huge proportion of extant Gandhāran art is without archaeological provenance. It largely comprises sculptures recovered without documentation over generations, whether through crude, earlier excavations, deliberate looting, or as the result of more casual finds which have ended up

[1] The University of Oxford's OUP John Fell Fund provided a proof-of-concept grant for an exploratory workshop in 2013. This laid the ground for Gandhāra Connections and we are deeply grateful to the participants for helping to define the research focus of the present project.

on the market. Textual and literary evidence is comparatively thin, notwithstanding the circumstantial evidence afforded by the study and publication of Gāndhārī manuscripts in recent years (which still promise the potential for new information directly relevant to art). It is indicative of the problem that some of the most valuable written sources for the chronology of Gandhāra are ancient Chinese texts, not those of Central Asia or even India (Falk 2015; Chavannes 1907; Zürcher 1968).

However, a still more fundamental problem lies with the instability of the very framework in which any fixed dates would be placed. Even the handful of explicitly dated Gandhāran sculptures that have survived have been difficult to pin down because of uncertainty and debate about the conventional eras – the ancient dating systems – to which their inscriptions make reference. In particular, for many years there has been disagreement about the date of the Kushan ruler Kaniṣka I, whose accession marked year one in a new era repeatedly used in Gandhāran and other Kushan inscriptions. This doubt has significantly limited the utility of a sculpture like the Mamāne Ḍherī stela (Figures 1 and 2 in Juhyung Rhi's chapter of this volume), a votive relief representing the seated Buddha in the Indraśaila cave, whose inscription lucidly dates it to 'the year 89' (but when is that?). This sculpture is discussed further below by Juhyung Rhi alongside the complexities of other dated sculptures.

Over decades a range of more or less circumstantial evidence has been enlisted to date the start of the Kaniṣka era, which is pivotal in considerations of Gandhāran chronology, to altogether different years, the principal candidates being AD 78, AD 127/8, and AD 227.[2] The latest of the three, AD 227, and other dates in contention around AD 230 were propounded by scholars, particularly numismatists, such as Nikolaus Schindel (2009; 2014) and Robert Göbl (1999), who largely base their arguments on iconographical and stylistic comparison between Kushan, Kushano-Sasanian and Roman coins. The year AD 78 as the start of Kaniṣka era was a result of equating this era to the well-known Śaka era known to commence in that year, which was used by the Western Kṣatrapas who were Kaniṣka's vassals in Ujjain. This equation was made on a variety of grounds, mainly epigraphic, literary (Chinese, Central Asian and Indian) and archaeological. Principal scholars who propounded this date include Johanna van Lohuizen-de-Leeuw (1949; 1968), James Fergusson (1880) and Sergei Tolstov (1968).

In the last twenty years, Joe Cribb and Harry Falk in particular have marshalled disparate but complementary evidence, from Central Asian numismatics and Indian and Chinese literature, to consolidate the case for AD 127 as the start of Kaniṣka era. In 2001 Falk published a paper reassessing passages from a Sanskrit astronomical text, the *Yavanajātaka* of Sphujiddhvaja, which mentions the Kushan era in relation to Śaka era (Falk 2001). The passages from this text demonstrate that this Kushan era does not correspond to the Śaka era. It states that by adding 149 to the Śaka era one can obtain the Kushan era (with a one year margin of error depending on the role of elapsed or current years in the calculation) – therefore ostensibly *c.* AD 227. Falk proposes that Sphujiddhvaja was living in the second century of the Kushan era, which is taken to be identical with the era founded by Kaniṣka. Consequently his formula for converting dates from the Śaka era to his own assumes the dropping of the first century, a practice previously suggested by Van Lohuizen-de Leeuw (1949: 235-262; 1986) and attested in other contexts. On that basis the formula actually converts to the second Kushan century, with the real date for the start of the Kushan era, as founded by Kaniṣka, being AD 127.

This proposal corresponds with the implications of other sources for the date of Kaniṣka, including his lineage recorded in the famous Rabatak inscription, which also attests to his creation of an era (Falk 2001: 127; Sims-Williams & Cribb 1995). Van Wijk (1927) had already suggested AD 128/9 for the start of the Kaniṣka era on the basis of calculation of the Indian Nakṣatra years. As Falk emphasizes, the Chinese sources also support the dating of Kaniṣka's reign to this period, as does a careful consideration of the

[2] For a critical overview of the main evidence and competing claims see esp. Golzio 2018; Bracey 2017.

numismatic evidence. Two decades ago, Cribb (1997) embarked on an attempt to align the 'Azes era' with the Kaniṣka era and suggested that by working out the length of the gap between the two eras one could establish the Gandhāran chronology. Numismatic research has contributed to a growing belief in the AD 127 date. In his magisterial opening chapter for this volume, Cribb builds on his previous research in seeking definitively to put a limit on the beginning and end of the gap between the Azes and Kaniṣka eras and consolidating Gandhāran chronology across several centuries. One of the key factors in Cribb's adherence to the AD 127 date is his earlier calculation of the start of the Azes era to 46 BC (Cribb 2005). Using this date, Cribb reviews and analyzes coin sequences from the Indo-Parthian to Kushano-Sasanian periods in combination with dated inscriptions associated with these kings.

Falk's and Cribb's conclusion of AD127 as the start of Kaniṣka era has not been universally accepted; for example it is still opposed in Fussman (1980 and 2004, maintaining the AD 78 date) and Bracey (2017) has been sceptical while accepting that AD 127 is very plausible. Nevertheless, a consensus has started to develop around this later date. Particularly in the light of the additional evidence and arguments presented here, the AD 127 date must surely now be regarded as settled beyond reasonable doubt. It should be noted that no one who participated in the Gandhāra Connections workshop, either as a speaker or a member of the physical and online audience, dissented from this date.

All of the issues mentioned so far have been connected with hard chronology – the challenge of arriving at or near absolute dates and of establishing historical eras. These are of obvious importance in locating Gandhāran works in relation to each other and understanding the development of their tradition. They are also centrally important in any effort to interpret the relationship between Gandhāran art at its Graeco-Roman relations. For example, the availability of relatively fixed dates for sculptures found in the Swat Valley has demonstrated that at least some of the earliest Gandhāran sculptures, confidently placed at least as early as the mid first century AD, are the least 'classical' in appearance; their linear, somewhat abstract style, which Domenico Faccenna dubbed the 'drawing style' (*stile disegnativo*) is more closely related to contemporary narrative sculpture in India than to the Hellenistic Greek or Roman traditions (Filigenzi 2006; 2008; Faccenna 1964).

Besides absolute chronology, however, Gandhāran art is surrounded by other, more subtle problems of chronological interpretation. Firstly, it is surprisingly difficult to construct a relative chronology of Gandhāran art. Certain broad assumptions are generally accepted: that the narrative reliefs which attract so much attention within the study of Gandhāran art are a comparatively early phenomenon (let us say, *c.* first and second centuries AD), which gradually yields to an emphasis, in the adornment of stupas and other devotional reliefs, on the image of the Buddha himself as a transcendental figure, largely detached from history, in iconic, frontal representations. Kurt Behrendt's use of architectural history lends weight to the perception of this trend (Behrendt 2003). Similarly, it is widely assumed that the numerous extant stucco and terracotta sculptures, many of which are markedly classical in appearance, are characteristic of the later tradition in the sculpture of the Greater Gandhāran region (the chapter in this volume by Anna Filigenzi and Luca Olivieri casts some light on the emergence of these sculptures). Nevertheless, beyond such generalizations, it is almost impossible to position the surviving sculptures with any confidence in a coherent narrative of stylistic development, a challenge which Juhyung Rhi's paper seeks to explore using images of the Buddha.

Other chronological questions remain open. Why did the flourishing tradition of figural, architectural decoration that we call 'Gandhāran sculpture' emerge when it did? Why not earlier, given that narrative Buddhist art is so strikingly attested at early Indian sites such as Bharhut, Sanchi and whose foundations could be dated to some time between the third and second centuries BC (Cunningham 1854; 1879; Maisey 1892; Hawkes 2008; Willis 2000; Mackenzie 1823; Elliot 1872; Shimada 2013). How should Gandhāran art be calibrated with neighbouring artistic traditions and later developments in the art of Central Asia?

Are our methodological tools, such as the traditional art-historical mainstay of stylistic comparison, fit for purpose in the examination of a tradition like that of Gandhāra? And how should we try to reconcile different methodologies, particularly methodologies derived from the diverse disciplines implicated in the study of Gandhāra – archaeology, art history, numismatics, epigraphy, Buddhology, philology and literary studies – when they converge on the chronology of Gandhāran art? Such questions were in the minds of the contributors to the Gandhāra Connections workshop and inform many of the observations in their chapters presented here.

A notable result of the workshop was that new problems were highlighted even as some of the older ones came closer to resolution. For example, if the date of Kaniṣka or the character of post-Kushan sculpture came into focus through new analysis and fieldwork, some of the old assumptions were unsettled by scrutiny of the relationship between Gandhāra and India. As a consequence we expect and hope that these proceedings will do as much to stimulate debate and further investigation, as to solidify the existing foundations of the subject. This introduction is intended to sketch the background of what follows and no further summary of the chapters is offered here. They will speak for themselves. It remains only to say that their order broadly reflects the themes outlined above. The initial three chapters look closely at the contributions that different forms of evidence can make to the study of chronology – numismatics (Cribb), the sculptures themselves (Rhi), and inscriptions on other artefacts (Baums). The focus then shifts to relevant archaeological evidence from specific sites, including results of recent fieldwork (Olivieri and Filigenzi, Rienjang), and then to a consideration of chronological problems in relation to material from India which complicates the story (Zin, Lo Muzio, Bracey). Finally, Kurt Behrendt's concluding chapter takes account of a later period of construction and reconstruction at Buddhist sites during the third to fifth centuries AD, challenging us to see the extant evidence through the lens of a flourishing late period of devotional activity, after the time of the Kushans.

References

Behrendt K. 2003. *The Buddhist Architecture of Gandhāra*. Leiden: E.J. Brill.

Bracey R. 2017. The Date of Kanishka Since 1960. *Indian Historical Review* 44/1: 21- 61.

Chavannes E. 1907. Les pays d'occident d'après le Heou Han Chou, T'oung Pao. *T'oung Pao* 8: 149-234.

Cribb J. 1997. Numismatic Perspectives on Chronology in the Crossroads of Asia. Pages 215-30 in E. Errington, N. Kreitman, R. Allchin and B. Allchin (eds), *Gandharan Art in Context: East-West Exchanges at the Crossroads of Asia*. New Delhi: Regency Publications for the Ancient India and Iran Trust.

Cribb J. 2005. The Greek Kingdom of Bactria: Its Coinage and its Collapse. Pages 207-226 in O. Bopearachchi and M.F. Boussac (eds), *Afghanistan, ancien carrefour entre l'est et l'ouest*. Turnhout: Brepols.

Cunningham A. 1854. *The Bhilsa Topes, or, Buddhist Monuments of Central India*. London: Smith Elder.

Cunningham A. 1879. *The Stūpa of Bharhut: A Buddhist Monument Ornamented with Numerous Sculptures Illustrative of Buddhist Legend and History in the Third Century BC*. London: W.H. Allen.

Elliot W. 1872. Archaeology in the Krishna District. *The Indian Antiquary* 1: 346-348.

Faccenna D. 1964. *Sculptures from the Sacred Area of Butkara I (Swāt, W. Pakistan)*. IsMEO Report and Memoirs, 2.2 and 2.3. Rome: Istituto Poligrafico dello Stato, Libreria dello Stato.

Falk H. 2001. The *Yuga* of Sphujiddhvaja and the era of the Kuṣânas. *Silk Road Art and Archaeology* 7: 121-136.

Falk H. (ed.) 2015. *Kushan Histories: Literary Sources and Selected Papers from a Symposium at Berlin, December 5 to 7, 2013*. Bremen: Hempen Verlag.

Fergusson J. 1880. On the Saka, Samvat, and Gupta eras. *Journal of the Royal Asiatic Society* 12: 259-285.

Filigenzi A. 2006. Ānanda and Vajrapāṇi: An Inexplicable Absence and a Mysterious Presence in Gandhāran Art. Pages 270-302 in P. Brancaccio and K. Behrendt (eds), *Gandharan Buddhism: Archaeology, Art, Texts*. Vancouver: UBC Press.

Filigenzi A. 2008. Sculptures from Swat. Pages 197-199 in D. von Drachenfels and C. Luczanits (eds), *Gandhara, the Buddhist Heritage of Pakistan: Legends, Monasteries and Paradise.* Mainz: Zabern.

Fussman G. 1980. Nouvelles inscriptions śaka: ère d'Eucratide, ère d'Azès, ère vikrama, ère de Kaniṣka. *Bulletin de l'École française d'Extrême- Orient* 67: 1-43.

Fussman G. 2004. Les Kouchans dans l'histoire de l'Asie centrale et de l'Inde. *Bibliothèque en ligne Clio* <http://www.clio.fr/BIBLIOTHEQUE>

Göbl R. 1999. The Rabatak Inscription and the Date of Kanishka. Pages 151-175 in M. Alram and D.E. Klimburg-Salter (eds), *Coins, Art and Chronology: Essays on the Pre-Islamic History of the Indo-Iranian Borderlands.* Wien: Verlag der Österreichischen Akademie der Wissenschaften.

Golzio H.K. 2008. Zur Datierung des Kusana-Königs Kaniska I. Pages 80-91 in D. Dimitrov, M. Hahn, and R. Steiner (eds), *Bauddhasāhityastabakāvalī: Essays and Studies on Buddhist Sanskrit Literature, Dedicated to Claus Vogel by Colleagues, Students, and Friends.* Marburg: Indica et Tibetica Verlag.

Hawkes J. 2008. Bharhut: A Reassessment. *South Asian Studies* 24: 1-14.

Lohuizen-de Leeuw J.E. van 1949. *The 'Scythian' Period: An Approach to the History, Art, Epigraphy and Palaeography of North India from the 1st century B.C. to the 3rd Century A.D.* Leiden: E.J. Brill.

Lohuizen-de Leeuw J.E. van 1968. The Date of Kaṇiska and Some Recently Published Images. Pages 126-133 in: A.L. Basham (ed.), *Papers on the Date of Kaniṣka Submitted to the Conference on the Date of Kaniṣka, London, 20-22 April, 1960.* Leiden: E.J. Brill.

Lohuizen-de Leeuw J.E. van 1986. The Second Century of Kaniṣka era. *South Asian Studies* 2/1: 1-9.

Mackenzie C. 1823. Ruins of Amurvarty, Depaldina, and Durnakotta. *Asiatic Journal* 15: 464-478.

Maisey F.C. 1892. *Sánchi and its Remains.* London: Kegan Paul, Trench, Trübner & Co.

Schindel N. 2009. Ardashir II Kushanshah and Huvishka the Kushan: Numismatic Evidence for the Date of the Kushan King Kanishka I. *Journal of the Oriental Numismatic Society* 198: 12-14.

Schindel N. 2014. Ardashir I Kushanshah and Vasudeva the Kushan: Numismatic Evidence for the Date of the Kushan King Kanishka I. *Journal of the Oriental Numismatic Society* 220: 27-30.

Shimada A. 2013. *Early Buddhist Architecture in Context: The Great Stūpa at Amarāvatī.* Leiden: E.J. Brill.

Sims-Williams N. and Cribb J. 1995. A New Bactrian Inscription of Kanishka the Great. *Silk Road Art and Archaeology* 4: 75-142.

Tolstov S.P. 1968. Dated Documents from Toprakala Palace, and the Problem of the 'Śaka era' and the Kaniṣka era. Pages 304-26 in A.L. Basham (ed.), *Papers on the Date of Kaniṣka Submitted to the Conference on the Date of Kaniṣka, London, 20-22 April, 1960.* Leiden: E.J. Brill.

Wijk W.E. van 1927. On Dates in the Kaṇiska era. *Acta Orientalia* 5: 168-170.

Willis, M. 2000. *Buddhist Reliquaries from Ancient India.* London: British Museum Press.

Zürcher E. 1968. The Yüeh-chih and Kaniṣka in Chinese Sources. Pages 346-90 in: A.L. Basham (ed.), *Papers on the Date of Kaniṣka Submitted to the Conference on the Date of Kaniṣka, London, 20-22 April, 1960.* Leiden: E.J. Brill.

Numismatic evidence and the date of Kaniṣka I

Joe Cribb

The dating of sculpture from Gandhāra and its related regions is a difficult thing. As there are only a handful of sculptures bearing dates, all in unspecified eras, any attempts at dating have to rely on a series of understandings, based on archaeological context, material and stylistic analysis, and iconographic development. What is often presumed without comment is the underlying chronological structure which gives such dating a relationship with the eras in use today. This structure has largely been constructed from four sources of evidence: dated inscriptions, numismatic sequences, the scarce references in historical texts, and attempts to match the era used by the Kushans with other Indian eras. Unfortunately the underlying chronological structure built from these has been in a state of flux since it was first attempted. The proposal made in 2001 by Harry Falk that Kaniṣka I's first year was in AD 127, based on the information about the relationship between the Kushan and Śaka eras in an astrological text, the *Yavanajātaka* by Sphujiddhvaja (Falk 2001), was the first to call on a relatively contemporary source with concrete evidence. This proposal has become widely accepted, even though its implications have not yet been fully assimilated into the discourse on Gandhāran art. This date has also not yet been applied to the broader chronological structure, as it comes from a different form of evidence. So parts of the chronological structures are still attached to earlier solutions, based on different resolutions of the evidence. This paper attempts to show that the solution reached by Falk from the astrological text can also be demonstrated by recourse to the use of numismatic and inscriptional evidence, thereby suggesting that Falk's proposal has important implications for solving the problem of Gandhāran chronology and accordingly that of Gandhāran art too.

A key date in Gandhāran chronology: the accession date of Kaniṣka I

It is now widely accepted that the proposal made in 2001 by Harry Falk dating Kaniṣka I's year 1 to AD 127 provides a satisfactory basis to underpin the chronology of Gandhāra and establishes a framework for dating Gandhāran sculpture and its relationship with Buddhist art created elsewhere in the subcontinent. Falk's proposal for dating Kaniṣka I's era was based on his interpretation of a passage in the relatively contemporary Indian astrological text, the *Yavanajātaka* which describes the relationship between the Śaka era and a Kushan era beginning in AD 227 (Falk 2001; 2004; 2007; see also Mak 2013: 96–98).[1] Falk interpreted the Kushan era as the second century of the era begun by Kaniṣka I a century earlier, i.e. in AD 127.[2] There are, however, still some scholars who prefer to stick to the former linking of Kaniṣka I's year 1 with the Śaka era (e.g. Chakravarty 2014: 47, 51–52; Singh 2009: 376–377), making its year 1 equal to AD 78, even though the text refers to a Kushan era which is different to the Śaka era. Mukherjee (1982; 2004: 395–405) was the first to bring the *Yavanajātaka* to the attention of Kushan studies, but vehemently adhered to the dating of Kaniṣka I's first year to AD 78. There is also a minority

[1] Pingree (1959: 282; 1961) dated the text to year 191 of the Śaka era, i.e. AD 269, and Falk initially concurred with this dating (Falk 2001: 121–122), but later questioned it (2007: 143). Mak (2013: 68–71) has since demonstrated this to be a mistaken reading of the manuscripts. The early date of the text which the manuscripts preserve, however, seems assured on the basis that it makes reference to a third century AD usage of a Kushan era.

[2] Falk's rereading of the *Yavanajātaka* showed that the ancient astrologer used the Śaka era, beginning in AD 78, to calculate the beginning of a heavenly cycle and as an afterthought added that the same calculation could be done using the Kushan era if one reckoned on the basis that the Kushan era began 149 years after the Śaka era (Falk 2001: 127), i.e. the Kushan era began in AD 78 + 149 = AD 227. Falk then reasoned that this was not the date of year 1 of Kaniṣka I's era, but year 1 of a second century with the hundreds dropped, therefore Kaniṣka I's year 1 was a hundred years earlier, i.e. AD 127 (Falk 2001: 130).

view (Schindel 2009; 2011; 2012; 2014) which accepts Falk's reading of the text of the *Yavanajātaka*, but identifies the Kushan era as Kaniṣka I's era without any adjustment for allowing for a second century.

The purpose of this paper is to demonstrate from other data, particularly numismatic and epigraphic, that Falk's proposal that Kaniṣka I's era began in AD 127 is sufficiently sound to accept it as the basis for constructing Gandhāran chronology. Various recent discoveries and insights have added to our understanding of the chronology of the Kushan era used by Kaniṣka I and his successors. The first of these is the Rabatak inscription, discovered in 1993 (Sims-Williams & Cribb 1995/6; Sims-Williams 2004), which gives explicit confirmation that the Kushan era was introduced by Kaniṣka I and lists the first four Kushan kings, Kujūla Kadphises, Wima Takto, Wima Kadphises and Kaniṣka I, in a direct line of descent. The second is Rukhuṇa's reliquary inscription which documents a synchronism between two eras used by the Kushans before Kaniṣka I, the year 73 of the Azes era, introduced by an Indo-Scythian king Azes, and year 201 of a Greek era, of uncertain origin (Salomon 2005[3]). This shows that Azes era year 1 = Greek era year 129. The others are the less obvious, but equally significant, series of coin overstrikes[4] which create external chronological links for the beginning and end of the Kushan period.

The chronology presented here differs radically from previous suggestions about Kushan chronology as it seeks to create a framework into which all evidence, early and late, can be fitted. The majority of earlier proposals focus on just one aspect of the problem, such as linking Kaniṣka I's era to the Śaka era, or trying to explain the limited references in Chinese sources to such a dating or any other, without taking account of the fact that, whatever date for the first year of Kaniṣka I's era is selected, the beginning and the end of the dynasty also need to link into contemporary events. What the AD 127 date proposed by Falk offers is a precision in constructing the framework.

The Kushan era

Falk's view that the Kushan era mentioned in the *Yavanajātaka* is a second century of the era commenced by Kaniṣka I is based on his view that, in the light of other evidence, AD 227 is too late for Kaniṣka I. He accepted the views of Van Lohuizen-de Leeuw (1949: 235; 1986) and Rosenfield (1967: 106) that the surviving inscriptional dates can be divided into two separate centuries, one following the other.[5] The second century was suggested on the basis of their analysis of the artistic style of dated sculptures. It can also be demonstrated by the coins of Vasiṣka, as first identified by Robert Göbl (1965). Vasiṣka's dated inscriptions cover years 20–30 and until the coins were identified he was identified as a co-ruler with Kaniṣka I, years 1–23, and Huviṣka, years 25–60. His coins, however, make it clear that he ruled after Vāsudeva I whose inscriptions cover the years 68–98, so his dates are in the Kushan era starting *c.* AD 227 as used in the *Yavanajātaka*, i.e. the second century of the era initiated by Kaniṣka I in AD 127.

As well as locating the reign of Vasiṣka, analysis of the designs, style and control marks of the coinage, has also positioned two other kings mentioned in inscriptions dated in the second century. Kaniṣka II has inscriptions dated years 4–18 and Kaniṣka III, son of Vasiṣka, has an inscription dated year 41. Later

[3] <https://www.Gāndhārī.org/a_inscription.php?catid=CKI0405> (accessed 1 January 2018).

[4] An overstrike occurs when a pre-existing coin is reused as the blank for making a new coin and overstruck with new dies with new designs. An overstrike can be recognized by having evidence of its original designs alongside its new ones. Its value is in indicating the sequence of production between the old understruck and the new overstruck designs. Overstrikes normally take place through the reuse of current coins, but can take place after a long gap between production of the old and new coins. When several examples of overstrikes of one design on the same under type have been found it suggest that the understruck coins were in circulation when the overstriking was done.

[5] Van Lohuizen-de Leeuw (1949: 235) suggested that the second century was an extension of the first century of Kaniṣka I's era with a missing hundred; Rosenfield (1967: 106) suggested a second era was commenced about 100 years after the start of Kaniṣka I's era. See also Bracey 2017: 33.

Kushan rulers known from coins, but not from inscriptions follow Vasiṣka: Vāsudeva II, Mahi, Ṣaka and Kipunadha (Oddy & Cribb 1998).

The *Yavanajātaka* offers contemporary evidence of the use of the Kushan era, even though Mak (2013: 68–71) has dismissed the interpretations of the text which suggested internal evidence for the date of its composition in AD 269. The citing of a Kushan era of AD 227, however, suggests that the composition of the text took place in the period AD 227–326, because if written later its author would be prompted to refer to a Kushan era in a later century, i.e. in AD 327, 427, 527 and so on.[6]

The Kushan king list

The Rabatak inscription, discovered in Afghanistan in 1993 and translated by Nicholas Sims-Williams (Sims-Williams & Cribb, 1995/6; Sims-Williams 1998 and 2004), provides a list of the first four Kushan kings, describing them as in direct succession, from father to son: Kujūla Kadphises, Wima Takto, Wima Kadphises and Kaniṣka I.[7] Change and continuity in the designs used on Kushan coins enable a sequence of issues to be established from the beginning to the end of the dynasty. The coins of the first three Kushan kings can be ordered by their gradual movement from diversity to uniformity of design, by denomination systems and their script styles (Cribb 2014: 94; 100–101). The order in which they were issued corresponds with the sequence presented by the Rabatak inscription. The final issue of gold coins by Wima Kadphises uses the same exceptional script style for its Greek inscriptions as the first issue of Kaniṣka I (Göbl 1984: types 18 and 19 linked with types 25–28; Bracey 2009: 41).

The coin sequence is based on a number of factors relating to the denomination system, metal quality, weight standards, design content and style, inscription language, script and style. For example (Table 1) an approximate sequence for the Kushan kings can be determined through the inscriptions on the coins. The first three kings use Greek and Gāndhārī (Kharoṣṭhī script) inscriptions with some coins using only Greek. The fourth king starts with Greek inscriptions but then replaces them with Bactrian inscriptions (Greek script). The fifth and sixth king use Bactrian, but during the sixth king's reign Brāhmī control marks are introduced. Bactrian inscriptions and Brāhmī control marks continue to be used by the seventh to tenth kings. The tenth king also added the first part of his name in Brāhmī in place of one of the control marks. By the end of his reign the Bactrian inscriptions had become illegible. The eleventh and twelfth kings' coins continued to feature the king's name in Brāhmī together with illegible Bactrian inscriptions. The late coins of the twelfth king and those of the thirteenth king no longer included an illegible Bactrian inscription.

According to the coin sequence, the direct successor of Kaniṣka I is Huviṣka, confirmed by an overlapping of the use of a coin die between these reigns (Göbl 1984: types 80 and 314). Likewise there is an overlapping coin die between Huviṣka and his successor Vāsudeva I (Cribb & Bracey in preparation; cf. Göbl 1984, types 277 and 510). The sequence of the king list created by the coins from Kaniṣka I to Vāsudeva II is confirmed by the Kaniṣka I era dates found in the inscriptions naming them: years 1–23 for Kaniṣka I, 25–60 for Huviṣka and 64–98 for Vāsudeva I.

[6] The practice of using an era which restarts a new century every hundred years is similar to another era still known of as the Laukika in modern India. There is such a close relationship between the Laukika as used today and the Kushan era, with a gap between them of just 3 to 4 years that it seems very likely that they are the same era which has shifted its century start date since its inception (Bracey 2017: 44). This attribution of the Kushan era convincingly argued by Bracey is not new as it was already proposed in a previous century by Smith (1903: 7): 'This long-standing problem I propose to solve by referring this series of [Kushan] dates to the Laukika or popular era...'

[7] Mukherjee's (1998) attempt to reread and retranslate the Rabatak inscription (in a language and script in which he had little expertise) sought to reflect his views on the chronology of the Kushans rather than the realities of the text as read and translated by Sims-Williams, who was able to confirm and extend his readings by direct examination of the inscription in Kabul (Sims-Williams 2004).

Table 1. Example of sequence of coin issues – according to use of languages/scripts.

	King	Greek and Gāndhārī	Greek	Bactrian	Bactrian/ Brāhmī control marks	Bactrian and Brāhmī name and control marks	Brāhmī name and control marks but illegible Bactrian	Brāhmī name and control marks
1	Kujūla Kadphises	x	x					
2	Wima Takto	x	x					
3	Wima Kadphises	x	x					
4	Kaniṣka I		x	x				
5	Huviṣka			x				
6	Vāsudeva I			x	x			
7	Kaniṣka II				x			
8	Vasiṣka				x			
9	Kaniṣka III				x			
10	Vāsudeva II				x	x	x	
11	Mahi						x	
12	Ṣaka						x	x
13	Kipunadha							x

The coin sequence also creates an order for the kings following Vāsudeva I, through their shared use of control marks and stylistic features. The last issues of Vāsudeva I (Göbl 1984: types 532–536) have a small Brāhmī *ha* control mark also continued on Kaniṣka II's first issues (Göbl 1984: types 539–546). The last issues of Kaniṣka II (Göbl 1984: types 548, 550, 552, 553 and 554) and the first issues of Vasiṣka (Göbl 1984: types 554 and 556) use the Brāhmī control marks *vi* and *tha* and the Kharoṣṭhī control mark *pa*. The last issues of Vasiṣka (Göbl 1984: types 567, 568) and the first issue of Vāsudeva II (Göbl 1984: type 569) share the Brāhmī control mark *khu*. The position of Kaniṣka III appears to place him as Vāsudeva II's early contemporary, suggesting a succession dispute which Vāsudeva II won. Kaniṣka III's coins (Göbl 1984: types 634 and 635) continue the Brāhmī *ga* control mark used by Vasiṣka (Göbl 1984: 563 and 564), but are then replaced by coins in the name of Vāsudeva II with which they share the Brāhmī control mark *gha* (Göbl 1984: types 628,[8] 629, 630, 631, 633, 634 and 635). The inscriptions of Vasiṣka have dates from years 24 to 30, but the sequence of coins shows his reign fell after Vāsudeva I and Kaniṣka II, hence the suggestion that there is a second century of Kushan dates. Although the picture is less clear for the reign of Kaniṣka II, because his dates in a second century correspond with the dates of Kaniṣka I in the first century, there is broad agreement that some inscriptions dated between year 4 and year 18 could

[8] Falk (2015: 127) links some of these coins (Göbl 1984: types 628, 630 and 631) with the inscription dated in the reign of a king *vaskuṣānasya*, dated year 22 (i.e. early among the inscriptions of Vasiṣka) because they bear variations of the corrupt inscription ÞAONANO ÞAO BAZKOÞANO. The earliest (Göbl 1984: type 633, with the same control marks as the last coins of Kaniṣka III, Göbl 635) correctly written coins of these types have the name of Vāsudeva II ÞAONANO ÞAO BAZ[O]ΔHO KOÞANO, and the progression to the corrupt version can be traced (the die engraver mistook the end of the king's name for the beginning of KOÞANO and then filled the resulting space at the end of the inscription with a repeat of KOÞANO). These coins were issued after coins in the name of Kaniṣka III, who succeeded Vasiṣka in part of his realm. They should not be anachronistically linked with an inscription from the beginning of the reign of Vasiṣka.

fall in the second century and therefore represent dates in the reign of Kaniṣka II (Falk 2015: 126–127).[9] The reign of Kaniṣka III is represented by one inscription dated year 41, which must fall in the same era as those of Vasiṣka, who is identified in the inscription as his father (the Ara inscription, Konow 1929: 162–165). There are no inscriptions which can be assigned to the reign of Vāsudeva II,[10] but the coin sequence suggests that his reign began, like that of Kaniṣka III, after that of Vasiṣka, so commenced somewhere between the years 30 and 41 of the second century.

The coin sequence after Vāsudeva II is not based on shared monograms, but on stylistic criteria. All the gold coins of the last Kushan kings have identical designs, showing the king standing making an offering at a small fire altar on the obverse and an enthroned goddess Ardochsho on the reverse. The sequence can be demonstrated through minor stylistic adjustments of the design (Cribb and Bracey in preparation) and moves from Vāsudeva II's last issues (Göbl 1984, types 576 and 577) to the issues of Mahi (Göbl 1984, types 582 and 588) and the first issues of Ṣaka (Göbl 1984, types 580 and 589). The late issues of Ṣaka (Göbl 1984, type 593) are followed by the first issue of Kipunadha (Göbl 1984, type 595), whose last issue (Göbl 1984, type 596) is followed by Kidarite issues (Göbl 1984, types 598–601, 603 and 605).

The later Kushan kings are not known from inscriptions, but are reconstructed from their coin inscriptions. On the basis that the coins of Vāsudeva II have his name written on them in Bactrian BAZOΔHO and in Brāhmī *vasu*, the kings who follow are named after their Brāhmī inscriptions: *mahi*, *ṣaka* (or *ṣāka*), *kipunadha*. Ṣaka should be a contemporary of the first Gupta emperor Samudragupta and seems to be referred to in his Allahabad inscription as *daivaputra ṣāhi-ṣāhānuṣāhi-śakamuruṇḍaiḥ*, as one of the tributaries of the Gupta king (Fleet 1888: 8, line 23). The spelling of the king's name as *śaka* in place of *ṣaka* is problematic, but could represent two different transliterations into Sanskrit from the name in the Bactrian language used by the Kushans. The titles used are those of the Kushan kings. The word *muruṇḍa* could represent the second half of the king's name in the same way that Vāsudeva's name was only represented by its first half in the Brāhmī inscription on the coins. The Sanskrit inflection of *muruṇḍaiḥ* giving a plural form has been used to suggest translating the inscription as representing various peoples, but the use of plural here could simply be honorific.

Apart from shared control marks and stylistic features, the coin sequence is also supported by two other factors, the falling gold content of the gold coinages from Wima Kadphises to the end of the dynasty (Oddy and Cribb 1998; Bracey and Oddy 2010) and the falling weight standard of the copper coinage from Kaniṣka I to the end (Jongeward & Cribb 2015: 7–8, 151; Bracey 2017: 30).

The Greek era

The discovery of Rukhuṇa's reliquary inscription (Salomon 2005; Baums 2012: 212–213) added another feature to the sequencing of the early Kushan kings. The discovery of a Greek era which could be dated in relation to the Azes era (Azes era year 1 = Greek era year 129) suggested the identity of the dates in the inscriptions of the second and third Kushan kings (Cribb 2005: 213–4; 221–3) as representing the Greek era. The first king's inscriptions appear to be dated in the Azes era, so the relationship between their dated inscriptions could be quantified. The inscriptions of Kujūla Kadphises (Panjtar inscription of year 122, Konow 1929: 67–70; Taxila inscription of year 136, Konow 1929: 70–77; Baums 2012: 237, no. 30) do not name him directly, but use the appellation Kushan, with which he was identified on coins of the Heraus type (Cribb 1996) and the Sind type (Mitchiner 2004, vol. 1: 619). The attribution of the inscriptions in the name of king (of kings) Kushan to Kujūla Kadphises are reinforced by the inscription

[9] Some caution should, however, be applied to this consensus, as it is based on very thin evidence (Bracey 2017: 35, 52 n. 121).

[10] The inscription dated in the reign of Vāsudeva, read by Mukherjee (1987; 2004b) as year 140 or 170 of the era of Kaniṣka, has now been convincingly reread by Falk (2002/3: 41–45) as dated to year 80 of the Kaniṣka I era.

of year 126 (Priyavamsa's reliquary, Baums 2012: 235–6, no. 28) which lacks a royal name but states that it was inscribed in the reign of the *yaua*, a Kushan title (Kushan yabgu) used only by Kujūla Kadphises.[11]

The dated inscriptions of the second and third king Wima Takto and Wima Kadphises are in a different era with dates for both in the 200s. Wima Takto's inscription (Dasht-e Nawar; Sims-Williams and Cribb 1995/6: 95) is dated 279 and Wima Kadphises' inscription (Khalatse; Konow 1929: 79–81, Cribb 1997: 230 n.32) is dated 287.

Among the Kushan period inscriptions at Mathurā there are two further inscriptions which appear to be in the same era and refer to unnamed kings: year 270 (Lüders 1961: 162–4, no. 77A/123) and year 299 (Lüders no 78; Konow 1934). Given the family relationship between Kujūla Kadphises and these two kings these dates cannot be in the Azes era. The most plausible explanation is to identify them as dates in the Greek era (Cribb 2005: 214, 222). Using the relationship expressed in Rukhuṇa's reliquary inscription, there are only six years between the last of Kujūla Kadphises Azes era inscriptions and the earliest Kushan inscription in the Greek era at Mathurā, suggesting that it be attributed to the reign of Wima Takto.[12] The Azes era inscriptions of Kujūla Kadphises and the Greek era inscriptions of his son and grandson can now be calculated within a common system (Table 2).

The gap between the Azes era and Kaniṣka I's era

In a paper presented in 1992 (not published until 1997; Cribb 1997: 223–226) I suggested that calculation of the chronological framework for Gandhāran history should be based on the relationship between the Azes and Kaniṣka I eras, which together provided a continuous dating system over almost three hundred years. The only uncertainty was how to join the two eras into a single sequence. In 1992, many of the important recent discoveries about the period, such as the Rabatak inscription and the Rukhuṇa reliquary inscription had not yet been made, but what was clear was the gap between the two eras. The proposed identity the dating system used in pre-Kaniṣka I inscriptions of the reigns of Wima Takto and Wima Kadphises as the Greek era allows a more precise definition of that gap, as its length appears to now depend on the length of the reign of Wima Kadphises. In my 2005 article (Cribb 2005: 214), I suggested that the gap between these two sets of dates was probably very small. If Wima Kadphises reign had begun by Greek era year 287 and still continued until year 299, then his reign was at least 13 years long. The closed gap between Wima Kadphises and Kaniṣka I led me to suggest in the same article that the new era started by Kaniṣka I could be a continuation of the Greek era, as his era's year 1 and

[11] The attribution of these inscriptions to Kujūla is further reinforced by the evidence that Kujūla Kadphises was the first Kushan ruler whose coins circulated in Taxila (Khan & Cribb 2012) and that he issued coins simply using the name Kushan in Bactria (Cribb 1996) and in Sind (Mitchiner 2004: no. 1910) and was so named in the inscription on his son Wima Takto's portrait sculpture at Mathurā (*kuṣāṇaputro* son of Kushan).

[12] The palaeographic style and the content of both inscriptions places them early in the Kushan period as such inscriptions only began to appear at Mathurā during the previous period of satrapal rule in the city (Salomon 1998: 143–4) and continued into the Kushan period. There are no royal inscriptions of this kind before the Kushan period so the attribution of the dates in these inscriptions to the Kushans is suggested by the use of royal titles in both inscriptions. The first Kushan king to rule in Mathurā appears from coin finds (Cribb 2014: 98) to be Wima Takto, so the year 270 inscription, dated before his Dasht-e Nawar inscription of 279, should be during his reign. The year 299 inscription, made after Wima Kadphises' year 287 inscription, but before the adoption of the Kaniṣka I era at Mathurā, was most likely inscribed during Wima Kadphises' reign.
The Yavanarājya era year 116 inscription (Mukherjee 1992; Fussman 1993: 111–117) found at Mathurā appears to belong to a different Greek era to that of the Rukhuṇa reliquary inscription. Its script style, hybrid Prakrit-Sanskrit language and its content place it among the dedicatory inscriptions which were made at Mathurā during the period of satrapal and early Kushan rule, i.e. during the first to early second century AD (Salomon 1998: 87–88). Fussman (1993; 117) proposed to date the inscription to an era based on the reign of Menander, i.e. 116 = *c.* 39 BC. Mukherjee (1992) suggested it should be dated in the Azes era, giving a date *c.* AD 59. The dating of the inscription to the period of the satraps and early Kushans is more in accord with Mukherjee's identification of this Greek era with the Azes era, which would give a date for the inscription *c.* AD 70 (based on the revised start of the Azes era to *c.* 46 BC).

Table 2. Coin and epigraphic sequence.

	King	Rabatak king list	dated inscriptions	die links	shared control marks	shared stylistic features
1	Kujūla Kadphises	x	Azes era 122, 126, 136			x
2	Wima Takto	x	Greek era 270 = Azes era 142 Greek era 279 = Azes era 151			x
3	Wima Kadphises	x	Greek era 287 = Azes era 159 Greek era 299 = Azes era 171			x
4	Kaniṣka I	x	Kaniṣka era 1–23	x		x
5	Huviṣka		Kaniṣka era 25–60	x		x
6	Vāsudeva I		Kaniṣka era 64–98	x	x	x
7	Kaniṣka II		Kushan era [4–18]		x	x
8	Vasiṣka		Kushan era 22–30		x	x
9	Kaniṣka III		Kushan era 41		x	x
10	Vāsudeva II				x	x
11	Mahi					x
12	Ṣaka					x
13	Kipunadha					x

the Greek era's year 301 must have coincided or been so close that such a resolution could be used as a working hypothesis.

When this solution is coupled with Falk's proposal that Kaniṣka I's era began in AD 127, as I proposed in 2005, an absolute chronology for about three hundred years can be achieved for the Gandhāra region, starting with the accession of the Indo-Scythian king Azes I in *c.* 46 BC and reaching through till *c.* AD 267 in the reign of Kaniṣka III. Subsequently, using different evidence, it has been suggested that the Azes era began in *c.* 47 BC (Falk & Bennett 2009).

The other widely held dating systems for Kaniṣka I's year 1 and Azes' year 1 cannot create a sensible solution for the gap between the reign of Wima Kadphises and Kaniṣka I as is now indicated by the evidence of the Rukhuṇa reliquary inscription's relationship between the the Azes era year 73 and the Greek era year 201. The most widespread alternative for the start date of Kaniṣka I's era is the identification of it with the Śaka era beginning in AD 78 (Salomon 1998: 182–4; Chakravarti 2014: 46–50; Singh 2009: 376–7). This proposal would make the Azes era begin c. 93 BC (i.e. AD 78 minus 171 years of the Azes era before Kaniṣka year 1), too early for the evidence we have for Azes I from his coins. The Azes era has been widely identified as the Vikrama era beginning in 58 BC (Salomon 1998: 182; Fussman 2015: 16) which points to a date for Kaniṣka era year 1 after AD 113. This dating excludes the possibility of Kaniṣka I's era being identical with the Śaka era, but the Azes era = the Vikrama era of 58 BC remains possible, dating the 171 inscription (Greek era 299) to AD 113, only a 14 year gap before Falk's date of *c.* AD 127 for year 1 of Kaniṣka I's era. The alternative dating of the Azes era year 1 to *c.* 47/46 BC closes the gap further to 2 or 3 years. The length of Wima Kadphises' reign would therefore be 25 years if Azes year 1 = 58 BC, or 13 or 14 years if Azes year 1 = 47/46 BC.

Schindel's suggestion that the Kushan era mentioned in the *Yavanajātaka*, beginning in AD 227 is the era of Kaniṣka I (Schindel 2011: 6) creates a different form of conflict with the evidence of the Rukhuṇa reliquary inscription. His suggestion results in an implausible gap of 102/3 (Azes era year 1 = 46/7 BC) or more years between Wima Kadphises and his son Kaniṣka I (see further below).

External corrobation – the numismatic context of the early Kushans

The construction of the Kushan king list using Falk's dating of the Kaniṣka I era year 1 = AD 127 and my suggestion of a date of 46 BC for year 1 of the Azes era and the connection between both these eras and the Greek era (Kaniṣka era year 1 = Greek era year 301 = Azes era 173) produces a coherent account of the progression of the Kushan dynasty to which AD dates can be attached (Table 3). A test of the reliability of this can be made using the numismatic context of the coins of these kings.

The connections between the coins of the first Kushan king and those of the first Indo-Parthian king Gondophares have long been recognized. Kujūla Kadphises' coins have been reported overstruck on coins of Gondophares (Figures 1a, 1b and 2; Mitchiner 1976, VIII: 681–2, type 1044c; Widemann 1972). Gondophares coins have also been seen overstruck by coins of the Indo-Scythian satrap Zeionises (Mitchiner 1976, VII: 594, type 883d). One series of Kujūla Kadphises (bull and camel type; Jongeward & Cribb 2015: 35–36, no. 114–124) copper coins copied the designs of Zeionises' coins, including retaining a blundered version of Zeionises' inscription. This positions Kujūla Kadphises' reign as starting after the commencement of the reigns of Gondophares and Zeionises.[13] The coins of Gondophares can be dated by comparison with Parthian coins. One issue of Gondophares copper coins (Senior 2001, II: 151, type 215) uses a design (Sellwood 1980: 202, type 63; king on horseback being approached by a standing goddess), featured on silver coins of the Parthian king Artabanus II (AD 10–38), issued in AD 27. The portrait used on Gondophares coins (Senior 2001, II: 149, type 210) has the loop of his diadem ties in triangular form containing a circular loop, which is the variety featured on coins of Artabanus II (Sellwood 1980: 200,

Table 3. Kushan king list.

	King	**dated inscriptions**	**AD**
		Azes era year 1 = 46 BC Kaniṣka era year 1 = AD 127	
1	Kujūla Kadphises	Azes era 122 Azes era 126 Azes era 136	76 80 90
2	Wima Takto	Greek era 270 = Azes era 142 Greek era 279 = Azes era 151	96 105
3	Wima Kadphises	Greek era 287 = Azes era 159 Greek era 299 = Azes era 171	113 125
4	Kaniṣka I	Kaniṣka era 1–23	127–149
5	Huviṣka	Kaniṣka era 25–60	151–186
6	Vāsudeva I	Kaniṣka era 64–98	190–224
7	Kaniṣka II	Kushan era [4–18]	230–244
8	Vasiṣka	Kushan era 22–30	248–256
9	Kaniṣka III	Kushan era 41	267
10	Vāsudeva II		
11	Mahi		
12	Ṣaka		
13	Kipunadha		

[13] The inscription of Zeionises found at Taxila has frequently been misunderstood as containing a date, but its context makes it clear that the numerals *ka 191* record the weight in kārshāpaṇas of the silver vessel on which they are written (Cribb 1999: 196).

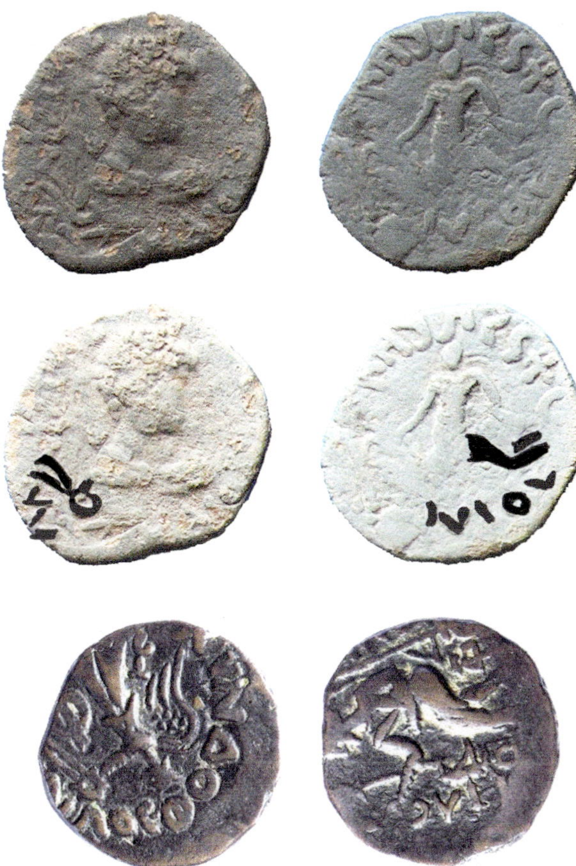

Figure 1a. Copper tetradrachm of Kushan king Kujūla Kadphises imitation Hermaeus Heracles type (Jongeward & Cribb 2015: 30–31, plate 3, nos. 45–56), Taxila Museum 558.01 (Sirkap find), 7.20g, 24mm (Khan & Cribb 2012: 153, 197, no. 1360), overstruck obverse on reverse on copper coin of Indo-Parthian king Gondophares (as Figure 2). (Photograph courtesy of Professor Dr. Gul Rahim Khan.)

Figure 1b. Drawing of Figure 1a showing traces of undertype.

Figure 2. Copper coin of Gondophares, enthroned king/ Nike type (Senior 2001: 150, type 214), British Museum 1859,0220.142, 7.03g, 22mm. (Photo: courtesy of the Trustees of the British Museum.)

type 62), issued in AD 21–22. Likewise the triangular diadem loop, with a single line within, on another of his issues (Senior 2001, II: 149, type 212) resembles that on the coins of Artabanus II's predecessors Phraataces (AD 2 BC – AD 4), dated AD 2 (Sellwood 1980: 189, type 58) and Vonones I (AD 8–12), dated AD 9 and 10, (Sellwood 1980: 194, type 60; 197, type 61). The Nike reverse design of some of Gondophares coins (Senior 2001, II: 149–150 and 158; types 212, 213, 214 and 222) also derives from Parthian silver issues of Vonones I (Sellwood 1980: 194–195, type 60).[14]

The dating of the prototypes of Gondophares' coins places his reign in the first century AD, aligning them with that of two other sources of evidence for dating his reign. Firstly an inscription datable to the Azes era year 103 also records the 26th year of Gondophares' reign (Takht-i-Bāhī inscription; Konow 1929: 57–62). Using the dating for the Azes era discussed above the reign of Gondophares should have begun in AD 32 and he was therefore still ruling in Gandhāra in AD 57. This places his dated inscription of Azes era 103 nineteen years before Kujūla Kadphises inscription dated Azes year 122. Secondly the dating created by the links with Parthian coin designs supports the historical significance of the less reliable reference to a first century AD king Gondophares in the early third century Syriac text *Acts of St Thomas* (Moffett 1998: 25–36).

[14] Senior 1997: 4–8 and 2001, I: 108–110 has argued against dating of Gondophares coins to the first century AD, placing them in the second half of the first century BC, ruling until *c.* 19 BC on the basis of the similarity of their fabric with Parthian coins of that period, rejecting the links outlined here.

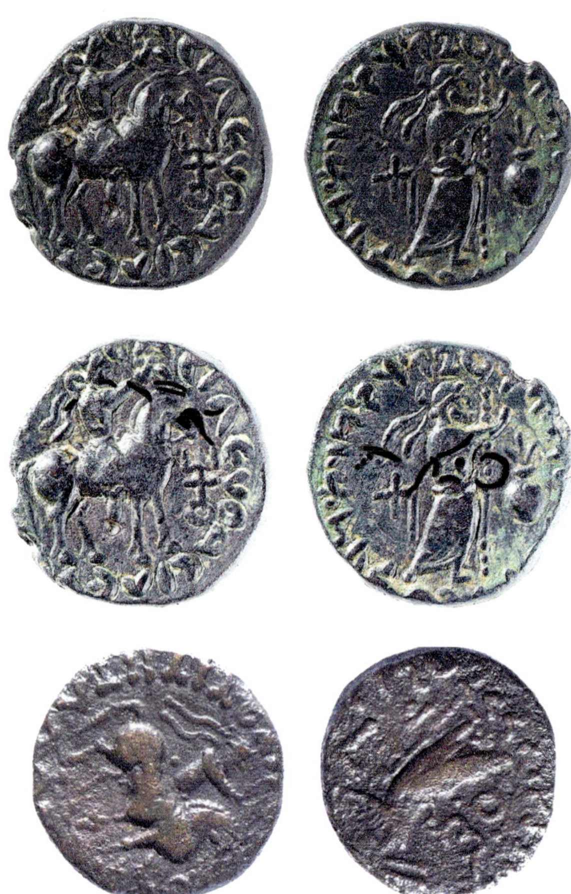

Figure 3a. Base silver tetradrachm of Wima Takto, bilingual king on horseback/ Zeus type (Cribb 2014: 113, 127, figure 27), British Museum 1894,0506.797, 8.89g 21mm, overstruck on base silver tetradrachm of Indo-Parthian king Sasan (as Figure 4). (Photo: courtesy of the Trustees of the British Museum.)

Figure 3b. Drawing of figure 3a showing traces of undertype.

Figure 4. Base silver tetradrachm of Sasan, king on horseback/ Zeus type (Senior 2001: 169–171, type 242) British Museum 1990,0515.181, 8.65g, 21mm. (Photo: courtesy of the Trustees of the British Museum.)

The relationship between Gondophares and Kujūla Kadphises is further confirmed by the relationships between the coins of his successors and both later Kushan coins and Parthian coins. Overstrikes by Wima Takto's Soter Megas types on coins of a later Gondopharid king Sasan[15] (Figures 3a, 3b and 4; Sims-Williams and Cribb 1995/6: 120, type 1; fig. 11b; Cribb 2014: 97, figs. 27–28; Cribb 2015: 29; Senior 2009) show the continuing chronological relationship between the first Kushan kings and their Indo-Parthian neighbours.[16] In turn Wima Takto's coins were overstruck by a later Indo-Parthian king Pakores (Senior 2001, II: 184 n. 3). The designs of Indo-Parthian coins also continue to relate to Parthian coins. The silver coins of Pakores (Senior 2001, II: 184), Abdagases II (Senior 2001, II: 166) and Sanabares (Senior 2001, II: 182) all possess a feature (Pahlavi letters in obverse field) first appearing on Parthian coins late in the reign of Vologases I (AD 51–78) (Sellwood 1980: 231, type 71) and continuing into the reign of Vologases II (c. AD 77–80) (Sellwood 1980: 234, type 72). Another late Indo-Parthian king Ubouzanes (Senior 2001, vol. 2: 181) is depicted on his coins wearing the same crown as Vologases II (Sellwood 1980: 234, type 72). Early Kushan and Indo-Parthian coins also circulated together. Silver drachms of several Indo-Parthian kings including Sasan were found in a hoard along with similar coins of Kujūla Kadphises (Marshall 1951, I: 160). Coins of Sasan have been reported overstruck on coins of the Satrapal ruler of western India Nahapāna (Cribb 1992: 133, 144, 145), whose reign is thought to be in the mid first century AD, *c.* AD 40–78. The numismatic context of the early Kushan kings (Table 4) corroborates the chronological framework (Table 3) suggested by the epigraphic evidence outlined above, and contradicts both the widespread dating of Kaniṣka I's year 1 to AD 78 and Senior's proposal that Gondophares' reign was in the first century BC.

[15] Sasan is also named Gondophares Sasan on most of his coin types (Senior 2001: 167–174).

[16] Senior (2009:19) published this coin as an overstrike by Sasan on a late Soter Megas coin datable to the reign of Wima Takto, but the nature of the overstriking makes the opposite more likely and plausible.

Table 4. Parthian, Indo-Parthian and Kushan coin connections (o/s = overstruck).

Parthian kings	**Indo-Parthians Gandhāra coin sequence**		**Indo-Parthians Arachosia coin sequence**	**coin sequence**	**Kushans**
Phraataces (2 BC–AD 4)					
Vonones I (AD 8–12) AD 10					
Artabanus II (AD 10–38) AD 27 Vardanes I Gotarzes II Vonones II Vologases I	Gondophares year 1 = Azes era 78 = Greek 206	Gondophares year 26 = Azes era 103 = Greek era 231	Gondophares	Gondophares copying coins of Vonones I and Artabanus II. Zeionises o/s by Gondophares; imitated by Kujūla Kadphises. Gondophares o/s by Kujūla Kadphises.	
Vologases II AD 77–80	Abdagases		Orthagnes Ubouzanes Sarpedanes	Kujūla Kadphises issues coins based on Sarpedanes issues in Sind.	Kujūla Kadphises o/s on Gondophares Azes era 122, 126 and 136 = Greek 250, 254 and 264]
	Sasan		Sasan	Sasan Gandhāran issues in o/s by and imitated by Wima Takto. Sasan Sind issues o/s on Nahapana, c. AD 40–78.	Wima Takto Azes 142 = Greek 270 Azes 151 = Greek 279
			Satavastres Abdagases II Pakores Sanabares	Satavastres o/s by Nahapana. Pakores o/s on Wima Takto. Indo-Parthian kings imitating coins of Vologases I and II.	Wima Kadphises Azes 159 = Greek 287 Azes 171 = Greek 299

External corrobation – the numismatic context of the late Kushans

A similar framework can be created from Iranian parallels with the late Kushan period. At the end of the reign of Vāsudeva I the Kushan kingdom came under threat from the newly established Sasanian kingdom in Iran. According to the Persian historian al-Ṭabarī (C.E. Bosworth *The History of al-Ṭabarī*, 1999, II: 15, section I. 820), the Kushan king offered submission to the new Sasanian king Ardashir I (224–240), probably in the last decade of Ardashir I's reign. Soon after this the Sasanians took western Bactria, including Balkh, from the Kushans and established their own Kushan king (Kushanshah) there (Cribb 1990). The Sasanian Kushanshahs' coinage is normally referred to in numismatic literature as Kushano-Sasanian. The coin sequence of the Kushanshahs (Table 5) has been established using the same criteria as outlined above for the Kushan sequence. There are various links between the two sequences which give some indication of an absolute chronological framework. Both Sasanian Kushanshahs and the Kushans were succeeded by Kidarite Huns which extends the evidence for the absolute chronology of the Kushan king sequence.

The first indication of a change in the Kushan coinage brought about by the Sasanian intervention into Kushan territory is the cessation of the coinage of gold coins in Bactria during the first years of the reign of Kaniṣka II. Prior to this the main gold mint of the Kushans had been in continuous operation in Bactria since the time of Wima Kadphises. From the first year of Kaniṣka II's reign the mint, which had previously been a subsidiary gold mint located south of the Hindu Kush, took over as the main centre for the production of Kushan gold coins. The last gold issue attributable to the Kushan mint in Bactria is known only from two coins (Göbl 1984: type 538; Göbl 1993: pl. 16, types 538 and 538A, pl. 56, no. 596). The copper coins of Kaniṣka II continued to circulate into Bactria. This suggests that early in the reign of Kaniṣka II western Bactria, including the capital Balkh, fell into the hands of the Sasanians. The main Kushan mint at Balkh however continued to issue gold coins imitating the designs of Vāsudeva I and in the name of the Kushan kings Vāsudeva I (Göbl 1984: types 644–659 and 666–699) or Kaniṣka II (Göbl 1984: types 661–665 and 700), apparently under Sasanian control. Alongside these the Sasanian authority also issued copper coins copying the obverse design of Kaniṣka II and the reverse design of Vāsudeva I (Göbl 1984: types 1008–1010; these coins are commonly referred to as 'Vāsudeva imitations'). There are also three coin types issued by the Sasanians for Kushan territory during the same period. The first is issued by a king, wearing a fish-tailed eagle crown, whose name is not yet read, but who appears to have the titles Marvshah and Kushanshah (Göbl 1984: type 1029). The Sasanian emperor Ardashir I appointed one of his sons also named Ardashir to be Marvshah (*'rthštr mrgw MLKA*) to rule in the territory he had captured around the ancient city of Merv (Kaᶜba-ye Zardošt inscription line 41: Huyse 1999: 54). The name on this coin type was read by Göbl (1984: 114) as Ardashir, but, although the context suggests he was correct, I have been unable to find a legible specimen among more than twenty examples examined. The second and third types (Göbl 1984: types 1028 and 1114) are inscribed with the name Ardashir Kushanshah, but with a different crown, with three floral projections, surmounted by a hair ball. It is unclear whether the unidentified king and the king named Ardashir represent the same ruler.

The third series of Kushanshah coins were issued in the name of a king called Peroz Kushanshah. His gold coins in Bactria start using the same designs as the imitation Vāsudeva gold coins, showing the king in Kushan crown and armour, with a change of inscription (Göbl 1984: gold type 702, copper types 1101–1103), giving his name and title in Bactrian. Later issues adopt a new lion-head crown design and Sasanian style armour (Göbl 1984: gold type 703–706, copper types 1105–1110). South of the Hindu Kush his coins used a different flat crown (Göbl 1984: gold type 555, copper types 1115–1119 and 1123), giving his name, and on the gold his title, in Bactrian. A rare Bactrian type (Göbl 1984: type 1112) uses the same crown, but with a Pahlavi inscription. A copper coin of Peroz's southern series has been reported overstruck on a copper coin of the imitation Vāsudeva series (Figures 5a, 5b and 6; British Museum 1981,0735.2; Cribb 1985: 314) and another overstruck on a Merv mint coin of Shapur I (Figures 7a, 7b and 8; BM 1996,0608.1; Cribb and Bracey in preparation). An example of Peroz's early Bactrian copper coins with Kushan crown and armour has also been recorded overstruck on a coin of Shapur I's Merv mint (Figures 9a, 9b and 10; Loeschner 2007).[17] In turn Peroz's southern copper coins were also overstruck by Kushan coins issued early in the reign of Vāsudeva II (Figures 11a, 11b and 12; British Museum 1981,0735.1; Cribb 1985: 309, 314).

Peroz I's gold coins issued south of the Hindu Kush (Göbl 1984: type 555) represented the king in Sasanian flat crown and dress, but in the same posture as Kushan kings. On the reverse of these coins the Kushan goddess Ardochsho offers a Kushan crown. The treatment of her drapery and her throne suggest the design was copied from coins of Kaniṣka II (see particularly Göbl 1984: type 539).

[17] Loeschner did not recognize the undertype of this overstruck coin and interpreted the visible features differently.

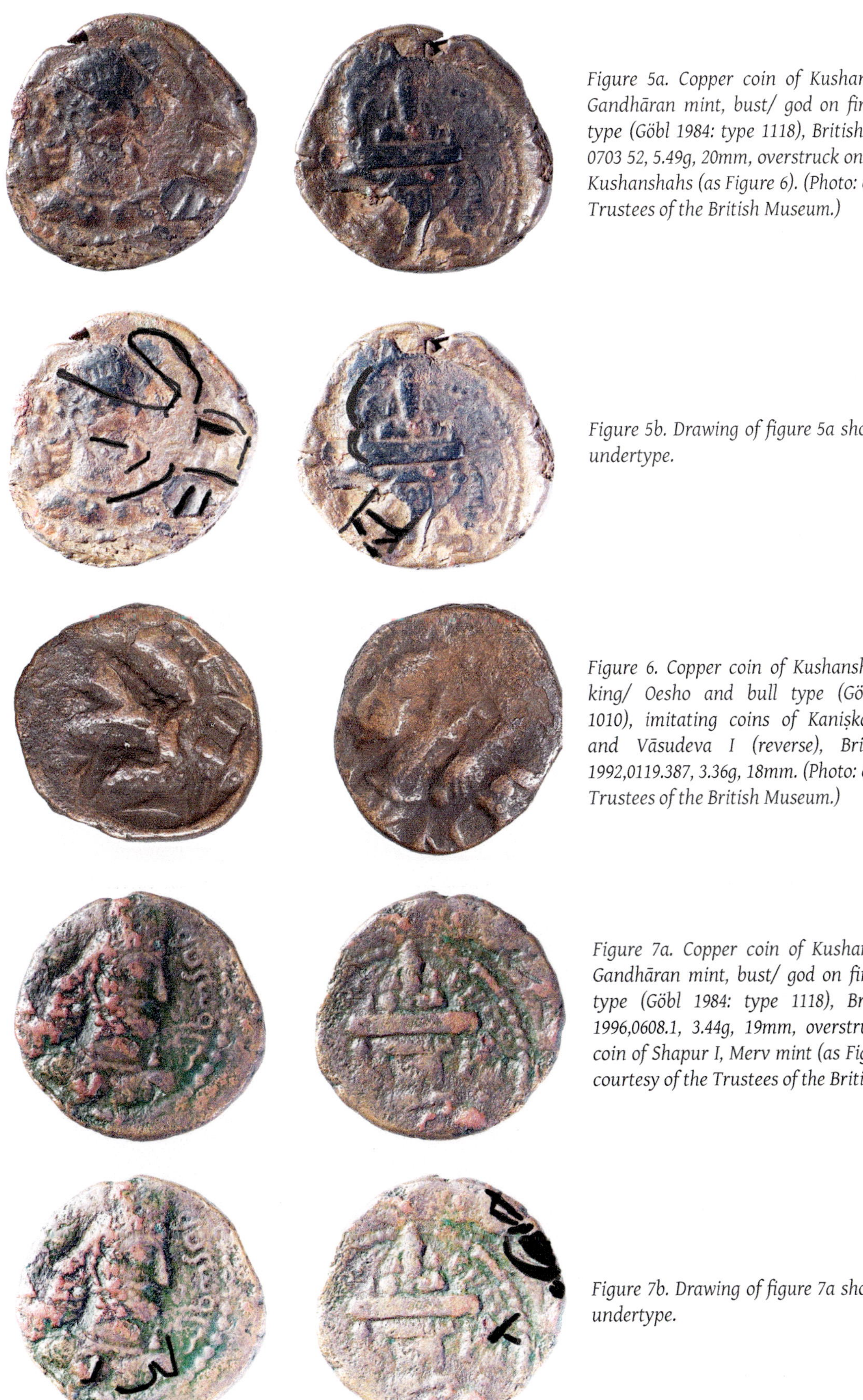

Figure 5a. Copper coin of Kushanshah Peroz I, Gandhāran mint, bust/ god on fire altar-throne type (Göbl 1984: type 1118), British Museum 1981 0703 52, 5.49g, 20mm, overstruck on copper coin of Kushanshahs (as Figure 6). (Photo: courtesy of the Trustees of the British Museum.)

Figure 5b. Drawing of figure 5a showing traces of undertype.

Figure 6. Copper coin of Kushanshahs, standing king/ Oesho and bull type (Göbl 1984: type 1010), imitating coins of Kaniṣka II (obverse) and Vāsudeva I (reverse), British Museum 1992,0119.387, 3.36g, 18mm. (Photo: courtesy of the Trustees of the British Museum.)

Figure 7a. Copper coin of Kushanshah Peroz I, Gandhāran mint, bust/ god on fire altar-throne type (Göbl 1984: type 1118), British Museum 1996,0608.1, 3.44g, 19mm, overstruck on copper coin of Shapur I, Merv mint (as Figure 8). (Photo: courtesy of the Trustees of the British Museum.)

Figure 7b. Drawing of figure 7a showing traces of undertype.

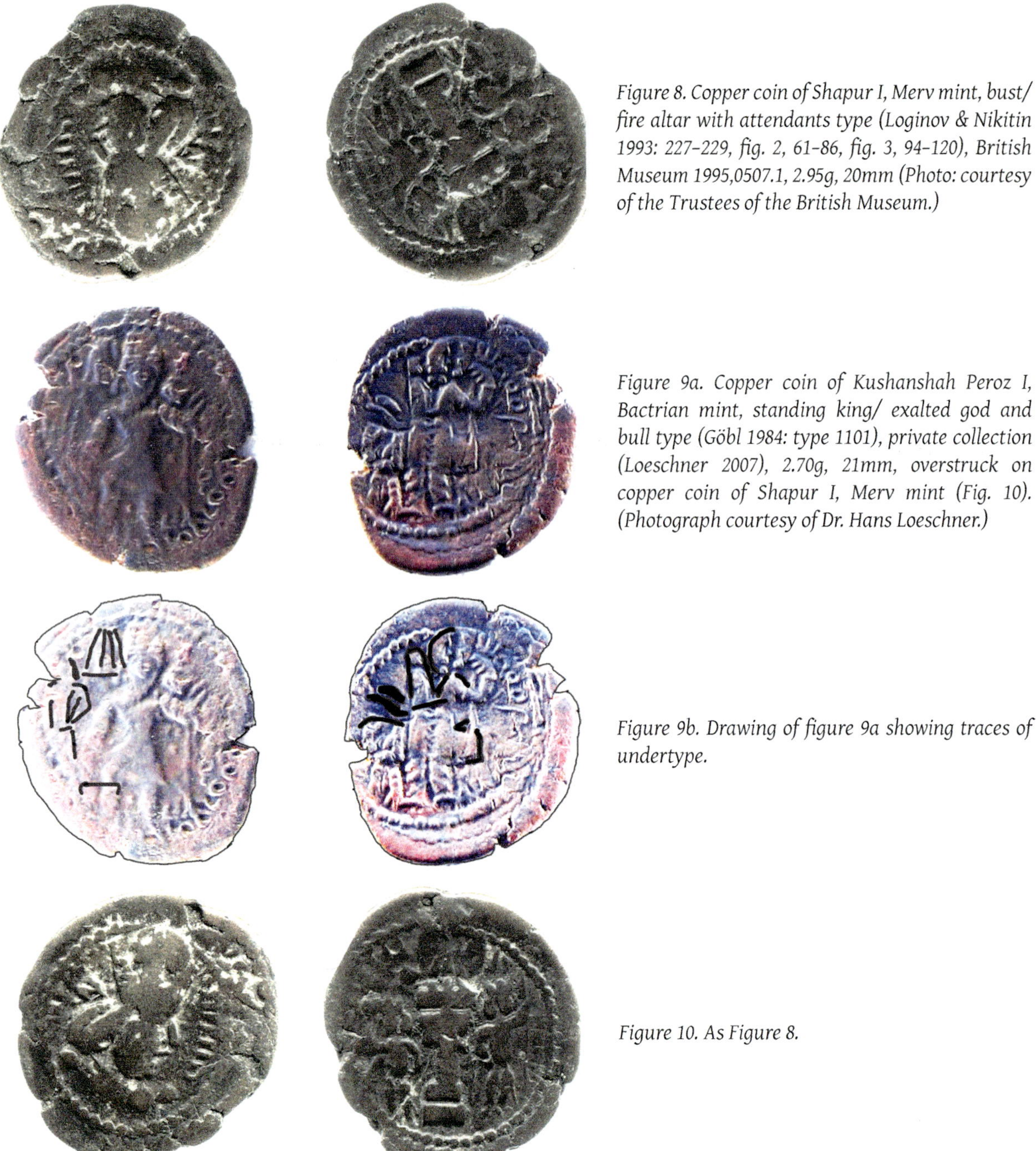

Figure 8. Copper coin of Shapur I, Merv mint, bust/ fire altar with attendants type (Loginov & Nikitin 1993: 227–229, fig. 2, 61–86, fig. 3, 94–120), British Museum 1995,0507.1, 2.95g, 20mm (Photo: courtesy of the Trustees of the British Museum.)

Figure 9a. Copper coin of Kushanshah Peroz I, Bactrian mint, standing king/ exalted god and bull type (Göbl 1984: type 1101), private collection (Loeschner 2007), 2.70g, 21mm, overstruck on copper coin of Shapur I, Merv mint (Fig. 10). (Photograph courtesy of Dr. Hans Loeschner.)

Figure 9b. Drawing of figure 9a showing traces of undertype.

Figure 10. As Figure 8.

The situation suggested by the designs of Peroz I's coins, and the related overstrikings, links him with the Sasanian kings Ardashir I (fire altar/throne) and Shapur I (overstrikes), and the Kushan kings Kaniṣka II (Ardochsho design, Vāsudeva imitation overstrike) and Vāsudeva II (overstrike). The initiation of coinage south of the Hindu Kush under Peroz I can also be linked with the claim by Shapur I that he ruled the Kushan kingdom up to Peshawar (kwšnhštr *HN* prhš OL pškbwr, Kaᶜba-ye Zardošt inscription line 3; Huyse 1999: 24 and 36). The links with the Kushanshahs and their Sasanian overlords for the period of Kushan rule from Kaniṣka II to Vāsudeva II place it in the period *c.* AD 224–270, matching closely the dating of this period, *c.* 230–270 calculated from the dating of Kaniṣka

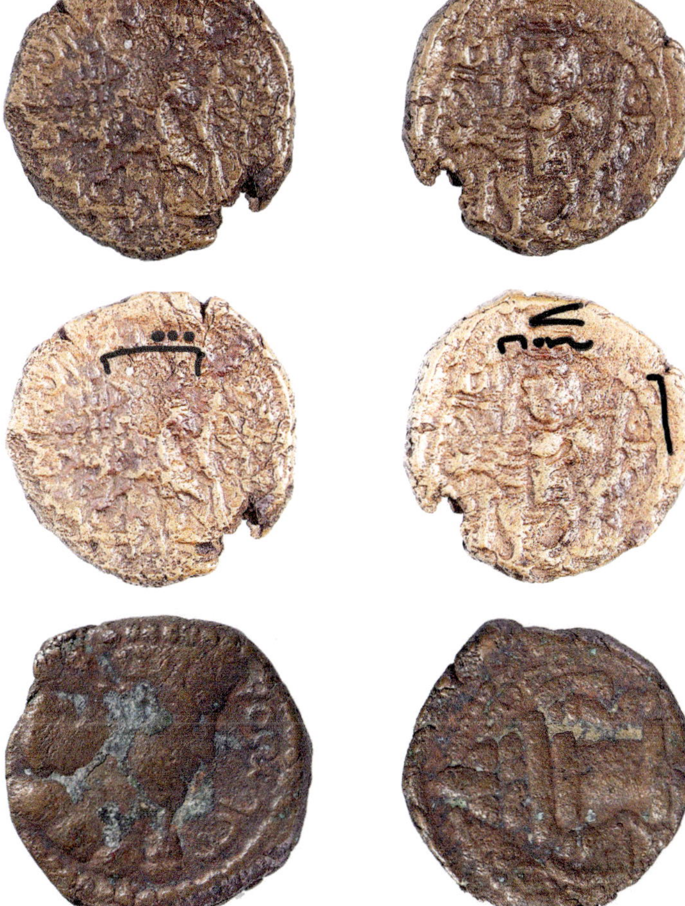

Figure 11a. Copper coin of Kushan king Vāsudeva II, standing king/ enthroned goddess type (Göbl 1984: type 1021), British Museum 1981,0735.1, 2.80g, 16mm, overstruck on copper coin of Kushanshah Peroz I (as Figure 12) (Photo: courtesy of the Trustees of the British Museum.)

Figure 11b. Drawing of figure 11a showing traces of undertype.

Figure 12. Copper coin of Kushanshah Peroz I, Gandhāran mint, bust/ god on fire altar-throne type (Göbl 1984: type 1118), British Museum 1980,1003.1, 4.60g, 17mm. (Photo: courtesy of the Trustees of the British Museum.)

I year 1 in AD 127. The conquest of territory south of the Hindu Kush during the reign of Shapur I is also corroborated by the Rag-i Bibi relief discovered in Afghanistan in 2002 (Grenet et al. 2007). The relief shows a horse-rider, whose surviving details suggest a ruler of the period of Shapur I, if not Shapur I himself, hunting Indian rhinoceroses. He is accompanied by various figures including one in Kushan dress. If this relief is read as a statement of Shapur I's rule 'up to Peshawar' (Grenet et al. 2007: 259), then it would correspond with the extension of Kushanshah rule under Peroz I south of the Hindu Kush.[18]

The close link with the chronology of the Kushan kings continues into the reign of the next Kushanshah Hormizd I, whose early copper coins from south of the Hindu Kush were overstruck by Vāsudeva II's later coins in large quantities (Figures 13a, 13b and 14; Cribb 1981: 106; Cribb 1985: 311–315; Jongeward & Cribb 2015: 172–173). A late coin of Hormizd I has also been reported overstruck on a coin of Vāsudeva II (Cribb 1985: 311–315). The synchronism of the Sasanian, Kushanshah and Kushan kings also supports Bivar's (1979: 324–327) argument that the Kushanshah Hormizd I was the brother of the Sasanian emperor Varahran II who led a revolt against his brother *c.* AD 283 reported in Latin

[18] The existence of coins issued by the Sasanian emperor Varahran I (AD 273–276) with the mint name Balkh (Alram & Gyselen 2012: 458–459, types A55–A57) has been invoked (Grenet et al. 2007: 258–260) as a reason to contradict the proposal that Kushanshahs ruled in Bactria from the time of the Sasanian king Ardashir I. Their existence does not prevent Kushanshah coins being issued in Balkh at an earlier date as no consideration has been given to the possibility that these coins represent a brief intrusion into Kushanshah territory, rather than a period of continuous direct Sasanian rule before Sasanian Varahran I, in the same way that Hormizd I Kushanshah's coins interrupt production of Sasanian coins at Merv.

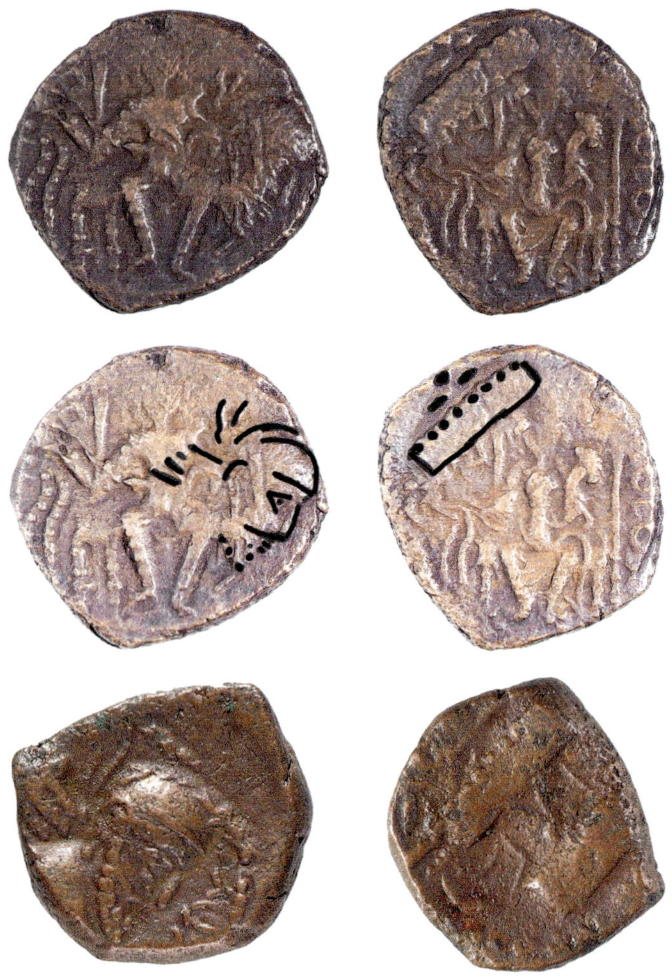

Figure 13a. Copper coin of Kushan king Vāsudeva II, enthroned king/ enthroned goddess type (Göbl 1984: types 1022–1024), British Museum, 1992,0119.23, 4.42g, 19mm, overstruck on copper coin of Kushanshah Hormizd I (as Figure 14). (Photo: courtesy of the Trustees of the British Museum.)

Figure 13b. Drawing of figure 13a showing traces of undertype.

Figure 14.Copper coin of Hormizd I, Kavad, Gandhāran mint, bust/ god on fire altar-throne type (Göbl 1984: type 1124), British Museum, 1990,0921.98, 3.76g, 15mm. (Photo: courtesy of the Trustees of the British Museum.)

sources.[19] During Hormizd I's reign he issued gold coins with the title 'king of kings' in Pahlavi and the mint name Merv (Göbl 1984: type 1026), suggesting a usurpation of the Sasanian king's title. Some of his coins issued in Bactria had the same title in Bactrian or Pahlavi.

The next Kushanshah ruled briefly as he is only known from a single gold coin and a limited number of copper coins from both Bactria and south of the Hindu Kush. His crown is identical to that of Sasanian Varahran II and very similar to that of Sasanian Hormizd II. It has been suggested (Bivar 1979: 320) that Sasanian Hormizd II may have previously ruled as Hormizd II Kushanshah because of this similarity. Hormizd II's link with the Kushanshahs is also suggested by his being the first Sasanian ruler to adopt a coin design feature, the placing of a divine bust in the flames of the fire altar on the reverse, which had already been used by the Kushanshahs Peroz I, and Hormizd I and II. This practice seems to have been developed in the Kushanshahs' mint as a means of combining the Sasanian fire altar/throne design with the Kushan reverse design of a god or goddess (in the same way that Sasanian Ardashir I's coinage combined Parthian throne with Persis fire altar in a unified throne/fire altar design). The first issue of Peroz I presented such a design with two different deities: Oesho labelled 'exalted god' in Bactrian (ΒΑΓΟ ΒΟΡΖΟΟΑΝΔΟ) and Nana labelled 'goddess Nana' (ΒΑΓΟ ΝΑΝΑ) (Cribb 1985: 309, 311 and 319–320). Initially the Sasanian version followed the Kushano-Sasanian coinage in presenting the deity frontally, but by the end of Hormizd II's reign in the Sasanian version the divine image was represented in profile.

[19] Scriptores Historiae Augustae, *Carus* 8: 'Nullo sibi occurrente Mesopotamiam Carus cepit et Ctesiphontem usque pervenit occupatisque Persis domestica seditione imperatoris Persici nomen emeruit.' *XII Panegyrici Latini*, III.17: 'Ipsos Persas ipsumque regem adscitis Sacis et Rufiis et Gelis petit frater Ormies nec respicit vel pro maiestate quasi regem vel pro pietate quasi fratrem.'

The next Kushanshah Peroz II was the last ruler to issue coins in both Bactria and south of the Hindu Kush. His successor in the southern territory was the Sasanian emperor Shapur II (AD 309–379), but in Bactria the Kushano-Sasanian state continued under Varahran Kushanshah. South of the Hindu Kush the Sasanians also established a mint to strike regular Sasanian silver drachms (the 'Kabul' mint, Schindel 2004) which continued through into the reigns of Ardashir II (379–383) and Shapur III (383–388) and also issued Kushano-Sasanian style copper coins in the name of Shapur II. The coinage of Varahran Kushanshah went through several phases, apparently under the authority of the Kidarite Huns, whose *tamga* featured on his coins from its second phase. The Kidarites also issued silver coins in Gandhāra in the name of Varahran Kushanshah until his name was replaced by that of the Kidarite king Kidara who took over from Varahran the title Kushanshah. Kidara also replaced the name of Varahran on the coins issued in Bactria. The intervention of the Kidarites also took place in Kushan territory as the coins of the last Kushan king Kipunadha were copied by the first Kidarite king Kirada. Kirada's coins were followed by issues of the Kidarite king Peroz, the immediate predecessor of Kidara (Cribb 2010).

The Kidarite incursions into Bactria and Gandhāra can be seen as a possible cause of the direct Sasanian involvement south of the Hindu Kush. The Sasanians were in their turn also replaced presumably before 388 by Huns, the so-called Alkhano (Alchon) Huns who issued coins in imitation of the issues of Shapur II and Shapur III (Vondrovec 2014, I: 170, types 36A and 36 B; Pfisterer 2013: 32, types 36A and 36B). The cessation of the 'Kabul' mint before the reign of Varahran IV (388–399) suggests a terminus ante quem for the Alkhano takeover during the reign of Shapur III.

The end of the reign of Shapur III also provides a terminus ante quem for the reign of Kidara as his coins (Figure 15) were found alongside 'Kabul' mint coins of Shapur II, Ardashir II and Shapur III in the Tepe Maranjan hoard found near Kabul (Curiel 1953). The reign of Kidara had probably ended by the end of the reign of Shapur III as the hoard also includes a coin with the same design, but the name of his successor in Bactria, Orolano (Figures 16 and 17; ΒΑΓΟ ΟΡΩΛΑΝΟ ΚΟÞΑΝΟ Þ[Α]ΥΟ; Göbl 1984: type 738.1). Orolano was followed by three other coin issuing Kidarite kings in Bactria: Pidoko (Figure 18; ΒΑΓΟ ΠΙΔΟΚΟ ΚΟÞΑΝΟ ÞΑ[ΥΟ]; Vondrovec 2014: 149, types 84-6 and 84-8), Tobazino (Figure 19; ΒΑΓΟ ΤΟΒΑΖΙΝΟ ΚΟÞΑΝΟ ÞΑΥΟ; Vondrovec 2014: 149, type 84-7) and Okilano ΒΑΓΟ ΩΚΙΛΑΝΟ ΚΟÞΑΝΟ [ÞΑΥΟ]; (Figure 20; provisional reading of name; Göbl 1984: type 740.1; Vondrovec 2014: 149, type 84-5). The reign of Tobazino can be approximately dated *c.* 420 as his coins copy issues of the Sasanian king Varahran IV and were overstruck on coins of Varahran IV and his successor Yazdgard I (399–420) (Vondrovec 2014:392–396). The reign of Okilano(?) can also be dated as his coinage was imitated and replaced by issues in the name of the Sasanian king Peroz who captured Balkh from the Kidarites in AD 467 (Figure 21; Chen, Doo & Wang 2006: nos. 838 and 839; see also the other type of Peroz, wearing his Sasanian crown, Vondrovec 2014: 152, type Peroz-1).

The evidence of the Tepe Maranjan hoard is also supported by the Kidarite coppers from Bactria found among the material collected by Charles Masson from the ancient site at Begram. The large number of small copper coins attributable to the period of Kidara found at Begram strongly suggests that it was during his reign that the Huns were driving the Sasanians out of the Kabul region (Khan, Errington & Cribb 2008: 68–70).

The framework created for the end of the Kushans through their Sasanian, Kushanshah and Kidarite Hun connections matches the framework created by the application of the dating of year one of Kaniṣka I in AD 127 to the numismatic sequence and epigraphic evidence. An alternative framework has been proposed by Schindel (2004; 2005; 2012; 2009), based on aspects of the iconographic details of Kushano-Sasanian, Sasanian and Kushan coins, earrings, diadem ribbons, crowns and firealtars. His main arguments for dating the relationship between Kushano-Sasanian, Sasanian and Kushan coinage was that the earrings depicted on the royal portraits of the Kushanshahs on their coins could only appear

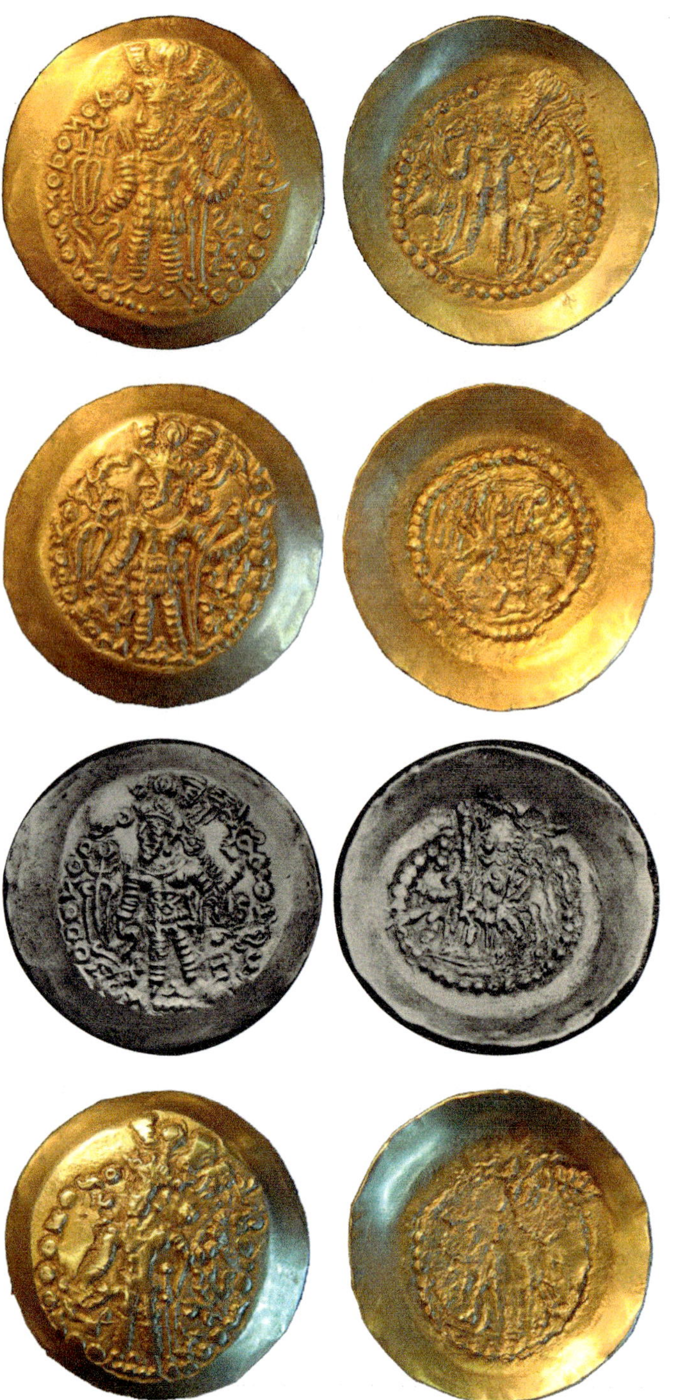

Figure 15.Gold dinara of Kidarite Hun king Kidara, Balkh mint, standing king/ exalted god and bull type, Bactrian inscription: ΒΑΓΟ ΚΙΔΑΡΑ ΟΟ ΟΑΖΑ[Ρ]ΚΟ ΚΟÞΑΝΟ ÞΑ[ΥΟ] (Lord Kidara Great Kushan King), British Museum 1847,1201.265, 7.69g, 34mm. (Photo: courtesy of the Trustees of the British Museum.)

Figure 16.Gold dinara of Kidarite Hun king Orōlano, Balkh mint, standing king/ exalted god and bull type, Bactrian inscription: ΒΑΓΟ ΟΡΩΛΑ - ΝΟ ΚΟÞΑΝΟ Þ[Α]ΥΟ (Lord Orōlano Kushan King), British Museum 1989,0625.4, 7.59g, 34mm. (Photo: courtesy of the Trustees of the British Museum.)

Figure 17.Gold dinara of Kidarite Hun king Orōlano, Balkh mint, standing king/ exalted god and bull type, Bactrian inscription: ΒΑΓΟ ΟΡΩΛΑ - ΝΟ ΚΟÞΑΝΟ Þ[Α]ΥΟ (Lord Orōlano Kushan King), Tepe Maranjan hoard, 7.48g, 35mm, Curiel 1953: 109 ('Ormizd'), plates XV, no. 5 and XVI, no. 12. (Photo: courtesy of the Trustees of the British Museum.)

Figure 18.Gold dinara of Kidarite Hun king Pidoko, Balkh mint, standing king/ exalted god and bull type, Bactrian inscription: ΒΑΓΟ ΠΙΔΟΚΟ - ΟΟ ΚΟÞΑΝΟ [ÞΑ]ΥΟ (Lord Pidoko Kushan King), British Museum 1982,0626.6, 7.41g, 33mm. (Photo: courtesy of the Trustees of the British Museum.)

after *c.* AD 271–273, when they first appeared on Sasanian coins and secondly, that the use of ribbed diadems by Huviṣka could only take place after they had been introduced in Sasanian coin portraits during the reign of the first Sasanian emperor Ardashir I (AD 224–240). He further identified the Kushan crown being bestowed by the goddess on the first Kushanshah (name uncertain) as the crown of Huviṣka (Schindel 2009). He has also identified the fire altar without projections on the coins of the Kushanshah Ardashir as a feature of Kushan coinage before the reign of Vāsudeva I (Schindel 2014),[20] arguing that

[20] Schindel based his argument on the side projections on the top of the fire altar which he mistook for flames (Ingholt & Lyons 1957: 166, fig. 432 which shows a relief from the Kalawan site, Taxila, featuring a fire altar with such corner projections and flames, attended by a Brahman).

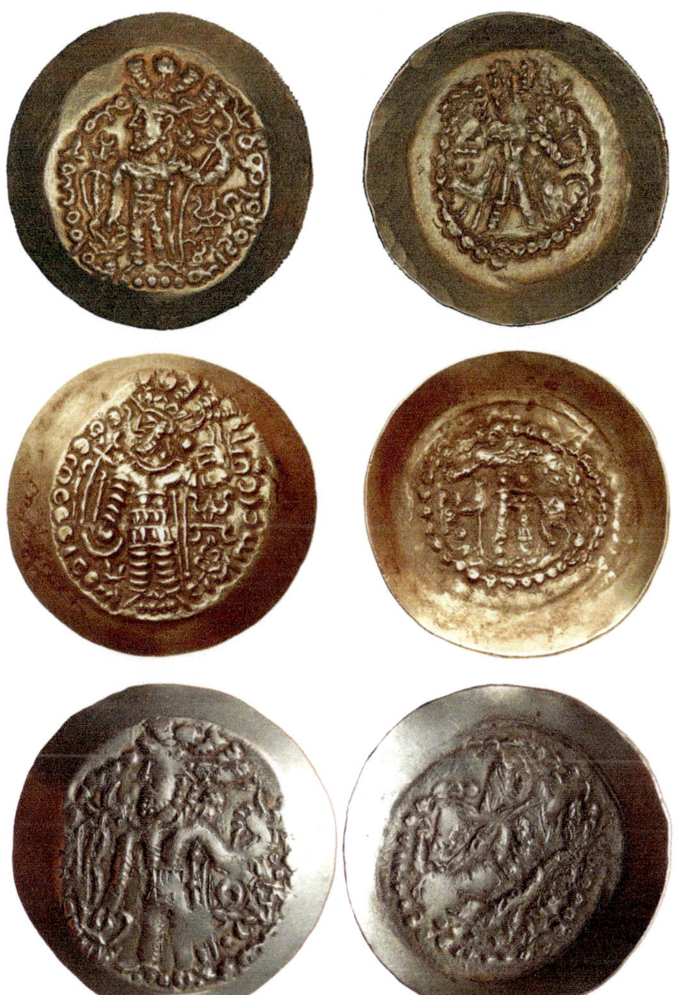

Figure 19. Gold dinara of Kidarite Hun king Tobozino, Balkh mint, standing king/ exalted god and bull type, Bactrian inscription: ΒΑΓΟ ΤΟΒΟΖΙΝΟ - ΚΟÞΑΝΟ ÞΑΥΟ (Lord Tobozino Kushan King), Aman ur Rahman collection (Vondrovec 2014, type 84-7), 7.41g, 34mm. (Photograph courtesy of Aman ur Rahman.)

Figure 20. Gold dinara of Kidarite Hun king Ōkilano, Balkh mint, standing king/ exalted god and bull type, Bactrian inscription: ΒΑΓΟ ΩΚΙΛΑ - ΝΟ ΚΟÞΑΟΝΟ ÞΑ[ΥΟ] (Lord Ōkilano Kushan King), British Museum archive file, 7.35g, 35mm. (Photo: courtesy of the Trustees of the British Museum.)

Figure 21. Gold dinara of Sasanian emperor Peroz, Balkh mint, standing king/ exalted god and bull type (illegible), Bactrian inscription: ΠΙΡΟΖΟ - ÞΑΟΝΑΝΟ ÞΑΟ (Peroz King of Kings), British Museum 1991,0640.17, 7.42g, 35mm.

the Kushanshah coin must therefore date to the period of Vāsudeva I or later as such projections appear on Kushan coins from this period onwards. He added that the representation of Ardashir Kushanshah wearing Sasanian dress also pointed to a date before Vāsudeva I. In both presentations on the coins of the earliest Kushanshahs he attributed them to the period of Huviṣka to argue that Kaniṣka I's year one was in AD 227. His logic was that the Kushanshah coins featuring portraits wearing earrings were issued after 271, therefore Huviṣka's reign was current in the 270s, a chronology only possible if the Kushan era starting in AD 227 was that of Kaniṣka I.

The main problem with Schindel's dating of the Kushans is the gap created between the rulers with inscriptions dated in Azes and Greek eras and those using the first and second centuries of the era of Kaniṣka I. Taking the later date for Azes era year 1, *c.* 46 BC as proposed above, the latest date in the reign of Wima Kadphises is *c.* AD 113 (Greek era 287) or if the anonymous Mathurā inscription is his *c.* AD 125 (Greek era 299). This creates a gap of a hundred years between Wima Kadphises and his son Kaniṣka I. In order to justify the third-century date for Kaniṣka I a new chronology would be needed for the early Kushan kings, drawing the first three kings forward into the late second to early third century. Such a late dating for their links with the Indo-Parthians and their Parthian contemporaries would be unreasonable. The fundamental argument that the dating of artistic details should rely only on coin designs seems improbable. Other sources of iconography are equally possible. Earrings, for example were already a feature in Iranian art before the Sasanian period.

Schindel also offers no rationale for suggesting that Kushanshahs were minting coins in Bactria, or that there was an issue of Balkh mint coins by Sasanian Varahran I during the reign of Huviṣka, as Huviṣka's gold coins were struck throughout his reign in Bactria and his gold and copper coins circulated there. The hoarding together of Kushanshah coins of the fourth Kushanshah Hormizd I and coins of Kushan king Vāsudeva II (Cribb 1981; 1985) clearly suggest that the Kushanshah coins were issued from the reign of Kaniṣka II and no earlier. The currency of the imitation Vāsudeva copper coins, which I have attributed to the early Kushanshahs, during the reigns of Kaniṣka II and Vasiṣka has also been reaffirmed by a hoard recently discovered in the Peshawar region (Cribb, Khan & Amanullah 2012).

The solution proposed by Schindel of dating Kaniṣka I's year one to AD 227 is also overturned by the overstrikes reported above. The direct links between the southern coins of the third and fourth Kushanshahs Peroz I and Hormizd I and the Kushan king Vāsudeva II, ruling from c. 141 years after Kaniṣka I year one, places their coins in the fourth century if Kaniṣka I's year one were c. AD 227, implausibly contemporary with both the Merv mint coins of Shapur I (240–270) (overstruck by Peroz I) and the last southern Kushano-Sasanian style coins in the name of Shapur II (309–379) (issued after the coins of the fifth and sixth Kushanshahs). Falk's assertion that 'hardly anyone would accept AD 227 as the date for the accession of Kaniṣka I to the throne' (Falk 2001:130) seems acceptable in the face of such implausible solutions for the chronology of the Kushano-Sasanian and Kushan kings.

Table 5. Kushan, Kushanshah and Sasanian links.

Kushan kings	**K1 = AD 127**	**Sasanian Kushanshahs and Kidarite Hun successors**	**Sasanian Emperors**	**Numismatic links**
Kaniṣka	K 1 = AD 127			
Huviṣka	K 25 = AD 151			
Vāsudeva I	K 64 = AD 190		Ardashir I 224–240	Vāsudeva sends embassy to China in AD 230
Kaniṣka II	K [1]05 = AD 231	Unknown king Ardashir		Issue of Kushan gold coins in Bactria stops. Sasanian imitations of Vāsudeva I gold and Kaniṣka II coppers. Copper coins issued by unidentified Kushanshah showing goddess Anahita offering king Kushan crown. Copper coins issued by Ardashir Kushanshah inscribed in Bactrian, copying Kushan coins of Kaniṣka II.
Vasiṣka	K [1]20 = AD 246	Peroz I	Shapur I 240–270 Record of conquest 'as far as Peshawar'	Peroz I Kushanshah issues coins copying the imitation Kushan coins and with new coin design based on Ardashir's throne/altar type. Examples of both types overstruck on copper coins of Shapur I from Merv mint. Gold coin shows Peroz being offered Kushan king by Kushan goddess Ardochsho in style of Kaniṣka II coins.

Kaniṣka III Vāsudeva II	K [1]41 = AD 268	Hormizd I	Bahram II 276–293 Brother of Hormizd I?	Early Vāsudeva II copper coin overstruck on Peroz I's copper coin. Late Vāsudeva II copper coins overstruck on Hormizd I's early coinages.
		Hormizd II	Narseh 293–303 Hormizd II 303–309	Hormizd II Sasanian emperor (wearing similar winged headdress to his Kushanshah predecessor) adopts bust on altar type from Kushanshahs' copper coinage.
Ṣaka		Peroz II	Shapur II 309–379	Shapur II takes direct control of part of Kushanshah domain, issuing Kushanshah style copper coins and Sasanian silver coins in Kabul region.
Kipunadha		Varahran		
		Kirada Peroz Kidara		End of Kushan coinage in Gandhāra. Kirada imitates Kipunadha coins in Gandhāra.
			Ardashir II 379–383	Peroz issues coins with ram horns in Gandhāra and with same crown in name of Varahran in Balkh. Kidara issued coins in Gandhāra and Balkh, replacing Varahran's name with his own and giving himself title Kushanshah. Coins issued in Gandhāra in the Kushan style with image of Kidara, but acknowledging Samudra[gupta] (c. AD 330–380). Kidara coins from Bactria in Tepe Maranjan hoard with coins of Shapur II, Ardashir II and Shapur III. Silver coins of Ardashir II issued in Kabul area.
		Orolano	Shapur III 383–388	Silver coins of Shapur III issued in Kabul area. Orolano coin from Bactria in Tepe Maranjan hoard with coins of Kidara and Shapur II, Ardashir II and Shapur III.
		Pidoko	Varahran IV 388–399	Alkhano silver coinage begins in Kabul region. Pidoko issuing gold coins in Bactria.
			Yazdgard I 399–420	
		Tobozino	Varahran V 420–438	Tobozino issuing gold coins in Bactria and imitating silver coins of Varahran IV and overstriking coins of Varahran IV and Yazdgard I.
		Okilano(?)	Yazdgard II 438–457	Okilano(?) issuing gold coins in Bactria.
			Peroz 457–484	Peroz imitating gold coins in Kidarite style of Okilano at Balkh 467–484.

A chronological framework for Gandhāran sculpture

The Kushan king list constructed around numismatic and epigraphic evidence combined with the rare references to the Kushan state in literary sources creates a framework for the chronology of Gandhāra within which Gandhāran sculpture can be examined. The framework positions the Kushans and the rulers who preceded and succeeded them in control of Gandhāra during the period of greatest activity in the creation of Buddhist sculpture in the region (Table 6). The few examples of Gandhāran art with dated inscriptions can then be positioned within this framework. The inscriptions in the three hundreds can be associated with the Greek era and dated accordingly. The inscriptions dated year 89 appear to be in the first century of Kaniṣka I era (127 + 88 = AD 215) and 5 (227 + 4 = AD 231) in the second century, but it cannot be ruled out that they could be moved a hundred years later in line with the recognized use for this era of a cycle of centuries (e.g. 227 + 88 = AD 315 and 327 + 4 = AD 331). It remains highly unlikely that the year 5 sculpture was made in the reign of Kaniṣka I (as Fussman 1974: 57; Fussman 1987: 72–75) as its marked difference from the Kaniṣka Buddha coins and the Kaniṣka casket and its stylistic similarity to the year 89 inscription sculpture both suggest a later date.

Although without specific dates there are three other representative examples of Gandhāran art which can be added to the framework as they can now be dated approximately in relation to the Kushan king list. The clarification of the date of the coins associated with the Bīmarān casket, as issues of the late first to early second century AD (Cribb 2015; 2018) suggests that the casket should be dated *c.* 100 or slightly later. The identification by Errington (2002) of a copper coin (or a clay copy of a coin) of Huviṣka among the finds associated with the Kaniṣka reliquary placed its deposit in the second half of Huviṣka's reign. There is now clear evidence from coins that the royal image represented on the casket is Kaniṣka I, as coins issued early in his reign (e.g. Göbl 1984: types 798, 803, 807, 814 and 818) show him with two of the features of the casket image, i.e. beardless with sideburns and with his left hand covered with

Table 6. Approximate framework for rulers of Gandhāra and adjacent regions.

BC/AD	Bactria	Begram/Kabul	Gandhāra	Taxila	Dated and datable Gandhāran images
AD10	**Da Yuezhi**	**Indo-Scythians**	**Indo-Scythian**	**Indo-Scythians**	
20			**Indo-Parthian**		
30			Gondophares	Satraps	
40	**Kushans**	**Kushans**			
50	Kujūla Kadphises				
60			Abdagases	**Kushans**	
70					
80			Sasan[1]		
90	Wima Takto			**Indo-Parthians**	
100			Kushans	Kushans	Bīmarān Casket (Cribb 2015)
110	Wima Kadphises				
120	Kaniṣka I				
130					
140					year 318 (Konow 1929: 106–107)
150	Huviṣka				Kaniṣka coins (Cribb 1999) and reliquary Errington

160					
170					
180					
190	Vāsudeva I				
200					
210					year 384 (Konow 1929: 117–119) year 89 (Konow 1929: 171–172)
220					year 399 (Konow 1929: 124–127)
230	**Kushanshahs**	Kaniṣka II			year 5 (Fussman 1974: 54–58; Harle 1974: 128)
240	?/ Ardashir	Vasiṣka			
250	Peroz I				
260		**Kushanshahs**	disputed by Kushans and Kushanshahs	Kaniṣka III/ VD II	
270	Hormizd I			Vāsudeva II	
280					
290					
300	Hormizd II			Mahi	
310	Peroz II			Ṣaka	[year 89]
320	Varahran				
330	**Kidarite Huns**[2]			Kipunadha	[year 5]
340	Kirada/ Peroz/ Kidara[3]	**Sasanian**	**Kidarite Huns**	**Kidarite Huns**	
350		Shapur II			
360					
370					
380		Ardashir II/ Shapur III			
390	Orolano	**Alchano Huns**	**Alchano Huns**	**Alchano Huns**	
400	Pidoko				
410					
420	Tobazino				
430					
440	Okilano(?)				
450					
460	**Sasanian**				
470	Peroz				
480	**Hephthalites**				

[1] Allied with the Apracarajas.
[2] Initially with Kushanshah as puppet.
[3] After initial period adopting title Kushanshah.

his sleeve. This suggests that the casket could have been created during Kaniṣka I's reign and deposited after a period of use. The gold and copper coins of Kaniṣka I showing the Buddha in the same style as the Buddha images on the Bīmarān casket can also be dated to the last years of his reign (Cribb 1999/2000).

The dating of Gandhāran art has long depended upon the broad frameworks created for the region through coins and inscriptions. The approximate dates used in books, exhibitions and museum websites make use of such frameworks. The shift by art historians and curators from using AD 78 to a later date of 100 or 127 (128, 129) for year one of Kaniṣka I is evident in the way that they date sculpture (Table 7). The broad tendency has been to date architectural features and toilet trays without obvious Buddhist content to the first century BC–first century AD, Buddhist stone sculpture to the first-fourth centuries AD and stucco sculpture to the fourth-fifth centuries AD. The framework outlined here can now be used to readdress these assumptions, particularly in relation to pieces bearing dates or found from excavated sites with numismatic dating material.

Acknowledgement

I would like to thank Peter Stewart, Director of the Classical Art Research Centre, University of Oxford, for his invitations to participate in the Gandhāra Connections project and to make this presentation at the workshop, *Problems of Chronology in Gandhāran Art*. I appreciate his encouragement to prepare it for publication here. I also thank my former colleagues at the British Museum, Elizabeth Errington, Robert Bracey and Kay Rienjang, Shailendra Bhandare of the Ashmolean Museum, my friends David Jongeward, Bob Senior, Harry Falk and Pankaj Tandon, and my partner Linda Crook for their support and encouragement. I am deeply indebted to Professors Nasim Khan and Gul Rahim Khan of University of Peshawar, Aman ur Rahman and Hans Loeschner for their help. Thanks also to Professor Nicholas Sims-Williams for his very welcome advice on the Bactrian inscriptions. I am also very grateful to Neil Kreitman for the support for my research he has generously given over the last three decades. I dedicate this paper to the memory of my much-missed old friend Professor A.K. Narain (1925–2013), who first introduced me to the mysteries of Kushan chronology in 1972.

Table 7. The impact of dating Kaniṣka I's year 1 on dating Gandhāran sculpture.

Publications/ websites featuring Gandhāran sculpture	Date used for Kaniṣka era year 1	Dating and number of examples of Gandhāran sculpture in each publication/website									
		1 BC	1 AD	1–2 AD	2 AD	2-3 AD	3 AD	3-4 AD	4 AD	4-5 AD	5 AD
Pal 1987	78		4	2	4	3	2				
Czuma 1986	78		16	2	16	4	6	3	2	6	
vam.ac.uk	78		2	2	10	5	7	15	4	3	
Errington & Cribb 1992	100	2	7	6	4	9	3		1	1	
Stančo 2001	100	1		1	14	16	4	2	1		
Mohatta 2009	100	2	11	2	6	28	1	13	2	11	1
britishmuseum.org	100		2	27	4	614		7		71	2
Jongeward 2003	127		1	2	12	3	13	1		13	
Berhendt 2007	129	5	7		5	3	4	2	1	12	6
Ali & Qazi 2008	128					321					
Luczanits 2008	128	1	13	17	27	53	20	24	7	10	1

References

Ali I. & Qazi M.N. 2008. *Gandhara Sculptures in the Peshawar Museum*. Peshawar: Peshawar Museum.

Alram M. & Gyselen R. 2012. *Sylloge Nummorum Sasanidarum Paris - Berlin - Wien*, vol. 2, *Ohrmazd I. - Ohrmazd II*. Vienna: Verlag der Österreichischen Akademie der Wissenschaften.

Baums S. 2012. Catalog and Revised Texts and Translations of Gandhāran Reliquary Inscriptions. Pages 200–251 in D. Jongeward, E. Errington, R. Salomon and S. Baums, *Gandhāran Buddhist Reliquaries* (*Gandharan Studies*, no. 1). Seattle: University of Washington.

Behrendt K. 2007. *The Art of Gandhara in the Metropolitan Museum of Art*. New York: Metropolitan Museum of Art.

Bivar D. 1979. The Absolute Chronology of the Kushano-Sasanian Governors of Central Asia. Pages 317–332 in J. Harmatta (ed), *Prolegomena to the Sources on the History of Pre-Islamic Central Asia*. Budapest: Academic Press.

Bracey R. 2009. The Coinage of Wima Kadphises. *Gandhāran Studies* 3: 25–74.

Bracey R. 2017. The date of Kanishka since 1960. *Indian Historical Review* 44.1: 21–61.

Bracey R. & Oddy W.A. 2010. The Analysis of Kushan Period Gold Coins by Specific Gravity. *Gandhāran* Studies 4: 31-39.

British Museum <http://www.britishmuseum.org/research/collection_online/search.aspx>.

Chakravarti R. 2014. The Kushanas. Pages 35–68 in D.K. Chakrabarti and M. Lal (eds), *History of Ancient India*, vol. IV, *Political History and Administration (C. 200 BC–AD 750)*. New Delhi: Aryan Books International.

Chen Xiejan, Doo R. & Wang Yue 2006. *Shanghai Museum's Collection of Ancient Coins from the Silk Road*. Shanghai: Shanghai Museum.

Cribb J. 1981. Gandharan hoards of Kushano-Sasanian and Late Kushan Coppers. *Coin Hoards* 6: 93–108.

Cribb J. 1985. Some Further Hoards of Kushano-Sasanian and Late Kushan Coppers. *Coin Hoards* 7: 308–321.

Cribb J. 1990. Numismatic Evidence for Kushano-Sasanian Chronology. *Studia Iranica* 19/2: 151–193, plates I–VIII.

Cribb J. 1992. Numismatic evidence for the date of the Periplus. Pages 131–145 in D. W. MacDowall, S. Sharma and S. Garg (eds), *Indian Numismatics, History, Art and Culture: Essays in Honour of Dr. P. L. Gupta*. Delhi: Agam Kala Prakashan.

Cribb J. 1996. The 'Heraus' Coins: Their Attribution to the Kushan King Kujula Kadphises, c. AD 30- 80. Pages 107-134 in M. Price, A. Burnett, R. Bland (eds), *Essays in Honour of Robert Carson and Kenneth Jenkins*. London: Spink and Son Ltd.

Cribb J. 1997. Numismatic Perspectives on Chronology in the Crossroads of Asia. Pages 215–230 in R. Allchin, B. Allchin, N. Kreitman & E. Errington (eds), *Gandharan Art in Context - East-West Exchanges at the Crossroads of Asia*. New Delhi: Regency Publications.

Cribb J. 1999. The Early Kushan Kings: New Evidence for Chronology: Evidence from the Rabatak Inscription of Kanishka I. Pages 177–205 in M. Alram and D.E. Klimburg-Salter (eds), *Coins, Art, and Chronology: Essays on the Pre-Islamic History of the Indo-Iranian Borderlands*. Vienna: Österreichische Akademie der Wissenschaften.

Cribb J. 1999/2000 Kanishka I's Buddha Image Coins Revisited. *Silk Road Art and Archaeology* 6: 151-89.

Cribb J. 2005. The Greek Kingdom of Bactria, its Coinage and its Collapse. Pages 207–226 in O. Bopearachchi and M.-F. Boussac (eds), *Afghanistan: ancien carrefour entre l'Est et l'Ouest* (*Indicopleustoi: Archaeologies of the Indian Ocean* 3). Turnhout: Brepols.

Cribb J. 2010. The Kidarites, the Numismatic Evidence. Pages 91–146 in M. Alram, D.E. Klimburg-Salter, M. Inaba and M. Pfisterer (eds), *Coins, Art, and Chronology II: the First Millennium in the Indo-Iranian Borderlands*. Vienna: Österreichische Akademie der Wissenschaften.

Cribb J. 2014. The Soter Megas Coins of the First and Second Kushan kings, Kujula Kadphises and Wima

Takto. *Gandhāran Studies* 8: 77–133.
Cribb J. 2015. Dating and Locating Mujatria and the Two Kharahostes. *Journal of the Oriental Numismatic Society* 223: 26–48.
Cribb J. 2018. The Bimaran Casket: The Problem of its Date and Significance. Forthcoming in J. Stargardt (ed) *Buddhist Relics*. London: British Museum.
Cribb J. & Bracey R. in preparation. *Kushan Coins - Catalogue of the British Museum Collection*.
Cribb J., Khan, F. & Amanullah 2012. Late Kushan Copper Hoard(?) from the Collection of the S.R.O. in Directorate of Archaeology and Museums Khyber Pakhtunkhwa. *Ancient Pakistan* 23: 117–143.
Curiel R. 1953. Le trésor du Tépé Maranjān. Pages 101–131 and plates 9–16 in R. Curiel & D. Schlumberger, *Trésors monétaires d'Afghanistan* (*Mémoires de la délégation archéologique française en Afghanistan* XIV). Paris: Imprimerie Nationale.
Czuma S.J. & Morris R. 1986. *Kushan Sculpture: Images from Early India*. Cleveland: Cleveland Museum of Art.
Errington E. & Cribb J. 1992. *Crossroads of Asia - Transformation in Image and Symbol*. Cambridge: Ancient India and Iran Trust.
Errington E. 2002. Numismatic Evidence for Dating the 'Kanishka' Reliquary. *Silk Road Art and Archaeology* 8: 127–146.
Falk H. 2001. The *Yuga* of Sphujiddhvaja and the Era of the Kuṣāṇas. *Silk Road Art and Archaeology* 7: 121–136.
Falk H. 2002/3. Some Inscribed Images from Mathurā Revisited. *Indo-Asiatische Zeitschrift* 6/7: 31–47.
Falk H. 2004. The Kaniṣka Era in Gupta Records. *Silk Road Art and Archaeology* 10: 167–176.
Falk H. 2007. Ancient Indian Eras: An Overview. *Bulletin of the Asia Institute*, New Series 21: 131-145.
Falk H (ed). 2015. *Kushan Histories - Literary Sources and Selected Papers from a Symposium at Berlin, December 5 to 7, 2013*. Bremen: Hempen Verlag.
Falk H. & Bennett C. 2009. Macedonian Intercalary Months and the Era of Azes. *Acta Orientalia* 70: 197–215.
Fleet J.F. 1888. *Corpus Inscriptionum Indicarum: Inscriptions of the Early Gupta Kings*, vol. 3. Calcutta: Central Publications Branch.
Fussman G. 1974. Documents épigraphiques kouchans. *Bulletin de l'École française d'Extrême-Orient* 61: 1–66.
Fussman G. 1987. Numismatic and Epigraphic Evidence for the Chronology of Early Gandharan Art. Pages 67–88 in M. Yaldiz & W. Lobo (eds), *Investigating Indian Art*. Berlin: Museum für Indische Kunst, Staatliche Museen Preussischer Kulturbesitz, Berlin.
Fussman G. 1993. Ménandre l'Indo-grec ou Paul Demiéville revisité. *Journal Asiatique* 281.1-2: 61–183.
Fussman G. 2015. Kushan Power and the Expansion of Buddhism beyond the Soleiman Mountains. Pages 153–202 in H. Falk (ed.), *Kushan Histories: Literary Sources and Selected Papers from a Symposium at Berlin, December 5 to 7, 2013*. Bremen: Hempen Verlag.
Göbl R. 1965. Vāsiška II, ein bisher unbekannter König der späten Kušān. *Anzeiger der philosophisch-historischen Klasse der Österreichischen Akademie der Wissenschaften* 100: 283–285.
Göbl R. 1984. *System und Chronologie der Münzprägung des Kušānreiches*. Vienna: Verlag der Österreichischen Akademie der Wissenschaften.
Göbl R. 1993. *Donum Burns - die Kušānmünzen im Münzkabinett Bern und die Chronologie*. Vienna: Fassbinder.
Grenet F., Lee J., Martinez P. & Ory F. 2007. The Sasanian relief at Rag-i Bibi (Northern Afghanistan). Pages 243–267 in J. Cribb & G. Hermann (eds), *After Alexander - Central Asia Before Alexander*. London: British Academy.
Harle J. C. 1974. A Hitherto Unknown Dated Sculpture from Gandhara: A Preliminary Report. Pages 128–135 in J. E. van Lohuizen-de Leeuw and J. M. M. Ubaghs (eds), *South Asian Archaeology 1973: Papers from the Second International Conference of the Association for the Promotion of South Asian Archaeology in Western Europe Held in the University of Amsterdam*. Leiden: Brill.
Huyse P. 1999. *Die Dreisprachige Inschrift Šābuhrs I an Der Ka'ba-I Zardušt (ŠKZ)* (*Corpus Inscriptionum Iranicarum* 3.1). London: School of Oriental and African Studies.
Ingholt H. & Lyons I. 1957. *Gandharan Art in Pakistan*. New York: Pantheon Books.

Jongeward D. 2003. *Buddhist Art of Pakistan and Afghanistan: The Royal Ontario Museum Collection of Gandhāra Sculpture*. Toronto: Royal; Ontario Museum.

Jongeward D. & Cribb J. 2015. *Kushan, Kushano-Sasanian and Kidarite: A Catalogue of Coins from the American Numismatic Society*. New York: American Numismatic Society.

Khan G.R. & Cribb J. 2012. Coins of Kujula Kadphises from Taxila. *Gandhāran Studies* 6: 81–219.

Khan M.N., Errington E. & Cribb J. 2008. *Coins from Kashmir Smast: New Numismatic Evidence*, Peshawar: M.N. Khan.

Konow S. 1929. *Corpus Inscriptionum Indicarum*, II.1, *Kharoshṭhī Inscriptions with the Exception of those of Aśoka*. Calcutta: Government of India.

Konow S. 1934. Note on the Mathurā Inscription of Samvat 299. Pages 172–173 in *Commemorative Essays Presented to Professor Kashinath Bapuji Pathak*. Poona: Bhandakar Oriental Institute.

Loeschner H. 2007. A New Oesho/Shiva Image of Sasanian 'Peroz' Taking Power in the Northern Part of the Kushan Empire. *Journal of the Oriental Numismatic Society* 192: 22–24.

Loginov S.D. & Nikitin A.B. 1993. Sasanian coins of the third century from Merv. *Mesopotamia* 28: 225–246.

Lohuizen-de Leeuw J.E. van 1949. *The 'Scythian' Period: An Approach to the History, Art, Epigraphy and Palaeography of North India from the 1st Century BC to the 3rd Century AD*. Leiden: Brill.

Lohuizen-de Leeuw J.E. van 1986. The second century of the Kanishka era. *South Asian Studies* 2: 1–9.

Luczanits C. 2008. *Gandhara - the Buddhist Heritage of Pakistan: Legends, Monasteries, and Paradise*. Mainz: Verlag Philipp von Zabern.

Lüders H. 1961 *Mathura Inscriptions*, edited by K.L. Janert. Göttingen: Vanderhoeck & Ruprecht.

Mak B.M. 2013. The last chapter of Sphujidhvaja's *Yavanajātaka* critically edited with notes. *SCIAMVS* 14: 59–148.

Marshall J. 1951. *Taxila: An Illustrated Account of Archaeological Excavations carried out at Taxila under the Orders of the Government of India between the Years 1913 and 1934* (3 volumes). Cambridge: Cambridge University Press.

Mitchiner M. 1976. *Indo-Greek and Indo-Scythian Coinage*, vol. 7 *Decline of the Indo-Scythians - Contemporaries of the Indo-Scythians*; vol. 8: *The Indo-Parthians*. London: Hawkins Publications.

Mitchiner M. 2004. *Ancient Trade and Early Coinage* (2 volumes). London: Hawkins Publications.

Moffett S.H. 1998. *A History of Christianity in Asia* (2nd edition), vol. 1. New York: Orbis Books.

Mohatta Palace Museum 2009. *Visions of Divinity: The Art of Gandhara*. Karachi: Mohatta Palace Museum.

Mukherjee B.N. 1982. The Yavanajātaka of Sphujidhvaja, the Śakakāla and the Kaniṣka Era. *Journal of the American Oriental Society* 102/2: 361-364.

Mukherjee B.N. 1987. A Mathura Image Inscription. *Indian Museum Bulletin* 22: 28–29.

Mukherjee B.N. 1992. Ob odnoj nadpisi iz Matxury i o ee značenii dlja problemy Javanov i šaka-paxlavov. *Vestnik Drevnej Istorii* 1: 87–88.

Mukherjee B.N. 1998. The great Kushan testament. *Indian Museum Bulletin* 32: 1–105.

Mukherjee B.N. 2004. *Kushāna Studies: New Perspectives*. Kolkata: Firma KLM Pvt. Ltd.

Oddy W.A. & Cribb J. 1998. Debasement and Sequence of Late Kushana Gold Coins. Pages 275–292 in A.K. Jha & S. Garg (eds), *Ex Moneta - Essays on Numismatics in Honour of Dr. David MacDowall*. New Delhi: Harman Publishing House.

Pal P. 1987. *Indian Sculpture*, vol. 1. Los Angeles: Los Angeles County Museum of Art.

Pfisterer M. 2013. *Hunnen in Indien*. Vienna: Österreichische Akademie der Wissenschaften.

Pingree D. 1959. A Greek Linear Planetary Text in India. *Journal of the American Oriental Society* 79/4: 282–284.

Pingree D. 1961. The Yavanajātaka of Sphujidhavaja. *Journal of Oriental Research, Madras* 31: 16–31.

Rosenfield J.M. 1967. *The Dynastic Arts of the Kushans*. Berkeley: University of California Press.

Salomon R. 1998. *Indian Epigraphy*. New York: Oxford University Press.

Salomon R. 2005. The Indo-Greek Era of 186/5 B.C. in a Buddhist Reliquary Inscription. Pages 359–401 in O. Bopearachchi and M.-F. Boussac (eds), *Afghanistan: ancien carrefour entre l'Est et l'Ouest* (*Indicopleustoi: Archaeologies of the Indian Ocean* 3). Turnhout: Brepols.

Schindel N. 2004. *Sylloge Nummorum Sasanidarum Paris - Berlin - Wien*, vol. 3, *Shapur II - Kawad*. Vienna: Vienna: Verlag der Österreichischen Akademie der Wissenschaften.

Schindel N. 2005. Adhuc sub iudice lis est? Zur Datierung der kushanosasanidischen Münzen. Pages 217–224 in H. Emmerig (ed.), *Vindobona docet. 40 Jahre Institut für Numismatik und Geldgeschichte der Universität Wien, 1965-2005* (*Numismatische Zeitschrift* 113/114). Vienna: Verlag der Österreichischen Numismatischen Gesellschaft.

Schindel N. 2009. Ardashir 2 Kushanshah and Huvishka the Kushan: Numismatic Evidence for the Date of the Kushan King Kanishka I. *Journal of the Oriental Numismatic Society* 198: 12–14.

Schindel N. 2011. The Era of the Bactrian Documents: A Reassessment. *Gandhāran Studies* 5: 1–10.

Schindel N. 2012. The Beginning of Kushano-Sasanian Coinage. Pages 65–73 in M. Alram & R. Gyselen, *Sylloge Nummorum Sasanidarum Paris - Berlin - Wien*. vol. 2, *Ohrmazd I. - Ohrmazd II*. Vienna: Verlag der Österreichischen Akademie der Wissenschaften.

Schindel N. 2014. Ardashir 1 Kushanshah and Vasudeva the Kushan: Numismatic evidence for the date of the Kushan king Kaniṣka I. *Journal of the Oriental Numismatic Society* 220: 27–30.

Sellwood D. 1980. *An Introduction to the Coinage of Parthia* (2nd edition). London: Spink and Son Ltd.

Senior R. 1997. *From Gondophares to Kanishka*. Glastonbury: R. Senior.

Senior R. 2001. *Indo-Scythian Coins and History*, vols. 1–3. London: Classical Numismatic Group.

Senior R. 2006. *Indo-Scythian Coins and History*, vol. 4. London: Classical Numismatic Group.

Senior R. 2009. Three Historically Important Indo-Greek and Indo-Scythian Coins. *Journal of the Oriental Numismatic Society* 199: 19–20.

Sims-Williams N. 1998. Further Notes on the Bactrian Inscription of Rabatak. Pages 79–92 in N. Sims-Williams (ed.) *Proceedings of the Third European Conference of Iranian Studies*, Part 1: *Old and Middle Iranian Studies*. Wiesbaden: Reichert.

Sims-Williams N. 2004. The Bactrian Inscription of Kanishka the Great: A New Reading. *Bulletin of the Asia Institute* 18: 53–68.

Sims-Williams N. & Cribb J. 1995/6. A New Bactrian Inscription of Kanishka the Great. *Silk Road Art and Archaeology* 4: 75–142.

Singh U. 2009. A History of Ancient and Early Medieval India. Delhi: Dorling Kindersley (India) Pvt. Ltd. (Pearson Education).

Smith V.A. 1903. The Kushan, or Indo-Scythian, Period of Indian History, *Journal of the Royal Asiatic Society* 1903.1:1–64.

Stančo L. 2001. Gandharan Sculpture of the Náprstek Museum', Prague. *Annals of the Náprstek Museum* 22: 31-64.

Tokyo National Museum 2002. *The Art of Gandhara, Pakistan*. Tokyo: Tokyo National Museum.

Victoria and Albert Museum <https://collections.vam.ac.uk/search>.

Vondrovec K. 2014. *Coinage of the Iranian Huns and their Successors from Bactria to Gandhāra (4th to 8th century CE)*. Vienna: Verlag der Österreichischen Akademie der Wissenschaften.

Widemann F. 1972 Une surfrappe de Gondophares sur Hermaios et une autre de Kozoulo Kadphises sur Gondophares qui apportent deux jalons numismatiques à la chronologie entre les Indo-Grecs et le début de l'empire Kouchan. *Bulletin de la Société Française de Numismatique* 27.1: 147-151.

Positioning Gandhāran Buddhas in chronology: significant coordinates and anomalies

Juhyung Rhi

In tackling the bewildering complexity surrounding the chronology of Gandhāran Buddhist imagery, we are naturally tempted to start with dated images, although we have to admit simultaneously that those dates are at the very centre of the complexity. Numerous scholars have examined, or at least commented on, the problem in previous scholarship,[1] and I am going to add yet another attempt to the list on this occasion (see further Stefan Baums's paper in the present volume, especially his Appendix 4). My approach may differ in that I will try to explore the problem in relation to five major visual types I have identified among Gandhāran Buddhas in my previous work (Rhi 2008). In particular, I am interested in positioning the dated images in conjunction with the five groups and discussing the ramifications of this placement for drawing a large chronological picture of Gandhāran Buddhist imagery. The following discussions will take two premises into consideration. First, the development of Gandhāran Buddhist imagery probably did not unfold in a single, linear process, which often formed an implicit basis of previous discussions on chronology. We have to take into consideration that there were a number of small and large formal series that had different origins temporally or spatially. Second, these formal series could often have coexisted chronologically, thus overlapping or being interrelated to one another, rather than a single, unified visual form monopolizing a given period of time.

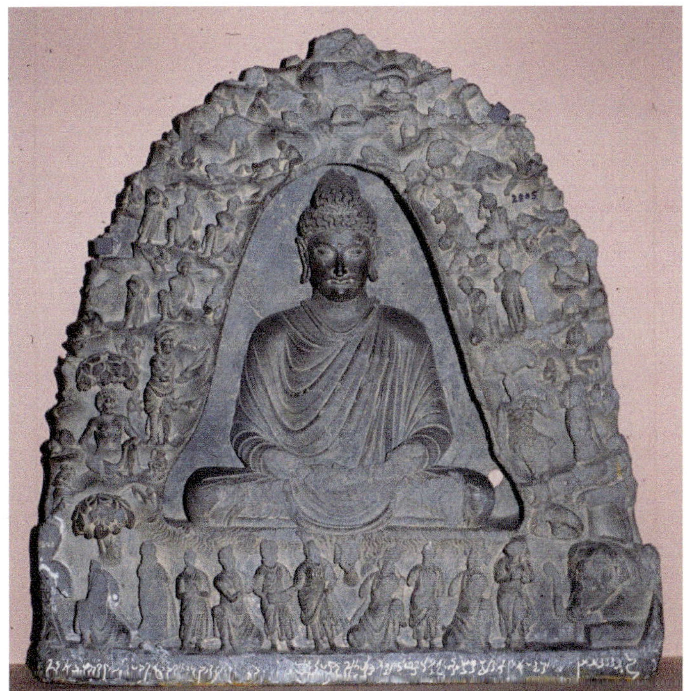

Figure 1. Indraśailaguhā. From Mamāne Ḍherī, Peshawar basin. Dated year 89. H. 76 cm. Peshawar Museum. (Photo: J. Rhi.)

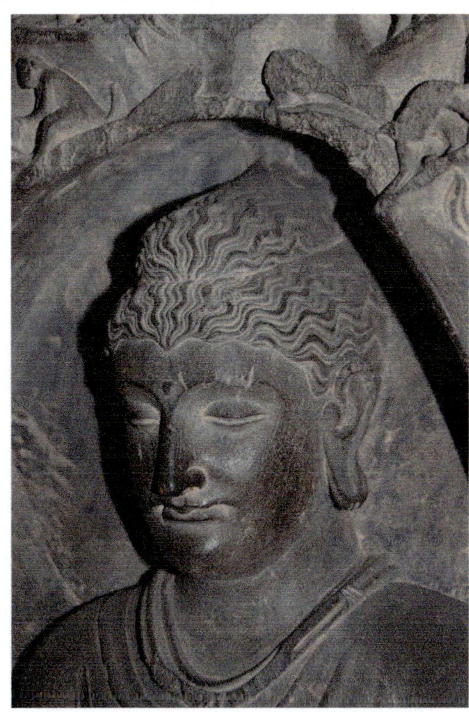

Figure 2. Detail of Figure 1. (Photo: J. Rhi)

* I would like to thank Professor Richard Salomon for making valuable comments on this paper, especially in the epigraphic assessment of the inscriptions.

[1] Some of the noteworthy attempts include: Vogel 1905; Foucher 1922: 490-491; Konow 1929; Rowland 1936; Van Lohuizen-de Leeuw 1949: Deydier 1950: 223-241; Soper 1951; Dobbins 1968; Fussman 1974: 41-42; Khandalavala 1985.

Although a fair number of objects from Gandhāra are known to bear inscribed dates, the majority of them are potsherds or reliquaries, and among Buddhist images it is commonly agreed that there are only five examples: (1) a seated Buddha stela from Mamāne Ḍherī (year 89; CKI 161) (Figures 1 and 2); (2) a standing Buddha from Loriyān Tangai (year 318; CKI 111) (Figures 9 and 10); (3) a standing Buddha from Hashtnagar (year 384; CKI 124) (Figures 7 and 8); (4) a standing Hārītī from Skārah Ḍherī (year 399; CKI 133; Lyons & Ingholt 1957: pl. II.3);[2] (5) a Buddha triad stela (year 5; CKI 232) (Figure 12).[3] Among them, perhaps the most secure reference point is the stela from Mamāne Ḍherī inscribed with the year 89. It represents the Buddha meditating inside Indra's cave, the theme of the so-called *Indraśailaguhā*. Its base is carved with an inscription in a single line, which reads:

> *saṃ 20 20 20 20 4 4 1 Margaśiraṣa masi 4 1 iśe kṣunami niryaïde ime deyadharme Dharmapriena ṣamanena piduno arogadakṣinae upajayasa Budhapriasa puyae samanuyayaṇa arogadakṣinae*[4]
>
> (In the year 89, in the month of Mārgaśiras, [the day] 5, at this term was bestowed this religious gift by the *śramaṇa* Dharmapriya, for the welfare of his father, in honor of his teacher Buddhapriya, for the bestowal of health on his fellow disciples.[5])

Despite some damage in the middle, the inscription is clearly legible. In particular, the reading of the year of its dedication is clear enough (Konow 1929: pl. XXXIV.1). With regard to the era to which it belongs, the majority of specialists agree that it was probably counted in the Kaniṣka era.[6] Among rare exceptions, Harald Ingholt suggests that the year 89 meant the year 489, with the omission of the digit 4 for hundreds, and converts it to AD 432 by applying the Vikrama era (Lyons & Ingholt 1957: 41). But his reasoning based on the presence of drapery folds consisting of paired, parallel lines in small subsidiary figures, which he interprets as a borrowing from Sasanian Persia, ignores many other elements in the configuration of this stela, and the omission of the digit for four hundreds seems groundless. Gritli von Mitterwallner (1987: 214, 220-221) dates it in the Gupta era, thus to AD 408, on the basis of its stylistic affinities she claims to find with Buddha images of the Gupta period from Mathurā, which seems dubious to me, not to mention the implausibility of the use of the Gupta era for such Gandhāran images.[7] There seems little possibility that this date was counted in anything other than the Kaniṣka era, and this is partly supported on the palaeographic grounds.[8] If we accept that it belongs to the Kaniṣka era and apply Harry Falk's suggestion regarding the era, which places its epoch in AD 127/8 CE (Falk 2001), the year 89 in this inscription will correspond to AD 216, as the month Mārgaśiras approximately coincides with November and December in the Gregorian calendar.[9]

---

[2] The Skārah Ḍherī Hārītī will not be discussed in this paper because I wish to focus on Buddha images, which are more homogeneous in formal configuration and thus will be more useful in comparing their traits, in addition to the fact that the Hārītī is stylistically a rather isolated piece.

[3] B.N. Mukherjee (1991) claims that there are two more examples in the Indian Museum, Kolkata: a seated bodhisattva (year 56) and a sculpted panel of Buddhas and bodhisattvas (year 400) (both reproduced in the last pages of the volume where Mukherjee 1991 is included). But Richard Salomon (personal communication) questions the interpretation of these inscriptions as recording dates.

[4] Konow 1929: 171-172; Konow 1933-1934; CKI 161; *IBHK* I: 982-983.

[5] Based on Konow (1929: 171-172), but modified according to Konow's revised reading in Konow (1933-34). In Konow's 1929 translation, the date is mistakenly printed as '85' instead of '89'.

[6] Konow 1929: 171-172; Rowland 1936: 396; Van Lohuizen-de Leeuw 1949: 111-115 (as in the Śaka era that she equates with the Kaniṣka era); Soper 1951: 308; Rosenfield 1967: 104; Dobbins 1968: 285-286; Harle 1974: 131; Czuma 1985: 35; Van Lohuizen-de Leeuw 1986: 4. See also Joe Cribb's paper in the present volume.

[7] Khandalavala also says that the Mamāne Ḍherī Buddha 'has a feeling of Gupta classicism' and suggests the Gupta era for the Buddha. But his points on the Buddha's formal affinities with Gupta images are simply based on mere uncritical impressions, as in the case of Mitterwallner—despite his claim of viewing the actual image, not photographs of it. Salomon (personal communication) suggests that the inscription cannot be that late on the palaeographic grounds. The Gandhāran catalogue of the 2008 Bonn exhibition dates it as '216 or 316' AD, implying the possibility of the omission of 100 in the year 89 (*GBHP* 232).

[8] Salomon (personal communication) points out, supporting the Kaniṣka era for the year 89, that the use of the dating formula *iśe kṣunami* ('at this time') is typical of (though not unique to) the Kaniṣka era.

[9] I deliberately count 'year zero' in calculating these dates in the Common Era throughout this paper.

The Buddha in the stela shows features quite common among Gandhāran Buddha images (Figures 1 and 2). It closely matches standard examples of a type that I identify as one of five major visual types of Gandhāran Buddhas, i.e. Type III (Rhi 2008: 57-63). The type is principally characterized by the hair arrangement in a wavy pattern, broadly undulating over the head, which is usually carved in low, flat ridges or incised lines. A close parallel to the Buddha in the Mamāne Ḍherī stela is found in a Buddha head from the site Sahrī-Bahlol Mound B in the Peshawar Museum (Figure 3). Though the Mamāne Ḍherī stela is only 96 centimeters high and thus its central Buddha is smaller than independent statues of usual sizes, the drapery folds are delicately rendered, consisting of alternating higher and lower ridges. In the drapery and the contour of the body, a seated Buddha in the National Museum of Scotland in Edinburgh is close to the best comparison (Figure 4). Slight differences are noticeable in the drapery covering the lower part of the body, especially that flowing from the left forearm, but they may be due to a smaller size and an optional variation in the Mamāne Ḍherī stela. Equivalents of this type among standing Buddhas can be found in such examples as one in Lahore Museum (Figure 5) and another in Peshawar Museum (Figure 6). Numerous images of this type exist in diverse qualities of craftsmanship, marking the most productive period of Gandhāran Buddhist icons.[10] The Mamāne Ḍherī stela is among the better specimens of this type, and those of similar quality may be considered contemporary with it. Most of them were discovered in the Sahrī-Bahlol and Takht-i-Bāhī areas near Charsadda, which I consider as the heart of the production of Gandhāran Buddhas in stone (Rhi 2008: 74-75), while Mamāne Ḍherī is also located in the Charsadda Tehsil. They must have been produced during decades around AD 216, though it may be hard to measure precisely how far they are spread in duration.

With this reference point in mind, we move to two other points of interest: two standing Buddhas inscribed with the years 318 and 384 respectively. The former (Figures 9 and 10) was discovered at Loriyān Tangai and entered the Indian Museum, Kolkata, along with a number of other finds from this site (Senart 1899) (Figure 11). The latter (Figure 7) was from Pālāṭū Ḍherī in Hashtnagar (near Charsadda), thus commonly called the 'Hashtnagar Buddha' (Smith 1889a; Smith 1889b: 144-146; Marshall & Vogel 1904: 160), but its current whereabouts are unknown except for its base acquired by the British Museum (Zwalf 1996, I: no. 172) (Figure 8). The inscriptions on the bases of these two images read:

Loriyān Tangai Buddha

sa 1 1 1 100 10 4 4 Proṭhavadasa di 20 4 1 1 1 Budhaghoṣasa daṇamu[khe] Saghorumasa sadaviyarisa[11]

(In the year 318, the day 27 of Prauṣṭhapada, gift of Buddhaghoṣa, the companion of Saṃghavarma.[12])

Hashtnagar Buddha

saṃ 1 1 1 100 20 20 20 20 4 Proṭhavadasa masasa divasaṃmi paṃcami 4 1[13]

(In the year 384, on the fifth, 5, day of the month Prauṣṭhapada.)[14]

The reading of the date in the Loriyān Tangai inscription is quite clear (Konow 1929: pl. XXI.1), and that of the Hashtnagar inscription is most plausible (Konow 1929: pl. XXII.10). It seems most likely that the years 318 and 384 were counted in the same era. The chronological positioning of these two Buddhas, and by corollary the era in which they are possibly dated, was often treated as holding a key

[10] Rowland (1936: 396) calls the phase of the Mamāne Ḍherī stela as 'the mature period', and Van Lohuizen-de Leeuw (1949: 113) as 'a flourishing period'. Soper (1951: 308) regards the stela as representing a more formalized stage when compared with another stela depicting the same theme from Jauliāñ at Taxila, a point with which I agree.

[11] Konow 1929: 106-107; CKI 111; *IBHK* I: 980.

[12] Based on Konow (1929: 107) with modification.

[13] Konow 1929: 117-119; CKI 124; *IBHK* I: 962.

[14] Based on Konow (1929: 119) with modification.

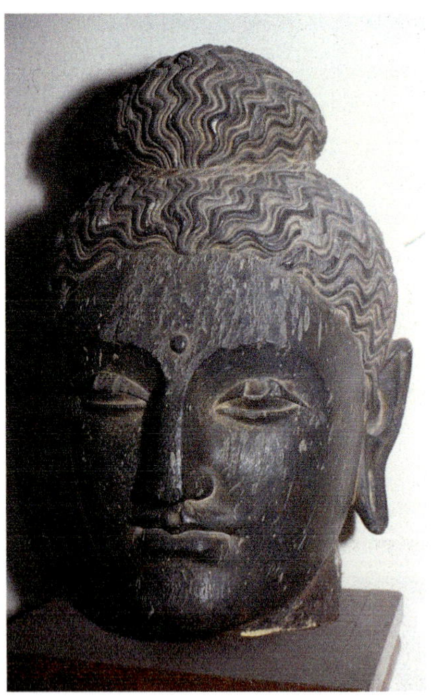

Figure 3. Buddha head. From Sahrī-Bahlol Mound B, Peshawar basin. H. 34 cm. Peshawar Museum. (Photo: J. Rhi.)

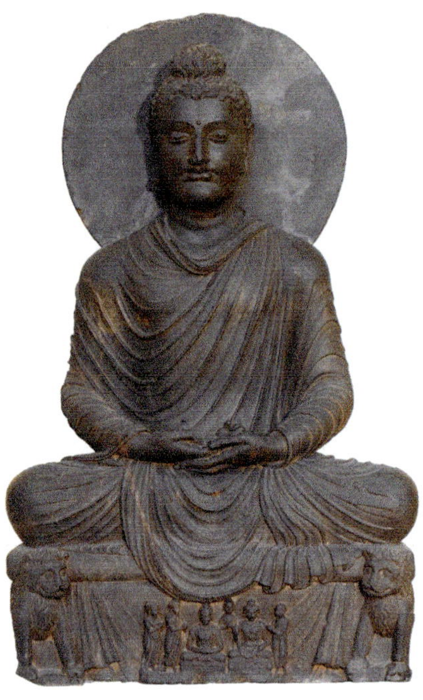

Figure 4. Buddha. Provenance unknown. H. 110.5 cm. National Museum of Scotland. (Museum photo.)

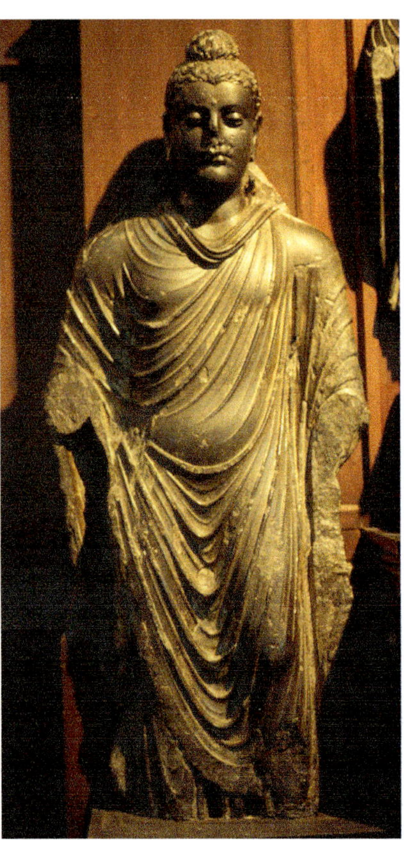

Figure 5. Buddha. From Jamālgarhī, Peshawar basin. H. 158 cm. Lahore Museum. (Photo: J. Rhi.)

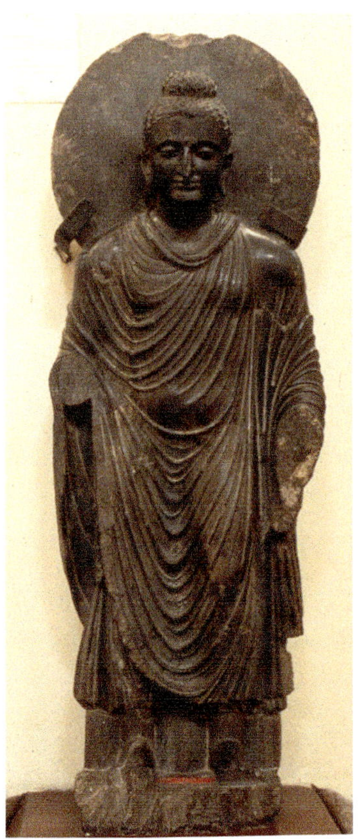

Figure 6. Buddha. From Sahrī-Bahlol Mound A, Peshawar basin. H. 165 cm. Peshawar Museum. (Photo: J. Rhi.)

in understanding the development of Gandhāran Buddhist imagery in the early scholarship. Besides rather outrageous suggestions such as the Seleucid era (321 BC; Vogel 1905: 259; Bachhofer 1929, I: 82-83), a noteworthy candidate supported by a number of scholars was the so-called 'Old Śaka era', which was first proposed by Sten Konow (1929: xci) as starting in 84/3 BC on the basis of a calculation by W.E. van Wijk (Konow & Van Wijk 1924: 79-83) and later revised by Konow himself to *c.* 145 BC (Konow 1933: 4). Benjamin Rowland (1936: 391) and Alexander Soper (1949: 253, n. 4; as noted by Dobbins 1968: 283) followed Konow's later date with a slight change to *c.* 150 BC, and J. E. van Lohuizen-de Leeuw (1949: esp. 95-96) presented another alternative of 129 BC. According to these old theories, the dates of the two Buddhas would be placed in AD 233 and 299 in Van Wijk's and Konow's initial assessment, or AD 167 and 233 in the revised theory based on *c.* 150 BC, or AD 188 and 254 in Van Lohuizen-de Leeuw's alternative theory, the last of which I once thought to be reasonable.

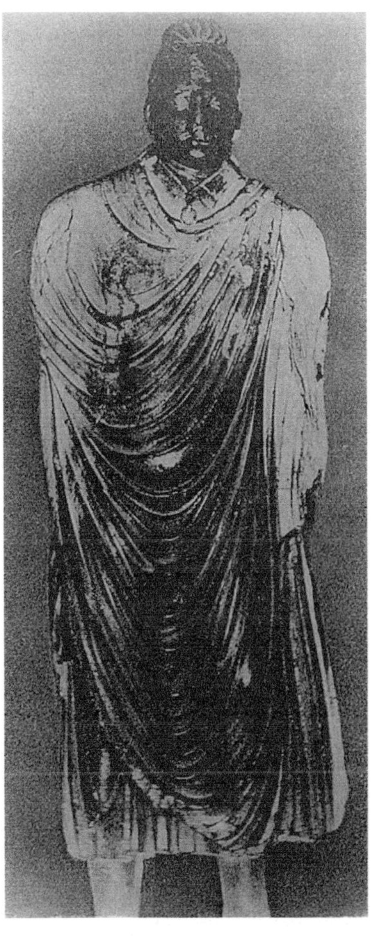

Figure 7. Buddha. From Pālāṭū Ḍherī, Peshawar basin. Peshawar basin. Current whereabouts unknown.

However, Richard Salomon (2005) recently proposed, based on a reliquary inscription of Queen Rukhuṇa recording triple dates, that five Kharoṣṭhī inscriptions known to us as bearing the years from 303 to 399 should be dated in the Yoṇa or Indo-Greek era of 186/5 BC. Salomon's suggestion has gained a wide acceptance, but Joe Cribb (2005: 213-15) and Harry Falk and Chris Bennett (2009, cf. Falk 2007[2012]) suggest slightly different dates, 174 and 175 BC respectively on the basis of their diverging assessments of the Azes era, which apparently dates 128 years later than the Yoṇa era according to the Rukhuṇa inscription (Salomon 2005: 363).[15] Cribb and Falk/Bennett's suggestions seem to make sense, and especially the latter seems more plausible to me.[16] If we apply this to the years 318 and 384, they will correspond to AD 143 and 209.

The Hashtnagar Buddha (dated year 384), or rather the statue itself, is known only through a single photo taken at the time when it was still worshipped as a Hindu icon (Figure 7). Not counting the head, which is not original, the body of the statue, even when seen in the photo alone, shows considerable affinities with the standing Buddha in Lahore (Figure 5) that I compared above with the Mamāne Ḍherī Buddha. The year AD 209 calculated through the application of the Yoṇa era is only seven years apart from the Mamāne Ḍherī Buddha and seems reasonable to accept.[17]

The Loriyān Tangai Buddha (dated year 318) (Figure 9), dedicated 56 years earlier if the date was counted in the same era, is very different from the Hashtnagar Buddha. It was discovered by Alexander Caddy

[15] Salomon's 2005 paper was originally presented at a conference held at Lattes in 2003 and published in the conference volume two years later. Cribb's 2005 paper was initially presented at the same conference, but its published version in the same conference volume of 2005 includes his alternative suggestion regarding the Yoṇa era in response to Salomon's original paper.

[16] Salomon (personal communication) is now inclined to agree with the revision proposed by Falk and Bennett.

[17] Citing Konow's assessment that the Hashtnagar Buddha is not notably different in style from the Mamāne Ḍherī Buddha, Rowland (1936: 396) assigns the two Buddhas to the mature period of Gandhāran art together with the vast quantity of finds from Jamālgarhī. Mainly based on the observation on small figures on the pedestal of the Hashtnagar and Loriyān Tangai Buddhas in comparison with subsidiary figures in the Mamāne Ḍherī stela, Dobbins (1968: 285) states that the Mamāne Ḍherī stela has more affinities with the Loriyān Tangai Buddha, but it is the Hashtnagar Buddha that is more comparable in the overall configurations of the body and drapery with standing Buddhas that can be grouped together with the Mamāne Ḍherī stela.

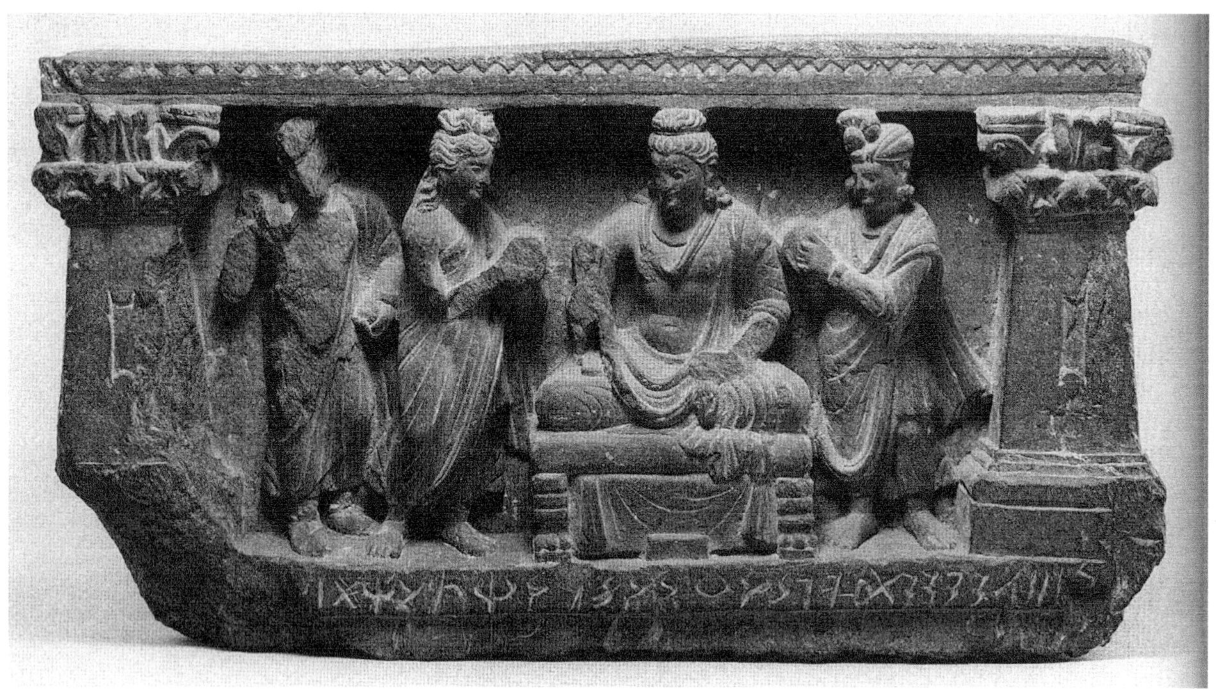

Figure 8. Pedestal of the Buddha (Figure 7). H. 20.5 cm. British Museum. (Photo: copyright the Trustees of the British Museum.)

at the site in 1896, and a now well-known excavation photo shows the Buddha standing in the right in the middle of dozens of images (Figure 11, marked A). Compared with the Hashtnagar Buddha and also with Mamāne Ḍherī Buddha, this Buddha is shorter and broader in proportion and thus looks heavier and more massive. The drapery is not as three-dimensional, and its folds are arranged in a monotonous way without the alternation of higher and lower ridges (Figure 10). The Buddha's head, which was already missing at the time of excavation, would have been relatively big and broad-jawed, perhaps as in another standing Buddha found at this site (Figure 11, marked B). These are features we commonly witness in the majority of the finds from Loriyān Tangai. I have had an impression that the finds from Loriyān Tangai show relatively late features, which may be characterized as reflecting the degeneration in quality in the process that gradually moved away from more classical prototypes and increasingly absorbed influence from India proper.[18]

However, the year AD 143 which we may assign for our Loriyān Tangai Buddha is more than seven decades earlier than the Mamāne Ḍherī Buddha and its related specimens, which apparently mark a high period in the production of Gandhāran Buddhist images. How do we explain this anomaly? There could be three possibilities. First, the Loriyān Tangai Buddha must be dated actually much later than

[18] Because of the probability that the dates were counted in the same era, most scholars simply accepted the precedence of the Loriyān Tangai Buddha and did not raise a question about this anomaly. But Vogel (1905: 259) already candidly noted its inferiority to the Hashtnagar Buddha. Bachhofer (1929, I: 82-83) notes, '. . . the drapery had been conceived as a separate volume. It is reproduced such as it is meant to be, namely as a piece of heavy, coarse stuff' but, probably due to the chronological inevitability, he adds, 'It is certainly older than the Chārsada Buddha, for it unmistakably manifests a clear and incorruptible sense of reality, the legacy of Bactrian Hellenism to its Central Asiatic heirs.' Rowland (1942: 224-226) notes: '. . . the canon of the proportions . . . must have been something like five heads to the total height; the robe of the figure falls in a series of loops, or swags of drapery, trailing from the left shoulder in a series of curves across the chest and then in more deeply cut folds falling over the lower limbs in a monotonously repeated succession of ridges and depressions. The garment has a hardness and stiffness that makes it look as though it had been hammered out of metal and is a far cry from the soft, clinging togas of the Hellenistic and Augustan periods.'

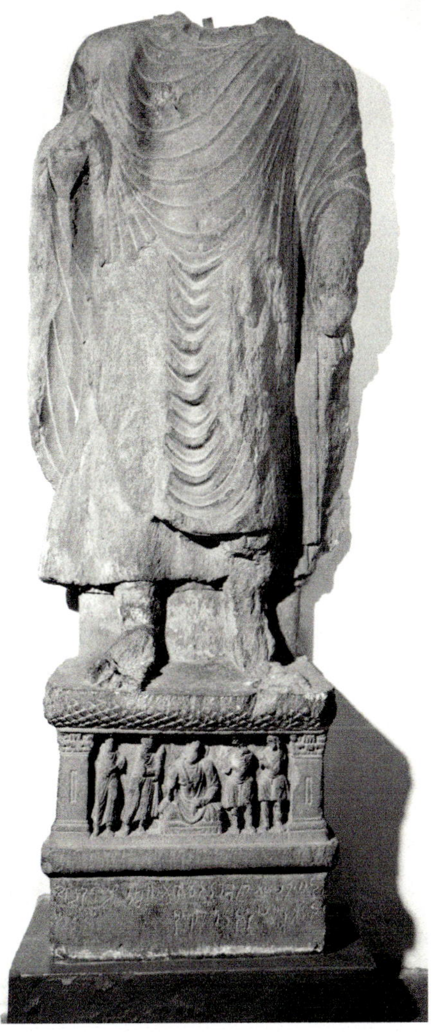

Figure 9. Buddha. From Loriyān Tangai, southern Swat. H. 168 cm. Indian Museum, Kolkata. (Photo: John C. Huntington.)

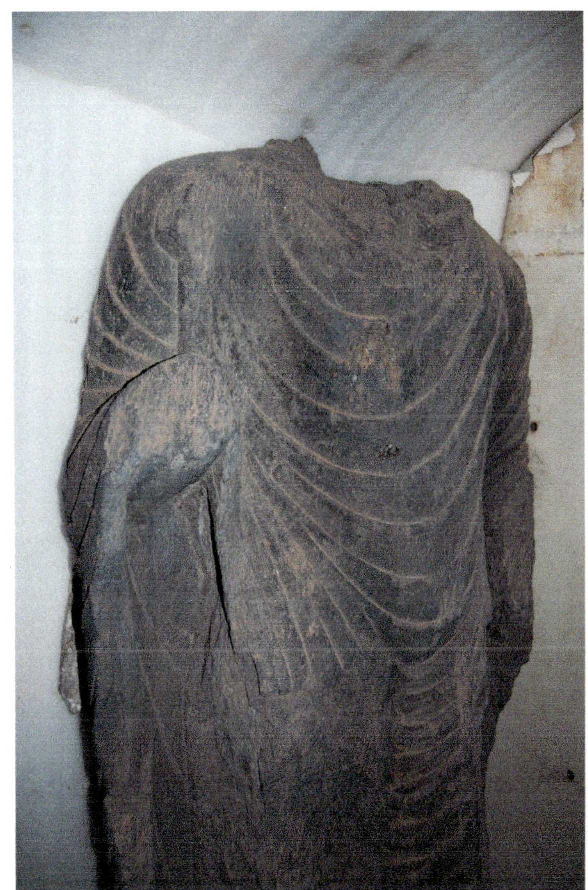

Figure 10. Detail of Figure 9. (Photo: J. Rhi.)

AD 143, perhaps to the late third or the early fourth century AD, and the era used in counting its date is not the Yoṇa era, but some later one, like the Azes era (46 or 47 BC) or the Vikrama era (58/7 BC), which would give the year AD 271/72 or AD 258/59, some fifty to forty years later than the Mamāne Ḍherī Buddha. In this case, we should be able to answer why the Yoṇa era, which seems neatly to explain a number of inscriptions dated with years in the 200s to 300s, may not be applicable to the Buddha images of the years 318 and 384. Another problem with this alternative is that, if we apply an era like the Azes era or the Vikrama era to the two Buddhas, the Hashtnagar Buddha would end up at the year AD 335/36 or 325/26, moving away from the Mamāne Ḍherī Buddha by as much as some 110 to 120 years. It is not impossible that this particular visual type persisted more than a century, but it seems unlikely. Second, there is a possibility that the two separate eras were used for the Loriyān Tangai Buddha and the Hashtnagar Buddha, but common sense tells us that this is only theoretically possible. Third, if the Loriyān Tangai Buddha indeed dates from AD 143, much earlier than the Mamāne Ḍherī Buddha, this may mean that there was a phase in Gandhāran Buddhist imagery in which a crude adoption or adaptation of classical prototypes took place around this time in the vicinity of Loriyān Tangai or which was already showing the signs of degeneration in standard. In this case, we still have to explain why many visual features displayed in the finds from Loriyān Tangai seem to look like later variations of those found in such images as the Hashtnagar Buddha or numerous finds from the Takht-i-Bāhī, Sahrī-Bahlol, and Charsadda area, and why iconographical features we may consider as a later phenomenon

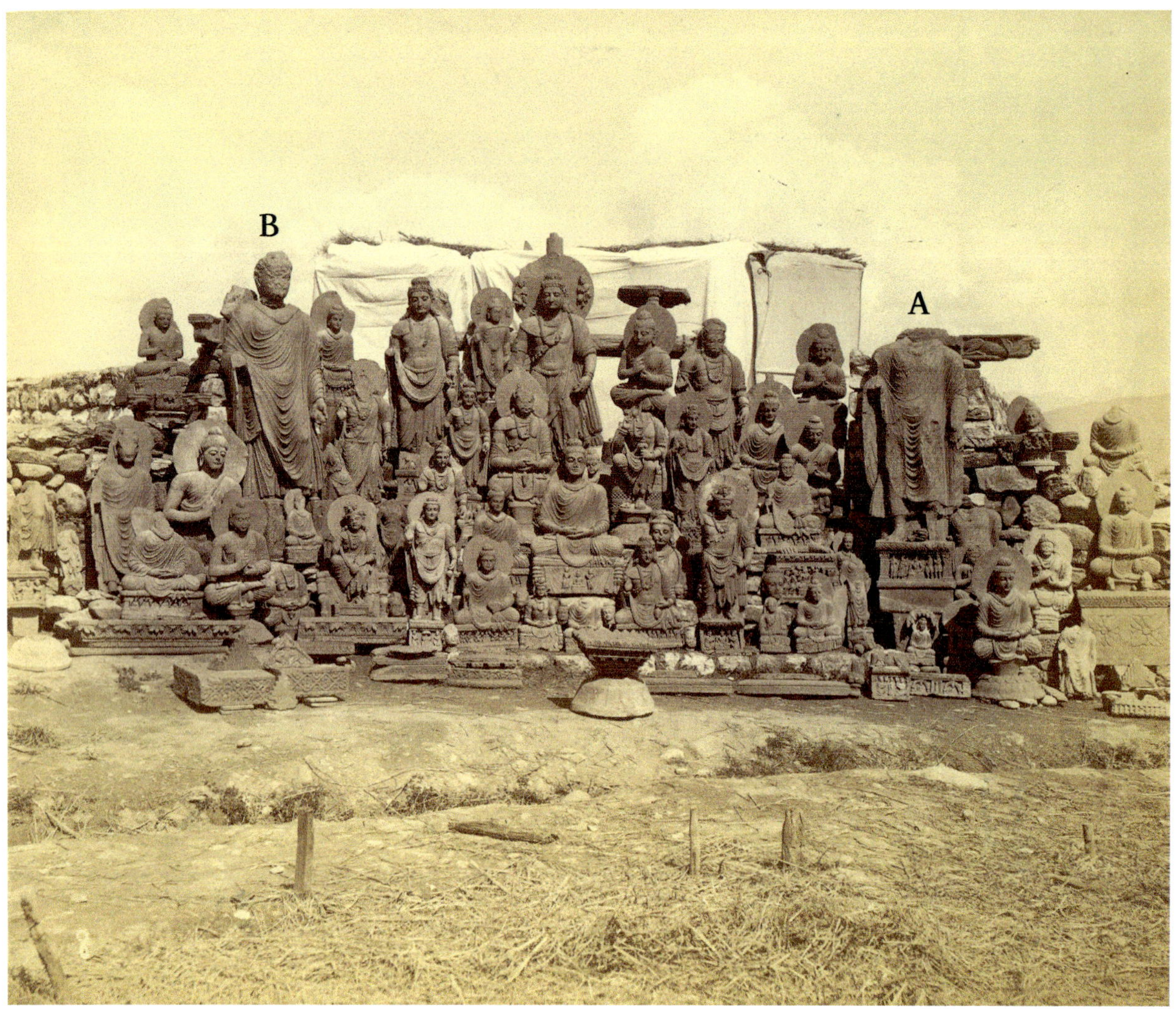

Figure 11. Excavated sculptures from Loriyān Tangai. Photo by Alexander Caddy, 1896. (Photo: courtesy of the British Library.)

in Gandhāran art already appear in this period.[19] I have to note that Loriyān Tangai is located to the north of the Peshawar valley beyond Buner and at the entrance to Swat valley and formed a regional unit in sculptural style distinct from that of the Takht-i-Bāhī, Sahrī-Bahlol, and Charsadda group. I do not rule out a possibility that some activity was going on in the Loriyān Tangai area during the first and second centuries AD preceding the major surge of sculptural activities in the Takht-i-Bāhī, Sahrī-Bahlol, and Charsadda group, while the local trend in the Loriyān Tangai area continued with maintaining its idiosyncratic features.[20]

[19] Sculptural finds yielded in the excavations conducted by the Italian mission at Barikot in Swat include several small stone images found in situ (Olivieri 2014: figs. 66, 85, 91, 119). They show features that we may usually consider to be distinctively late in the faces, contours and draperies, but the stratigraphical evidence indicates that they are datable to the second half of the third century AD, somewhat—at least a century—earlier than our usual presumption. Though they are not markedly early as the Loriyān Tangai Buddha, this also seems to support the possibility that carvings of rather clumsy or crude execution that we have often attributed to a chronological factor may actually, in some if not all cases, reflect regional variations at diverse technical levels. See also Filigenzi's and Olivieri's paper in the present volume.

[20] Rowland (1942: 226) explains the transition from the Loriyān Tangai Buddha to the Hashtnagar Buddha as elaborating a rigid formula of drapery design.

There is yet another interesting but controversial point among dated examples: a Buddha triad inscribed with the year 5 (Figures 12 and 13), commonly called 'Brussels Buddha' after the location of its initial collection.[21] The triad was first introduced in an advertisement published in 1973 (*Oriental Art*, spring 1973) and received the first scholarly treatments by Gérard Fussman (1974: 54-58) and James Harle (1974) in the following year. It drew attention for its dated inscription as well as its interesting iconographical configuration, especially a bodhisattva in the right bearing small Buddha in the headdress. The inscription reads:

> *sa[ṃ] 4 1 Phagunasa masasa di paṃcami Budhanadasa trepiḍakasa danamukhe madapidarana adhvadidana puyaya bhavatu*[22]
>
> (In the year 5, on the fifth day of the month Phālguna: the pious gift of Buddhananda, learned in the three *piṭakas*: may it be for the honoring of his deceased [?] father and mother.[23])

The inscription is clearly legible. Though the first *akṣara* may look somewhat ambiguous, there is no difficulty in reading it as '*saṃ*' meaning 'year'. Numerals for 5 are also clear.[24] Many specialists instantly linked the year 5 to the Kaniṣka era (Fussman 1974: 54; Harle 1974; 129; *LA* 1984: 191; Bussagli 1984:

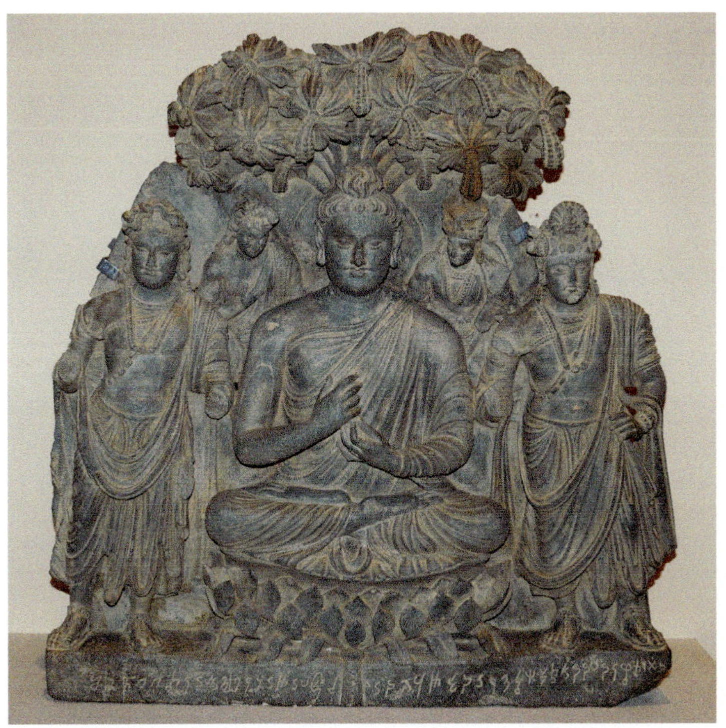

Figure 12. Buddha triad. Provenance unknown. H. 62 cm. Agonshū, Japan. (Photo: J. Rhi.)

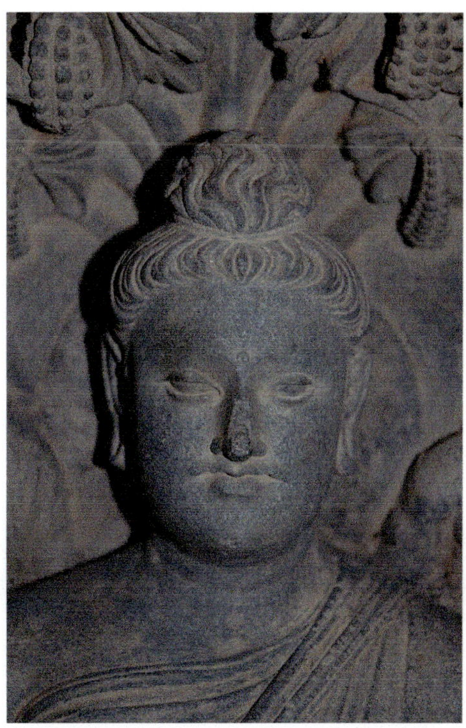

Figure 13. Detail of Figure 12. (Photo: J. Rhi.)

[21] When its existence first became publicly known, the triad was in the collection of Claude de Marteau in Brussels and thus has been commonly called 'Brussels Buddha'. Actually, it is now in the collection of a new Japanese Buddhist sect called Agonshū (*GBGI* 2007: 61), so the name 'Brussels Buddha' may not be appropriate. But respecting its first place of origin in modern collecting history and the common usage in previous scholarship, I will continue to use this appellation.

[22] Fussman 1974: 54; Harle 1974: 128; CKI 232; *IBHK* I: 961-962.

[23] Based on John Brough's reading and translation cited in Harle 1974: 128, with slight modification, in comparison with Fussman 1974: 54 and Salomon's suggestion.

[24] Harle (1974: 128-129) cites Brough as having reservations about the year, whether 4 or 5, but thinks that it appears to be 5. Fussman (1974: 54) excludes any doubt about the reading of the date.

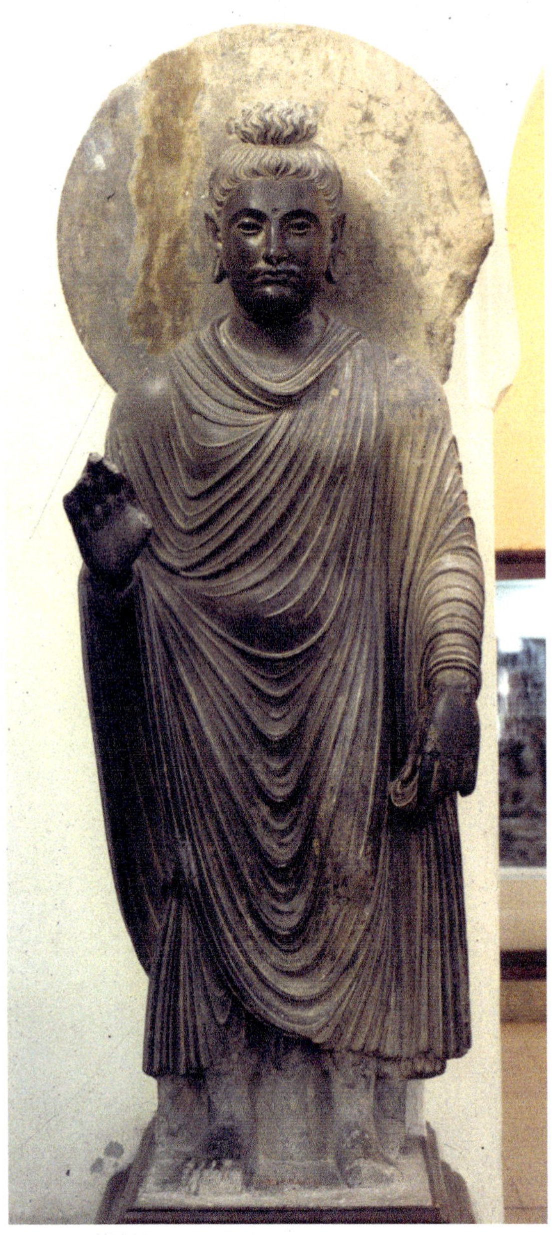

Figure 14. Buddha. From Sahrī-Bahlol Mound B, Peshawar basin. H. 264 cm. Peshawar Museum. (Photo: J. Rhi.)

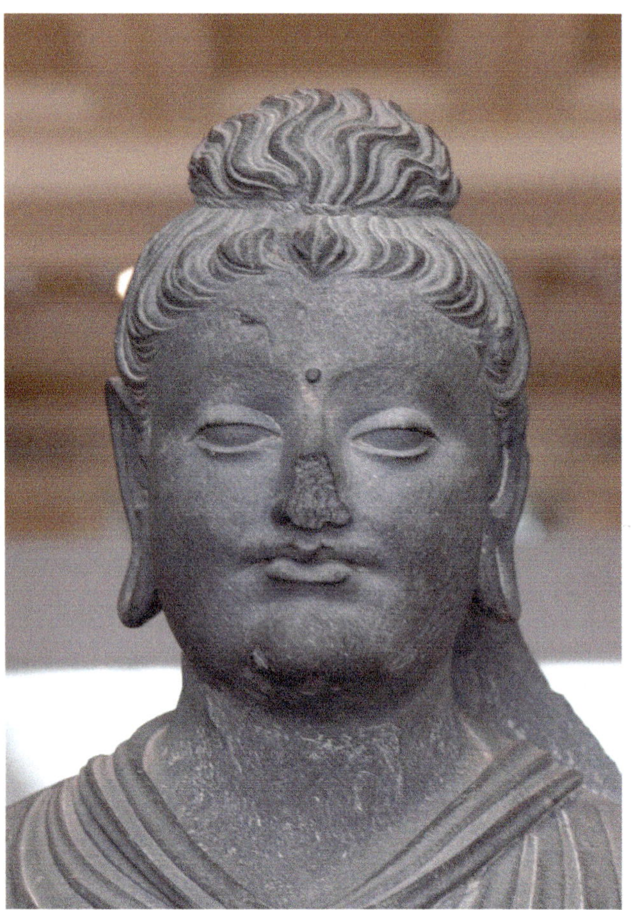

Figure 15. Standing Buddha (detail). Provenance unknown. H. 104 cm. British Museum. (Photo: J. Rhi.)

106), which thus could be converted to AD 82 when AD 78 is applied for the Kaniṣka era, as a number of specialists then believed, or to AD 132 according to the more popular estimation of the era in recent scholarship. But there was also hesitation based on concerns over whether the date might be too early for the stela. Therefore, some scholars attempted to push its date down by about a century by applying the so-called omitted-hundred theory and thus considering the year 5 as actually the year 105 of the Kaniṣka era (Van Lohuizen-de Leeuw 1986: 7) or treating the Kaniṣka era as an era allegedly founded by Kaniṣka II almost a century after the original Kaniṣka era (Czuma 1985: 198). Some scholars even dated it to the fourth or fifth century AD by applying other eras,[25] but this seems too late.

The grounds for some scholars' reluctance to accept its date as the fifth year of the Kaniṣka era is that the triad shows a number of features in style and iconography that seem too advanced for the date: for instance in iconography, the gesture of *dharmacakramudrā*, the lotus seat, and the bodhisattva

[25] Khandalavala (1985: 68-69) links the Brussels Buddha to the Gupta era, thus dating it to AD 324, and Mitterwallner (1987: 221-222) to the era of the Sita-Hūṇa king Khiṅgila, which she assigns to around AD 448, thus dating it to around AD 453.

image on the right bearing a small Buddha in the headdress.[26] The Buddha in the centre is stylistically related to the group that I identify as Type II (Rhi 2008: 50-57). A pair of gigantic standing Buddhas from Sahrī-Bahlol Mound B, currently in Peshawar Museum, are the most magnificent examples in this group (Figure 14). I would not be surprised if those two Buddhas can be dated to around the first decade of the Kaniṣka era, that is to say the era of Kaniṣka I. The Buddha in the Brussels triad appears to stand in the same line of development. However, as to whether or not such sophistication of iconography would have been possible around the first decade of the Kaniṣka era I cannot be certain. I should be more tempted to see such sophistication as coming somewhat later and to side with those who suggest a later date, perhaps year 105 of the Kaniṣka era (AD 232) with the admission of the omitted-hundred dating practice, or year 5 of the second Kaniṣka era (AD 229). Still, I admit that my supposition is based on a number of speculations and do not entirely exclude the possibility that such advancement in iconographical configurations was already current a century earlier.[27]

Initially, I even had a suspicion about the authenticity of the triad because it has so many details too good to be true. I was all the more surprised to see that such an exquisite piece was brought to public attention as late as 1973, and its history before that date had never been clearly stated despite the claim that it came from near Peshawar, which is simply a handy attribution of a source for a new Gandhāran object on the market. Katsumi Tanabe and Francine Tissot also raised the possibility of forgery.[28] Yet I cannot but concede that such an inscription, though conventional in content, would have been very hard to simulate even if any forger had a masterful knowledge of Kharoṣṭhī and Gāndhārī on the basis of available epigraphic materials; moreover, virtually no manuscript remains, except for the famous Gāndhārī *Dharmapāda*, had been known by the 1970s, and I respect the assessments of authorities in epigraphy such as Fussman and Salomon.[29] When I examined the piece in 2008 for a second time,[30] I thought that it looked better than in photos. The Buddha with its delicate face seems to compare better with such images as a standing Buddha in the British Museum (Figure 15) than the two Sahrī-Bahlol Buddhas (Figure 14). If the stela dates from the 105th year of the Kaniṣka era, it would date sixteen years later than the Mamāne Ḍherī Buddha. But this remains no more than a provisional speculation for now.

[26] Harle 1974: 129; Czuma 1985: 198.

[27] Fussman (1987: 72-73) staunchly defends a position to accept the date of the Brussels Buddha as it is.

[28] Tanabe (1988: 100, n. 18) presents the following three reasons for his doubts: (1) the reversal of the positions of two different types of bodhisattvas unlike the usual composition in similar triads, (2) the lack of a halo for a seated Buddha in the headdress of a bodhisattva, (3) the engraving of the beginning of the inscription in a slightly slanting position to avoid the broken part. Of the three, I do not think that the first point can be taken seriously because the placement of two bodhisattva types was not always consistent. The second point is interesting because small Buddhas in a bodhisattva's headdress in Gandhāra (though there exist only a handful of examples) are invariably marked with halos. There may be a possibility that the figure is actually not a Buddha because the place was not reserved only for a Buddha. The third point is notable because the inscription starts at the right end of the base of the stela slightly towards the upper side, but it is hard to tell whether this was due to a forger's deliberate arrangement, though one could have a suspicion. Tissot (2005: 396-398) also points out the reversed positioning of two bodhisattvas, which cannot be an indication of forgery. A more forceful reason for her suspicion is the Brussels Buddha's 'almost total similarity' with a triad stela in the Peshawar Museum (Tissot 2005: fig. 2; Lyons & Ingholt 1957: no. 253). However, despite many apparent similarities, the two pieces show differences as well in a number of features, and I cannot agree with her judgment that they are identical. Furthermore, even though there may be a significant degree of similarity, they cannot be a sign of forgery because a workshop or an artisan in the period could have produced a number of such small objects in the same shape for dedication. We have to keep it in mind that carvings from Gandhāra were not supposed to have the uniqueness as a work of art that is associated with modern and contemporary art

[29] Fussman (1974; 1987) never expresses any reservation about the authenticity of the inscription of the triad; Salomon (personal communication) is of the opinion that no forger would be capable enough of composing an inscription in such expertly Kharoṣṭhī. Recently, Ingo Strauch (2009[2013]: 209-212) notes a very special nature of the word *adhvadida* (*adhvatīta*) found in the Brussels Buddha's inscription and implies that the inscription, thus the triad itself, must be genuine if the problem of its 'astonishing similarity' with a triad stela in Peshawar (see n. 28 in this paper) can be resolved. As I have already pointed out, the 'astonishing similarity' cannot be a problem.

[30] The piece was shown in the exhibition of 'Gandhāran Art and the Bamiyan Site' held in Japan from December 2007 to July 2008 (*GBGI* 2007: 61).

There is another inscribed Buddha image worth considering here, though it is not dated. It is a standing Buddha in the Hirayama Ikuo Silk Road Museum in Yamanashi, Japan (Figures 16 and 17; cf. Tanabe 2007: II.2). The inscription, carved on a halo, was first reported by Harold Bailey in 1982 without referring to the image.[31] Bailey read the inscription as follows (Bailey 1982: 150-151):[32]

dhramatithaṇa-ṇagaraṃmi dhamara'i'aṃmi aśo-raya-pra'iṭhividami momadara'e bala-soma-bha-
ya'e saṃ-'aṇakara-bhaya'e daṇa-mukhe 'imiṇa kuśala-muleṇa
ṣarva-ṣatva ṇiva'iti
para

(In the city [*nagara*] Dharmātiṣṭhāna, at the Dhamra-rājika-[*stūpa*] established by Aśoka-rāja, the donation of the wife [*dara*] Moma, the wife Bala-soma, together with the wife 'Aṇakara. By this root of good all beings are brought to *nirvāṇa*.)

In 2007, Richard Salomon presented a revised reading and translation (Salomon 2007: 283; cf. CKI 256):

[tra]matithaṇaṇagaraṃmi dhamaraïaṃmi aśoraya-praïstavidami momadatae balasoma-bha-
yae suaṇakara-bhayae daṇamukhe imiṇa kuśalamuleṇa
ṣarva ṣatva <para>nivaïti

(The gift of Momadata, wife of Balasoma, wife of a goldsmith, in the Dharmarājika [*stūpa*] established by King Aśo(ka) at the capital city Trama. By this root of merit all beings are caused to attain *nirvāṇa*.)

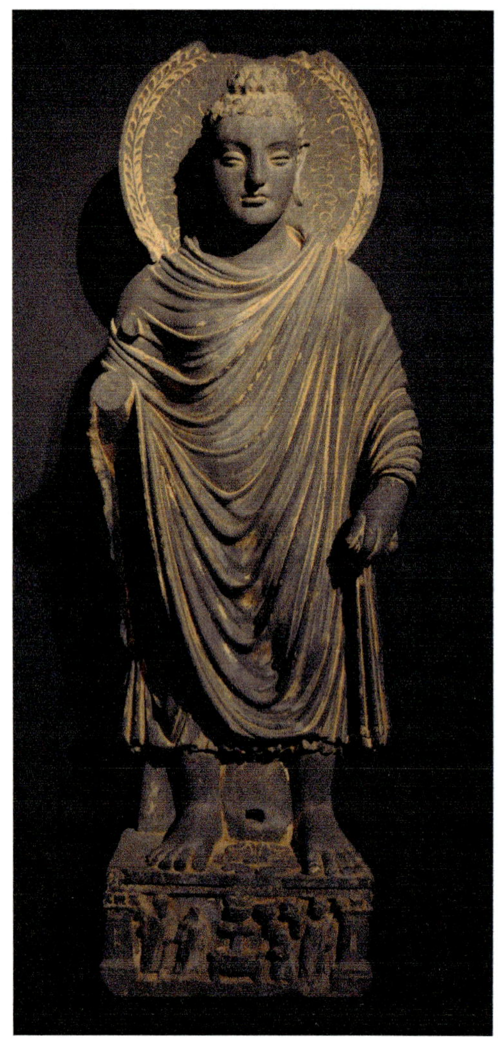

Figure 16. Buddha. Provenance unknown. H. 98 cm. Hirayama Ikuo Silk Road Museum, Yamanashi. (Photo: J. Rhi.)

Salomon reads *[tra]matithaṇaṇagaraṃmi* where Bailey read *dhramatithaṇaṇagaraṃmi*, and translates it as 'at the capital city Trama' instead of 'in the city Dharmātiṣṭhāna'. Then, he equates Trama with Tramaṇa/Tamaṇospa/Tramaṇospa, which he considers as the capital of the Apraca/Avaca dynasty. Based on the supposition that the dynasty was active in the Bajaur area during the first century AD, he suggests that the Buddha may also be dated to the period (Salomon 2007: 273-276, 281-282).[33]

To a number of specialists, this date may seem too early for the Hirayama Buddha. It is no surprise that some art historians expressed doubts about such an early date when Salomon first presented the idea at a conference in 2000 (Salomon 2007: 281). When I first saw the Buddha in publications from 1984 (Tanabe

[31] The image seems to have arrived in Japan in 1984, and in the same year Katsumi Tanabe wrote two articles: one (1984a) is a short note, which dated it to the late Kushan period, the latter half of the second century to the third century AD, and the other (1984b) is a monograph, which is devoted to the discussion of the Iranian features of the scene on the pedestal along with remarks on the content of the inscription.

[32] Cf. CKI 256; *IBHK* I: 1012-1013.

[33] Tsukamoto Keishō (*IBHK* I: 1012-1013) mistakenly equates 'Dharmarājikā' in the inscription with a monastery site in Taxila named as such by John Marshall (Marshall 1951, I: 234-235). Tanabe (1984B: 11) is also aware of the problem.

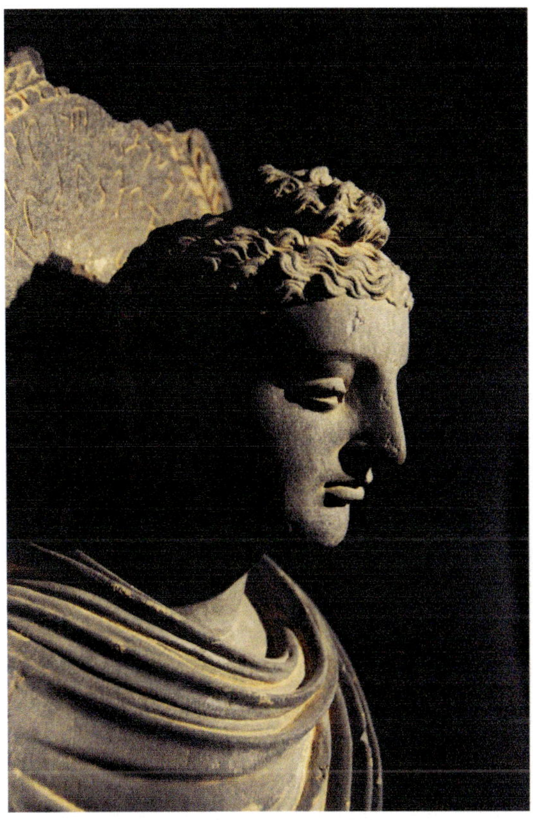

Figure 17. Detail of Figure 16. (Photo: J. Rhi.)

1984a; 1984b), I even wondered about its authenticity owing to its somewhat unfamiliar and clumsy-looking facial features and drapery as well as the long inscription carved on the halo, a peculiar arrangement very rarely noticed for such a long inscription in Gandhāran images.[34] However, I admit that it would have been very hard for a forger to compose such an inscription that contains quite specific information of a sophisticated nature about the circumstances of dedication.[35] If it is indeed genuine, this Buddha is comparable in hairstyle to Buddhas that I have identified as Type V (Rhi 2008: 69-74). Also, in proportion and overall drapery pattern, it is similar to a standing Buddha in Lahore Museum (Figure 18) among Type V Buddhas, although the drapery is more deeply carved. The Hirayama Buddha has a hole on the *uṣṇīṣa*, as a number of examples in Type V (Rhi 2005). Yet the face seems significantly different. Another interesting parallel is found in a standing Buddha in the Matsuoka Museum in Tokyo (Figures 19 and 20).[36] Especially the profiles of the heads show remarkable similarities, while they differ from other, more commonly found types of Gandhāran Buddhas. The Matsuoka Buddha is quite a refined piece both in expression and craftsmanship. It does not seem easily matched with any of the five visual groups I have identified and may form a small, separate group. The Hirayama Buddha might be related to the Matsuoka Buddha and loosely linked to my Type V, although this does not mean that Type V Buddhas are necessarily as early as the Hirayama Buddha (and perhaps the Matsuoka Buddha) – even if the last two Buddhas can be dated to the first century AD. Bajaur is located to the north-west of the Peshawar valley separated by the Malakand Range and to the west of the Swat valley. We know little about Buddhist art production there. Still, some reliquaries and scriptural manuscripts found in the area indicate that Buddhists were active in the area around the beginning of the Common Era (Falk & Strauch 2014). If we accept Salomon's suggestion, could the Hirayama Buddha as well as the Matsuoka Buddha have been among the early attempts in creating Buddha images in the Northwest, which did not leave a lasting impact? I do not think that this is entirely unlikely.

[34] I can recall three more examples: (1) the bust of a bodhisattva (Fussman 1980: 56-58 and pl. VII); (2) a standing bodhisattva (first on the market at Christie's, London on 12 April 1988, lot 212); (3) a seated Buddha (on the market at Christie's, New York on 16 September 2008, lot 341). Of these, Fussman treats the inscription of piece (1) as genuine, and I think that the image is also genuine; pieces (2) and (3) seem to me clearly fakes, while Salomon considers them so on epigraphic grounds.

[35] Conscious of the criticism about the dating of the Hirayama Buddha as contemporary with the Apraca dynasty, Salomon (2005: 281-282) takes a somewhat cautious stance at the end of his discussions on the Hirayama Buddha, saying: '. . . in light of the many uncertainties of the chronology of Gandhāran sculptures, a relatively early date for this piece should not be ruled out. Although the apparent connections of the Aśo-raya Buddha [as he calls the Hirayama Buddha] inscription with early inscriptions and documents cannot be claimed to prove an early date for it, they do suggest linkages with the pre-Kuṣāṇa world of the first century. But as to whether the image itself can be this early, I decline to give any opinion, and leave it to art historians to consider the issue further,' but he adds that the inscription probably dates from the first or second century on palaeographic grounds (Salomon 2005: 281, n. 55). If the Buddha was made at the former Apraca capital after the Apraca period, we should be able to explain the historical background for the information stated in the inscription. Regardless of this, Salomon is confident that the inscription is genuine, though he notes that Fussman disagrees with him (personal communication).

[36] This Buddha was originally in the Hagop Kevorkian collection in New York (Lyons & Ingholt 1957: pl. XVII4) and later purchased by the Matsuoka Museum (Matsuoka 1994: no. 2).

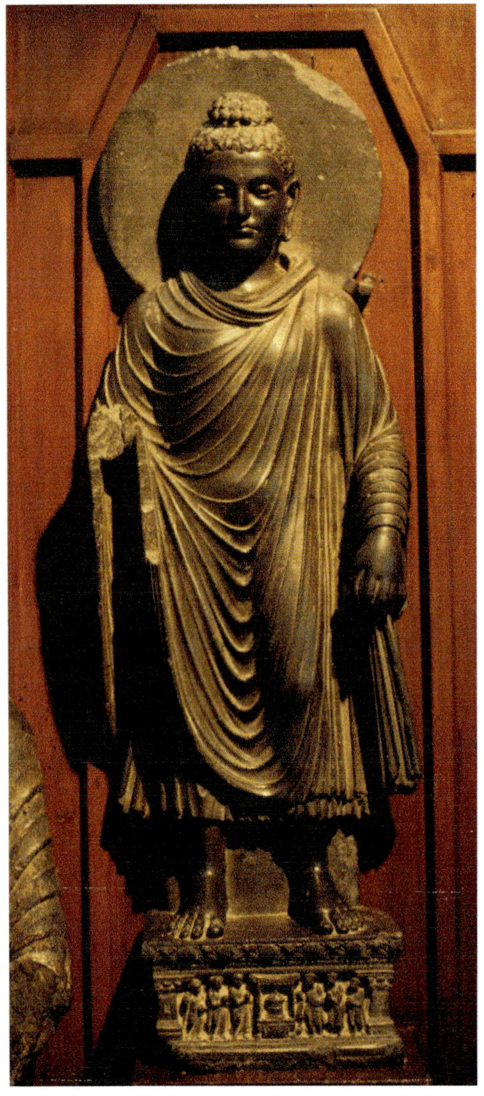

Figure 18. Buddha. Provenance unknown. H. 139 cm. Lahore Museum. (Photo: J. Rhi.)

Problems with the last two examples remind us of a thorny question: to what extent can we trust the expert opinion on the authenticity of inscribed objects? As an art historian, I tend to think that it would be far more difficult to forge an inscription in a convincing manner because it seems to require more sophisticated and articulated knowledge and any problems can be more easily detected—unlike visual images, which essentially resist reduction in verbal or quantitative terms—and that the task would be even harder when one works in an obsolete language and script. Therefore, I have felt compelled to give greater weight to the assessment of epigraphical specialists when the issue of forgery arises, as I did for the Brussels Buddha and the Hirayama Buddha. But when the opinions of most reliable epigraphical experts diverge, this makes me wonder how good the modern forgers are in their command of this ancient language and script.

On the premise that the Brussels Buddha and the Hirayama Buddha are genuine, the five examples I have discussed in this paper may be arranged in the following chronological order.

The Hirayama Buddha – first century AD?

The Loriyān Tangai Buddha (year 318) – 143 AD

The Hashtnagar Buddha (year 384) – 209 AD

The Mamāne Ḍherī Buddha (year 89) – 216 AD

The Brussels Buddha (year 5 = 105?) – 232 AD?

However, this could be misleading because it gives an illusion that they appeared in this linear sequence. If we consider the factor of provenances, we may have a more sensible picture.

Table 1. Comparison of dated Buddha figures by region.

Bajaur	Loriyān Tangai area in Swat	Charsadda, Takht-i-Bāhī, Sahrī-Bahlol area in the Peshawar basin		Chronological comparisons
• Hirayama Buddha, first century AD?				• Bīmarān reliquary. first century AD (Jalalabad)
		Rhi Type III	**Rhi Type II**	
			• Brussels Buddha 132 AD?	• Buddha on Kaniṣka coins (Peshawar?)
	• Loriyān Tangai Buddha, 143 AD			
		• Hashtnagar Buddha 209 AD		
		• Mamāne Ḍherī Buddha, 216 AD	• Brussels Buddha 232 AD?	

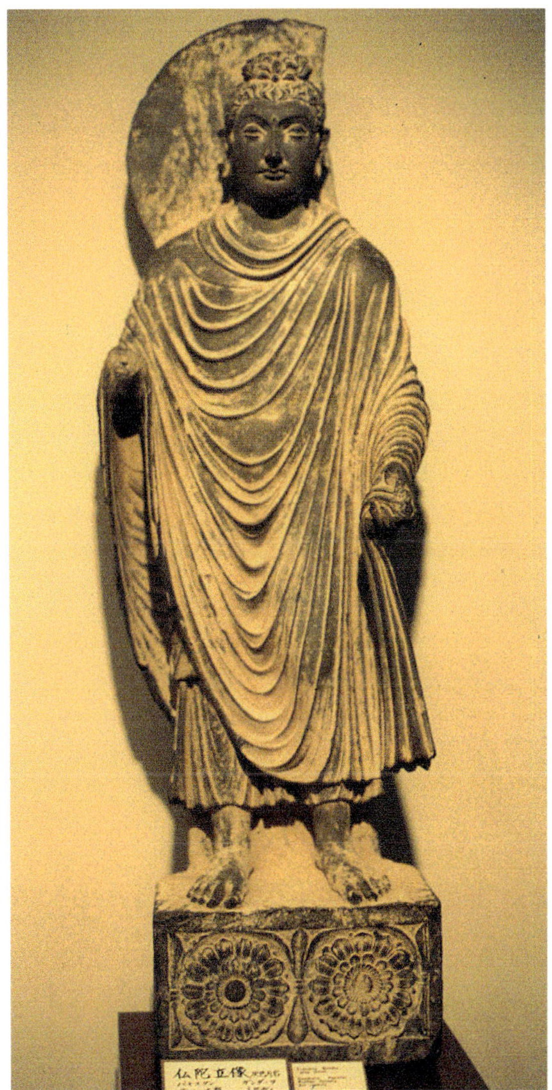

Figure 19. Buddha. Provenance unknown. H. 130 cm. Matsuoka Museum, Tokyo. (Photo: J. Rhi.)

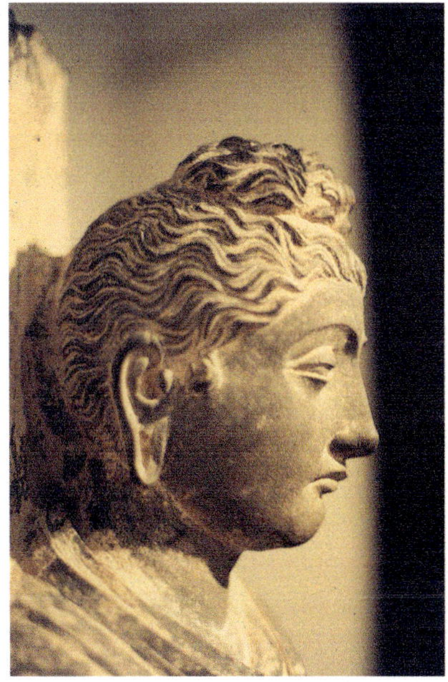

Figure 20. Detail of Figure 19. (Photo: J. Rhi.)

From this table I may be able to draw the following picture. The most standard specimens of my Type II Buddhas, as seen in the Mamāne Ḍheri Buddha and the Hashtnagar Buddha, were made in large numbers in the Charsadda, Takht-i-Bāhī, Sahrī-Bahlol area of the Peshawar basin during several, possibly more, decades spreading around AD 200. In the first half of the second century AD, a cruder type, as seen in the Loriyān Tangai Buddha, was produced in the Loriyān Tangai environs in the north, though we cannot specify the origin of the type; it may have continued in this area as a distinctive local style for another century while it was stylistically interacting with the dominant type from the Peshawar basin just mentioned. Perhaps during the first century AD, one of the early attempts of making Buddha images, as seen in the Hirayama Buddha, may have taken place in Bajaur. This may have been contemporary with another early attempt in the Jalalabad valley as witnessed in a famous reliquary from Bīmarān. It is interesting to note that Loriyān Tangai, Bajaur, and Jalalabad are all located at rather marginal areas when viewed from the Peshawar basin, but they were active in the dedication of relics, and possibly also of images, as well as the creation of Buddhist manuscripts from around the beginning of the Common Era. Back in the Peshawar basin, the production of some of my Type II Buddhas, such as the two gigantic standing Buddhas from Sahrī-Bahlol (Figure 14), may have been made during the second century and overlapped with that of the Type III Buddhas because the former often show indistinguishable affinities with the latter in the rendering of the body and drapery despite deliberate distinction in hairstyle (Rhi 2008). But whether more delicate-faced examples of this type, such as the Brussels Buddha, were products from the early third century AD or a century earlier remains a question. We must, of course, keep it in mind that this is only a provisional picture delineated on the basis of a handful of examples as well as some presumptions regarding the evolution of visual form.

In closing, I would like to stress again that Gandhāran Buddhist imagery probably did not unfold in a single, linear process. There must have been a number of different trends in diverse regional units, some dying out in a short span and some persisting for a longer period. Contacts with classical prototypes were not made at a single moment and did not proceed in a linear way. A new impact may have come later, and a new process could have started at a later date. The picture I have drawn on basis of the examination of dated images may seem complex and confusing, but I believe that this is exactly what we have to expect in charting the development of Gandhāran Buddhist imagery. Perhaps we need to be prepared to expect and tackle even greater complexity in sorting it out in as coherent a picture as possible.

References

Bachhofer L. 1929. *Early Indian Sculpture* (2 volumes). Paris: The Pegasus Press.

Bailey H.W. 1982. Two Kharoṣṭhī Inscriptions. *The Journal of the Royal Asiatic Society of Great Britain and Ireland*: 142–155.

Bussagli M. 1984. *L'Arte del Gandhara*. Torino: UTET.

CKI *Corpus of Kharoṣṭhī Inscriptions*, by S. Baums & A. Glass. https://www.gandhari.org/a_inscriptions.php

Cribb J. 2005. The Greek Kingdom of Bactria, Its Coinage and Its Collapse. Pages 207-225 in O. Bopearachchi and M.-F. Boussac (eds), *Afghanistan, ancien carrefour entre l'est et l'ouest*. Turnhout: Brepolis.

Czuma S. 1985. *Kushan Sculpture: Images from Early India*. Cleveland: The Cleveland Museum of Art.

Deydier H. 1950. *Contribution à l'étude de l'art du Gandhâra*. Paris: Adrien-Maisonneuve.

Dobbins K.W. 1968. Gandhāra Buddha Images with Inscribed Dates. *East and West* 18-3/4: 281-288.

Falk H. 2001. The *Yuga* of Sphujiddhvaja and the Era of the Kuṣāṇas. *Silk Road Art and Archaeology* 7: 121-136.

Falk H. 2007(2012). Ancient Indian Eras: An Overview. *Bulletin of the Asia Institute* 21: 131–145.

Falk H. & Bennett C. 2009. Macedonian Intercalary Months and the Era of Azes. *Acta Orientalia* 70: 197-216.

Falk H. & Strauch I. 2014. The Bajaur and Split Collections of Kharoṣṭhī Manuscripts within the Context of Buddhist Gāndhārī Literature. Pages 51-78 in P. Harrison & J.-U. Hartmann (eds), *From Birch Bark to Digital Data: Recent Advances in Buddhist Manuscript Research*. Vienna: Verlag der Österreichischen Akademie der Wissenschaften.

Foucher A. 1922. *L'Art gréco-bouddhique de Gandhâra* II.2. Paris: Impremerie Nationale.

Fussman G. 1974. Documents épigraphiques kouchans. *Bulletin de l'École Française d'Extrême-Orient* 61: 1–66.

Fussman G. 1980. Documents épigraphiques kouchans (II). *Bulletin de l'École Française d'Extrême-Orient* 67: 45-58.

Fussman G. 1987. Numismatic and Epigraphic Evidence for the Chronology of Early Gandharan Art. Pages 67-88 in M. Yaldiz and W. Lobo (eds), *Investigating Indian Art*. Berlin: Museum für Indische Kunst.

GBGI 2007. *Gandāra bijutsu to bāmiyan isekiten* (The exhibition of Gandhāran art and the Bamiyan site). Shizuoka: Shizuoka shinbunsha.

GBHP 2008. *Gandhara, The Buddhist Heritage of Pakistan: Legends, Monasteries, and Paradise*. Mainz: Verlag Philipp von Zabern.

Harle J.C. 1974. A Hitherto Unknown Dated Sculpture from Gandhāra: A Preliminary Report. Pages 128-135 in J. E. van Lohuizen-de Leeuw and J. M. M. Ubaghs (eds), *South Asian Archaeology 1973*. Leiden: E. J. Brill.

IBHK Tsukamoto K. 1996–98. *Indo bukkyō himei no kenkyū* (Study of inscriptions of Indian Buddhism) (3 volumes). Kyoto: Heirakuji shoten.

Khandalavala K. 1985. The Five Dated Gandhāra School Sculptures and Their Stylistic Implications. Pages 61-71 in F. M. Asher and G. S. Gai (eds), *Indian Epigraphy: Its Bearing on the History of Art*. New Delhi: American Institute of Indian Studies.

Konow S. 1929. *Khroshṭhī Inscriptions*. Calcutta: Manager of Publications.

Konow S. 1933. Notes on Indo-Scythian Chronology. *Journal of Indian History* 12/1: 1-46.

Konow S. 1933-34. A Note on the Mamane Dheri Inscription. *Epigraphia Indica* 22: 14-15.

Konow S. & Wijk W.E. van 1924. The Eras of the Indian Kharoṣṭhī Inscriptions. *Acta Orientalia* 3: 52-91.

LA 1984. *Light of Asia: Buddha Sakyamuni in Asian Art*. Los Angeles: Los Angeles County Museum of Art.

Lohuizen-de Leeuw J.E. van 1949. *The 'Scythian' Period*. Leiden: E.J. Brill.

Lohuizen-de Leeuw J.E. van 1986. The Second Century of the Kaniṣka Era. *South Asian Studies* 2: 1-9.

Lyons I. & Ingholt H. 1957. *Gandhāran Art in Pakistan.* New York: Pantheon Books.

Marshall, J. 1951. *Taxila: An Illustrated Account of Archaeological Excavations carried out at Taxila under the Orders of the Government of India between the Years 1913 and 1934* (3 volumes). Cambridge: Cambridge University Press.

Marshall J. & Vogel J.Ph. 1904. Excavations at Chārsada in the Frontier Province. *Archaeological Survey of India Annual Report 1902-03*: 104-184.

Matsuoka Museum of Art 1994. *Ancient Asian Sculptures from the Matsuoka Collection.* Tokyo: Matsuoka Museum of Art

Mitterwallner G. von 1987. The Brussels Buddha from Gandhara of the Year 5. Pages 213-247 in M. Yaldiz and W. Lobo (eds), *Investigating Indian Art.* Berlin: Museum für Indische Kunst.

Mukherjee B.N. 1991. Dated Inscriptions on Gandhāra Sculptures in the Indian Museum. Pages 149-152 in A. Sengupta and D. Das (eds), *Gandhara Holdings in the Indian Museum: A Handlist.* Calcutta: Indian Museum.

Oliveri L.M. 2014. *The Last Phases of the Urban Site of Bir-Kot-Ghwandai (Barikot), The Buddhist Sites of Gumbat and Amluk-Dara (Barikot).* Lahore: Sang-e-Meel Publications.

Rhi J. 2005. Images, Relics, and Jewels: The Assimilation of Images in the Buddhist Relic Cult of Gandhāra. *Artibus Asiae* 65-2: 169-211.

Rhi J. 2008. Identifying Several Visual Types in Gandhāran Buddha Images. *Archives of Asian Art* 58: 43-85.

Rosenfield J.M. 1967. *The Dynastic Arts of the Kushans.* Berkeley and Los Angeles: University of California Press.

Rowland B. 1936. A Revised Chronology of Gandhāra Sculpture. *Art Bulletin* 18: 387-400.

1942. Gandhāra and Late Antique Art: The Buddha Image. *American Journal of Archaeology* 46: 223-236.

Salomon R. 2005. The Indo-Greek Era of 186/5 B.C. in a Buddhist Reliquary Inscription. Pages 359-401 in O. Bopearachchi and M.-F. Boussac (eds), *Afghanistan, ancien carrefour entre l'est et l'ouest.* Turnhout: Brepolis.

Salomon R. 2007. Dynastic and Institutional Connections in the Pre-and Early Kuṣāṇa Period: New Manuscript and Epigraphic Evidence. Pages 267-86 in D. M. Srinivasan (ed), *On the Cusp of an Era: Art in the Pre-Kuṣāṇa World.* Leiden: Brill.

Senart É. 1899. Notes d'épigraphie indienne VII: Deux épigraphes du Svāt. *Journal asiatique* 9e série 13: 526-537.

Smith V.A. 1889a. A Dated Graeco-Buddhist Sculpture. *The Indian Antiquary* 18: 257-258.

Smith V.A. 1889b. Graeco-Roman Influence on the Civilization of Ancient India. *The Indian Antiquary* 21: 107-198.

Soper A. 1949. Aspects of Light Symbolism. *Archives of Asian Art* 12: 252-283.

Soper A. 1951. The Roman Style in Gandhāra. *American Journal of Archaeology* 55/4: 301-319.

Strauch I. 2009(2013). Inscribed Objects from Greater Gandhāra. *Bulletin of the Asia Institute* 23: 209-219.

Tanabe K. 1984a. Butsuda shakamuni (Buddha Śākyamuni). *Kokka* 1076: 25-26.

Tanabe K. 1984b. Karōshuti meikoku butsuda ritsuzō kō (On a standing Buddha image with a Kharoṣṭhi inscription). *Kokka* 1078: 7-24.

Tanabe K. 1988. Iconographical and Typological Investigations of the Gandhara Fake Bodhisattva Image Exhibited by the Cleveland Museum of Art and the Nara National Museum. *Orient* 24: 84-107.

Tanabe K. 2007. *Hirayama korekushon: Gandāra bukkyō bijutsu* (Hirayama collection: Buddhist art of Gandhāra). Tokyo: Kōdansha.

Tissot F. 2005. Remarks on Several Gandhāra Pieces. *East and West* 55/1: 395-403.

Vogel J.Ph. 1905. Inscribed Gandhāra Sculptures. *Archaeological Survey of India Annual Report 1903-04*: 245-260.

Zwalf W. 1996. *A Catalogue of the Gandhāra Sculpture in the British Museum* (2 volumes). London: British Museum Press.

A framework for Gandhāran chronology based on relic inscriptions

Stefan Baums

Introduction

Many Gandhāran relic containers have inscriptions attached to them or are otherwise associated with inscriptions belonging to the same relic deposit, and the majority of these inscriptions contain dating formulas.[1] My intent in the present article is to provide an overview of these, to discuss alternative means at our disposal for dating inscribed objects, and to arrange as many of the inscribed relic containers as possible in a single chronological sequence as a solid basis for further research on Gandhāran chronology. The article also provides an update to the corpus of Gandhāran relic inscriptions edited in Baums 2012 and since kept up to date as part of Baums & Glass 2002- a, adding six new inscribed relic containers and suggesting several improved readings.

Gandhāran relic inscriptions

Relic establishments played an especially prominent part in the spread of Buddhism to and within ancient Gandhāra (Fussman 1994; Falk 2005), with an emphasis on what the tradition calls *śārīraka* relics, that is bodily relics of the Buddha, called *dhātu*, *śarīra* or *dhātuśarīra* in the inscriptions themselves.[2] There are two other types of relic in the traditional classification (Strong 2004: 8-20). One of these consists of so-called *paribhoga* relics, i.e. items purportedly used by the Buddha during his final lifetime that came to be worshipped. Typical for Gandhāra are alms bowls of the Buddha in stone, often larger than life-size and sometimes inscribed. The others are *uddeśaka* relics, i.e. representational relics of the Buddha in a broad sense including images.[3] To these should be added dharma relics as a fourth type, that is a text or collection of texts representing the word and hence person of the Buddha. Apart from scriptural quotations in inscriptions (on which see below), probably the earliest example of a dharma relic we have is the Gāndhārī birch-bark manuscripts of the Senior collection, dated to *c.* AD 140 (Salomon 2003a). The inscription on the container that preserved them for us (CKI 245) closely follows the typical formula of relic inscriptions, providing a strong argument that already in antiquity they were considered a dharma-relic deposit.

The Gandhāran Buddhist imaginaire was well familiar with events surrounding the Buddha's death and the division of his relics into eight shares by the brahman Droṇa, as depicted in Gandhāran art (Jongeward 2012a), and as narrated at the end of the Pali *Mahāparinibbānasutta* (ed. Rhys Davids and Carpenter 1890-1911, II: 154-168) and its parallel versions in other languages. Moreover, Gandhāran Buddhists remained aware of the more proximate origin of their relic cult in the redistribution of relics under Aśoka, as evidenced in Gandhāran art by the depiction of Mauryan motifs such as lion-

[1] I thank Peter Stewart for inviting me to the workshop 'Problems of Chronology in Gandhāran Art' (University of Oxford, 23-34 March 2017) in which this article originated, and for seeing it to publication. Some of the material was previously presented at the 'Bīmarān Workshop' (Ancient India and Iran Trust, Cambridge, 11-12 September 2015) organized by Wannaporn Rienjang.
[2] For convenience, the present article gives technical terms in their Sanskrit form, and uses Gāndhārī only when directly quoting from an inscription or where a Sanskrit equivalent is unavailable or unclear.
[3] It is not clear that footprints of the Buddha – known from Gandhāra (for instance the inscribed set at Tirath, CKI 36), but also very prominent in Southeast Asian Buddhism – were considered *uddeśaka*, since usually they were taken to be actual marks left by the Buddha on a visit rather than artistic representations.

topped pillars (e.g. in the relief illustrated in Jongeward 2012a: 32 and the miniature *stūpa* in Jongeward 2012b: 76). Direct epigraphic evidence of this awareness is provided by the Indravarma casket in the Metropolitan Museum of Art (no. 8,[4] CKI 242), whose inscription specifically mentions that relics were taken from a *mauryakālīna* 'Maurya-period' *stūpa* and reestablished in a new *stūpa*.

The main physical types of Gandhāran stone relic containers have been categorized in Jongeward 2012b as small spherical, spherical, ovoid, cylindrical, and miniature *stūpas*. Occasionally, secular items were repurposed as reliquary containers, such as the two drinking cups that were combined to form the Indravarma silver reliquary (no. 25, CKI 564) and the incense container (*gandhakaraṇḍa*) that became the Kaniṣka casket (no. 45, CKI 145). All of these would open up, typically to reveal a smaller container made from crystal or precious metal containing the actual relic as well as donative objects. Relic inscriptions are found on the relic containers themselves, on metal scrolls inside the containers, on metal plates deposited next to the containers,[5] or on a slab of the relic chamber.

Regardless of which physical object of a deposit they are applied to, Gandhāran relic inscriptions all adhere to the same basic formula (cf. Salomon 2012b: 178-197): usually, a date, with or without era, is followed by the name of one or more donors, then an action verb or noun denoting the act of establishing the relics (almost always a derivative of *prati-ṣṭhā-*), then a term for the relic itself, often specified as a relic of the Buddha Śākyamuni. Optional elements include a place name (most of which we cannot localize where the find circumstances are unknown), a list of persons (almost always family) in honor (*pūjā*) of whom the establishment is made and an expression of the wish to reach nirvāṇa on behalf of the donor or, occasionally, all beings (*sarvasattva*). Some inscriptions highlight that the establishment occurred in a place where no relic establishment had been made before (*apratiṣṭhāpitapūrva pradeśa*), presumably because such an establishment was particularly meritorious.[6]

While staying within the parameters of this formula, relic inscriptions can vary greatly in size. The shortest known Gandhāran relic inscription, from Sanghol in the Panjab (no. 49, CKI 239), consists of only the two words *upasakasa ayabhadrasa* 'of the lay-follower Ayabhadra.' The longest relic inscriptions, on the other hand – the gold scroll of King Senavarma (no. 24, CKI 249) and the copper plates of Helaüta (no. 26, CKI 564) – come to no less than 14 and 29 long lines, respectively. They do so by adding extensive strings of canonical quotations and epithets of the Buddha to the basic formula, as well as, in the case of Senavarma, a historical introduction detailing the circumstances of the relic installation.[7] Individuals who had a formal role in the act of depositing relics also sometimes memorialized themselves by additions to the inscribed formula. One such role is the *navakarmika*, the monastic superintendent of construction, who is named both at the end of the Taxila copper plate (no. 12, CKI 46) and on the Manikyala relic-chamber slab (no. 37, CKI 149). The conclusion of the Senavarma inscription mentions the person who weighed (if Harry Falk's interpretation of *solite* as a mistake for *tolite* is correct) the gold of which the inscription is made.

[4] Here and in the following, I identify Gandhāran relic inscriptions by their running number in Baums 2012 in addition to their number in Baums & Glass 2002- a.

[5] A special case is the inscription of Helaüta (no. 26, CKI 564) on a set of bronze sheets that appears to imitate (or independently invent) the 'concertina' manuscript format (otherwise not known in early Gandhāra, cf. Baums 2014).

[6] As pointed out by Vincent Tournier in discussion during the workshop, this higher degree of merit would primarily have been available during the earlier phase of the expansion of Buddhism in Gandhāra. Once every major and minor town had a *stūpa* and a state of 'relic saturation' had been reached, all one could still do was add secondary *stūpas* and make minor dedications. This would explain why the liveliness of the Gandhāran relic cult appears to have abated in the third century AD (around the same time that Gāndhārī began to fall out of use as a literary language).

[7] The original Ekaüḍa Stūpa was hit by lightning. Senavarma, having succeeded his brother Varmasena, opened it up, excavated the rubble and opened the relic chamber. He took out the relic he found there next to an earlier relic inscription (*likhitaka*) which stated: 'Vasusena, son of Utarasena, king of Oḍi from the Ikṣvāku family, he establishes this Ekaüḍa.'

Comparison with image inscriptions

The donative inscriptions on Gandhāran images, by comparison, are much simpler than the relic-donation formula, but since images are one of the most prominent genres of Gandhāran art and four of the inscribed pieces do contain much-discussed dates, they warrant a brief discussion. Altogether, there are 34 inscriptions on Gandhāran images, 29 of them on pedestals, and five on halos. (The implications of the inscriptions on extant sculptures are further discussed in Juhyung Rhi's paper in the present volume.) The main formula types are: (1) name only (e.g. *ṣamanamitrasa*, CKI 76); (2) name and a word for 'donation' (e.g. *[hora]ṣadasa da[namukhe]*, CKI 54); (3) name, title and word for 'donation' (e.g. *budharakṣi[dasa] bhi[kṣusa] da[namu]kho*, CKI 77); (4) name, name of companion and word for 'donation' (e.g. *budhamitrasa [bu]dharakṣidasa sadayarisa daṇa[mukhe]*, CKI 113); (5) name, word for donation and place name (only example: *bu[dh]orumasa daṇamukh[e] khaṃda[vaṇatu]baga[mi]*, CKI 112); (6) name, word for donation and beneficiary (e.g. *[aṃ]bae savaseṭhabhariae daṇamukhe sa[rva](*sa)tvaṇa puyae spamiasa [ca a]ro[ga]dakṣiṇi(*ae)*, CKI 117); (7) label inscriptions (e.g. *kaśavo tathagato*, CKI 84); and (8) date inscriptions (e.g. *saṃ 1 1 1 100 20 20 20 20 4 proṭhavadasa masasa divasaṃmi paṃcami 4 1*, CKI 124). See Appendix 4 for texts and translations of the four dated image inscriptions.

Methods of dating

There are several ways, direct and indirect, in which inscriptions can be used to date the objects they are associated with.

(1) The inscription may contain an explicit date, and this date may or may not contain an explicit era.[8] To illustrate both the general date format and some possible complications, we may consider the inscription of the nun Utara (no. 35, CKI 226) whose date runs as follows:

> *saṃbatsara satapaṃ⟨*ca⟩ïśa 1 100 20 20 10 4 1 1 1 mase pr⟨*o⟩ṭha [1]*

The year (*saṃvatsara*; sometimes the abbreviation *saṃ* or the synonym *varṣa* are used) is 157 of an unspecified era, the value being given both as number word and as number sign, as is common practice in Gandhāran relic inscriptions. The inscription provides direct evidence for the occasional practice of omitting hundreds in that the number word does not spell out 'one hundred', but the number sign does. The next element of the date is the month. Two different systems of month names were in use in ancient Gandhāra: the Macedonian and the Indian (see Appendix 2, and the discussion below of different varieties of the Macedonian calendar). Here the Indian month name Prauṣṭha is used. The day is in this inscription indicated simply by the number sign *1*. In other inscriptions it is spelled out and usually preceded by the word *divase* or the abbreviation *di* 'day'. Certain days were auspicious dates and more popular for relic deposits than others (see Appendix 3).

(2) Historical figures may be referred to, which can help us date inscriptions and their objects when those figures are known from other sources. In ancient Gandhāra – contrasting with contemporary mainland India – we have from at least the first century AD onwards a strong sense of history that manifested in a desire on the part of donors to record who they were, when they lived and who they

[8] It is interesting to note that so many of the relic inscriptions from Gandhāra are in fact dated. One might wonder why this is the case, and even why the inscriptions were prepared at all. In what might be called the daily life of a relic – when it is not paraded as part of a ceremony – it resides deep inside a *stūpa* where it cannot be seen and where nobody can read an inscription. I think it can be argued nonetheless that relic inscriptions were meant for posterity, since those that installed them were evidently quite aware of the possibility of a *stūpa* being reopened in the future. This is apparent from the coins that were sometimes deposited in the *stūpa* shaft for future repairs and renovations to the structure. Even stronger evidence is provided by the Senavarma inscription quoted in the previous footnote, in which we have a concrete case of posterity reading and engaging with a relic inscription.

were related to. Combining the evidence from individual inscriptions (and, secondarily, the coinage) it becomes possible to draw up comprehensive family trees for two major sponsors of the Gandhāran relic cult, the Apraca royal house in Bajaur and the Oḍi dynasty in Swat (see Falk 1998: 107 and von Hinüber 2003: 33, respectively, for summaries of the latest state of our knowledge). A very common point of chronological reference was the Indo-Scythian king Azes and his eponymous era, which remained in use long after his death.[9] Sometimes, references to the wider frame of South Asian history also occur, such as when the Wardak vase (no. 43, CKI 159) mentions the overlord of the donor as 'the great king, chief king of kings Huviṣka'.

(3) The ideas expressed in the inscription, and the formulas used to do so, can sometimes be correlated with what we know from the literary tradition. Gandhāran relic inscriptions contain several examples of fixed phrases and literal quotations from Buddhist texts, both mainstream and Mahāyāna. (Falk 2010 calls these 'signature phrases' with the implication that their users had a personal affinity for the expression chosen and meant to showcase their learnedness and acquaintance with Buddhist literature.) The dating of literary texts is, however, usually very approximate itself and can thus provide at best a general classification of inscriptions as 'early' or 'late'. The best-known example of a canonical quotation in a Gandhāran inscription is the Kurram casket (no. 39, CKI 153), reproducing the formula of dependent arising (*pratītyasamutpāda*). It has to be noted that since this is a canonical formula which remained mostly unchanging through time, its usefulness for dating the casket is limited.

Another well-known example is the aforementioned Senavarma inscription, which within the framework of the usual dedication formula has a very extensive list of literary quotations attached as epithets to the expression 'relics of the lord, the Buddha'. A thorough discussion of these is provided in von Hinüber 2003, but it is worth highlighting one particular pair of terms that relates to the relics themselves. A distinction is drawn in the inscription between two 'bodies' of the Buddha, his *paścimaśarīra* and his *antimaśarīra*, both of which words on their own mean 'final' or 'last body'. In context, however, the former appears to be a reference to the body of the Buddha in his last human life, whereas the *antimaśarīra* (described as a *vajrasaṃghana* or 'diamond mass'; cf. Radich 2011) means the totality of his relics after his death. This is thus an explicit statement that the relics continued to be regarded as a body of the Buddha, though distinct (*visaṃyukta*) from his human body.

A final example of a literary quotation occurs in the Kopśakasa relic reestablishment (no. 21b, CKI 266), as read anew in Baums 2012 when I realized that it adapted a quotation from the Prajñāpāramitā literature:

> *to dhaduve ṇiṣehit[a aho ca] aparimaṇada du[khato] moi[d](*o) logo ce[va t](*e)ṇa pra[d̲i]moido*

'based on these relics I am liberated from the immeasurable suffering, and what is more, the world is liberated by him' (i.e. the Buddha, whose relics are being installed) or, more generally, 'through this' (i.e. this act of relic installation). The fact that the donor Kopśakasa emphasizes the liberation of the world over and above his own personal liberation can be considered a Mahāyāna notion.

(4) Palaeography is often looked to as a means of dating inscriptions, but the answers it provides are of an approximate and relative nature. The shape of certain Kharoṣṭhī letters that undergo a well-defined series of changes – most prominent among them the letter *s* – serve as indicators and help categorize inscriptions as 'early' (Indo-Greek), 'middle' or 'late' (Kushan), but can certainly not be used to assign them to any particular decade. The 'early' type of *s*, to stay with this example, has a head that is completely

[9] In his case the expressions *atīta*, *kālagata* or *abhyatīta* (see Strauch 2009: 209-213 for the Gāndhārī spelling *adhvadida*) are often attached to his name.

closed on its left, the 'middle' type is half open, and the 'late' type is not much more than a vertical squiggly line (cf. the discussion and illustrations in Glass 2000: 104–107), but the overall development is very gradual. We should also expect (and can observe in Gāndhārī manuscripts) that the writing of the same scribe varies from one task to another. Furthermore, writing for monumental purposes on a hard surface such as stone[10] can be expected to preserve a more formal, archaic character than contemporary manuscripts hands. The closest manuscript equivalent in terms of ductus to a carefully executed relic inscription would be something like the bold, precise hand of the scribe who produced the Anavataptagāthā (CKM 1) and other canonical manuscripts in the British Library collection. With all due caution, and focusing on the morphology of letters more than on impressionistic aspects of their shape (cf. the discussion of *bh* in Glass 2009), palaeography can be a useful weapon in the chronological armory.

(5) The language of Gandhāran inscriptions follows a general trajectory from Gāndhārī proper to a highly Sanskritized version of the language, and inscriptions can accordingly be placed in a tentative relative chronology (cf. Salomon 2001 and 2002 for descriptions of the process). Quite apart from this increasing Sanskritization, however, we can also observe the co-existence of several different approaches to orthography for writing Gāndhārī in the newly available body of manuscripts, ranging from a very precise phonetic spelling that employs numerous diacritics (and is thus reader-friendly) to a minimal orthography that leaves many phonetic distinctions, such as fricativization and nasalization, unmarked (making it easier to write than decipher). In principle, it should be possible to correlate the orthographic conventions we observe in the reliquaries with the systems distinguishable in the manuscripts and arrive at groupings representing scribal schools (or at least schools of orthographic thought). This has never been attempted, but should be no less informative than palaeographic analysis. It is complicated by the general problem of distinguishing temporal and regional variation.

(6) The materials, techniques, and style employed in the production of inscribed objects are the proper province of art history, but technical details of how text was inscribed can potentially also be put to chronological use under the assumption that they represent inventions made at particular points in time. Harry Falk in particular has pointed out that those in charge of the final execution of an inscription were not necessarily literate and able to write Kharoṣṭhī without help (e.g. Falk 1998: 87–88). A common division of labor would then be for a scribe to trace letters very slightly with a needle on the surface of the stone, and for a stonemason to carve them deeply following the scribe's outline.[11] This process was liable to produce errors such as missing or extraneous lines, which we can often still observe in the finished product: the reliquary of Utara (no. 10, CKI 254) provides several clear examples. Again, however, it is often difficult or impossible to separate regional from temporal variation.

(7) If organic material is associated with a relic deposit, this can in principle be radiocarbon-dated, though I am not aware of any such datings actually having been performed. One promising case that has been the focus of recent discussion is the Bīmarān reliquary (no. 52, CKI 50) and the organic remains inside its golden casket.[12] Another is the relic deposit of Ayadata (no. 22, CKI 401), which contained several samples of wood. But like all other means of dating, radiocarbon dating is not a silver bullet for solving chronological problems. It can only provide one or more date ranges, sometimes spanning many decades (cf. the report on birch-bark and palm leaf manuscripts in Allon, Salomon, Jacobsen and

[10] Specialized epigraphic writing techniques (such as pointillé on metal) further distort the shape of letters.

[11] During the workshop, Robert Bracey remarked on a similar procedure in the design of coins, with one person putting dots in those places where letters should go, and another person actually adding them as a separate step.

[12] The Bīmarān relic deposit is particularly important for correlating the epigraphic record of Gandhāra (represented by its stone relic container) with the art-historical (represented by its gold casket with images of the Buddha and the gods Brahma and Indra).

Zoppi 2006), and is thus not necessarily more precise than palaeographic dating, let alone an explicit date given in an inscription.

A general problem that has to be kept in mind regardless of the specific evidence used for dating is that Gandhāran relic deposits are invariably multi-object finds, including at a minimum a container and the relic itself, but often a series of nesting containers within a relic chamber, encasing a relic together with any number of additional donative goods such as inscribed metal foils, jewelry, metal flowers, precious textiles and others. If any one of these objects can be dated, this does not necessarily mean that all of the others were produced at the same time.[13] The only relative certainty is that they were interred at the same time and that any inscription relates to this moment, though the cases of re-interment discussed above complicate even this assumption.

Six new relic inscriptions and one new reading

Five years ago, I published my edition and translation of the corpus of fifty-eight inscribed Gandhāran reliquaries then known (Baums 2012). Work on this edition had started in 2006 and proceeded in tandem with the compilation of an illustrated online corpus and catalog of the same reliquaries on the website Gandhari.org, where the complete set is retrievable by filtering for type 'relic establishment' in the Inscriptions section of the *Catalog of Gāndhārī Texts* (Baums & Glass 2002- a). Since the publication of the print edition, I have kept this online corpus and edition of the Gandhāran reliquary inscriptions up to date, improved several readings and provided complete lexicographic coverage for it in the *Dictionary of Gāndhārī* (Baums & Glass 2002- b).

The online corpus now contains altogether sixty-six items, eight more than the book. Two of these were consciously excluded from Baums 2012 as being possible forgeries: a golden version of the silver sheet of Mahazada (CKI 332, cf. Baums 2012: 245 n. 100) and the Haḍḍa gold sheet (CKI 455, cf. Baums 2012: 201). This possibility remains, but it still seemed advisable to include them in the online corpus, if only because each of them has attracted a certain amount of discussion in the secondary literature.

An inscribed reliquary in the form of a *stūpa* surrounded by four worshippers had been omitted by oversight from *Gandharan Buddhist Reliquaries* and Baums 2012. The short inscription (CKI 267) as reproduced by its editor (Sherrier 1984) on the authority of Harold Bailey and Gérard Fussman is *śivarakṣidakasa thube sapariane*. Of the two interpretations given, I prefer the one that takes the last word descriptively as Skt. *saparijanaḥ*, and thus translate 'Śivarakṣidaga's *stūpa* with attendants.'

In 2013, a number of reliquaries, two of them inscribed, reached the Museum Fünf Kontinente in Munich from the collection of the late Gritli von Mitterwallner. I had the opportunity to inspect them in the museum soon after their arrival. In the following year, the museum journal published photographs and a discussion of these reliquaries (Falk 2014–15).

During my inspection, it was immediately apparent that one of the two inscribed reliquaries (no. 34, CKI 225) had been published previously in Salomon 1995 and reedited in Baums 2012. The reading and translation I gave there, following in all essentials Salomon's edition and followed in turn by Falk, were *sa[ṃ]vatsara satapacaïśa⟨*śa⟩da 1 100 20 20 10 4 1 1 1 mase proṭha sastehi sa[ta]viśati iśa kṣ[u]nami pratiṭhavati khadadata utara[ci]tathopo mahavanami matapitina pujartha sarvasatvana puyartha utarapuya[rtha]* – 'In the one-hundred-and-fifty-seventh – 157th – year, in the month Prauṣṭhapada, after twenty-seven days, at this moment Khaṃdadata establishes the *stūpa* built by Utara in the Great Forest (Monastery), in order to honor mother and father, in order to honor all beings, in order to honor Utara.'

[13] A case in point is the Bīmarān casket.

Using the new photographs and following my personal inspection of the inscription, I am now able to offer one improvement on this interpretation. The word *utara[ci]tathopo* always presented a problem: the expression and somewhat awkward compound were without parallel in the Gāndhārī epigraphic corpus, and it remained unclear what exactly it meant for a *stūpa* to be built (literally, 'piled up') by one person (Utara), but established by another (Khaṃdadata). As it turns out, however, the fourth akṣara of this expression is not actually a *ci*, but rather a clear *dhi* with an attached footmark (see Figure 1). Accordingly, I now read two words *utaradhita* and *thopo*, and interpret the sentence in question as 'Khaṃdadata, daughter of Utara, establishes a *stūpa*.'

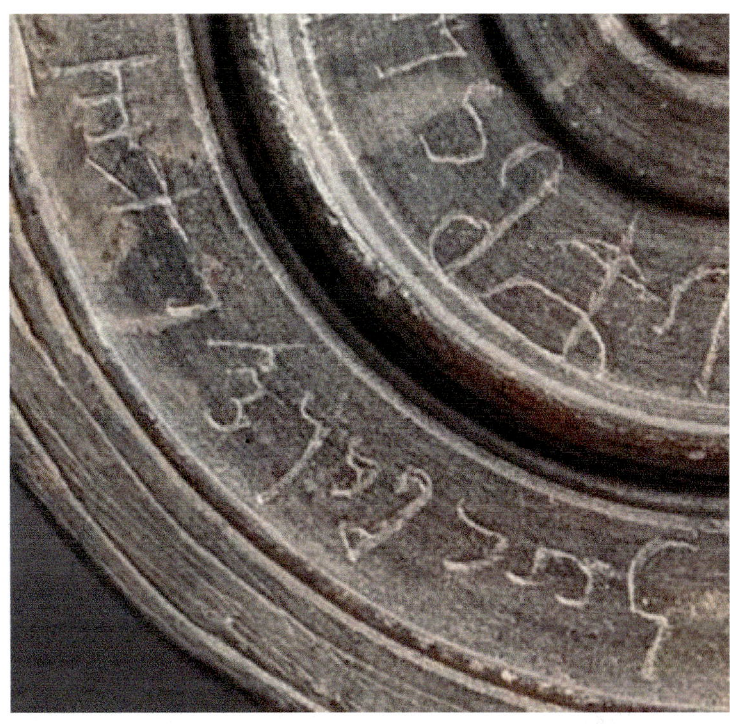

Figure 1. Detail of Khaṃdadata's relic inscription. (Photograph after Falk 2014–15.)

This can be compared with two other Gandhāran relic inscriptions in which the donor, in both cases a woman, identifies herself as the daughter of somebody else: *kumarasa viṣuvarmasa [a]teuria loṇa grahavadi[dhita]* – 'a (lady) of the women's quarters of prince Viṣuvarma, Loṇa, daughter of a householder' (no. 5, CKI 247), and *kamagulyaputravagamaregavihara[thu]ba ... khoḍadhida* 'at the stūpa of the Vagamarega-Son-of-Kamagulya Monastery ... the little daughter' (no. 44, CKI 509). Exactly as in the last-mentioned case (the second Wardak vase), Khaṃdadata's inscription thus recorded part of a joint parent-daughter donation, her mother's donation to the same monastery in the same year being recorded in no. 35, CKI 226. The special role of her mother Utara in the joint relic donation also explains why Khaṃdadata refers to her separately after she had arguably already been included in Khaṃdadata's collective expression of worship to her parents (*matapitina*). My complete new reading of Khaṃdadata's inscription (including some other minor improvements) is: *savatsara satapacaïśa⟨*śa⟩de 1 100 20 20 10 4 1 1 1 mase proṭha sastehi sataviśati iśa kṣunami pratiṭhavati khadadata utaradhita thopo mahavanami matapitina pujartha sarvasatvana puyartha utarapuya⟨*rtha⟩.*

The second inscribed reliquary in the Munich collection (CKI 240) is a miniature *stūpa*. This object was previously unknown, and my reading of the inscription (based on personal inspection and photographs) is: *priavaśabhayae pra[ṭh]iṭhavaṇe madapida puyaïta sarvasatva pu⟨*yaïta⟩* – 'The establishment of the wife of Priyavaṃśa. Mother and father are honored. All beings are honored.' This differs in a number of points from the reading given in Falk 2014–15: 150–157, among them my preference for the noun *pra[ṭh]iṭhavaṇe* over unclear *praḍiṭhavae*. The most substantial point of difference is, however, my reading of the name of the unnamed donor's husband as *priavaśa* rather than *priavaya*. This is supported by the occurrence of the same name Priyavaṃśa in another relic inscription (no. 28, CKI 331), there also spelled *priavaśa*, though we cannot be certain that reference is to the same person.

Also in the collection of von Mitterwallner was an inscribed copperplate (CKI 466). The plate had unfortunately been lost by the time the collection reached the museum, but Salomon 2014–15 was able to provide a reading based on photographs that von Mitterwallner and Robert Senior had sent him years earlier. In the photographs, the plate is heavily oxidized and only partly legible, but does appear to give a date without explicit era. The first of four number signs is *100*, the last two are *4 4*. Because of the way the Kharoṣṭhī number system works, the second number sign can only have been either *10* or *20*, making the year of the date either 118 or 128.

A new inscribed miniature *stūpa* in the private collection of Aman ur Rahman (CKI 827; Falk 2007: 138–140) appears to state that it was dedicated in the year 11 of an otherwise unknown *mahakṣatrapa* 'great satrap' Namipala (likely a misspelling for Nagapala; see below for a discussion of the era).

Another miniature *stūpa*, this one in the private collection of Pankaj Tandon (CKI 828; Falk 2007: 141–142), poses a different chronological puzzle. The date reads *sa atitie rayasa ayasa atitasa katiasa mase di pra*. Here *sa* is probably for 'year' (*saṃvatsara*), since *di* is doubtless an abbreviation for *divasa*, 'day'. The number of the day is likewise given in abbreviated form as *pra* for *prathama*, and the specification of the month Kārttika presents no problem. How are we, however, to interpret the number of the year spelled *atitie*? Falk proposes reasonably that we have to do with a misspelling of **aśitie*, 'eightieth', and one may add that this misspelling could be due to the following, similar-sounding word *atitasa*. The complete dating formula can then be translated: 'In the eightieth year of King Azes who has passed on, on the first day of the month Kārttika.'

The last addendum to the corpus of Gandhāran reliquary inscriptions (CKI 975) is on a fourth miniature *stūpa* in the private collection of Isao Kurita and was read *saṃghilakasa iṃdrakae ya iyo śariramuhe* – 'this is the foremost relic of Saṃghilaga and Iṃdraga' – by its editor (Falk 2014–15: 143–144). It is mentioned here for the sake of completeness, but does not contribute chronological information to the present survey.

etaye purvaye, *iśa kṣunaṃmi* and related expressions

Inscription no. 12 (CKI 46) contains, following the specification of the date by year, month and day and preceding the name of the donor, the expression *etaye purvaye*:

> *[saṃva]tsaraye aṭhasatatimae 20 20 20 10 4 4 maharayasa mahaṃtasa mogasa pa[ne]masa masasa divase paṃcame 4 1* ***etaye purvaye*** *kṣaha[ra]ta[sa cukhsa]sa ca kṣatrapasa liako kusuluko nama tasa [pu]tro pati[ko] ... bhagavata Śakamuṇisa śariraṃ (*pra)tithaveti ...*

A variant of the same expression (using the adverb *etra* for the inflected pronoun) occurs in the same position in no. 37 (CKI 149):

> *saṃ 10 4 4 [kartiyasa maze divase 20]* ***e[tra] purvae*** *maharajasa kaṇeṣkasa guṣaṇavaśasaṃvardhaka lala daḍaṇayago veśpaśisa kṣatrapasa horamurt[o] ... ṇaṇabhagavabudhaz[a]va p[r]atistavayati ...*

In both cases, Konow 1929 (29, 150) translated it 'on this first (*tithi*)', and I followed him in Baums 2012 (212, 241) with 'on this first (lunar day)'.

These translations are, however, untenable since in a system of lunar months, the fifth and twentieth day of the month, respectively, does not coincide with the 'first lunar day',[14] and in any case the expected word for 'first' would be *prathama*, not *pūrva*. The solution is provided by later Sanskrit inscriptions that contain phrases such as *asyāṃ saṃvatsaramāsadivasapūrvāyām* (sc. *velāyām*) 'at this aforementioned (time) of year, month and day' after the date proper 'by way of introducing the body of the document' (Salomon 1998: 176), exactly as in our Gāndhārī inscriptions.

[14] In Indian chronology, a month is subdivided into 30 *tithi*, during each of which the angle between moon and sun changes by 12 degrees. A *tithi* is thus only slightly shorter than a solar day (*divasa*), 29.5 of which make up a synodic month.

Understood thus, *etaye purvaye* and *etra purvaye* are in fact only variants of several similar expressions that occur with great regularity in the same position of other relic inscriptions. One of them is *iśa divase* or *aja divase* 'on this day':

no. 6 (CKI 454): *iśa divasami*
no. 13 (CKI 405): *iśa divasaṃmi*
no. 14 (CKI 251): *aja sudivase s[u]nakṣetre*
no. 16 (CKI 544): *iś[a] (*divasami)*
no. 22 (CKI 401): *[aja d](*i)va[sa]mi*[15]
no. 28 (CKI 331): *iśa divasami*
no. 30 (CKI 60): *iśa diva[se]*
no. 31 (CKI 563): *iśa divasa*

Another, equally frequent variant, involves the word *kṣuna* in the locative or instrumental case and occurs primarily in Kushan-period inscriptions:

no. 26 (CKI 564): *iśa kṣunami*
no. 29 (CKI 172): *imeṇa kṣuṇeṇa*
no. 34 (CKI 225): *iśa kṣunami*
no. 38 (CKI 152): *iś[e] kṣunaṃmi*[16]
no. 39 (CKI 153): *iś[e] kṣunaṃmi*
no. 40 (CKI 368): *iśe kṣuṇami*
no. 41 (CKI 155): *iśa kṣunaṃmi*
CKI 466: *[iśe kṣ](*u)[ṇaṃmi]*

Once, this (or maybe rather its Indian phonetic cousin *kṣaṇa* 'moment') occurs with the added specification *cetrike*, which is echoed in another inscription by simple *cetreṇa* and appears to make explicit a beginning of the year at the spring equinox (i.e. with the Indian month Caitra, cf. Appendix 2 and Baums 2012: 207 n. 15):

no. 8 (CKI 242): *imeṇa cetrike kṣ[a]ṇ[e]*
cf. CKI 455: *imeṇa cetreṇa*

The word *kṣuna* corresponds to Bactrian χþονο 'year', which itself has been interpreted as a loanword from Greek χρόνος 'time' by A. Thierfelder (Humbach 1966: 24, cf. Davary 1982 s.v. *xšono*). If this is correct, the Gāndhārī occurrences provide important evidence for the semantic specialization of this word from Greek 'time' over Gāndhārī 'date' to Bactrian 'year'.[17] A third variant, occurring only once, is *ghaḍiga* 'period of time' (Sanskrit *ghaṭikā*):

no. 43 (CKI 159): *imeṇa gaḏiḡeṇa*

Chronology

In the final part of this article, I will now in several steps arrange the inscribed Gandhāran reliquaries in a chronological sequence, making explicit the procedure that led to their their initial arrangement in Baums 2012 and adding the several new items to the corpus in their proper places.

[15] This is my own tentative reconstruction in light of no. 14. In his edition, Salomon 2003b: 44-45 noted that the heavily damaged first word remained unclear, but was certainly not *iśa*.

[16] I prefer this reading over Konow 1929: 152 *kṣunaṃṃi*, taking the horizontal line at the bottom of the third akṣara as a footmark. It is possible, however, that neither of these readings is correct since the inscription in question is lost and only an imprecise eye copy was available to Konow and myself.

[17] I am grateful to Nicholas Sims-Williams for discussing the Bactrian connection with me after the workshop.

In the last complete edition of Gandhāran reliquary inscriptions prior to Baums 2012, Sten Konow's 1929 *Kharoshṭhī Inscriptions*, the relic containers then known were arranged together with the other inscriptions under three rough chronological headings: (A) 'Inscriptions of Greek chiefs and unclassed North-Western records', (B) 'Inscriptions connected with the Old Saka era', and (C) 'Inscriptions connected with the Kanishka era' (followed by 'Inscriptions outside the Kharoshṭhī area' which, however, does not contain any relic inscriptions). As Konow sets out in his introduction (lxxxii–xciv), he did not believe that an equivalent of the Vikrama era was used in the inscriptions (nor that the term *ayasa* referred to King Azes), which left him with only two eras.

The modern scholarly consensus works with three major eras: the Greek era, the Azes era, and the Kushan era.[18] A considerable literature has grown around the question of the most likely starting points of these three eras as epigraphical, numismatic and literary pieces of evidence have continued to emerge (see also Joe Cribb's paper in the present volume).[19] It now seems certain from the information given in Sphujiddhvaja's third-century AD astronomical work *Yavanajātaka* that the Kushan era (the institution of which Kaniṣka proclaimed in the Rabatak inscription) commenced in AD 127 (Falk 2001).[20] The relic inscription of Aprakhaka (no. 33b, CKI 328) similarly provided persuasive new information for placing the commencement of the Azes era in 47 BC (Falk & Bennett 2009).[21] The beginning of the Greek era, finally, is synchronized with the Azes era by the triple dating formula of the relic inscription of Rukhuṇa (no. 13, CKI 405), placing it in 175 BC under the new dating of the Azes era (cf. Salomon 2012a).[22] While the dates adopted here – especially the linked dates for the Azes and Greek eras – are still subject to discussion, they seem to the present author the most reasonable in light of the available evidence and now preferable to the more conservative dates used in Baums 2012.

As a starting point for our chronological sequence, the fourteen inscriptions whose dates are explicitly in the Azes era can be put in a relative order. The inscriptions in question are nos. 8, 13, 14, 16, 17, 21, 23, 26, 28, 29, 30 and 31 in the numbering scheme of Baums 2012, together with the new inscription CKI 828 and the potential forgery CKI 455. The year values given in these inscriptions range from 39 to 139, with no. 8 (year 63) produced after the death of Azes (*maharayasa ayasa atidasa*), and cover a period of altogether 101 years.[23]

---

[18] I use this term in preference to 'Kaniṣka era' since it is used in Sphujiddhvaja's discussion of this era (Falk 2001a: 126).

[19] A selection of the main publications by the most prominent recent participants in this discussion is: Cribb 1997, 1999, 2000, 2005, 2008; Errington & Curtis 2007: 29-106; Falk 2001, 2002, 2006, 2007, 2008, 2010; Falk & Bennett 2009; Salomon 1998: 180-198, 2005, 2012.

[20] Technically speaking, Sphujiddhvaja states that in the second century of the Kushan era in which he was writing, the difference between the number of the Śaka year and the number of the Kushan year (with hundred omitted) was 149.

[21] Different varieties of the Macedonian month system were used in India and beyond, but there is only one – the Arsacid system – in which the month Gorpiaios functioned as one of two intercalary months once every nineteen years. Therefore, in Aprakhaka's inscription, which is dated to an intercalary month Gorpiaios (*gurpiya yaṃbulima*) of a year 172 in implied Azes era, the Arsacid calendrical system will be in use. The year 172 corresponds to a suitable year with intercalary Gorpiaos (the year AD 126) only if the start date of the era was 47 BC. (In principle, 66 BC and 28 BC would also be possible, but the former would yield too early a year for the Greek era, and the latter would place the Aprakhaka inscription in the year AD 146, when a dating in the Kushan era would be expected.) Based on the affinity between the Arsacid and Azes calendrical systems shown by this inscription, Falk & Bennett 2009: 209-211 suggest further that the Azes era may itself be a reinauguration of the Arsacid era of 248 BC in the first year of its third century.

[22] It is then possible that the Kushan era should be understood as a reinauguration of the Greek era since it commenced its fourth century, similar to the possible origin of the Azes era as a reinauguration of the Arsacid era (Cribb 2005: 214; Falk & Bennett 2009: 208-211).

[23] With the continued use of Azes regnal years after his death, turning them into an era proper, compare the continued issue of Azes-type coins for about one hundred years after the end of his reign (Cribb 2008: 66).

Two other eras are explicitly named in Gandhāran relic inscriptions: that of the Apraca king Vijayamitra - maybe regnal years rather than an era proper - and that of the Greeks. The former occurs in nos. 1c and 13 (years 5 and 27), the latter only in no. 13 (year 201).

The relic inscription of Rukhuṇa (no. 13, CKI 405; first edited in Salomon 2005) not only provides a synchronism between the Azes era and the Greek era (as noted above), but also with the Vijayamitra regnal years. This makes it possible to combine all 15 inscriptions discussed so far into a single sequence. Within this sequence, the earliest date (possibly spurious) is given as a (regnal?) year of Azes, followed after a gap of twelve years by a regnal year of Vijayamitra, which in turn is followed after a gap of another twelve years by the first explicitly posthumous date in the Azes era. The earliest date in the Greek era occurs another ten years later and, notably, is the very first year in the third century of this era.

In addition to these fifteen dated inscriptions with explicit era, there are eighteen dated inscriptions that do not give an era. These are nos. 6, 7, 19, 32, 33a, 33b, 34, 35, 36, 37, 38, 39, 40, 41, 42, 43 and 44, together with the new inscription CKI 466. The year values given in these inscriptions range from 18 to 303. In order to add these inscriptions to the sequence established so far, it is necessary to determine by circumstantial evidence which era is implicit in the date of each of them. In addition to the Greek, Vijayamitra and Azes eras, some of these eighteen inscriptions on the face of it belong to the Kushan period, and the Kushan era thus becomes a fourth possibility.

As a first step, those inscriptions belonging to the reign of Kaniṣka or later can be separated out using the following criteria:

(1) A ruler of this period is explicitly mentioned (nos. 37 and 43).

(2) A Macedonian month name is used. This is not an unequivocal sign of an inscription belonging to the reign of Kaniṣka or later, but Macedonian month names did become predominant in this time, and their occurrence can therefore serve as a dating criterion in conjunction with others. The cases in question are nos. 33b, 38, 39, 40, 41, 43 and 44.

(3) The Greek loanword *kṣuna* ('date') or the Iranian loanword *sasta* ('day') are used. As with the month names, this is a strong tendency from the reign of Kaniṣka onwards and can be used as a dating criterion in conjunction with others. The cases in question are nos. 33b, 38, 39, 40, 41, 43 and 44.

(4) A year value above 300 is likely to be in the Greek era and belong to the time after the beginning of Kaniṣka's reign. This applies to no. 36, dated in the year 303.

(5) For a low year value, the type of object may decide that an inscription belongs to the second century AD (Kushan era) rather than the first century BC (Azes era) or the first century AD (Vijayamitra year). This appears to be the case with the clay pot no. 42 (cf. Strauch 2007: 81-82).

In sum then, the following ten inscriptions are certain or likely to be from around the beginning of the reign of Kaniṣka or later: nos. 33b, 36, 37, 38, 39, 40, 41, 42, 43 and 44. Of these, no. 36 is most likely dated in the era of the Greeks, no. 33b in the Azes era, and the remainder in the Kushan era.

Of the remaining eight pre-Kaniṣka inscriptions with date but without explicit era, no. 19 must belong to the era of Vijayamitra since the donor is his consort Prahodi. Inscriptions nos. 6, 7, 32, 33a, 34 and 35, together with the new inscription CKI 466, are most likely to belong to the Azes era, with year values ranging from 50 (or 60) to 157. (For two of these, nos. 32 and 35, use of the Greek era and a date in the late first century BC cannot be entirely excluded, but in the absence of positive evidence that Greek-era years lower than 201 were used in Gandhāran inscriptions, this seems less safe to assume.)

At this point, we have thirty-two inscriptions that can be assigned to the Greek, Azes, Vijayamitra, or Kushan eras. Of these, twenty-four are in a secure single sequence thanks to the synchronism for the first three of these eras provided by Rukhuṇa's inscription (no. 13, CKI 405). Applying AD 127 as the commencement of the Kaniṣka era, we can next combine all thirty-two into a single chronological sequence and make several summary observations.

The overall range of dated Gandhāran relic inscriptions is from 9/8 BC (CKI 455, if genuine, otherwise AD 3/4 or 13/14, no. 6) to AD 177/178 (no. 44), assuming that all dates in the Kushan era can be assigned to its first century.[24] Within this span of 185 (or 174 or 164) years, the Azes era is used predominantly until just before the beginning of Kaniṣka's reign (no. 33b: AD 125/126). The only exceptions at this point of our discussion are three dates in years of Vijayamitra (nos. 1c, 13 and 19), which can probably all be considered current regnal years rather than an era proper, and one date in the era of the Greeks (no. 13), used in conjunction with dates using the Azes era and a Vijayamitra regnal year, presumably because the year in question was notable for being the very first in the third century of the era of the Greeks. The very first available date after the accession of Kaniṣka is again given using the era of the Greeks (year 303 = the second year of Kaniṣka).[25] Use of the Kushan era itself in the relic inscriptions commences in AD 144/145 (with year 18), after which it is used exclusively until the end of the observable period.

Seven Gandhāran relic inscriptions contain dates that cannot be linked up precisely with the sequence of thirty-three inscriptions established so far. Potentially the oldest preserved relic inscription from Gandhāra, the primary inscription on the Shinkot casket (no. 1a), almost certainly contains a damaged reference to the mid-second-century BC Indo-Greek king Menander. Its position in the date formula (... *minedrasa maharajasa kaṭiasa divasa 4 4 4 1 1*) indicates that it specified the year in which the donation was made, though whether this was in terms of a regnal year or an otherwise unattested era of Menander is unclear. Some doubt has also surrounded the genuineness of this inscription (Falk 2005), and it does contain many peculiarities of wording. To me, however, the way the number signs for the day are corrected from one evidently popular date (*4 4* '8th') to another (*4 4 4 1 1* '14th') rings true, and its deviations from the standard formula could follow from its early date. As archaic as the palaeography of the Shinkot casket is that of the Gomitra relic-chamber slab (no. 2), which in its broken beginning contains the value of a year ('current twelfth year') with lost further specification (*? + + .[u] ? ... [va]ṣe vatamane ya [d]u[va]ḏaya ? ? ? ?*), and this slab may therefore also belong to the second or first century BC.

The above-mentioned miniature *stūpa* of the eleventh year of Namipala (CKI 827) is so similar in terms of its decoration, formula, and palaeography to an inscribed plate of year 9 of Azes (CKI 459) that its year 11 should probably also refer to the Azes era, whether as a simple case of renaming or as an independent reuse of the Arsacid era (following Falk 2007: 140). If this is the case, then this would be by far the earliest use of the Azes era in a relic inscription, predating no. 6 by thirty-nine or even forty-nine years. A somewhat parallel case is the well-known copper-plate inscription of Patika dated to the year 78 'of Maues' (no. 12: *[saṃva]tsaraye aṭhasatatimae 20 20 20 10 4 4 maharayasa mahaṃtasa mogasa*). If this refers to an otherwise unattested era of Maues, then it would date to the early years of the first century AD (Baums 2012: 211, n. 23), which would make it one of the oldest dated relic inscriptions. If, on the other hand, here too we have to do with the Azes era under another name, then the date of the copper plate would be AD 31/32.

[24] Five inscriptions (nos. 38, 39, 40, 41 and 42) could conceivably – with omission of the number sign 100 – belong to the second century of the Kushan era and would then date from between AD 244/245 and 270/271. There is no positive evidence to support this, however, and the resultant chronological gap in the reliquary record of at least 67 years between AD 177/178 (no. 44) and AD 244/245 (no. 38) would be highly unlikely.

[25] It is the (expected) third year if – with Falk & Bennett 2009: 208-209 – we assume that Kaniṣka established the Kushan era with reference to a (hypothetical) Bactrian ('Macedonian') version of the era of the Greeks in which the year started at the autumn equinox following the spring equinox of the corresponding Gandhāran era of the Greeks.

The last major piece of the chronological puzzle concerns the position of the Oḍi kings vis-à-vis the other eras. In Baums 2012 (209-210 n. 20), I proposed an argument for the approximate synchronization of the Oḍi kings with the main chronological sequence. In the following, I slightly reformulate this argument for the later date of Azes used in the present article.

The three known inscriptions of the Oḍi royal house are all dated by regnal year only: year 4 of Ajidasena (no. 11), year 5 of his son Varmasena (no. 22), and year 14 of the latter's brother Senavarma (no. 24). The inscription of Senavarma mentions Kujūla Kadphises as 'great king, chief king of kings' and is accordingly to be dated in the latter's reign, some time between AD 40 and 90 or 95 (Errington and Curtis 2007: 54, Bopearachchi 2008: 52). If Suhasoma, the minister mentioned in Senavarma's inscription, is the same person as Suhasoma, the co-donor of the earthenware pot inscription CKI 369 associated with the British Library collection of Gāndhārī manuscripts, then this suggests a dating around the middle of the first century AD. Such a dating would receive further support if Vasavadata, wife of Suhasoma and main donor in CKI 369, is the same person as Vasavadata, sister of Indravarma I in relic inscription no. 8, since for the latter we have the firm dates AD 16/17 and 26/27. Both possible correlations point to an earlier rather than later point in the reign of Kujūla Kadphises for Senavarma's inscription. If Senavarma ascended the throne around AD 35, then an approximate date for the accession of his brother Varmasena would be AD 25, and one for his father Ajidasena AD 5. Their three inscriptions would then date from approximately AD 9 (no. 11), AD 30 (no. 22) and AD 39 (no. 24).

Of the remaining twenty-eight Gandhāran relic inscriptions that contain no date at all, some mention persons that we can at least associate with other, dated material: two inscriptions (nos. 3 and 4) are conspicuous for their archaic palaeography, and the donors of both are meridarchs, suggesting they belong to the Indo-Greek period of the second to first centuries BC. Nos. 20a and 20b (the two inscriptions on the Mathurā Lion Capital) relate to the family of the satrap Śuḍasa and thus belong to the second half of the first century BC. Its unusual concertina format associates the copper-plate inscription no. 27 with no. 26. Six inscriptions (nos. 1b, 5, 9, 10, 18 and 25) mention members of the Apraca royal house and thus belong to the first half of the first century AD. For no. 45, the find context included coins of Huviṣka and suggests a date during his reign. The relic container no. 15 was found together with the dated relic-chamber slab no. 14 and is possibly (though not certainly) contemporary with it.

After all is said and done, we are left with fifteen relic inscriptions (nos. 45-59 and the new inscription CKI 975) that provide none of the evidence used above and that, in the present state of our knowledge, can at best be assigned to the 'early', 'middle' or 'late' phase of the Gāndhārī epigraphic record, based mostly on palaeographic impressions (as done in Baums 2012).

Appendix 1: chronological sequence of Gandhāran relic inscriptions

The following table lists the thirty-four Gandhāran relic inscriptions for which precise datings can be suggested. The first column gives each inscription's number in Baums 2012 (where available), the second its number in Baums & Glass 2002- a. The third column provides the year and era, including in parentheses elements that are only implied. The last column contains a keyword (most often the name of the donor) to help the reader more quickly identify the inscription in question.

Table 1. Chronological sequence of Gandhāran relic inscriptions.

no.	CKI	Year	Date	Keyword
—	827	11 Namipala (= Azes?)	37/36 BC(?)	Balamitra
—	455	39 Azes(?)	9/8 BC(?)	Tora et al.
6	454	50 or 60 (Azes)	AD 3/4 or 13/14	Naganaṃda
1c	176	5 Vijayamitra	AD 4/5	Vijayamitra (II)
7	403	60 (Azes)	AD 13/14	Saṃgharakṣida
8	242	63 Azes	AD 16/17	Iṃdravarma (I) et al.
13	405	73 Azes 27 Vijayamitra 201 Greeks	AD 26/27	Rukhuṇa
14	251	74 Azes	AD 27/28	Ramaka
16	544	76 Azes	AD 29/30	Gunyar Slab
17	257	77 Azes	AD 30/31	Śatruleka
19	359	32 (Vijayamitra)	AD 31/32	Prahodi
—	828	80(?) Azes	AD 33/34(?)	Diśaśpa Stūpa
21	266	83 Azes	AD 36/37	sons of Dhramila et al.
23	358	98 Azes	AD 51/52	Ariaśrava
—	466	118 or 128 (Azes)	AD 71/72 or 81/82	Sazaṃduṣa et al.
26	564	121 Azes	AD 74/75	Helaüta
28	331	126 Azes	AD 79/80	Priavaśa
29	172	134 Azes	AD 87/88	Caṃdrabhi
30	60	136 Azes	AD 89/90	Urasaka
31	563	139 Azes	AD 92/93	Year 139 Reliquary
32	536	147 (Azes)	AD 100/101	Relic Cube
33a	328	156 (Azes)	AD 109/110	Sataṣaka and Muṃji
35	226	157 (Azes)	AD 110/111	Utara
34	225	157 (Azes)	AD 110/111	Khaṃdadata
33b	328	172 (Azes)	AD 125/126	Aprakhaka
36	178	303 (Greeks)	AD 128/129	'Macayemana'
37	149	18 (Kushan)	AD 144/145	Lala
38	152	18 (Kushan)	AD 144/145	Box Lid
39	153	20 (Kushan)	AD 146/147	Śveḍavarma
40	368	20 (Kushan)	AD 146/147	Mitravarma
41	155	28 (Kushan)	AD 154/155	Saṃghamitra
42	511	44 (Kushan)	AD 170/171	Budhapriya and others
43	159	51 (Kushan)	AD 177/178	Vagamarega
44	509	51 (Kushan)	AD 177/178	daughter of Vagamarega

Appendix 2: months of relic establishments

The following table provides an overview and concordance of the two systems of month names – Macedonian (Babylonian) and Indian – that are used interchangeably in Gandhāran inscriptions, and shows how often each month name is attested in the corpus of relic inscriptions. Like the Indian year, the Babylonian year began at (or close to) the spring equinox. Most variants of the Macedonian calendar began at the autumn equinox, but for the Arsacid variant as used in Gandhāra a beginning of the year in spring is here assumed (following Falk & Bennett 2009, also for the correspondence of Babylonian and Macedonian month names in this variant). The month name *ira* (no. 33a) is here interpreted as Babylonian Aiaru (with Falk & Bennett 2009 and Baums 2012), but could phonetically also correspond to a Greek month name Ἡραῖος (attested at Delphi and elsewhere, cf. Liddell & Scott 1940 s.v., as an equivalent of Ὑπερβερεταῖος, but not to my knowledge in Macedonian calendars). The month name *ulo* (no. 40) has here been taken as Ὀλώιος (so also in Falk & Bennett 2009 and Baums 2012), but could also represent the Babylonian month name Ululu (a possibility considered in Falk 2003: 72–73).

Table 2. Concordance of month names used in relic inscriptions.

Macedonian (Babylonian)	**Indian**
Ξανδικός (Nisannu) (1)	Caitra (1)
Ἀρτεμίσιος (Aiaru) (4)	Vaiśākha (1)
Δαίσιος (Simanu)	Jyaiṣṭha (2)
Πάνημος (Du'zu) (1)	Āṣāḍha (6)
Ὀλώιος (Abu) (1)	Śrāvaṇa (6)
Γορπιαῖος (Ululu) (1)	Prauṣṭhapada (2)
Γορπιαῖος ἐμβόλιμος (1)	
Ὑπερβερεταῖος (Tashritu)	Āśvayuj (1)
Δίος (Araḫsamnu)	Kārttika (6)
Ἀπελλαῖος (Kislimu) (1)	Mārgaśīrṣa
Αὐδυναῖος (Tebetu) (1)	Tiṣya (1)
Περίτιος (Shabatu)	Māgha
Δύστρος (Addaru)	Phālguna
Δύστρος ἐμβόλιμος	

Appendix 3: days of relic establishments

The following is a list of the days of the month specified in Gandhāran relic establishments and of how often each of them occurs. Babylonian and Macedonian months begin with the day following the new moon, so that the full moon falls into the middle of the month. In India, both this practice (*amānta*) and the beginning of months with the day after the full moon (*pūrṇimānta*) were and are used. In the following table, the *amānta* system is assumed, at least as predominant. This is supported by the evidence of inscription no. 6 (CKI 454), where day 24 of the month Kārttika correponds to the lunar mansion (*nakṣatra*) Hasta, and no. 26 (CKI 564), where day 13 of the month Gorpiaios corresponds to the lunar mansion Uttara-Proṣṭhapada. Inscription no. 14 (CKI 251), however, where day 3 of the month Āśvayuj corresponds to the lunar mansion Aśvayuj, would seem to indicate *pūrṇimānta* reckoning. Under our assumption of predominantly *amānta* dates, the popularity of, especially, the 8th and the middle (15th) of the month are conspicuous, probably due to being waxing half and full moon days as well as Buddhist *uposatha* days (cf. Brough 1961: 520–522).

1 (2×), 3, 4, 5 (2×), 8 (5×), 9, 10 (3×), 13, 14 (2×), 15 (5×), 16, 20 (2×), 21, 23 (2×), 24 (4×), 25, 27, 30

Appendix 4: dated Gandhāran image inscriptions

The readings in this appendix follow those adopted in Baums & Glass 2002- b. See Baums & Glass 2002- a for bibliographical coverage of alternative proposals.

sa[ṃ] 4 1 phagunasa masasa di paṃcami budhanadasa trepiḍakasa danamukhe madapidarana adhvadidana puyaya bhavatu

'Year 5, on the fifth day of the month Phālguṇa. Donation of the master of the three collections Budhanaṃda. May it be in honor of his mother and father who have passed on.' (CKI 232, 'Brussels Buddha', 5 Kushan = AD 131)

sa 1 1 1 100 10 4 4 proṭhavadasa di 20 4 1 1 1 budhaghoṣasa daṇamu[khe] saghorumasa sadaviyarisa

'Year 318, on the 27th day of Prauṣṭhapada. Donation of Budhaghoṣa, the companion of Saṃghavarma.' (CKI 111, Loriyān Tangai, 318 Greeks = AD 143/144)

saṃ 1 1 1 100 20 20 20 20 4 proṭhavadasa masasa divasaṃmi paṃcami 4 1

'Year 384, on the fifth – 5th – day of the month Prauṣṭhapada.' (CKI 124, Hashtnagar, 384 Greeks = AD 209/210)

saṃ 20 20 20 20 4 4 1 margaśiraṣa masi 4 1 iśe kṣunami niryaïde ime deyadharme dharmapriena ṣamanena piduno arogadakṣinae upajayasa budhapriasa puyae samanuyayaṇa arogadakṣinae

'Year 89, on the 5th of the month Mārgaśira. On this date this donation is offered by the monk Dharmapriya for the reward of health of his father, in honor of his teacher Budhapriya, for the reward of health of his fellow pupils.' (CKI 161, Mamāne Ḍherī, 89 Kushan = AD 215/216)

References

Allon M., Salomon R, Jacobsen G. & Zoppi U. 2006. Radiocarbon Dating of Kharoṣṭhī Fragments from the Schøyen and Senior Manuscript Collections. Pages 279-291 in J. Braarvig (ed.), *Buddhist Manuscripts, Volume III* (Manuscripts in the Schøyen Collection). Oslo: Hermes Academic Publishing.

Baums S. 2012. Catalog and Revised Texts and Translations of Gandharan Reliquary Inscriptions. Pages 200-251 in D. Jongeward, E. Errington, R. Salomon and S. Baums, *Gandharan Buddhist Reliquaries* (Gandharan Studies, vol. 1). Seattle: Early Buddhist Manuscripts Project.

Baums S. 2014. Gandhāran Scrolls: Rediscovering an Ancient Manuscript Type. Pages 183-225 in J.B. Quenzer, D. Bondarev and J.-U. Sobisch (eds), *Manuscript Cultures: Mapping the Field* (Studies in Manuscript Cultures, vol. 1). Berlin: De Gruyter.

Baums S. & Glass A. 2002- a. *Catalog of Gāndhārī Texts* <https://gandhari.org/catalog>

Baums S. & Glass A. 2002- b. *A Dictionary of Gāndhārī* <https://gandhari.org/dictionary>

Bopearachchi O. 2008. Les premiers souverains kouchans: chronologie et iconographie monétaire. *Journal des savants*: 3–56.

Brough J. 1961. A Kharoṣṭhī Inscription from China. *Bulletin of the School of Oriental and African Studies* 24: 517-530.

CKI = Corpus of Kharoṣṭhī Inscriptions, part II of Baums and Glass 2002- a.

CKM = Corpus of Kharoṣṭhī Manuscripts, part I of Baums and Glass 2002- a.

Cribb J. 1997. Numismatic Perspectives on Chronology in the Crossroads of Asia. Pages 215-230 in R. Allchin, B. Allchin, N. Kreitman and E. Errington (eds), *Gandharan Art in Context: East-West Exchanges at the Crossroads of Asia*. New Delhi: Regency Publications.

Cribb J. 1999. The Early Kushan Kings: New Evidence for Chronology: Evidence from the Rabatak Inscription of Kanishka I. Pages 177–205 in M. Alram and D.E. Klimburg-Salter (eds), *Coins, Art, and*

Chronology: Essays on the Pre-Islamic History of the Indo-Iranian Borderlands. Vienna: Österreichische Akademie der Wissenschaften.

Cribb J. 2000. Early Indian History. Pages 39-54 in M. Willis, *Buddhist Reliquaries from Ancient India*. London: British Museum Press.

Cribb J. 2005. The Greek Kingdom of Bactria, Its Coinage and Its Collapse. Pages 207-225 in O. Bopearachchi and M.-F. Boussac (eds), *Afghanistan: ancien carrefour entre l'Est et l'Ouest: actes du colloque international organisé par Christian Landes & Osmund Bopearachchi au Musée archéologique Henri-Prades-Lattes du 5 au 7 mai 2003* (Indicopleustoi: Archaeologies of the Indian Ocean, 3). Turnhout: Brepols.

Cribb J. 2008. Die Chronologie Gandharas anhand der Münzen. Pages 64-69 in C. Luczanits (ed), *Gandhara: das buddhistische Erbe Pakistans: Legenden, Klöster und Paradiese*. Mainz: Verlag Philipp von Zabern.

Davary G.D. 1982. *Baktrisch: ein Wörterbuch auf Grund der Inschriften, Handschriften, Münzen und Siegelsteine*. Heidelberg: Julius Groos Verlag.

Errington E., & Sarkhosh Curtis, V. 2007. *From Persepolis to the Punjab: Exploring Ancient Iran, Afghanistan and Pakistan*. London: British Museum Press.

Falk H. 1998. Notes on Some Apraca Dedicatory Texts. *Berliner indologische Studien* 11-12: 85-108.

Falk H. 2001. The Yuga of Sphujiddhvaja and the Era of the Kuṣâṇas. *Silk Road Art and Archaeology* 7: 121-136

Falk H. 2002. Frühe Zeitrechnung in Indien. Pages 77-105 in: H. Falk (ed), *Vom Herrscher zur Dynastie: zum Wesen kontinuierlicher Zeitrechnung in Antike und Gegenwart* (Vergleichende Studien zu Antike und Orient 1.). Bremen: Hempen Verlag.

Falk H. 2003. Five New Kharoṣṭhī Donation Records from Gandhāra. *Silk Road Art and Archaeology* 9: 71-86.

Falk H. 2005. The Introduction of Stūpa-Worship in Bajaur. Pages 347-358 in: O. Bopearachchi and M.-F. Boussac (eds), *Afghanistan: ancien carrefour entre l'Est et l'Ouest: actes du colloque international organisé par Christian Landes & Osmund Bopearachchi au Musée archéologique Henri-Prades-Lattes du 5 au 7 mai 2003*, Indicopleustoi: Archaeologies of the Indian Ocean. Turnhout: Brepols.

Falk H. 2006. The Tidal Waves of Indian History: Between the Empires and Beyond. Pages 145-166 in P. Olivelle (ed), *Between the Empires: Society in India 300 BCE to 400 CE* (South Asia Research). New York: Oxford University Press.

Falk H. 2007. Ancient Indian Eras: An Overview. *Bulletin of the Asia Institute* 21: 131-145.

Falk H. 2008. Zeitrechnung in Gandhara. Pages 70-71 in C. Luczanits (ed), *Gandhara: das buddhistische Erbe Pakistans: Legenden, Klöster und Paradiese*. Mainz: Verlag Philipp von Zabern.

Falk H. 2010. Signature Phrases, Azes Dates, Nakṣatras and Some New Reliquary Inscriptions from Gandhāra. 創価大学国際仏教学高等研究所年報 13: 13-33.

Falk H. 2014-15. Buddhistische Reliquienbehälter aus der Sammlung Gritli von Mitterwallner. *Journal Fünf Kontinente: Forum für ethnologische Forschung* 1: 128-161.

Falk H. & Bennett C. 2009. Macedonian Intercalary Months and the Era of Azes. *Acta Orientalia* 70: 197-216.

Fussman G. 1994. Upāya-kauśalya: l'implantation du bouddhisme au Gandhāra. Pages 17-51 in F. Fukui and G. Fussman (eds), *Bouddhisme et cultures locales: quelques cas de réciproques adaptations* (Études thématiques 2). Paris: École française d'Extrême-Orient.

Glass A. 2000. A Preliminary Study of Kharoṣṭhī Manuscript Paleography. M.A. thesis, University of Washington.

Glass A. 2009. Bha. *Bulletin of the Asia Institute* 23: 79-86.

Hinüber O. von. 2003. *Beiträge zur Erklärung der Senavarma-Inschrift*. (Akademie der Wissenschaften und der Literatur, Abhandlungen der geistes- und sozialwissenschaftlichen Klasse, 2003, no. 1.) Stuttgart: Franz Steiner Verlag.

Humbach H. 1966. *Baktrische Sprachdenkmäler, Teil I*. Wiesbaden: Otto Harrassowitz.

Jongeward D. 2012a. The Buddha's Last Days as Portrayed in Gandharan Sculpture. Pages 9-38 in D. Jongeward, E. Errington, R. Salomon & S. Baums, *Gandharan Buddhist Reliquaries* (Gandharan Studies 1). Seattle: Early Buddhist Manuscripts Project.

Jongeward D. 2012b. Survey of Gandharan Reliquaries. Pages 39-110 in D. Jongeward, E. Errington, R. Salomon & S. Baums, *Gandharan Buddhist Reliquaries* (Gandharan Studies 1). Seattle: Early Buddhist Manuscripts Project.

Konow S. 1929. *Kharoshṭhī Inscriptions with the Exception of Those of Aśoka.* (Corpus Inscriptionum Indicarum, Vol. II, Part I). Calcutta: Government of India Central Publication Branch.

Liddell H.G. & Scott R. 1940. *A Greek-English Lexicon* (9th edition). Oxford: Clarendon Press.

Radich M. 2011. Immortal Buddhas and Their Indestructible Embodiments: The Advent of the Concept of Vajrakāya. *Journal of the International Association of Buddhist Studies* 34: 227-290.

Rhys Davids T.W. & Estlin Carpenter J. 1890-1911. *The Dīgha-Nikāya.* Pali Text Society. London: Luzac & Company.

Salomon R. 1995. Three Dated Kharoṣṭhī Inscriptions. *Bulletin of the Asia Institute* 9: 127–141.

Salomon R. 1998. *Indian Epigraphy: A Guide to the Study of Inscriptions in Sanskrit, Prakrit, and the Other Indo-Aryan Languages.* (South Asia Research.) New York: Oxford University Press.

Salomon R. 2001. 'Gāndhārī Hybrid Sanskrit': New Sources for the Study of the Sanskritization of Buddhist Literature. *Indo-Iranian Journal* 44: 241-252.

Salomon R. 2002. Gāndhārī and the Other Indo-Aryan Languages in the Light of Newly-Discovered Kharoṣṭhī Manuscripts. Pages 119-134 in N. Sims-Williams (ed), *Indo-Iranian Languages and Peoples.* (Proceedings of the British Academy 116.) Oxford: Oxford University Press.

Salomon R. 2003a. The Senior Manuscripts: Another Collection of Gandhāran Buddhist Scrolls. *Journal of the American Oriental Society* 123: 73-92.

Salomon R. 2003b. Three Kharoṣṭhī Reliquary Inscriptions in the Institute of Silk Road Studies. *Silk Road Art and Archaeology* 9: 39-69.

Salomon R. 2005. The Indo-Greek Era of 186/5 B.C. in a Buddhist Reliquary Inscription. Pages 359-401 in O. Bopearachchi and M.-F. Boussac (eds), *Afghanistan: ancien carrefour entre l'Est et l'Ouest: actes du colloque international organisé par Christian Landes & Osmund Bopearachchi au Musée archéologique Henri-Prades-Lattes du 5 au 7 mai 2003* (Indicopleustoi: Archaeologies of the Indian Ocean, 3). Turnhout: Brepols.

Salomon R. 2012a. The Yoṇa Era and the End of the Maurya Dynasty: Is There a Connection? Pages 217-228 in P. Olivelle, J. Leoshko & H.P. Ray (eds), *Reimagining* Aśoka: Memory and History. New Delhi: Oxford University Press.

Salomon R. 2012b. Gandharan Reliquary Inscriptions. Pages 164-199 in D. Jongeward, E. Errington, R. Salomon & S. Baums, *Gandharan Buddhist Reliquaries* (Gandharan Studies 1). Seattle: Early Buddhist Manuscripts Project.

Salomon R. 2014-15. Eine auf Kharoṣṭhī beschriebene Kupfertafel aus der Sammlung Gritli von Mitterwallner. *Journal Fünf Kontinente: Forum für ethnologische Forschung* 1: 162-169.

Sherrier 1984. An Important Relic Stūpa with Four Free-Standing Figures. *South Asian Archaeology* 1981: 254–256.

Strauch I. 2007. Two Inscribed Pots from Afghanistan. *Gandhāran Studies* 1: 77–88.

Strauch I. 2009. Inscribed Objects from Greater Gandhāra. *Bulletin of the Asia Institute* 23: 209-219.

Strong J.S. 2004. *Relics of the Buddha.* (Buddhisms.) Princeton: Princeton University Press.

On Gandhāran sculptural production from Swat: recent archaeological and chronological data

Luca Maria Olivieri and Anna Filigenzi

Introduction

This paper is based on the results of the latest archaeological excavations carried out in Swat by the Italian Archaeological Mission in Pakistan (IAMP). It will illustrate the archaeological background of some significant cultic monuments, the stratigraphy-based chronology of their decorative assemblage, and the wider context of implications of the fresh information available, particularly in relation to the chronological and cultural stages of the 'Gandhāran artistic idiom' in Swat. For the sake of brevity, it will not deal with the stylistic, iconographic, and iconological aspects of the sculptural material, which are the object of ongoing study.

[L.M.O. and A.F.]

Recent advances in knowledge: fresh data from Barikot

As confirmed by both archaeological and radiocarbon data, the fortified urban settlement at Barikot (lower area and acropolis) was established around the mid-first millennium BC on the ruins of an Early Iron age proto-urban settlement dated to the eleventh-eighth centuries (Olivieri & Iori, forthcoming; Terrasi et al. forthcoming). A city (Figure 1) was clearly established at the site around the sixth century BC. The site was re-fortified in a mature phase of the Indo-Greek kingdoms, around the mid-second century BC, with a massive defensive wall, which remained in use until the beginning of the second century AD (Olivieri 2015a). At this time maintenance ceased and the disrupted wall, although still marking the limit of the urban area, was utilized simply as a retaining structure throughout the second half of the third century AD, the period which corresponds to the last phases of urban occupation of the site. The lower quarters of the ancient city were eventually abandoned at the end of the third century after massive destruction caused by the combined

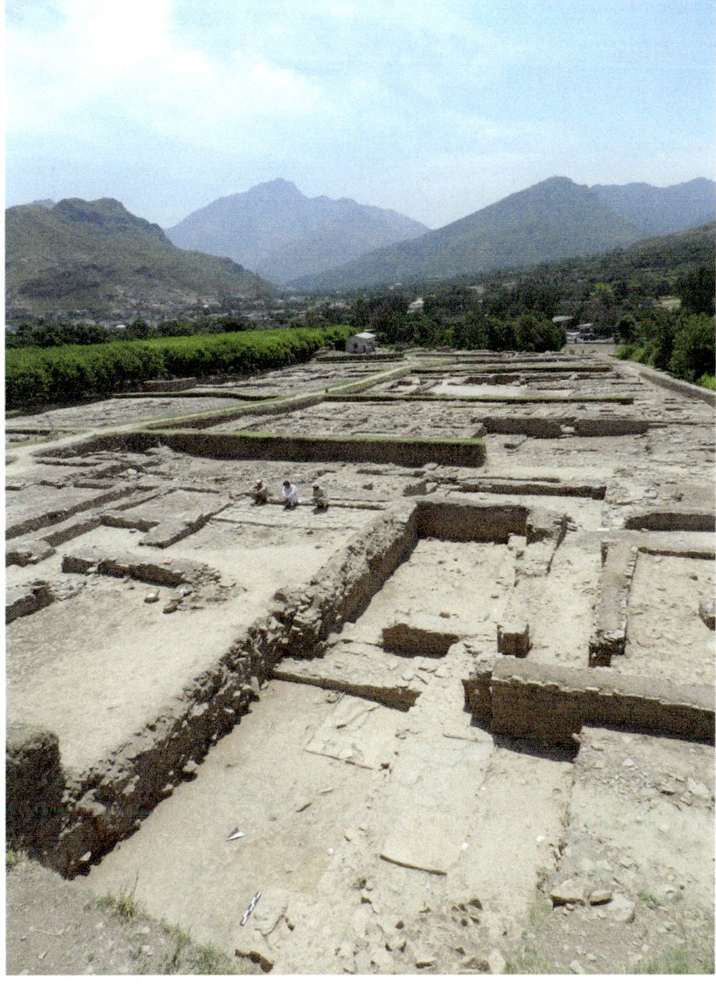

Figure 1. A panoramic view of Barikot. (Photo: copyright IAMP.)

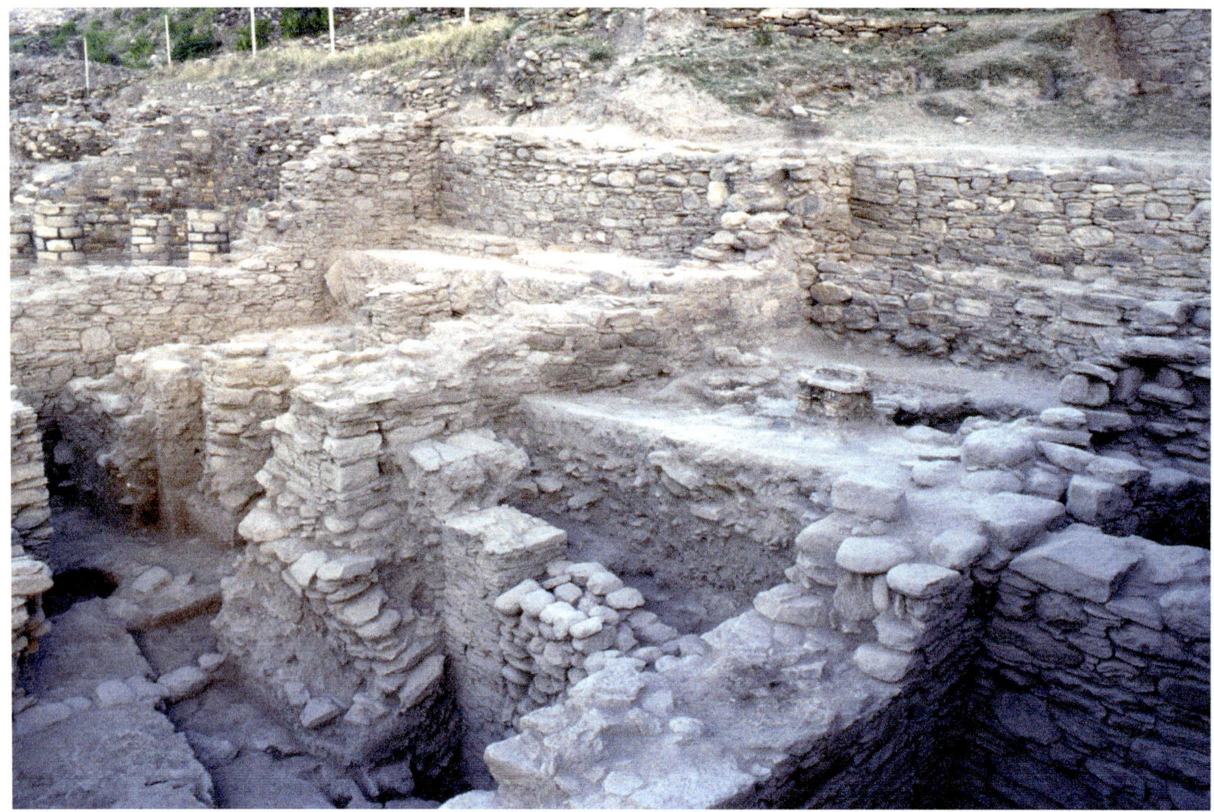

Figure 2. A partial view of the area of BKG 2. (Photo: copyright IAMP.)

effects of two earthquakes and other factors, which will be described later. With the area now nothing more than a field of ruins, it was briefly re-occupied by non-urban settlers (squatters), and definitively deserted by the mid-fourth century (Cupitò & Olivieri 2013). Meanwhile, a smaller fortified cluster of buildings was built at the foot of the ancient acropolis (BKG 2) and lasted – through a well-documented Shahi phase – until Ghaznavid times (Callieri et al. 2000; Figure 2).

Although Buddhist sacred areas began to be established in Swat as early as the third century BC (at Butkara I, see below), the earliest physical evidence of a Buddhist presence in the city is represented by a small Buddhist sacred area, consisting of a *stūpa* surrounded by minor chapels, dated to the early/mid-second century AD (Figure 3). Unfortunately, apart from a very few fragments, the decorative assemblage had already disappeared by the time of excavation, since the monument had already been plundered by illegal diggers (Callieri et al. 1992: 27-33, fig. 8, pls. XII-XIV).

However, a possible hint of an even earlier Buddhist presence in the city is afforded by the recent discovery of a fine black ware bowl from the Śaka-Parthian levels bearing a Kharoṣṭhī inscription which has been studied by Stefan Baums. We refer to his work for further details, limiting ourselves here just to mentioning the presence in the inscription of the genitive singular of the monastic title *ṣamaṇera* (Sanskrit *śrāmaṇera*) 'novice' (Baums, forthcoming).

Both palaeography and stratigraphy suggest an early first-century date for the bowl. This piece of information perfectly matches the data gathered in the survey of the Barikot countryside, where more than one hundred monastic settlements were documented in less than 100 square kilometres. The sites were not all contemporary, but the pottery assemblages clearly indicate that the majority of them were founded before the second century AD (Olivieri, Vidale et al. 2006).

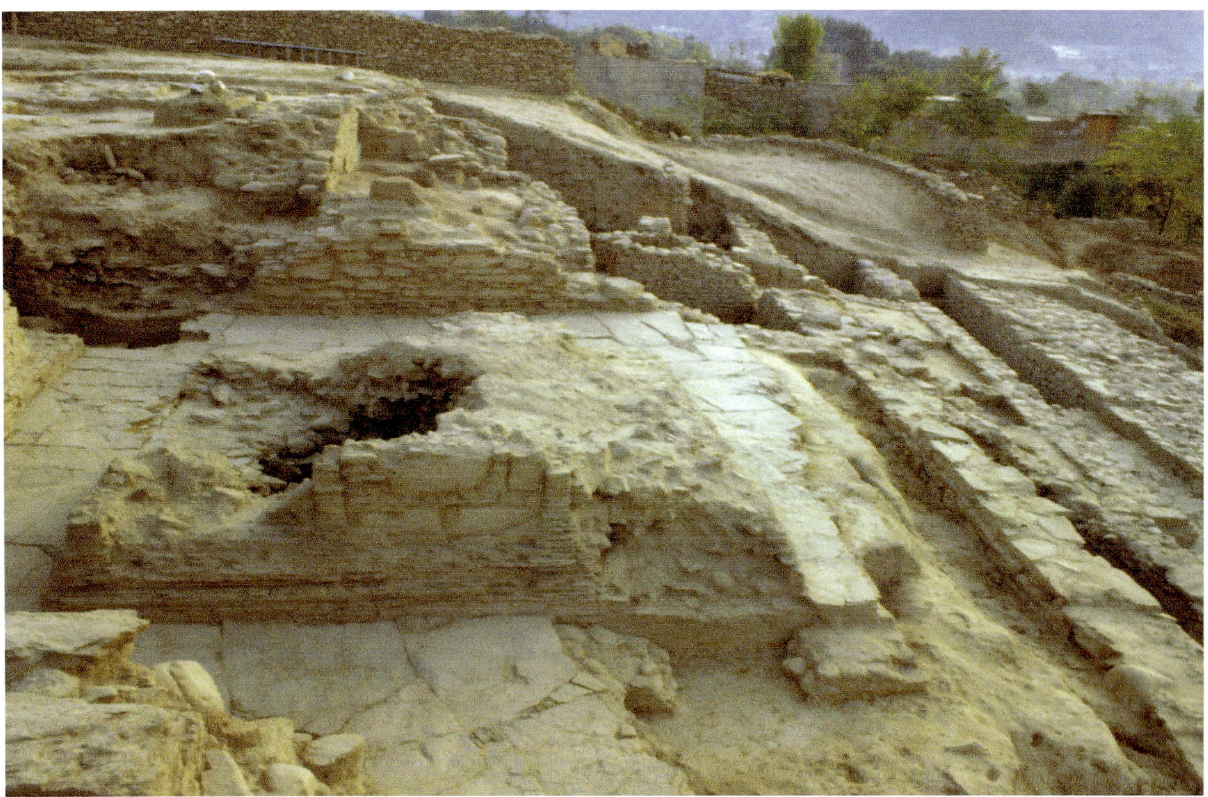

Figure 3. Barikot: the small Buddhist sacred area within the urban perimeter. (Photo: copyright IAMP.)

At Barikot, during the final urban phases (i.e. during the third century), the south-western quarter of the city was divided into several dwelling units of different sizes (ranging from 300 to 700 square metres), all arranged around a central courtyard, and in some cases provided with domestic worship areas (Figure 4). The blocks were served by a network of communicating streets, while the main street ran *intra muros* along the western section of the defensive wall. Two of these blocks or units are entirely dedicated to worship purposes (Olivieri et al. 2014; Olivieri 2011 [2015]; Olivieri 2013 [2017]).

Dwelling Unit B is characterized by a large cultic complex organized into two main buildings (Figure 5). One of them ('Sacred Building B') is a large rectangular shrine which opens onto a walled courtyard with niches and an altar. One of the niches yielded a set of small Buddhist stelae, three of which fixed to the walls by means of iron clamps (Figure 6). In front of the altar (with ex-votos) there was a large stone alms-bowl. Along two sides of the courtyard runs a bench, on top of which a large amount of intentionally broken shell bangles and Golden Slip and Fashion Ware pottery was deposited (on Fashion Ware, see Callieri & Olivieri, forthcoming). A few metres to the north, the 2016 excavation revealed a second building ('Temple B'), which was connected to the previous one through a raised corridor (Olivieri 2013 [2017]; Moscatelli et al. 2016). Temple B features a raised rectangular paved space closed on three sides and open to the east (and not to the north, a *lapsus calami* in Olivieri 2018: 191). The building had a tetrastyle façade. A rough altar was placed right in the lower space between the second and the third base. A flight of steps at the southern end of the platform gave access to a lower courtyard with a rectangular tank. Close to the tank, a condenser was found *in situ*, while two fire-places were documented a few steps from the central altar. A small stela representing *Hārītī* was found in the debris of the courtyard (Figure 7).

Of special interest is the central courtyard of Dwelling Unit D. Also used as a cooking area, it nevertheless housed a small Buddhist shrine in the collapse debris of which an assortment of reused sculptural

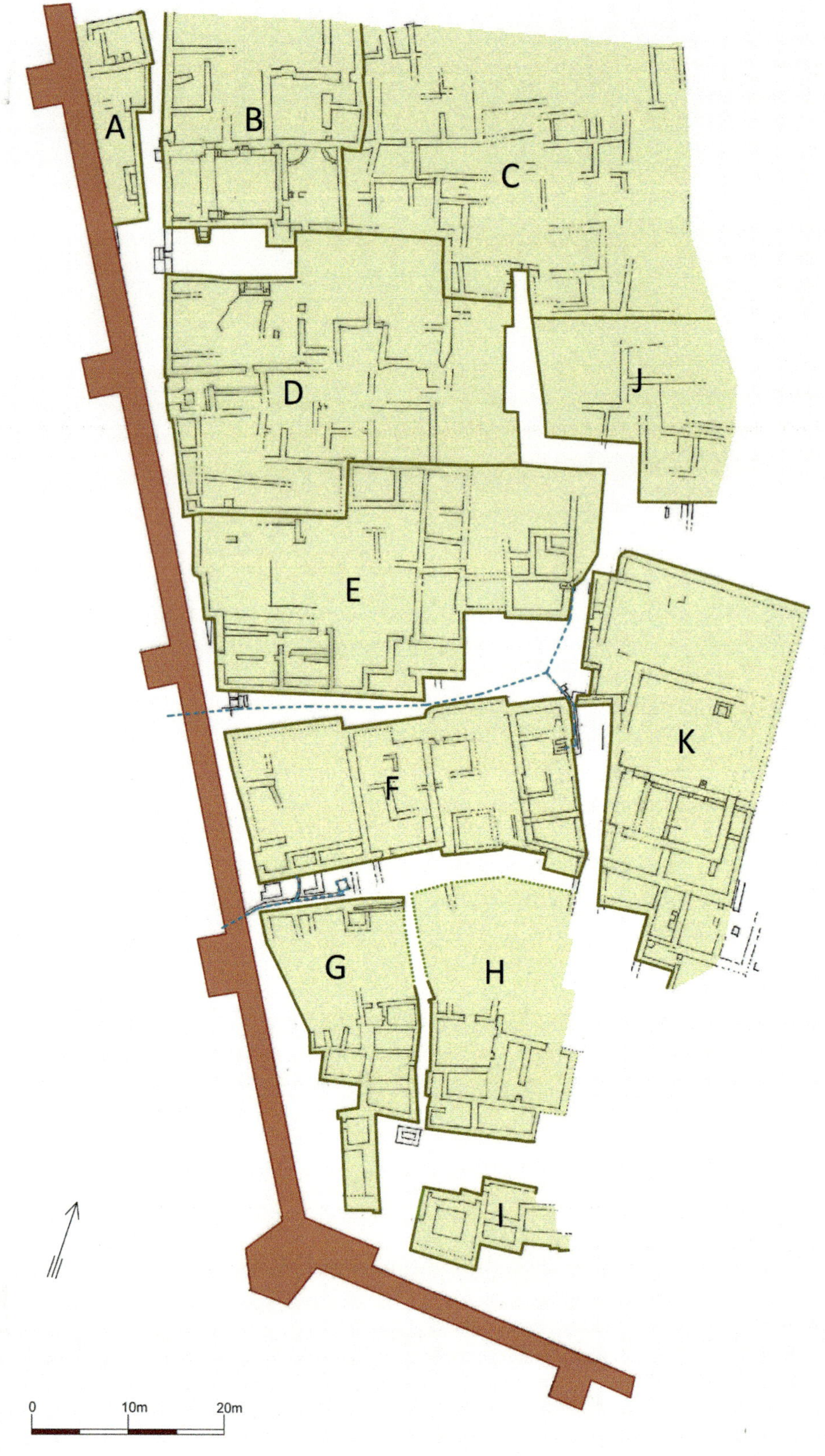

Figure 4. Barikot: dwelling units in the south-western quarter of the city. (Copyright IAMP.)

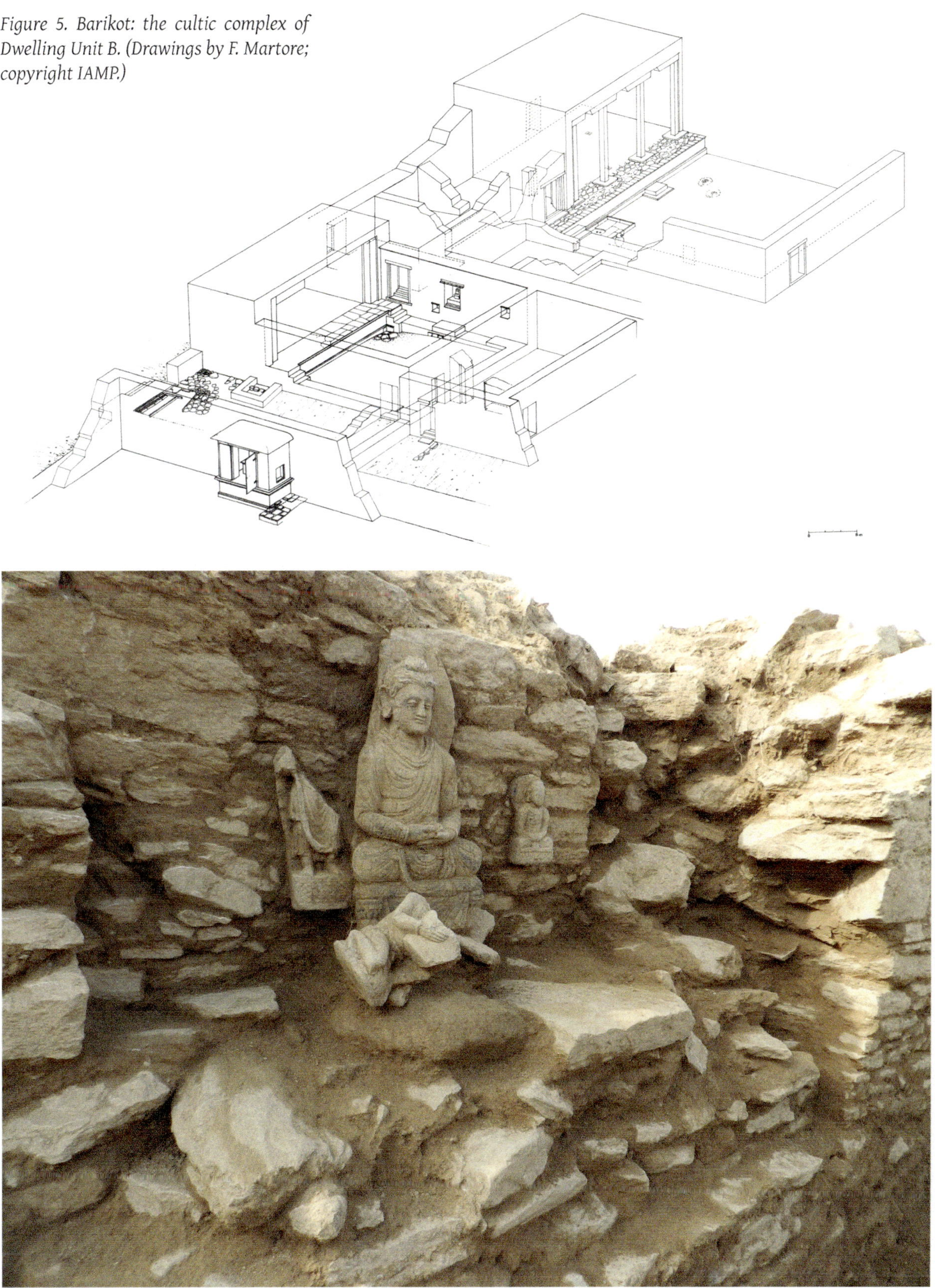

Figure 5. Barikot: the cultic complex of Dwelling Unit B. (Drawings by F. Martore; copyright IAMP.)

Figure 6. Barikot: the niche with small Buddhist stelae (BKG 2347, 2343, 2361 and 2364; Swat Museum, Saidu Sharif, Swat) in 'Sacred Building B'. (Photo: copyright IAMP.)

materials was found. In the corridor leading from the main street to the courtyard, inside a small stone cist beside a fireplace, a small stela was found. It depicts an unknown bearded male deity seated in European fashion and holding a chalice and a goat's head (Olivieri 2011 [2015]; Figure 8). This stela finds close comparison with a stratigraphically coeval icon brought to light at Barikot during a previous excavation campaign, whose subject is a goddess holding a bunch of flowers and the goat-headed finial of a lost object, possibly a cornucopia (Callieri et al. 1992: 35, pl. XIX.4; Figure 9). This discovery has however much wider implications, insofar as it provides a common frame of reference for a group of small Gandhāran stelae lacking archaeological context.

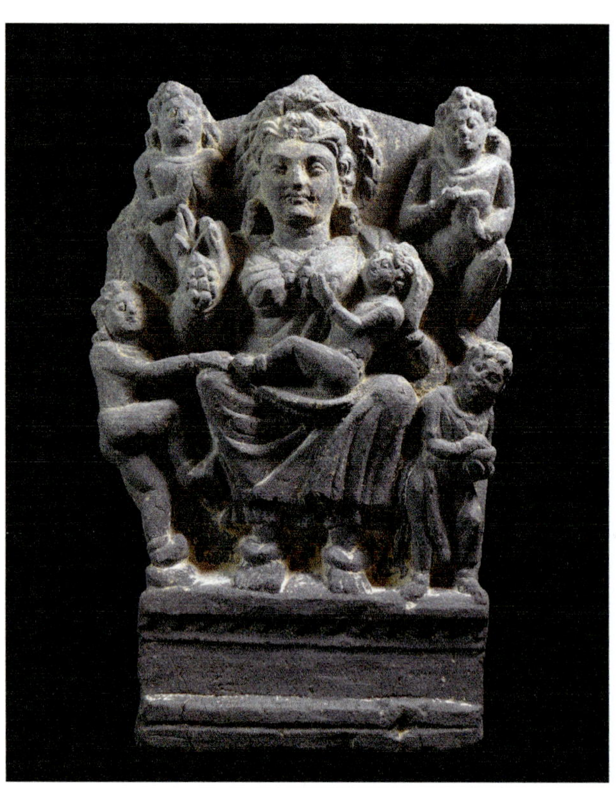

Figure 7. Barikot: a small stela representing Hārītī from the debris of the courtyard of 'Temple B' (BKG 3636; Swat Museum, Saidu Sharif, Swat). (Photo copyright IAMP.)

One of these originally belonged to Major-General Henry Lawrence Haughton – a member of a military family active in British India – who probably visited Swat (see Olivieri 2015b: 210 [document 154]) and 'acquired' there part of his famous Gandhāran collection. The stela represents a male bearded god holding attributes which are no longer recognisable (Olivieri et al. 2014: fig. 74a; Buchtal 1945: fig. 45).

Even more noteworthy are the similarities with a group of goddesses who, like the Barikot god, hold a beaker and the severed head of a goat (Taddei 1987). In one case, the strong connection between the *devī* and the goat is expressed by the anthropo-theriomorphic aspect of the former (see Zwalf 1996: no. 105). All these dispersed pieces of evidence can now be regarded as belonging not only to one and the same ideological and chronological horizon but also to one and the same chain of sculptural production, which has found a unifying benchmark in the archaeological sequence of Barikot.

The second unit dedicated to cultic activities is Dwelling Unit K (Figure 10). It consists of a rectangular enclosure with a central courtyard and with a distyle building open to the north. In front of the latter, in the courtyard, stands a small shrine. As attested by several fragments found at the spot, the shrine was originally provided with stucco decorations and wooden hinged doors. Almost completely reconstructed after a collapse, in its first phase it housed a miniature *stūpa*, the remains of which were partly recovered during the excavation. Inside the shrine, a Buddhist stela was found (Figure 11). Both inside and in the immediate vicinity of the shrine numerous ex-votos were found, in particular, horse figurines originally with (now missing) riders and lion figurines.

The distyle building ('Temple K') has an open antecella, a cella, and a side corridor leading to a rear chamber (that can be accessed also via the cella), in which a deposit of valuable objects, no doubt donations, was discovered. The assemblage of votive gifts includes luxury goods such as Golden Slip and Fashion Ware pottery (Figure 12), a glass ampulla and an elephant's tusk (see more details in Olivieri 2013 [2017]).

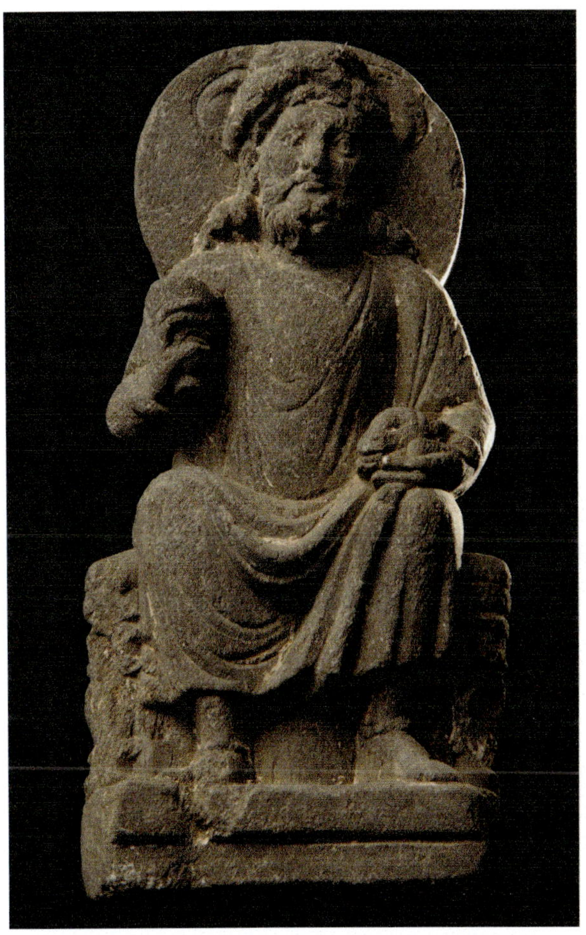

Figure 8. Barikot: a bearded male deity holding a chalice and a severed goat's head from Dwelling Unit D (BKG 2304; Swat Museum, Saidu Sharif, Swat). (Photo: copyright IAMP.)

Figure 9. Barikot: goddess holding a flower and a cornucopia (BKG 1591; Swat Museum, Saidu Sharif, Swat). (Photo: copyright IAMP.)

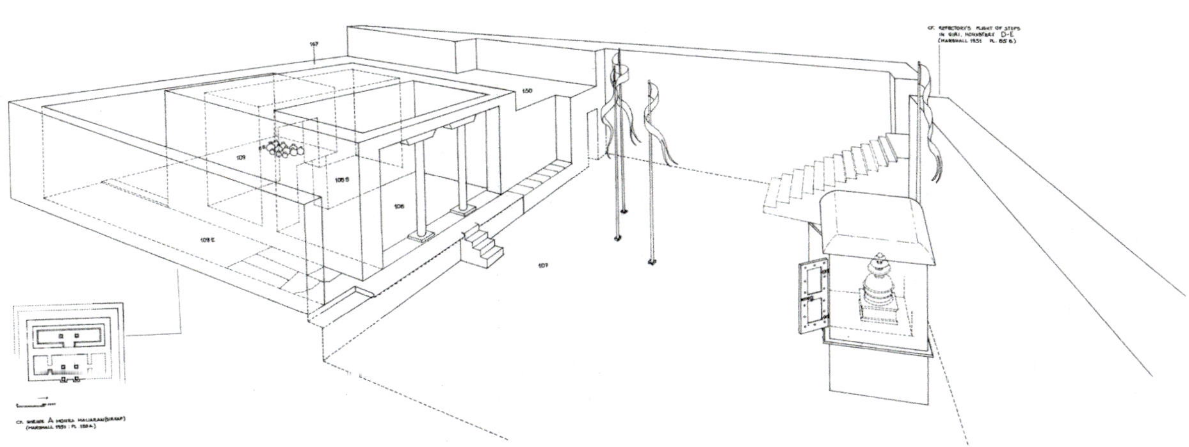

Figure 10. Barikot: Dwelling Unit K. (Drawings by F. Martore; copyright IAMP.)

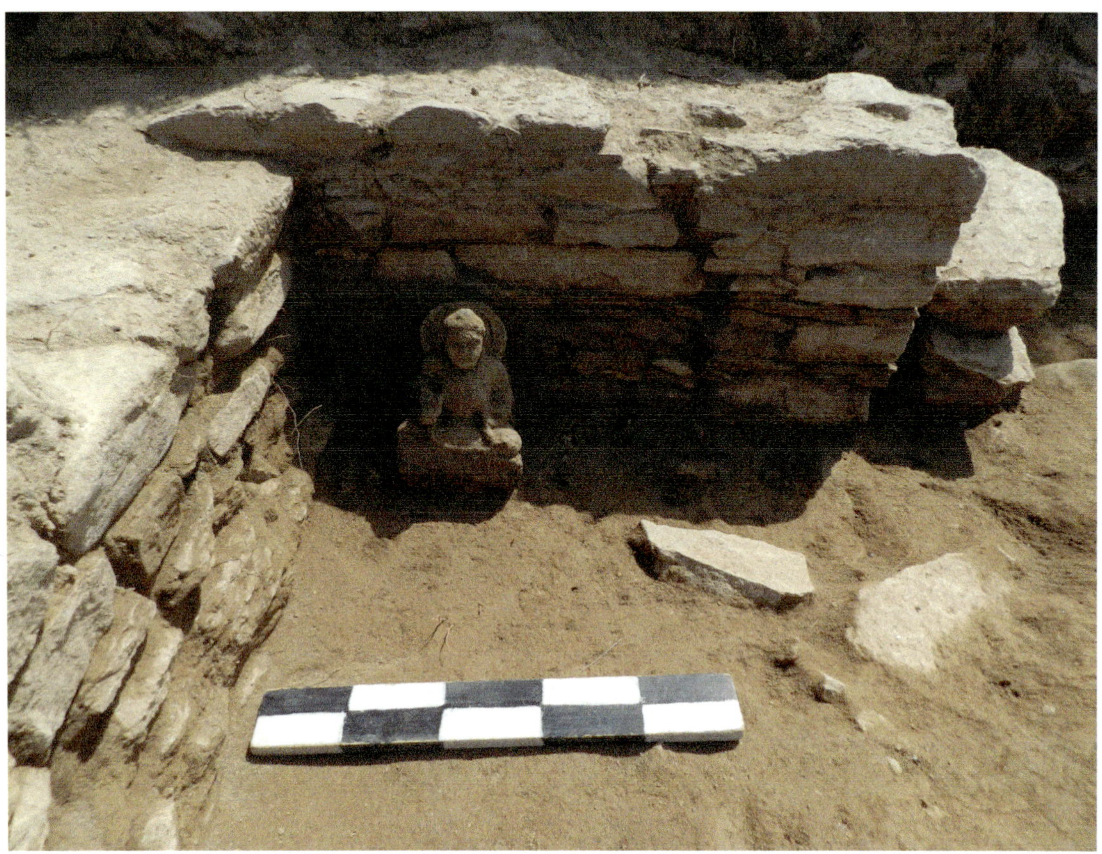

Figure 11. Barikot, Dwelling Unit D: a Buddhist stela (BKG 2344) inside the shrine. (Photo: copyright IAMP.)

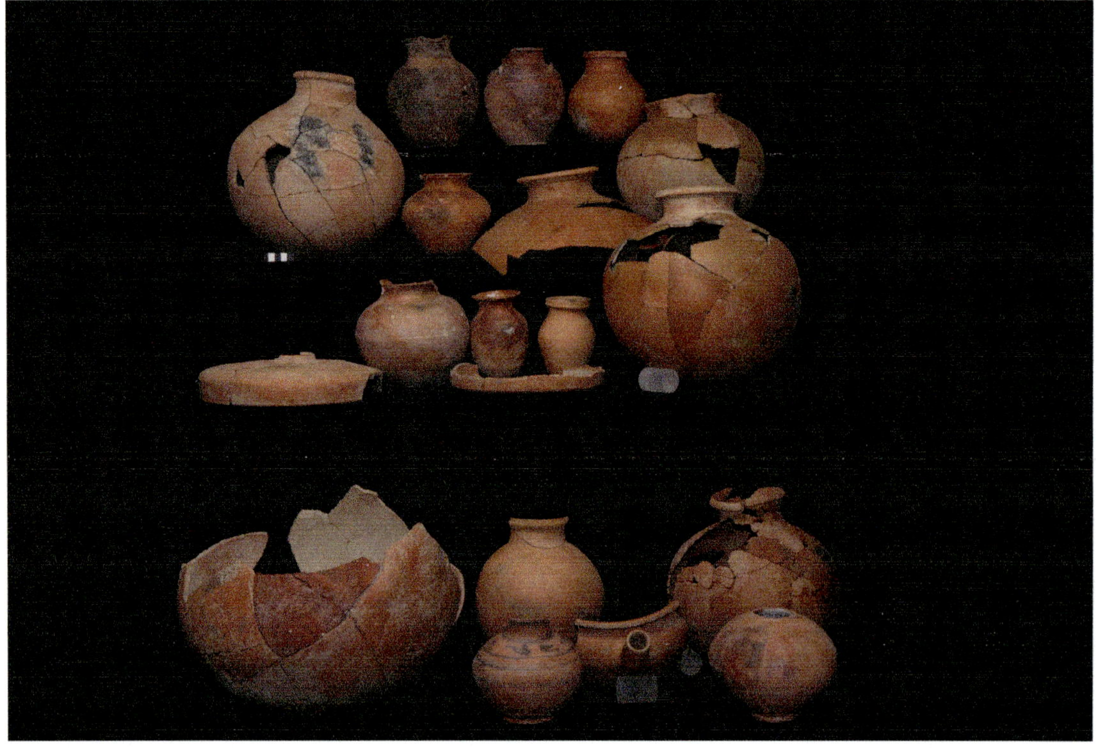

Figure 12. Barikot: Golden Slip, Fashion Ware, and Slip Ware pottery from 'Temple K' (Swat Museum, Saidu Sharif, Swat. (Photo: copyright IAMP.)

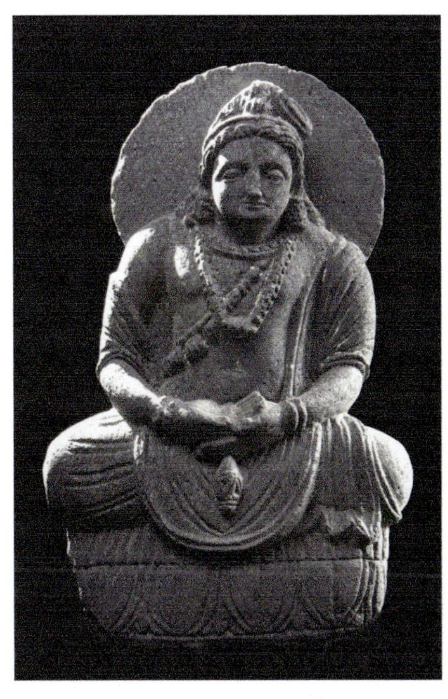

Figure 13. Barikot: a small stela depicting Maitreya from inside a jar in Unit E (BKG 2210; Swat Museum, Saidu Sharif. (Photo: copyright IAMP.)

Several more stelae were recovered *in situ* in various dwelling units or in collapse layers, all belonging to the same chronological phase, among which a Maitreya from inside a jar in Unit E (Figure 13) and an unusual miniature stele from Unit F (Olivieri et al. 2014: 42-46, figs. 15-17, 66, 119); two bodhisattvas from a deep masonry tank or bath in Unit G (in an area close to the small Buddhist sacred area) (Callieri et al. 1992: 35, pls. VIII.1, XVIII.1-2); and the female deity with a cornucopia already mentioned, from a niche in the same Unit. Other stelae were found in collapse layers in other loci of the same chronological context (see Olivieri et al. 2014).

Periods/Phases	Macrophases	earlier	Kushan	Late Kushan	Kushano-Sasanian	sub- Kushan	other	erratic
				BKG 11, BKG 12				
Period X	6	1	3	11	1	10	-	1
Period IX		-	1	13	6	13	1	-
Period VIII	5	3	15	13	7	7	-	
Period VII		1	7	7	-	-	-	-
				BKG 4-5				
Period X	6	-	-	-	-	-	-	-
Period IX	5	-	-	3	-	-	-	-
Period VIII		1	12	12	6	6	-	-
Periods VII		-	8	4	4	5	-	-
				BKG 3				
Period IVB-Phase 2b	5	-	-	11	14	-	-	-
Phase 2A2		-	-	8	-	-	-	-
				BKG 1				
Period VIII	5	-	-	-	-	1	-	-
Period VII		1	-	-	-	-	-	-
Total		1	4	24	7	23	1	1
Total		6	42	58	31	19	-	-
		earlier	Kushan	Late Kushan	Kushano-Sasanian	sub- Kushan	other	later

Figure 14. Table of coins found in the late phases at Barikot.

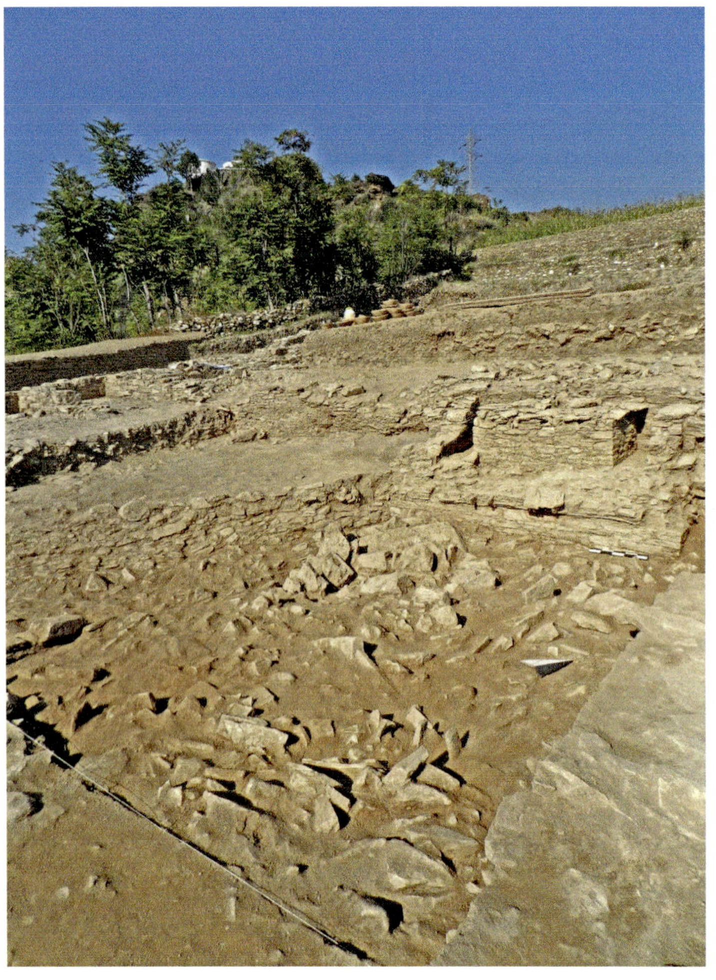

Figure 15. Barikot: evidence relating to the first earthquake. (Photo: copyright IAMP.)

The numismatic assemblage of the last structural period of the city is clearly defined by three copper types: the Vāsudeva-type issues, the Kushano-Sasanian coins and the so-called sub-Kushan coins. The latter, probably minted locally as convertible metal values, were equivalent to 1/8 of the Late Kushan issues and to a quarter of the Kushano-Sasanian issues (McDowall and Callieri 2004; Olivieri et al. 2014; Figure 14). Two major earthquakes within the space of less than 50-70 years have been clearly documented in these last phases of the city (Figure 15). This fact, alongside the political earthquake represented by the contemporary collapse of the Kushan Empire, eventually led to the abandonment of the city (Olivieri 2012), whereas, in the country areas the Buddhist communities managed to cope with the general crisis.

Of special interest in this regard are two recently excavated sacred areas near Barikot - Gumbat and Amluk-dara - two major Buddhist sites, both founded between the first and the second century AD, which not only survived the crisis but underwent extensive renovation. Moreover, the archaeological sequence documented in both sites offers much food for thought with regard to the shift from schist to stucco in sculptural decoration, and to the related production chain.

The site of Gumbat (Figure 16) (five kilometres southwest of Barikot) comprises three monumental terraces, the first characterized by a large stepped substruction wall and three flanking monuments of the same size: two *stūpas*, of which only part of the first storey was preserved, and a central shrine (Figure 17). The latter was probably constructed as early as the late first century AD, as suggested by the radiocarbon dating of the wooden lintel of one of the upper loopholes of the cell (Figure 18). The dating obtained for three other beams found during the restoration work to prop up the inner dome have a later dating (second century AD) (Olivieri et al. 2014: 310-14; Meister et al. 2016). The terrace was enhanced with brightly coloured and heavily-stuccoed lesser monuments in the two later structural phases. The complex seems to have been abandoned at around the tenth century.

The Main Stūpa of the Buddhist sacred area of Amluk-dara (Figures 19 and 20) (five kilometres southeast of Barikot) is one of the most majestic and best conserved in Gandhāra. The monument evinces a complex sequence of renovation and reuse spanning a long period of time, from the second to the tenth century AD (Olivieri et al. 2014).

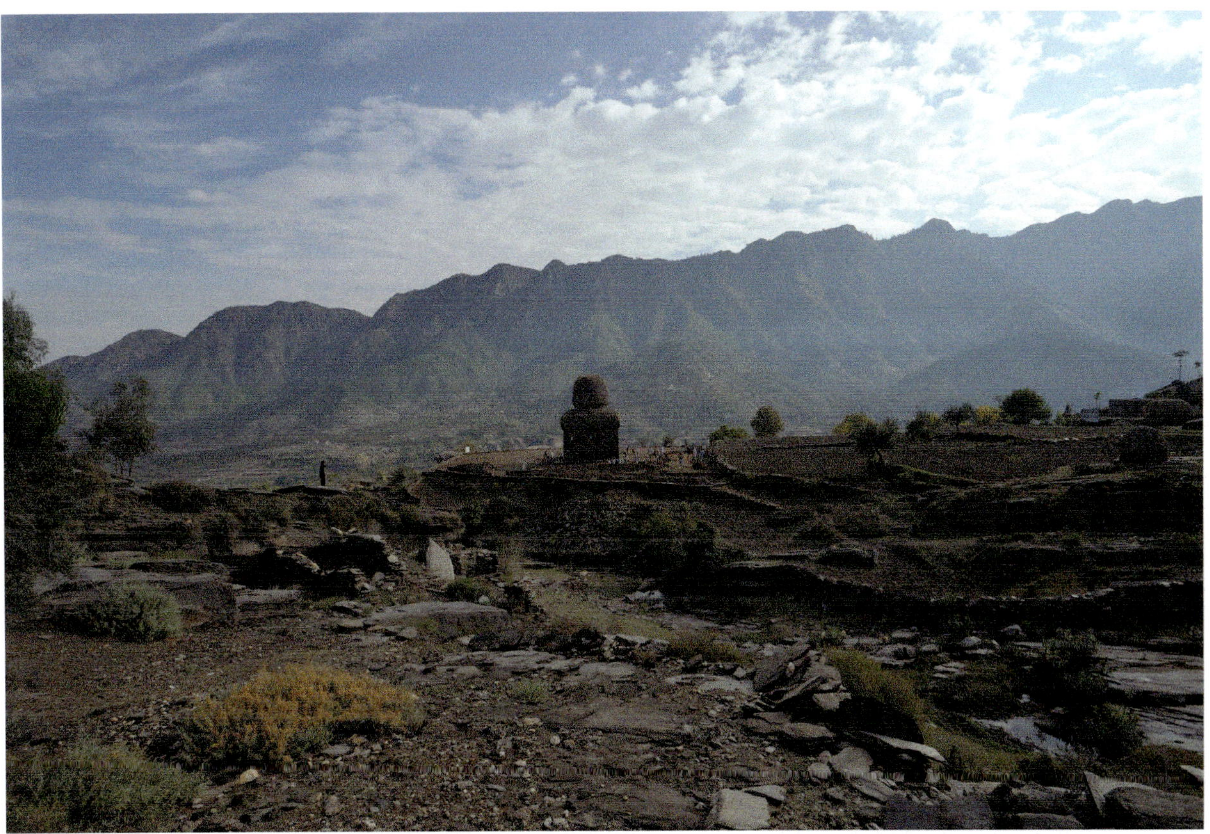

Figure 16. Panoramic view of Gumbat from the west. (Photo E. Loliva; copyright IAMP.)

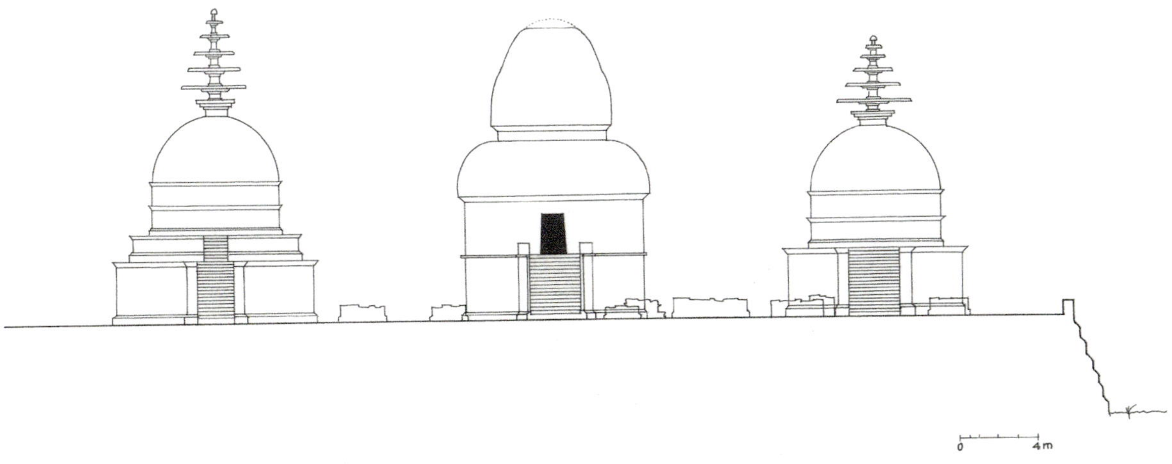

Figure 17. Gumbat: the monuments on the first terrace; view from east (drawing by F. Martore; copyright IAMP.)

Originally provided with a bluish schist decoration, the main monument was completely reshaped in the mid-third century, possibly after damage caused by the same seismic events responsible for the desertion of the nearby Barikot. The staircase with its monumental entrance (two well-sculpted step-side elements) (Figure 21), was further lengthened. Pilasters, modillions and most of the false brackets of the podium and upper storeys of the Main Stūpa were remade in kanjur (organogenic limestone) and copiously stuccoed and painted (Figure 22). Now we understand that stucco was certainly a by-product of kanjur stone workmanship.

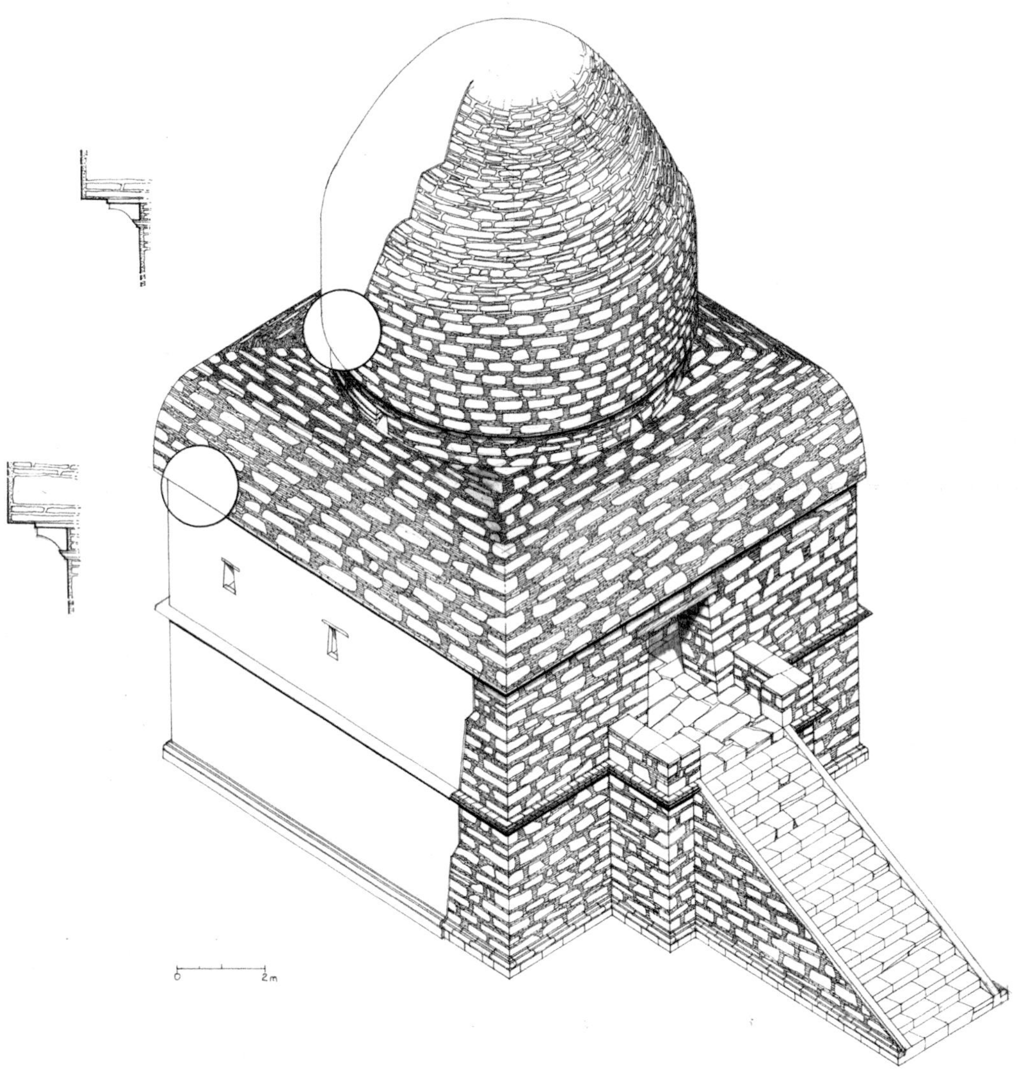

Figure 18. Gumbat, first terrace: axonometric view of the central shrine (drawing by F. Martore; copyright IAMP.)

As introduction to the following section, on the basis of the evidence yielded by both the urban site of Barikot, and the Buddhist complex of Amluk-dara, we may draw the following preliminary conclusions:

1 – schist is widely available and quarried in Swat;

2 – in the third century kanjur and stucco appear together in Swat;

3 – the massive appearance of stucco decoration during the course of the third century AD both at Barikot (e.g. in the shrines of Units B and K), and at Amluk-dara and Gumbat, finds a chronological comparison with recent data from coeval Kushano-Sasanian evidence yielded at Termez (Ferreras et al. 2014);

4 – kanjur is not a local stone (it is instead extensively quarried in the rocky reliefs south and south-east of Swat, in Buner, Mardan, Swabi and Taxila);

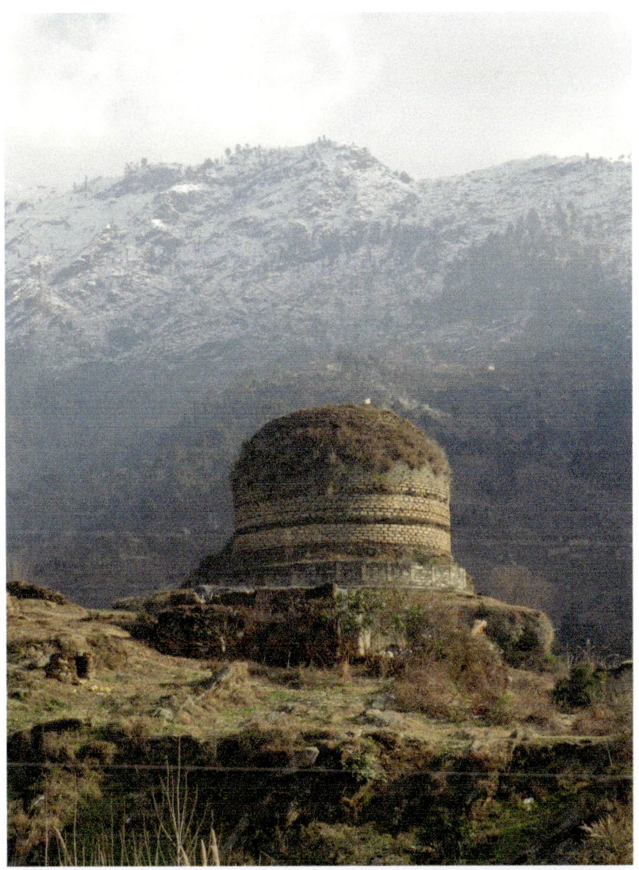

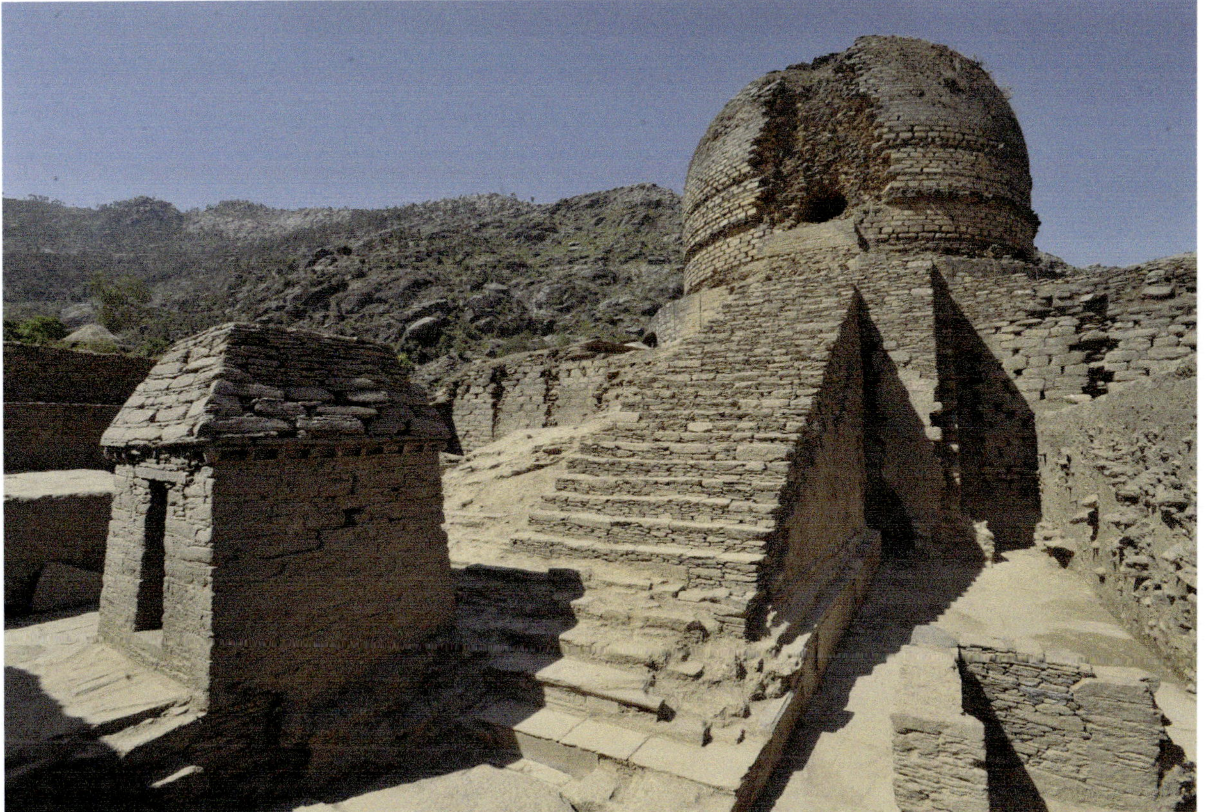

Figures 19 and 20. Amluk-dara: the Main Stūpa before and after excavation and restoration (Photo E. Loliva; copyright IAMP.)

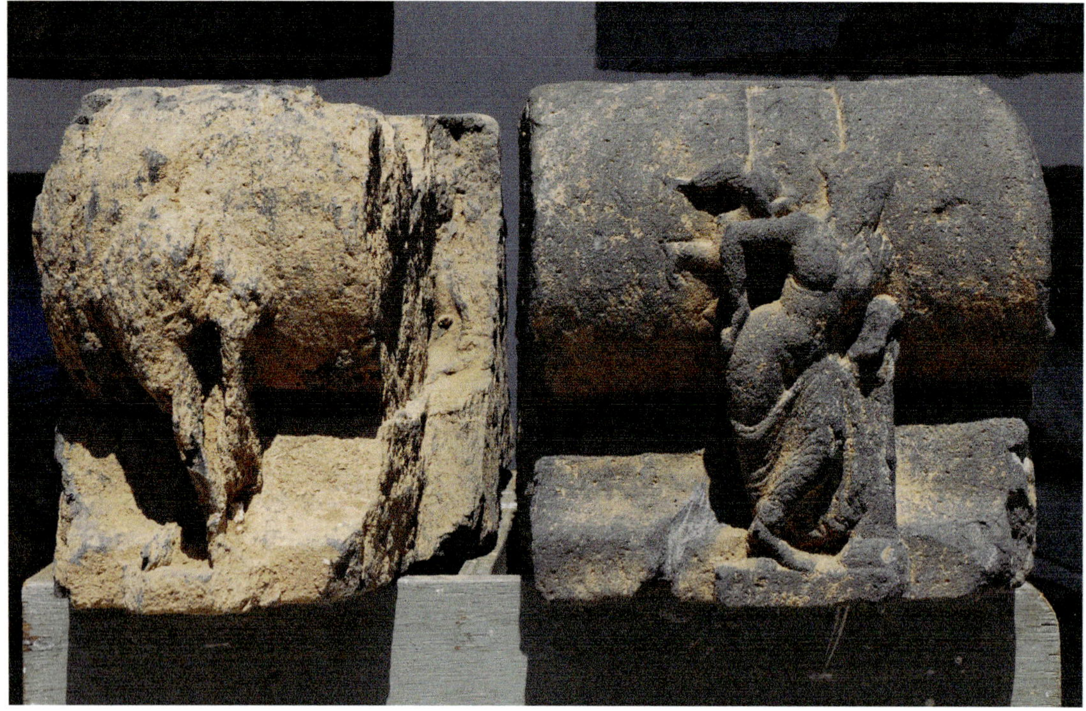

Figure 21. Amluk-dara: step-side elements from the monumental staircase of the Main Stūpa (AKD 97 and 98; Swat Museum, Saidu Sharif, Swat). (Photo: copyright IAMP.)

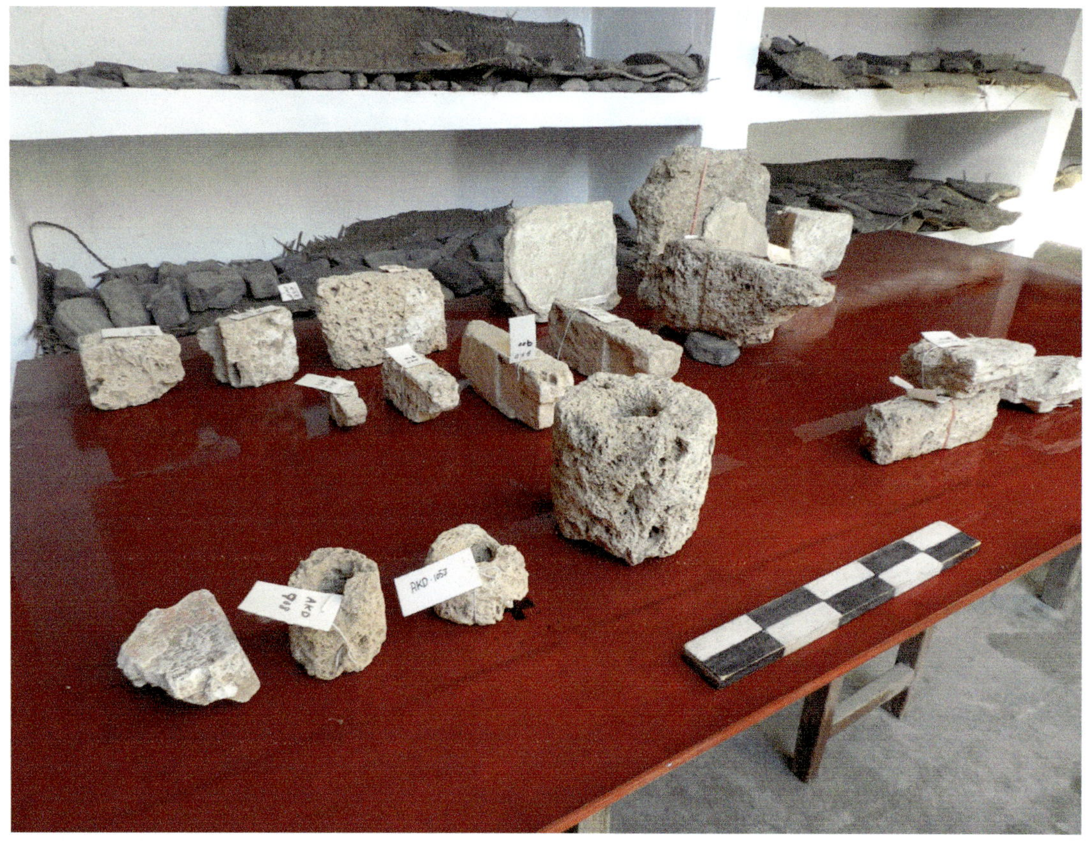

Figure 22. Amluk-dara: fragments of the architectural decoration in kanjur of the Main Stūpa and other monuments (Swat Museum, Saidu Sharif, Swat) (Photo: copyright IAMP.)

5 - the above may imply that the local schist quarry areas of Swat were closed or, most probably, that they were working at a very low pace, maybe just for the only surviving contemporary production, i.e. the stelae that we have found in plenty at Barikot;

6 - the shift to kanjur - which requires a completely different sculptural skill and, by its nature, implies a massive role for stucco modelling - tells us that the large sculptural ateliers in Swat also had to face a tremendous challenge.

[L.M.O.]

From stone to stucco: some observations on technical and cultural patterns

The information potential of the newly available data is multiplied by spatial triangulation with the archaeological sequence reconstructed in other sites. Particularly significant is their congruence with the key Buddhist site of Butkara I (Figure 23). Identified with the Tolo visited by Songyun and the Dhumat'ala of the Tibetan pilgrim O rgyan pa (Tucci 1978: 60-61; Faccenna 1980-81: [4] 756, n. 1.), Butkara I was excavated and painstakingly recorded by Domenico Faccenna from 1956 to 1962 (Faccenna 1980-81).

The long archaeological sequence, stretching from the third century BC to the tenth/eleventh century AD, was divided into five main building periods, corresponding to the construction and four successive reconstructions of the Great Stūpa (Figure 24), which reflect changes in sculptural and architectural patterns throughout an unbroken continuity of physical and cultural identity.

At Butkara I, a shift towards plastic materials and related techniques can be observed on a large scale during the Period of Great Stūpa 4, which covers a long time span (from the end of the second/early third century to the seventh century AD), and encompasses crucial moments of change, enrichment and embellishment (Faccenna 1980-81: [1] 77–127; [3] 632-664; Filigenzi 2010).

It seems that at the time of Great Stūpa 4, Butkara I - the most important and richest artistic centre of the region - was not able, or not inclined, to obtain newly-made stone sculptures. Side by side with the increasing use of calcareous stone as building material, stucco sculptures and decorations began to predominate, while stone sculptures became an ever rarer commodity. Stone from collapsed monuments was collected and re-used, often as filling material, sometimes re-cut and reworked; less frequently it was re-employed in the decoration of the monument, with the missing parts reintegrated by means of stucco additions.

Such is the case of Great Stūpa 4 in which sixteen earlier green schist panels depicting scenes of the Buddha's life were inserted into niches that interrupt the wall of the lower storey (Figure 25). The re-use evinces very little interest in the original setting and subject matter of the sculptures. However, their ornamental function, enhanced by the sharp contrast between their dark green colour and the white surface of the plaster, harmonised by painted decorations (Faccenna 1980-81: [1] 704 ff. and Figure 337; [5.1] pls. XIV, 70, 88e, 90-97, colour pls. F-Hb; Figure 26), cannot be dissociated from their being valued as precious, timeless sacred relics.

The religious implications of such a re-use are also highlighted by the unusual presence of a reliquary recess just behind each niche. As the archaeological evidence shows (Faccenna 1980-81: [1] 84 ff.; [3] 680 ff., pls. XIII XIV, XVII; [5.1] pls. 75-78), the recesses are contemporary with the erection of Great Stūpa 4 and intentionally meant as a ritualistic device in connection with the niches and their reliefs. The coin deposits in the reliquaries give important chronological clues.

We refer to Faccenna's detailed report on the coin finds, where their relative archaeological sequence and stratigraphic cross-validation is most accurately illustrated and made available for numismatic

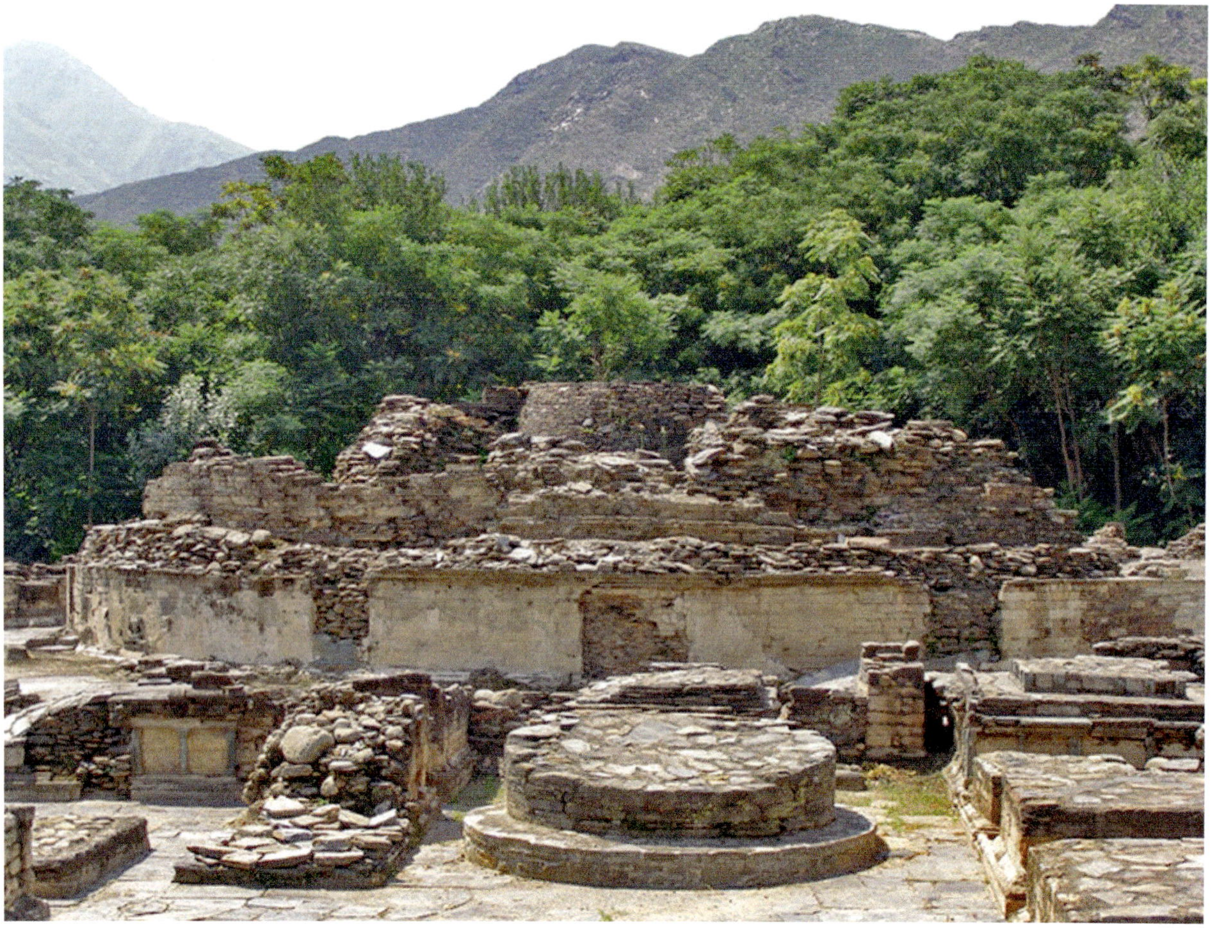

Figure 23. Panoramic view of the Buddhist sacred area of Butkara I (Photo: copyright IAMP.)

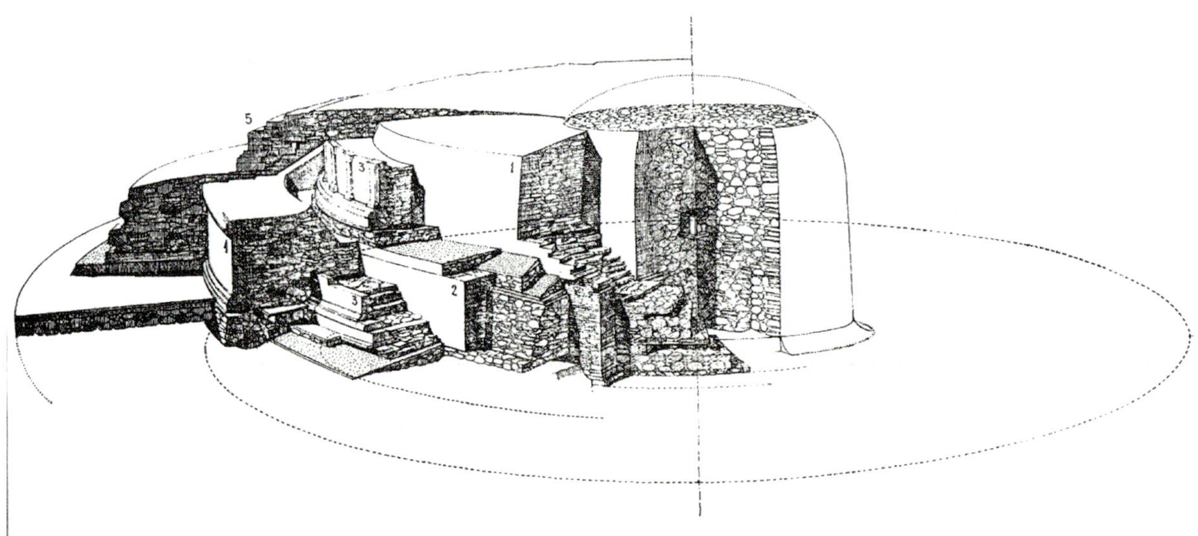

Figure 24. Butkara I: isometrical view showing the five periods of Great Stūpa (after Faccenna 1980-1981: [1] pl. V).

debate (Faccenna 1962: 78 ff. [nos. 1-26], 158 ff. [nos. 27-50]; Göbl 1976). On this occasion, we will limit ourselves to pointing out the significance of Huviṣka and Huviṣka type coins in the erection of Great Stūpa 4, and of the coins of Kavād I, a governor under Shapur II (dated by Göbl to about AD 356/360) for

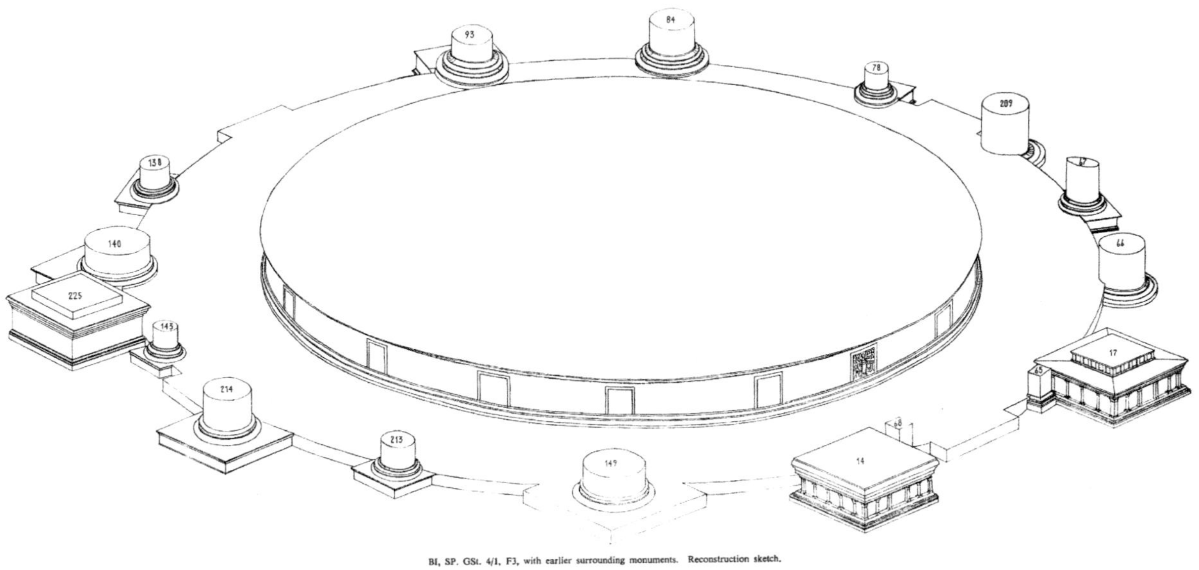

Figure 25. Butkara I: reconstruction sketch of Great Stūpa 4 with earlier surroundings monuments (after Faccenna 1980-1981: [3] pl. XII).

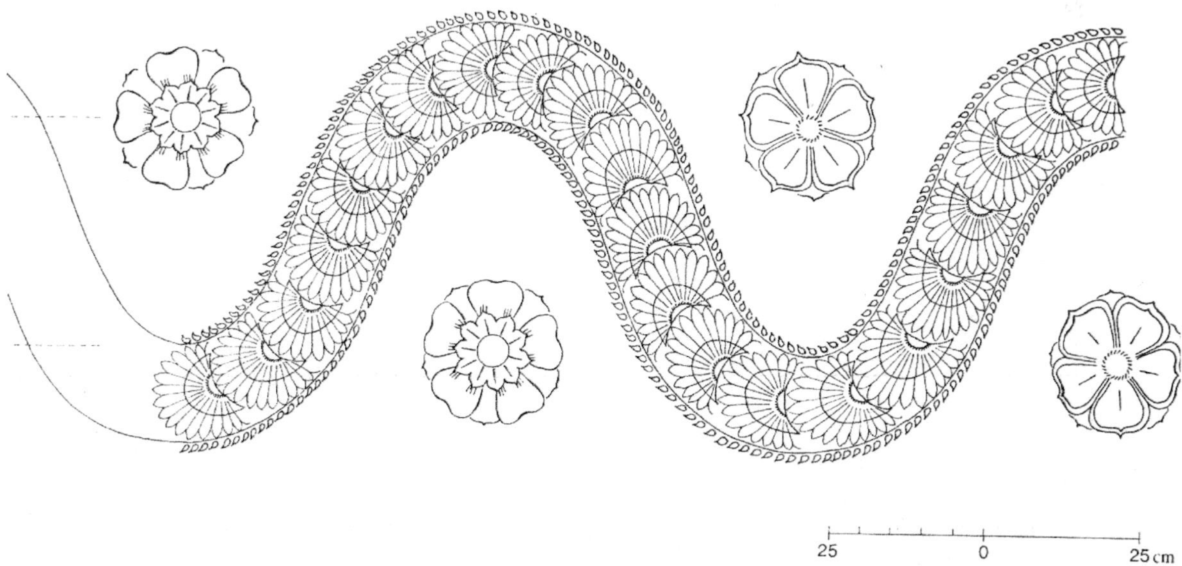

Figure 26. Butkara I: a painted decoration of the Great Stūpa 4 showing a curvilinear festoon (after Faccenna 1980-1981: [1] fig. 337).

its Phase 4, when a secondary deposit of coins accompanied the re-positioning and restoration of the relief panel sealing one of the niches, in the framework of extensive building and restoration activity after widespread collapse and damage, most probably caused by an earthquake (Faccenna et al. 1993).

On the whole, the period of Great Stūpa 4 sheds full light on a dramatic change of taste, techniques and materials, which is most clearly traceable in Phases 4 and 5, when vigorous building activity and striking sculptural and pictorial embellishment is documented by the scanty – and yet most telling – surviving evidence. This magnificent vision of the sacred space, where the tendency towards verticality, colour and gilding must have played a prominent role, is nonetheless embedded in the initial project of Great Stūpa 4 itself, whose decoration included, most probably since the very beginning, stucco sculptures – now lost – that rested against it, as shown by sockets in the wall (some of them certainly earlier than the second coat of plaster of Phase 4), and by some still-preserved bases (Faccenna 1980-81: [1] 709; [5.1] pls. 70, 92a, 101, colour pl. Hc; Figure 27).

The surface of the *stūpa*, the enclosure wall and, over time, also floors, were coated with plaster, which has been found to exist in numerous layers. Although only scant traces of paint survive, we may safely assume that the extensive use of both plaster coats and stucco sculptural decorations was inseparable from a lively polychromy and, ultimately, from the pursuit of an overall electric effect (Faccenna 1980-81: [3] 678-679).

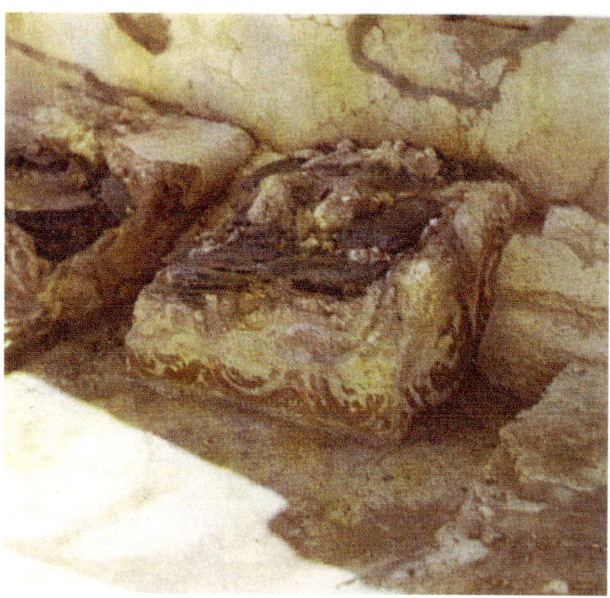

Figure 27. Butkara I; a painted base resting against Great Stūpa 4 (B37; after Faccenna 1980-81: [5.1] pl. Hc).

As for the figurative apparatus, the Period of Great Stūpa 4 yielded extremely fragmentary evidence of stucco sculpture, which nonetheless bespeak the richness and variety of artistic forms. With very few exceptions, such as the rare sculptural remains *in situ* (Faccenna 1980-81: [1] 689; [5.1] pl. 87a; Figure 28), the surviving fragments cannot be precisely correlated to the various phases. Nevertheless, comparative analysis suggests a distribution throughout the whole period (Figures 29-32).

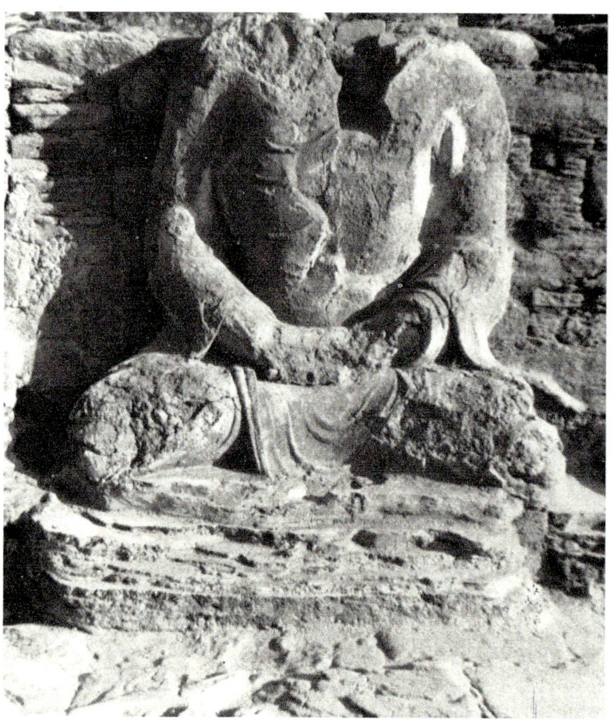

Figure 28. Butkara I, period of Great Stūpa 4: a stucco image of Buddha in situ (B 4492; after Faccenna 1980-81: [5.1] pl. 87a).

One extremely important integration with this cultural-chronological sequence is now offered by the small Buddhist architecture of Barikot. Despite their scarcity and fragmentary state of preservation, the remains of stucco sculpture recovered from these areas are of utmost importance for the chronological patterning of Gandhāran art. The clear and datable stratigraphic context in which they were found is a reliable clue to an early introduction of stucco decorations, since at Barikot this predates the natural calamities that determined the crisis of the city. Thus we may say that the *increasing* use of media such as local soapstone, kanjur, and stucco has significant correlations with periods of economic distress, which may have favoured the adoption of cheaper building options based on low-cost materials and processing techniques.

Nevertheless, the stratigraphic history of events also warns us that other triggering factors of cultural significance may have stimulated the change; first of all, we may assume, a new aesthetics, possibly radiating from Afghanistan, Southern Central Asia, and Xinjiang, where strong and captivating artistic forms, characterised by smoothness of volumes, pathos, polychromy and gilding were developed precisely because of the large-scale use of malleable materials (Figure 33).

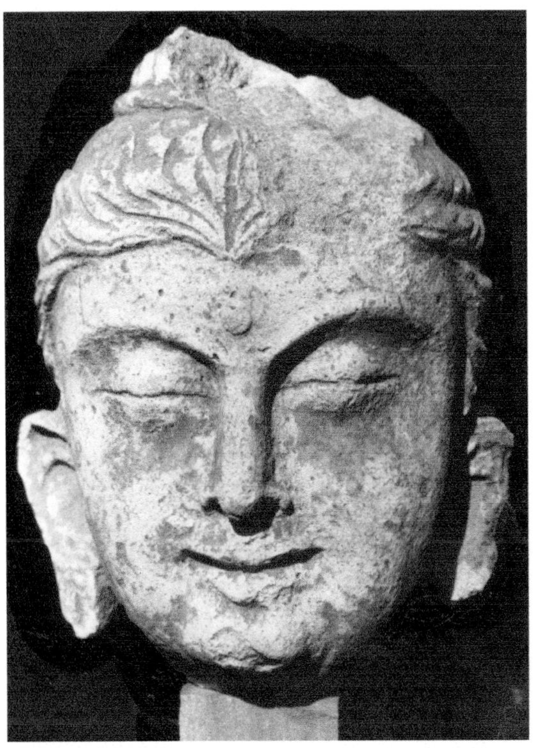

Figure 29. Butkara I: a Buddha head in stucco (B 59; Swat Museum, Saidu Sharif, Swat). (Photo: copyright IAMP.)

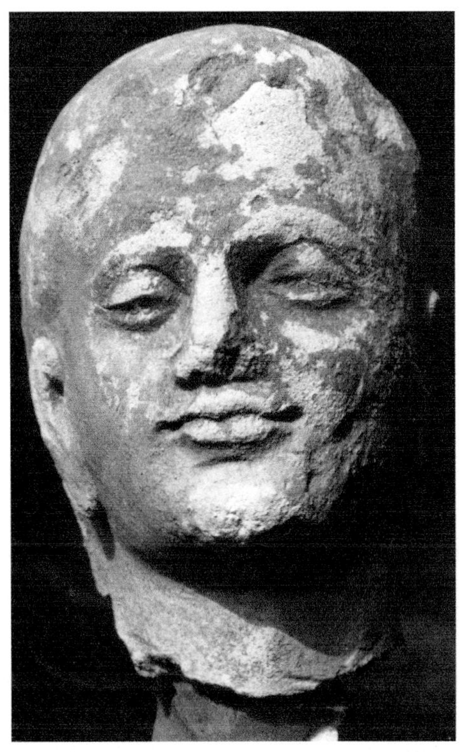

Figure 30. Butkara I: a monk's head in stucco (B 7641; Swat Museum, Saidu Sharif, Swat). (Photo: copyright IAMP.)

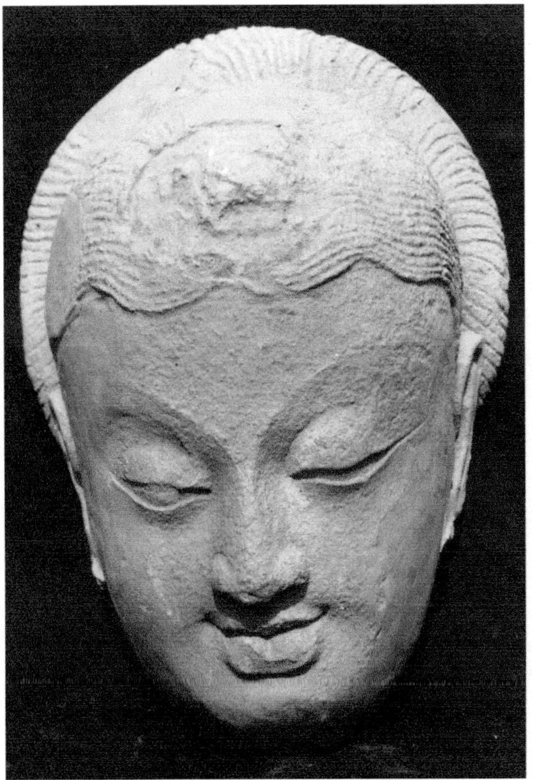

Figure 31. Butkara I: a female head in stucco (B 4533; Swat Museum, Saidu Sharif, Swat). (Photo: copyright IAMP.)

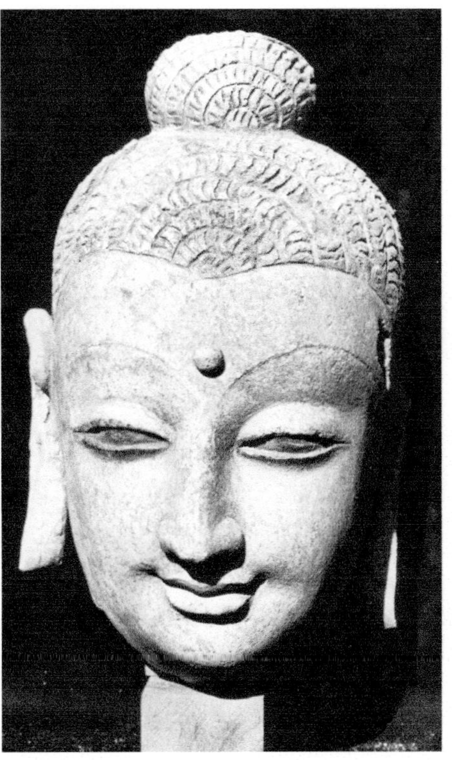

Figure 32. Butkara I: a Buddha head in stucco (B 4598; Swat Museum, Saidu Sharif, Swat). (Photo: copyright IAMP.)

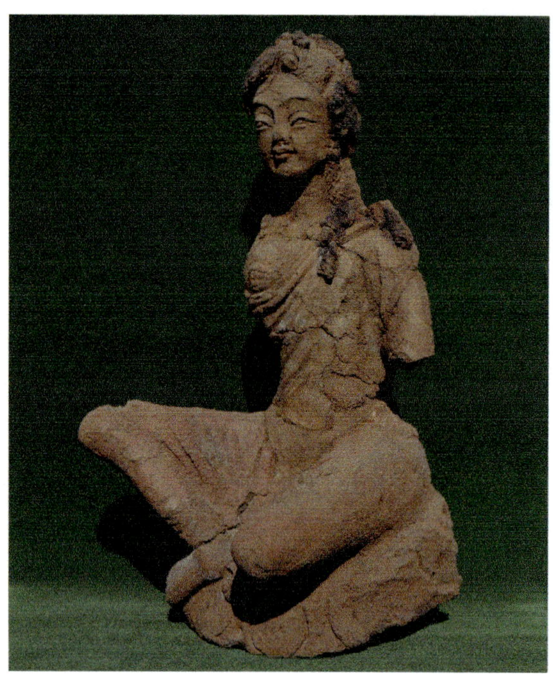

Figure 32. An image of a bodhisattva in polychrome clay, from Tapa Sardar, Afghanistan (TS 1500; Kabul National Museum; Dep. CS, MNAOR 3734).

The new trends in sculpture and architecture pose challenges to archaeological interpretation, since their real magnitude and impact are extremely difficult to verify. In most cases, changes are only insufficiently documented by partial additions that overlap existing layouts. Moreover – as old installations in stone have often survived where later additions made of more short-lived materials have almost disappeared – our reconstructions of the Gandhāran phenomenon risk being flawed by insufficient recognition of relevant evidence (Filigenzi 2015: 43-47). It is clear that even the most careful investigation will not be able to fill all the gaps completely. Hasty excavations, often carried out in the framework of rescue archaeology, further aggravate this problem.

The period of Great Stūpa 4 at Butkara I is a precious reference model for the ephemeral and yet stunning dimension of what we may call a 'non-stone aesthetics'. Besides, the data from the last urban phases at Barikot, which rely on the cross-validation of stratigraphy, numismatic evidence and radiocarbon analyses, confirm that important changes start taking place in Swat in a quite early period. They prove that during the third century AD, side by side with the introduction of stucco, figurative art in the urban cultic complex is represented only by small stelae (Figures 7-9, 13), and by re-used Gandhāran materials. Moreover, on the whole, the stelae display features that would have probably been assigned to a later date if judged on the grounds of style only. However, this matter deserves a separate treatment, which is beyond our present scope.

For the time being, let us conclude saying that, as archaeological research progresses and further tasks take shape, we see more and more clearly the need for a *modus operandi* capable of efficiently and consciously tackling objective difficulties. However, a change of cultural mentality is also advisable, which can induce us, archaeologists and art historians, not to overemphasise and somehow freeze the 'classical' Gandhāran art and architecture in stone at the expense of their still little-known, and perhaps under-evaluated, cultural, aesthetic and technical dynamism.

[A.F.]

References

Baums S. Forthcoming. Inscribed Pottery. Kharoṣṭhī and Brāhmī – 2. In P. Callieri and L.M. Olivieri (eds), *Ceramics from the Excavations in the Historic Settlement at Bīr-koṭ-ghwaṇḍai (Barikot), Swat, Pakistan (1984-1992)* (ACT Reports and Memoirs, Special Volume 2). Lahore: Sang-e-Meel Publisher.

Buchtal 1945. *The Western Aspects of Gandhara Sculpture* (From the *Proceedings of the British Academy* 31). Oxford: Oxford University Press.

Callieri P., Brocato P., Filigenzi A., Nascari M., and Olivieri L.M. 1992. *Bīr-koṭ-ghwaṇḍai 1990-1992. A Preliminary Report on the Excavations of the Italian Archaeological Mission, IsMEO. Annali dell'Istituto Universitario Orientale di Napoli* 52.4, Suppl. 73.

Callieri P., Colliva L., Micheli R., Abdul Nasir, and Olivieri L.M. 2000. Bīr-koṭ-ghwaṇḍai, Swāt, Pakistan. 1998-1999 Excavation Report, *East and West* 50, 1-4: 191-226.

Callieri P. and Olivieri L.M. Forthcoming. Inscribed Pottery. Kharoṣṭhī and Brāhmī - 2. In P. Callieri and L.M. Olivieri (eds), *Ceramics from the Excavations in the Historic Settlement at Bīr-koṭ-ghwaṇḍai (Barikot), Swat, Pakistan (1984-1992)* (ACT Reports and Memoirs, Special Volume 2). Lahore: Sang-e-Meel Publisher.

Cupitò M. and Olivieri L.M. 2013. Architectural and Infra-structural Evidence of Re-use of Residential Units in Macro-Phase D, Sector W of Bīr-koṭ-ghwaṇḍai/Barikot. *Journal of Asian Civilizations* 36, 1: 41-81.

Faccenna D. 1962. Mingora, Site of Butkara I. In D. Faccenna and G. Gullini, *Reports on the Campaigns in 1956-58 in Swāt (Pakistan)* (IsMEO Reports and Memoirs I). Rome: Istituto Poligrafico dello Stato, Libreria dello Stato.

Faccenna D. 1980-81. *Butkara I (Swāt, Pakistan) 1956-1962* (IsMEO Reports and Memoirs III 1-5.2). Rome: IsMEO.

Faccenna D., Göbl R., and Khan M.S. 1993. A Report on the Recent Discovery of a Deposit of Coins in the Sacred Area of Butkara I (Swat, Pakistan). *East and West* 43: 95-114.

Ferreras Martínez V., Ariño Gil E., Gurt Esparraguera J.M., and Pidaev S. 2014. The Enclosure of Tchingiz-Tepe (Ancient Termez, Uzbekistan) During the Kushan and Kushan-Sassanian periods. Archaeological Stratigraphy and 14C Dating Analyses. *Iranica Antiqua* 49: 736-764.

Filigenzi A. 2010. Post-Gandhāran/Non-Gandhāran: Archaeological Inquiry into a Still Nameless Period. Pages 389-406 in M. Alram et al. (eds), *Coins, Art and Chronology II: The First Millennium C.E. in the Indo-Iranian Borderlands*. Vienna: Verlag des Österreichischen Akademie der Wissenschaften.

Filigenzi A. 2015. *Art and Landscape. Buddhist Rock Sculptures of Late Antique Swat/Uḍḍiyāna*. With contributions by L.M. Olivieri and P. Rockwell. Vienna, Österreichische Akademie der Wissenschaften (Open access: <http://hw.oeaw.ac.at/7241-3?frames=yes>].

Göbl R. 1976. *A Catalogue of Coins from Butkara I (Swāt, Pakistan)* (IsMEO Reports and Memoirs IV). Rome: IsMEO.

McDowall D.W. and Callieri P. 2004. *A Catalogue of Coins from the Excavations at Bīr-koṭ-ghwaṇḍai 1984-1992.* Bīr-koṭ-ghwaṇḍai Interim Reports II. Pages 27-90 in (IsIAO Reports and Memoirs, New Series III). Rome: Istituto Italiano per l'Africa e l'Oriente.

Meister M.W., Olivieri L.M., and Vidale M. 2016. Gumbat Balo-Kale (Swat): Architectural Analysis, Conservation, and Excavation (2011-2012). Pages 551-566 in V. Lefèvre, A. Didier, and B. Mutin (eds), *South Asian Archaeology and Art* 2012/2. Turnhout: Brepols.

Moscatelli C., Olivieri L.M., and Syed Niaz Ali Shah 2016. A Late Kushan Urban Temple from Bazira/Vajīrasthāna. Data from the 2016 Excavation Campaign at Barikot, Swat. *Pakistan Heritage* 8: 49-61.

Olivieri L.M. 2011[2015]. The Last Phases at Barikot: Domestic Cults and Preliminary Chronology. Data from the 2011-2012 Excavation Campaigns in Swat, *Journal of Inner Asian Art and Archaeology* 6: 1-40.

Olivieri L.M. 2012 [2017]. The Last Phases at Barikot: Urban Cults and Sacred Architecture. Data from the Spring 2013 Excavation Campaign in Swat. *Journal of Inner Asia Art and Archaeology* 7: 7-30.

Olivieri L.M. 2012. When and Why the Ancient Town of Barikot was Abandoned? A Preliminary Note Based on the Last archaeological data, *Pakistan Heritage* 4: 109-120.

Olivieri L.M. 2013 [2017] The Last Phases at Barikot: Urban Cults and Sacred Architecture. Data from the Spring 2013 Excavation Campaign in Swat, *Journal of Inner Asia Art and Archaeology* 7: 7-30.

Olivieri L.M. 2015a. Urban Defenses at Bīr-koṭ-ghwaṇḍai, Swat (Pakistan). New Data from the 2014 Excavation Campaign. *Ancient Civilizations from Scythia to Siberia* 21/1: 183-199.

Olivieri L.M. 2015b. *Sir Aurel Stein and the 'Lords of the Marches'. New Archival Material* (ACT Report and Memoirs, Archival Studies 1). Lahore: Sang-e-Meel Publisher.

Olivieri L.M. 2018. Vajīrasthāna/Bazira and Beyond. Foundation and Current Status of the Archaeological Work in Swat. Pages 173-212 in H.P. Ray (ed), *Buddhism and Gandhara. An Archaeology of Museum Collections*. London and New York: Routledge.

Olivieri L.M. and Iori E. Forthcoming. Beginnings and Abandonment of an Early-Historic Town in the

North-West of the Subcontinent. Data from the 2015 and 2016 excavation campaigns at Bīr-koṭ-ghwaṇḍai, Swat (Pakistan). In A. Hardy and L. Rose Greaves (eds), *Proceedings EASAA 23rd Biennial Conference* (Cardiff, July 4-8, 2016).

Olivieri L.M., Vidale M. et al. 2006. Archaeology and Settlement History in a Test-Area of the Swat Valley. Preliminary Report on the AMSV Project (1st Phase). *East and* West 44/1-4: 73-150.

Olivieri L.M. et al. 2014. *The Last Phases of the Urban Site of Bir-kot-ghwandai (Barikot). The Buddhist Sites of Gumbat and Amluk-dara (Barikot)* (ACT Reports and Memoirs II). Lahore: Sang-e-Meel Publisher.

Taddei M. 1987. Non-Buddhist Deities in Gandhāran Art: Some New Evidence. Pages 349-363 in M. Yaldiz and W. Lobo (eds), *Investigating Indian Art: Proceedings of a Symposium on the Development of Early Buddhist and Hindu Iconography held at the Museum of Indian Art Berlin in May 1986*. Berlin: Staatliche Museen Preussischer Kulturbesitz.

Terrasi F., Olivieri L.M., Iori E., Marzaioli F., Micheli R., Passariello I, and Vidale M. Forthcoming. New Chronology for Late Protohistory and Early Historic Urbanization Phases at Barikot, Swat (NW Pakistan). In *The 14th International Conference on Accelerator Mass Spectrometry* (Ottawa, August 14-18, 2017).

Tucci G. 1978. *La via dello Swat*. Rome: Newton Compton. [first ed. Bari 1963].

Zwalf W. 1996. *A Catalogue of the Gandhāra Sculpture in the British Museum*. London: British Museum.

The chronology of *stūpa* relic practice in Afghanistan and Dharmarājikā, Pakistan, and its implication for the rise in popularity of image cult

Wannaporn Rienjang

Introduction

The Buddhist complex of Dharmarājikā is located in the fertile valley of Taxila, in the present day province of Punjab, northern Pakistan. The site was excavated by Sir John Marshall between 1913 and 1916. The excavations revealed the main *stūpa* and several smaller, subsidiary *stūpas*, chapels and monasteries (Figure 1) (Marshall 1916; 1918; 1920; 1951). Of the approximately forty excavated subsidiary *stūpas* and twenty chapels, only eighteen *stūpas* and three chapels yielded deposits.[1] Information on these *stūpa* and chapel deposits has been obtained from the published excavation reports: *Archaeological Survey of India Annual Reports* between 1913 and 1916, and *Taxila: An Illustrated Account of Archaeological Excavations Carried out at Taxila under the Orders of the Government of India between the Years 1913 and 1934* (Marshall 1918; 1918; 1920; 1951).

Information on almost all *stūpa* deposits in eastern Afghanistan has been obtained from records of the nineteenth century explorers: Charles Masson (1800-1853), Martin Honigberger (c. 1975-1868), James Gerard (1795-1835), and Lieutenant Robert Pigou (1816-1841) (Errington 1987; 2017). Most of the information on these *stūpa* deposits comes from Charles Masson who excavated more than fifty *stūpas* (Errington 2017). Masson is also the most systematic amongst his contemporaries, whose published and unpublished records, drawings, and sketches provide sufficient detail on the finds, including associated coins and their find spots in each *stūpa* (Errington 1999; 2017).

Not all *stūpa* deposits contained coins. At the Dharmarājikā, of approximately forty subsidiary *stūpas* excavated, ten contained coins (approximately twenty-five percent), while coins were not found in any of the chapel deposits. In eastern Afghanistan, however, a larger proportion of *stūpa* deposits containing coins is evident. Out of the sixty-four excavated Afghan *stūpas*, twenty-seven contained coins (approximately forty percent).[2] This paper investigates the changing nature of *stūpa* deposits over time. It achieves this by analyzing the coins and associated finds in *stūpa* deposits across the Dharmarājikā Buddhist complex and eastern Afghanistan. The paper proposes that the decreased numbers and the poorer nature of *stūpa* deposits that were found with coins whose dates are later than the second century AD may imply that after this period different modes of merit-gaining or worship may have become more popular than establishing relics inside *stūpas*.

[1] At the time of Marshall's excavations, all that were left on the subsidiary *stūpas* were the drums and circular or square bases (Marshall 1951: 240). It is therefore possible that some *stūpas* may have contained deposits above the drums which were no longer extant by then. As for the main *stūpa*, parts of its dome, drum and base were present at the time of Marshall's excavation. Marshall mentioned that the main *stūpa* was, however, looted prior to his excavation, as evidenced by a trench driven through the centre of the *stūpa* dome (Marshall 1951: 238, pl. 47 a, b).

[2] The identification of coins from approximately twenty *stūpa* deposits in Afghanistan that are in the British Museum was carried out by Elizabeth Errington and Joe Cribb (Errington 2017; Errington & Cribb 1992). The re-identification of Kushan coins from *stūpa* deposit of Tepe Maranjan 2 in Kabul, Afghanistan, excavated by the Afghan Institute of Archaeology and briefly published by Gérard Fussman (2008), was carried out by Joe Cribb upon examining photographs of the coins in combination with their dimensions and weights (personal communication, August 2015).

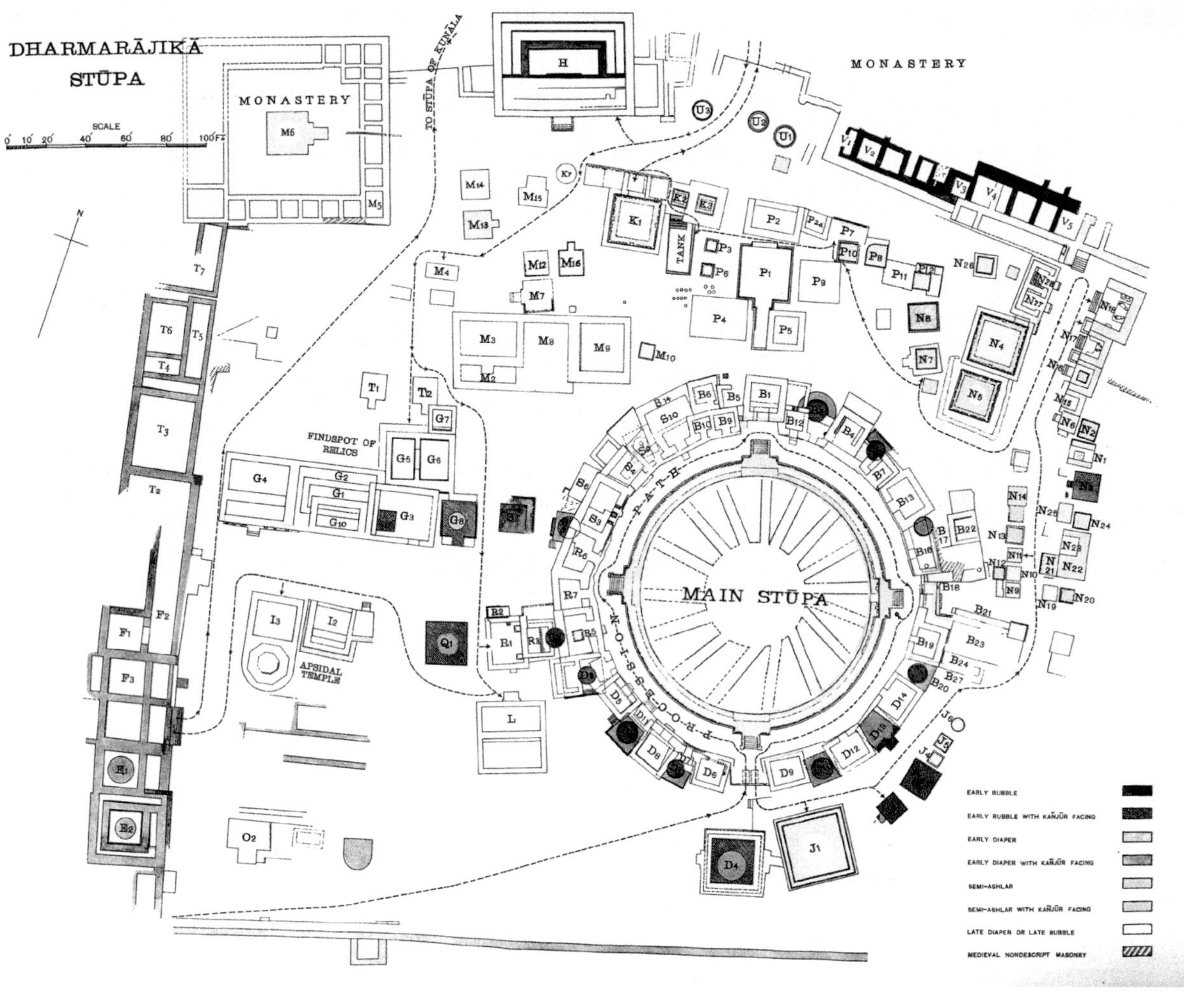

Figure 1. Site plan of the Dharmarājikā Buddhist complex (after Marshall 1951: pl. 45).

Coin groups

Upon analysing coin distribution patterns across *stūpa* deposits at the Dharmarājikā and eastern Afghanistan, it is evident that in general only coins of similar date range were included in each deposit. Only in rare instances were coins of much different date ranges mixed in the same deposit. In addition, there are also chronological correlations between the coins and their associated objects, and in the case of Dharmarājikā, the chronological correlation between coins, associated objects and the structures in which they were found. It is possible therefore to say that coins in general were included when still current, and thus can be used to help date the deposits.

Based on their distribution pattern, it is possible to divide coins in *stūpa* deposits into nine groups, ranging in date between mid-first century BC and seventh century AD (Table 1).[3] The first group (A) belongs to coins of the Indo-Greeks and the Indo-Scythians, whose issue dates range from early to mid first century BC. The second and third coin groups belong to coins of the Indo-Scythians. Their issue dates range from early first century BC to early first century AD. The fourth coin group (D) includes coins of the first Kushan king, Kujūla Kadphises (*c.* AD 40-90) and a local satrap ruling in Jalalabad, Mujatria, whose dates range between late first and early second century AD (Cribb 2015a). These coins (group D) are the earliest in date found within *stūpa* deposits of eastern Afghanistan.

[3] The dates of coin issuers used in this paper follow those published in Errington & Curtis (2007) and Jongeward & Cribb (2015).

Table 1. Coins in stūpa deposits.

Coin group	Date range of coins	Issuers and their ruling dates
A	c. 75 BC-50 BC	-Maues (*c*. 75-65 BC) -Apollodotus II (*c*. 65-50 BC) -Vonones with Spalahores (*c*. 65-50 BC)
B	*c*. 75 BC-1 BC	-Maues (*c*. 75-65 BC) -Azes I (*c*. 46-1 BC)
C	31 BC to *c*. AD 30	-Augustus (31 BC-AD 14) -Azilises (*c*. 1 BC-AD 16) -Azes II (*c*. AD 16-30)
D	*c*. AD 32 to early 2nd century AD	-Gondophares (*c*. AD 32-60) -Kujūla Kadphises (*c*. AD 40-90) -Mujatria (*c*. late first to early second century AD)
E	*c*. AD 90-113	-Kujūla Kadphises (*c*. AD 40-90) -Wima Takto (*c*. AD 90-113) (Soter Megas coins in the Darūnta)
F	*c*. AD 113-190	-Domitian (AD 81-96) -Trajan (AD 98-117) -Sabina (*c*. AD 128-36) -Wima Kadphises (*c*. AD 113-27) -Kaniṣka (*c*. AD 127-150) -Huviṣka (*c*. AD 150-90)
G	*c*. AD 190-227	- Vāsudeva I (*c*. AD 190-227)
H	*c*. AD 230-350	- 'Late Kushan' (*c*. AD 230-350) - Vāsudeva II (*c*. AD 280-320)
I	*c*. mid-3rd to 7th century	- Shapur I (*c*. AD 240-272/3) -Imitation of Shapur II (AD 309-379) -Imitation of Shapur III (AD 390-410) -Varhran IV (AD 388-99) -Varhran V (AD 420-438) -Yazdagird II (AD 439-457) -Peroz (AD 457/9-84) -Imitation of Theodosius II (AD 409-450) -Imitation of Marcianus (AD 450-457) -Imitation of Leo (AD 457-474) -Kidara (*c*. AD 340-345) -Kidara 'Kushanshah' (*c*. AD 370-400) -Alchon (5^{5th}century AD) -Khingila (5th century AD) -Sri Sailanavirya (King of Kashmir) (5th - early 6th century AD) -Nezak Huns Kabul mint (*c*. AD 515-650)

The fifth coin group (E) covers a short period, belonging to the so-called Soter Megas coins, whose issue dates could have started towards the end of Kujūla Kadphises (*c*. AD 40-90) and continued during the reign of his successor, Wima Takto (*c*. AD 90-113) (Cribb 2014; 2015b). The sixth coin group (F) comprises coins of the third to the fifth Kushan kings, Wima Kadphises (*c*. AD 113-127), Kaniṣka (*c*. AD127-150) and Huviṣka (*c*. AD 150-90).[4] The seventh group (G) belongs to the coins of the sixth Kushan king, Vāsudeva

[4] In the *stūpa* deposit of Ahinposh, eastern Afghanistan, there are also Roman gold coins of Domitian (AD 81-96), Trajan (AD 98-117) and Sabina (*c*. AD 128-36) found together with the gold coins of the three Kushan kings in coin group F (Simpson 1879; 1880).

I (*c.* AD 190-227), and the eighth group (H) to the coins of the so-called 'late Kushans' (*c.* AD 230-350). *Stūpa* deposits found with these two coin groups (G and H) are fewer in number and their nature poorer than those found with coins of earlier dates. The last coin group (I) comprises coins of the Sasanians and the Huns, covering a period of approximately three centuries (*c.* AD 240 to *c.* AD 650).

Types of *stūpa* deposits

The above coin groups were almost invariably found associated with objects inside *stūpas*, and different types of deposits across the Dharmarājikā and eastern Afghanistan can be observed. To facilitate the analysis, deposits of these two areas are categorized into types. Three main elements used in the categorization are corporeal remains, relic containers, and other associated objects including coins.

There are two main types of *stūpa* deposits at the Dharmarājikā and in eastern Afghanistan: deposits that did not contain relic container(s) and those that did. Within each type, three and four variations can be observed, respectively (Table 2).

Deposits that did not contain relic containers, can comprise corporeal remains alone without any accompanying objects (1.1), corporeal remains with accompanying objects (1.2), or simply objects without any corporeal remains (1.3). Corporeal remains that were found alone without accompanying objects generally were larger pieces of bone, recorded as human bones or skeletons, as well as a skull (Masson 1841). These corporeal remains were almost always laid on the ground inside the *stūpa*. It is to be noted that there are no report of larger pieces of bones from *stūpa* deposits at the Dharmarājikā, and when reported from *stūpas* in Afghanistan, none of them were found accompanied with objects. This type of deposit (1.1) therefore is likely to be sepulchral in nature rather than being for the purpose of worship. In this respect, they are not considered as relic deposits. On the contrary, corporeal remains that were accompanied with objects (1.2), are generally smaller pieces of bones or ashes. Sometimes earth and charcoal were reported from *stūpa* deposits and they were probably mixed with ashes. The most consistent kinds of objects in *stūpa* deposits are beads and coins. This type of deposit (1.2) is considered be a relic deposit. While coins were generally placed outside relic containers, beads were almost always placed mixed with corporeal remains inside relic containers, and in most cases, inside caskets.[5] *Stūpa* deposits that only contained objects (1.3) are also considered relic deposits.

Table 2. Varieties of relic deposit.

Deposit type	Deposit sub-type	Nature of deposit sub-type
1. Without relic container	1.1	Corporeal remains
	1.2	Corporeal remains, objects
	1.3	Objects
2. With relic container	2.1	Relic container, corporeal remains
	2.2	Relic container, corporeal remains, objects
	2.3	Relic container, objects
	2.4	Relic container
Note: 'Relic container' refers to the outermost container, while 'objects' refer to any items, apart from relic containers and corporeal remains that were found in the *stūpa* deposits.		

[5] Caskets are smaller containers, often made of precious metal, placed inside relic containers. One relic container can contain one or more caskets. In case of more than one casket, often they were placed inside one another, making layers of caskets. See a compilation of relic containers and caskets from Pakistan and Afghanistan in Jongeward et al. 2012: appendix.

Stūpa deposits that contained relic containers are by and large richer in nature, in that they often contained objects such as beads of gemstone and occasionally gold ornaments. In addition, the arrangement of the corporeal remains (when present) in relation with the associated objects is more elaborate than in the deposits that did not contain relic containers. The corporeal remains found inside relic containers are almost invariably bone fragments or ashes, or organic substances such as charcoal, earth or moulds, which were probably mixed with ashes. Deposits that contained relic container(s) are considered relic deposits. The relic containers can contain corporeal remains (2.1), corporeal remains with accompanying objects (2.2), objects without corporeal remains (2.3), or nothing inside (2.4). It will be seen below that this richest and most elaborate type of deposit (2.2) was generally found associated with coins early periods, i.e. from the Indo-Greeks to Huviṣka (coin groups A to F).

Five phases of relic practice: changing natures in relic deposits

Upon analysing the above coin groups and their associated deposits, it has become apparent that there are chronological correlations between coin groups and deposit types. It is possible therefore to tentatively establish a chronology for the development of *stūpa* relic practices (Table 3). This chronology is divided into five phases according to the changing natures of the *stūpa* deposits. The first phase covers the period of the Indo-Greeks and the Indo-Scythians (coin groups A-C). Deposits during this phase only belong to the richest and the most elaborate type (2.2). Corporeal remains during this phase were almost invariably recorded as bone fragments and in a few instances, ashes. The objects accompanying the bone relics were mostly beads of various materials including gemstone, pearl and ivory. The elaborate arrangement of the relics is attested by the placement of the bone relics inside one or two caskets[6] made of precious metals (gold, silver, copper). These caskets were in turn placed inside relic containers, which were mostly made of stone.

The second phase covers the period of the first two Kushan kings, Kujūla Kadphises and Wima Takto and a local satrap in Jalalabad, Mujatria (coin groups D and E). By and large, *stūpa* deposits of this phase continued in the same fashion as those in the first phase, with the richest and the most elaborate deposit type 2.2 being most dominant. Relic containers were still made of stone and the corporeal relics[7] were often placed inside one or more caskets, accompanied with objects such as beads and other types of ornaments.

Table 3. Chronology of stūpa relic practices.

Phase	Coin Group	Deposit Type	Corporeal Remains	Relic Container	Casket	Beads
I	A	2.2	All	Stone	None	All
	B	2.2	All	Stone	Gold	All
	C	2.2	All	Stone	Gold / Bronze	All
II	D	2.2/2.3	Some	Stone	Gold / Silver	Some
	E	1.2/2.2	Some	Stone/Metal	Gold / Silver	Some
III	F	1.2/2.1/2.2/2.3	Some	Stone/Metal/Clay/ Bone/ Ivory/Wood	Gold / Silver	Some
IV	G	2.3	None	Clay	None	None
	H	1.3	None	-	None	None
V	I	2.2/2.3	One or two	Metal/Clay	Gold/ Silver / Gilt copper	Some

[6] When there was more than one casket, the smaller casket(s) were almost always placed inside the larger one(s).

[7] Corporeal relics at the Dharmarājikā continued to be, by and large, bone fragments. The same is true in eastern Afghanistan, where other types of corporeal relics were also reported. These include ashes, charcoal, earth and moulds, the last three could have been mixed with ashes.

The third phase covers the period of three Kushan kings, Wima Kadphises, Kaniṣka, Huviṣka (coin group F). This is the phase that witnessed the most variety of *stūpa* deposits. Coins of these three Kushan rulers occurred in *stūpa* deposits in a large area of Afghanistan, from the Jalalabad plain to the Kabul region, indicating that *stūpa* relic cult was widely practised in Afghanistan during the periods of these three rulers.[8] Relic containers of this phase were made of a variety of media, including stone, metal, bone, ivory, wood and clay. The richest and the most elaborate type of *stūpa* deposit (2.2) continued into this phase, but a larger number of deposits belong to type 2.3, which share the same elements as type 2.2, except that they do not yield corporeal remains.[9] Beads continued to appear in *stūpa* deposits of this phase but are much less in quantity compared to the previous two phases.

The fourth phase covers the period of the successor of Huviṣka, Vasudeva I (*c.* AD 190-227), and the late Kushan kings (*c.* AD 230-350) (coin groups G and H). This is the period that witnessed a clear change in the nature of *stūpa* deposits. The number of relic deposits found with coins of this phase decreased,[10] and they are much poorer in nature compared to those found with coins of earlier phases. This poorer nature is manifested in the general absence of corporeal remains, caskets, beads and other ornaments in *stūpa* deposits. Some *stūpa* deposits appear to have only contained coins.[11] Stone relic containers appear to have gone almost completely out of fashion, giving ways to the cheaper media such as clay. The fifth phase covers the period of the Sasanians and the Huns (coin group I). Similar to Phase IV, the number of *stūpa* deposits that contained coins of this phase is less than in the previous Phases I to III.[12] Their nature, except for one deposit,[13] is also poorer than those in Phases I to III.

Implications

There are many possible interpretations for the limited number and the poorer nature of relic assemblages associated with coins of Phases IV and V. One of them could be that after the second century AD, relic deposits of earlier periods may have been re-consecrated, whereby the earlier *stūpa* could have been enlarged or the old relics were re-located to a new *stūpa*.[14] Another possible explanation could be that other kinds of religious activities became more widely practised. Such activities may have included the display of relics and image cult. The Chinese pilgrim Faxian (mid fourth to early fifth century AD) mentions a display of relics in Haḍḍa and Nagarahāra and the involvement of royal elites (Legge 1991), suggesting that the display of relics was already being practised and received royal patronage by the fourth century AD, the period contemporary with Phases IV and V.

Faxian states that in Haḍḍa, for example, the bone relic of the Buddha, which he describes as a flat bone of a skull, was kept inside a shrine (*vihāra*) and brought out during the day, for public display

[8] It is to be noted that Darūnta is the only area in Afghanistan whose *stūpa* deposits did not yield coins of these three Kushan kings.

[9] It should be noted that the information on corporeal remains was mostly obtained from the nineteenth- and early twentieth-century records, so it is possible that there were corporeal remains inside relic containers that escaped the attention of the excavators. However, it is unlikely that bone or ash relics that were placed inside minute caskets would have escaped their attention, for they were almost always recorded when found in such contexts.

[10] None in Darūnta, three in Jalalabad plain, two in Kabul region, and one at the Dharmarājikā.

[11] These are *Stūpas* nos. 6, 8, and 9 in Haḍḍa, Afghanistan, excavated by Charles Masson (Masson 1841).

[12] None in Darūnta, one in Jalalabad plain, one in Kabul region, and two at the Dharmarājikā.

[13] This is the *stūpa* deposit of Haḍḍa Stūpa no. 10 (Masson 1841)

[14] This is evident in two *stūpa* relic deposits in eastern Afghanistan. One is the Tepe Maranjan 2 (Fussman 2008), where there were a mixture of coin groups D and H, whose issue dates are almost two centuries apart (see the re-identification of the coins from this *stūpa* deposit under the above footnote 2). The other is the deposit of a *stūpa*, probably from Wardak based on the inscription on its relic container (Falk 2008; Baums 2012: 245-46). It contained coin groups F and I, whose issue dates are almost five centuries apart. The characters of the two *stūpa* relic deposits are similar to those found with coins of earlier dates (groups D and F), suggesting that the contents of the original relic deposits were not discarded, but coins, and perhaps more items, were added during the re-consecration. It must not be forgotten, however, that the practice of re-dedicating the 'old' relics without adding new coins may have also played a role in the decreased number of relic deposits with coins of later periods.

on a platform (Legge 1991:37-38). Offerings, which included flowers and incense, were made to the relics during the display. He also mentions the daily participation of 'the king of the country' and the safeguarding of the relics (that were kept inside an accessible shrine) by 'great families of the kingdom' as well as the offerings made to the relics by 'the kings of various countries' (Legge 1991: 37-38).

Other forms of worship that may have come into in practice alongside the public display of relics include the cult of image. Kurt Behrendt (2003) has proposed four chronological phases for Buddhist architecture in Gandhāra. In his chronology, Behrendt distinguishes the periods before and after Huviṣka; one difference between pre- and post-Huviṣka periods is the presence and absence of image shrines. Behrendt notes that image shrines started to appear after the second century AD, and the size of the images placed inside the shrines became larger over time. An example of an image shrine with large images can be seen at the Dharmarājikā, which holds two life-size Buddha images and one over-life size image, all made of stucco (Figure 2). The shrines were built with semi-ashlar type of masonry, a masonry type common to structures of post-Huviṣka period.

It is known that the representation of the Buddha in anthropomorphic form already took place on coins towards the end of the reign of Kaniṣka (*c.* AD 127-150) (Cribb 1982; 1984; 1985; 1999/2000) (Figure 3). It is therefore not impossible that by the time of the late Kushans (*c.* AD 230-350), image cult may have become popular within Gandhāra and adjoining areas. This form of practice may not have been limited to images placed inside shrines for veneration, but may have also included images attached to *stūpas.* While relics continue to be the central point of rituals, the use of anthropomorphic objects to represent the Buddha could have become more popular. Commissioning sculptures that 'represent' the Buddha and bodhisattvas could also be an easier way to make merit than acquiring their relics.

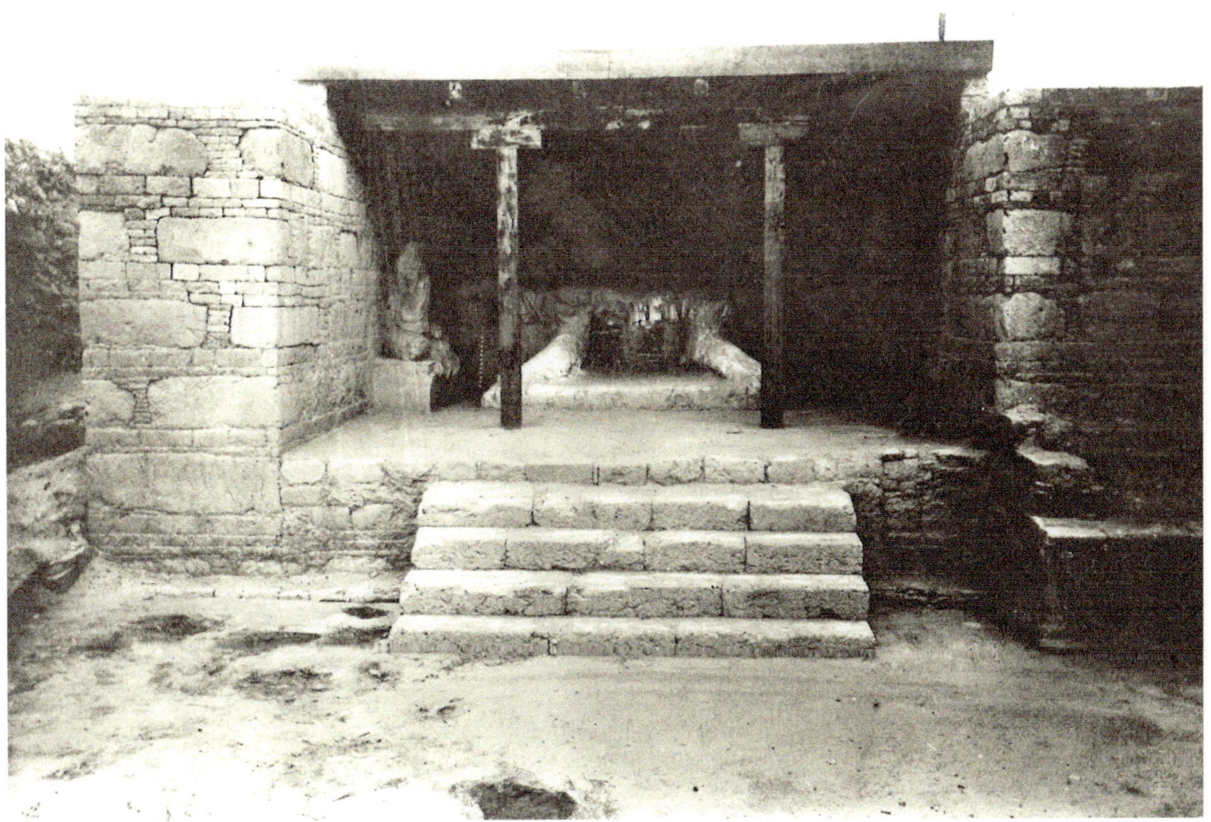

Figure 2. Chapel N18 at the Dharmarājikā (after Marshall 1951: Pl. 59.c).

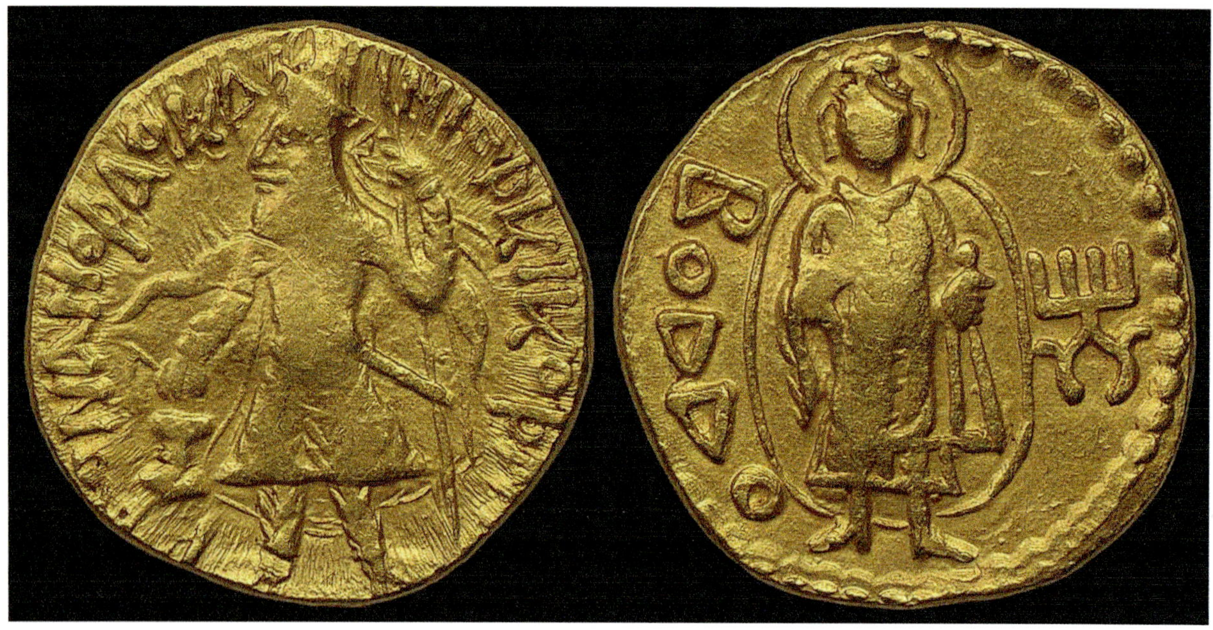

Figure 3. Gold coin of Kaniṣka I, with Buddha image on the reverse. (Photo: Heritage Image Partnership Ltd/ Alamy Stock Photo.)

Summary

To sum up, *stūpa* relic deposits found with coins whose issue dates are later than the second century AD are much less in number, and generally poorer in nature than those found with coins of earlier dates. One possible explanation for such a transition could be that other forms of worship or merit-making may have become more popular than establishing relics inside *stūpas*. These new forms of worship and merit-making may have included the display of relics and the image cult. That the practice of involving visual representations of the Buddha and bodhisattvas was likely to have become more popular than establishing relics inside *stūpas* may also explain why some of the excavated *stūpas* did not yield any deposits. Some stone and many stucco images, particularly large ones, may in fact have been produced during the period in which these alternatives became popularized, some time after the second century AD.

References

Baums S. 2012. Catalog and Revised Texts and Translations of Gandhāran Reliquary Inscriptions. Pages 201-251 in D. Jongeward, E. Errington, R. Salomon & S. Baums. *Gandhāran Buddhist Reliquaries.* Seattle: University of Washington Press.

Behrendt K. 2003. *The Buddhist Architecture of Gandhāra.* Leiden: Brill.

Cribb J. 1982. Kanishka's Buddha Coins – the Official Iconography of Sakyamuni and Maitreya. *Journal of the International Association of Buddhist Studies* 3: 79-88.

Cribb J. 1984. The Origin of the Buddha Image – the Numismatic Evidence. Pages 231-244 in B. Allchin (ed). *South Asian Archaeology 1981: Proceedings of the Sixth International Conference of the Association of South Asian Archaeologists in Western Europe, held in Cambridge, 5-10 July 1981.* Cambridge: Cambridge University Press.

Cribb J. 1985. A Re-examination of the Buddha Images on the Coins of King Kanishka. Pages 59-86 in A.K. Narain (ed) *Studies in Buddhist Art of South Asia.* New Delhi: Kanak Publications.

Cribb J. 1999/2000. Kanishka I's Buddha Image Coins Revisited. *Silk Road Art and Archaeology* 6: 151-189.

Cribb J. 2014. The Soter Megas Coins of the First and Second Kushan Kings, Kujula Kadphises and Wima Takto. *Gandhāran Studies* 8: 77-134.

Cribb J. 2015a. Dating and Locating Mujatria and the Two Kharahostes. *Journal of the Oriental Numismatic Society* 223: 26-48.

Cribb J. 2015b. Introduction. Pages 1-20 in D. Jongeward & J. Cribb. *Kushan, Kushano-Sasanian, and Kidarite coins. A catalogue of coins from the American Numismatic Society.* New York: The American Numismatic Society.

Errington E. 1987. The Western Discovery of the Art of Gandhāra and the Finds of Jamalgarhi (PhD dissertation). School of Oriental and African Studies, London.

Errington E. 1999. Rediscovering the Collections of Charles Masson. Pages 207-238 in M. Alram & D.E. Klimburg-Salter (eds) *Coins, Art and Chronology. Essays on the Pre-Islamic History of the Indo-Iranian Borderlands.* Wien : Verlag der Österreichischen Akademie der Wissenschaften.

Errington E. 2017. *Charles Masson and the Buddhist Sites of Afghanistan. Explorations, Excavations, Collections 1832-1835.* London: British Museum Press.

Errington E. & Cribb J. (eds) 1992. *The Crossroads of Asia: Transformation in Image and Symbol.* Cambridge: Ancient India and Iran Trust.

Errington E. & Curtis V. (eds) 2007. *From Persepolis to the Punjab: Exploring Ancient Iran, Afghanistan and Pakistan.* London: British Museum Press.

Falk H. 2008. Another Reliquary Vase from Wardak and Consecrating Fire Rites in Gandhāra. Pages 63-80 in C. Bautze-Picron (ed) *Religion and Art: New Issues in Indian Iconography and Iconology.* London: British Association for South Asian Studies.

Fussman G. 2008. *Monuments Bouddhiques de la region de Caboul,* Vol. 2. *Memoires de la Delegation Archeologique Française en Afghanistan,* LXXVI. Paris: Diffusion de Boucard.

Jongeward D., Errington E., Salomon R. & Baums S. 2012. *Gandhāran Buddhist Reliquaries.* Seattle: University of Washington Press.

Jongeward D. & Cribb J. 2015. *Kushan, Kushano- Sasanian, and Kidarite Coins. A Catalogue of Coins from the American Numismatic Society.* New York: American Numismatic Society.

Legge J. 1991. *A Record of Buddhistic Kingdoms.* London: Constable.

Marshall J. 1916. Excavations at Taxila. Pages 1-52 in *Annual Report of the Archaeological Survey of India 1912-1913.* Calcutta.

Marshall J. 1918. Excavations at Taxila. Pages 1-38 in *Annual Report of the Archaeological Survey of India 1915-1916.* Calcutta.

Marshall J. 1920. Excavations at Taxila. Pages 1-35 in *Annual Report of the Archaeological Survey of India 1914-1915.* Calcutta.

Marshall J. 1951. *Taxila: An Illustrated Account of Archaeological Excavations Carried out at Taxila under the Orders of the Government of India between the Years 1913 and 1934* (3 volumes). Cambridge: University Press.

Masson C. 1841. A Memoir of the Buildings Called Topes. Pages 55-118 in H. H. Wilson (ed) *Ariana Antiqua. A Descriptive Account of the Antiquities and Coins of Afghanistan.* London: East India Company.

Simpson W. 1879. Coins from the Ahin Posh Tope near Jelalabad. *Journal of the Asiatic Society of Bengal* 48: 77-79.

Simpson W. 1880. Buddhist Architecture in the Jelalabad Valley. *Transaction of the Royal Institute of British Architects 1879-80*: 37-58.

Buddhist art's late bloomer: the genius and influence of Gandhāra

Monika Zin

The intention of this paper is to place the art of Gandhāra in the context of the other schools of Buddhist art. As a student devoted to Andhra, Ajanta, and Kucha, I do not feel that I am in a position to address questions concerning the absolute datings of individual Gandhāran reliefs and can only provide some general – naïve and possibly controversial – remarks concerning the supposed earliest and latest specimens, while leaving a detailed investigation to the specialists.

As for the beginnings of the Gandhāran artistic production, congresses were held to establish characteristics of these earliest pre-Kushan reliefs (Srinivasan 2007). The reliefs have their own style and are ruled by their own compositional principles which do not always correlate with the principles used to establish an early dating of the 'classical' Gandhāran reliefs. Marshall proposed credible characteristics which allow us to date some reliefs early. These include cases where the figures do not overlap one another, or where the figures surrounding the Buddha are shown in the same scale as the Buddha instead of being shown much smaller (e.g. Marshall 1960: 41-42 regarding what is known as the 'Mardan group' of reliefs). These characteristics are not valid for the pre-Kushan art of Swat. Here, the Buddha might be twice as large as his worshipers, and people in the images are depicted standing in several rows. Pointing to similarities between the pre-Kushan reliefs and the earliest art of the subcontinent (e.g. Miyaji 2008) can certainly provide answers, although probably not for all questions. The iconography of the bare-chested early Gandhāran Buddhas (similar to Mathurā?),[1] which did not carry on over time or develop, leaves us with riddles.

Some issues concerning the early reliefs deserve comparative investigation. The aniconic representation of the Buddha's descent from the Trāyastriṃśa Heaven discovered in Butkara I (Figure 1),[2] is taken as coming from Gandhāra's uniconical period (cf. e.g. Van Lohuizen-de Leeuw 1981: 389-90). The relief, however, represents a monastic figure – this is probably the nun Utpalavarṇā awaiting the Buddha on earth – differently from all other early representations. Note the conventionalized representation of the *pāṃśukūla*, the patchwork robe, familiar from Mathurā. One should probably say: 'already conventionalized'. As for the oldest Indian art, in not only the Buddha's descent from the Trāyastriṃśa Heaven but also in all other representations from the aniconic period, monks and nuns were not represented. They do not appear a single time in Bharhut, Sanchi, in old Ajanta paintings, etc. They only appear in art where the image of the Buddha had already been established, even though it might not always have been represented. Is the Gandhāran relief the single exception to this general rule? In my opinion, this is probably not the case. A comparison of the descent from the Trāyastriṃśa Heaven from Butkara with other reliefs from Faccenna's early 'drawing group' (e.g. Faccenna 2007: 190-191) which do represent the Buddha or the Bodhisatva in person shows no considerable stylistic differences.[3] Furthermore, the appearance of Indra and Brahma in the relief is not dissimilar to some representations of scenes of Indra and Brahma entreating the Buddha

[1] Van Lohuizen-de Leeuw (1981) understands them as being an adaptation of the earliest Mathurā Buddhas which she dates into first century BC.

[2] Butkara I, Saidu Sharif; Swat Museum, no. 2524. Illustrated e.g. in: Faccenna 1962-64, II: pl. 233; Van Lohuizen-de Leeuw 1981: fig. 21; Faccenna 2007: pl. 7.39.

[3] Cf. e.g. a certainly early relief showing the Bodhisatva riding to school, illus. in: Faccenna 1962-64, II: pl. 234; Faccenna 2007: fig. 7.38.

(depicted as a person) to preach.[4] The descent from the Trāyastriṃśa Heaven excavated in Butkara I is certainly early; it appears, however, very doubtful that it can be considered as belonging to the time before the creation of the Buddha image. It should not be forgotten that Taddei (2006: 43) provided an argument for a much later dating of the 'drawing group'.

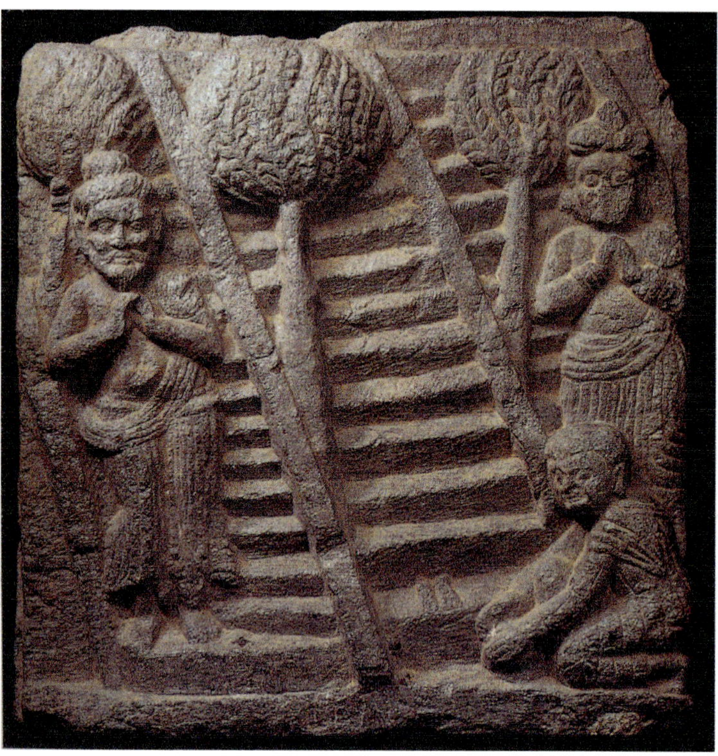

Figure 1. The Buddha's descent from the Trāyastriṃśa Heaven in a relief from Butkara I, Saidu Sharif (Swat Museum, no. 2524). (Photo: courtesy Isao Kurita).

As an outsider to research on Gandhāra, I must risk posing a sacrilegious question: could the characteristics of this 'drawing group' be signs of a specific regional style influenced by Central India, rather than an indication of their age? Comparable questions have been raised regarding several centres in Andhra, where e.g. the reliefs from Chandavaram - which appear very archaic - turned out instead to have been the products of a district which was separated from the prominent (and 'royal') centres of art (Arlt 2016). As for Gandhāra, a question arises: why was the core of the 'archaic' style in Swat and not in the capital? With this, we come to the crucial question: why was Gandhāran art so late?

We are all aware of good evidence which shows that Buddhism had an early influence in the region of Gandhāra, even if we take into consideration the fact that the archaeological evidence may not go as far back as expected.[5] However, an early Gandhāran school of art - contemporary to Bharhut, Bodhgayā, or early Amaravati - did not emerge.[6] Buddhism is not an exception here; neither Brahmanical representations, nor - and this is really astonishing - statues of *yakṣas* or *nāgas* have been recorded from Gandhāra. It is hardly imaginable that here, in the region associated with several narratives of *nāgas*[7] or *yakṣas* being subjugated by the Buddha,[8] such deities had not been worshipped. It is also hardly imaginable that the pan-Indian deities - primarily Kubera, the ruler of the North - were not venerated either. The protective deities must have been worshipped, but representations of these deities were not customary. The area, which will become one of the most prolific centres of Indian art in the second century AD - and where the *nāgas* are also depicted[9] - seems not to have an earlier artistic tradition.

[4] Faccenna 2007: fig. 7.41; Kurita 2003, I: figs. 245, 247; several examples in Van Lohuizen-de Leeuw 1981.

[5] The Dharmarājikā *stūpa* in Taxila, believed to be an Aśokan foundation, turned out to be a post-Mauryan monument, cf. Thapar 2012: 5.

[6] Cf. e.g. Rosenfield 2006: 22, 'Surprisingly, however, this was not the case in Gandhara. No significant works of art datable prior to the first century AD have been found there, even though excavations at Taxila and in the Swat Valley provide abundant evidence of Buddhist religious activity as early as the third century BC.'

[7] For the narrative of Apalāla of Swat cf. Zin 2006: no. 3.

[8] For Hārītī cf. Zin 2006: no. 2; the earliest literary sources naming Hārītī seems to be a Kharoṣṭhī inscription of Senavarma, king of Oḍi from the 1st century, cf. Hinüber 2003.

[9] Cf. Zin 2009; the massive statues of the *nāgas* were, however, never produced in the area.

It cannot be supposed that this lack of depictions can be traced back to a deficiency in the skills of the local artisans, but instead is probably due to the religious framework which prevented the development of visual arts. The framework here was evidently quite different from how it was in other areas of South Asia and is probably linked to the predominant supremacy of Brahmanism.

In his controversial book *Greater Magadha*, Johannes Bronkhorst points to the deep dissimilarities between the culture of this area and the Vedic culture of the 'land of the Āryas' (*āryavarta*) which was defined by the grammarian Patañjali (after 150 BC) as a region to the east of where Sarasvatī disappears, to the west of the Kālaka forest, south of the Himalayas, and north of the Pāriyātra mountains.[10] Even if the designation of the western and southern limits is not clear, it is evident that the *āryavarta* was limited to certain territory. This territory was expanding; in the second century AD, in the *Mānava Dharma Śāstra* 2.22, it is defined as the land between Himalaya and Vindhya reaching from the eastern to the western sea. Using an impressive number of quoted sources, Bronkhorst delivers several examples illustrating vast dissimilarities between the areas, and the intellectual culture of 'Greater Magadha' as area of emergence of heterodox movements. The distinctions are revealed through the language, as Māgadhī was apparently not easy to understand for people from other areas.[11] The differences in cultures can, according to Bronkhorst, be identified through several aspects, such as in the differing approaches to medicine, which was 'magico-religious, using sorcery, spells and amulets' in the west and 'empirico-rational' in the east (Zysk 1991; Bronkhorst 2007: 56-60). Another difference could be found in the funerary praxis: the *Śatapatha Brāhmaṇa* (13.8.1.5) orders sepulchral monuments in the form of the four-cornered burial places and adds: 'those who are of Asura nature, the Easterners and others, make them round (*parimaṇḍala*)'. The forms of the sepulchral monuments are indeed different in the west, a fact which is documented in representations in art.[12] The most important distinction in the culture of the 'Greater Magadha' makes its appearance in the territories of the religious movements based on a belief in rebirth and karmic retribution – a Sāṃkya philosophy, which is connected with the sage Rishi Kapila (*īśvaramaharṣi*), Ājīvikism, Jainism and Buddhism.

Bronkhorst's book faced critical opinions, such as for example the fact that there is no evidence to support the claim that all the changes and innovations leading to the appearance of heterodox movements based on a belief in rebirth came solely from the 'Greater Magadha' (Neelis 2008). This critique is convincing, and many of the features presented by Bronkhorst as Magadhan in nature might well stem from much a larger cultural group over a longer period of time. The present paper does not ask, however, about the 'Greater Magadha' but is concerned instead with its counterpart, the land of the Āryas. The intellectual culture of this land, as Bronkhorst has shown, stood in opposition to the outer world – including the 'Greater Magadha' and a much larger territory beyond them.

In Appendix VII of his book, *Brahminism in Gandhāra and Surrounding Areas*, Bronkhorst (2007: 357-362) lists some interesting references. The *Baudhāyana Śrautasūtra* (18.13) lists the names of the tribes which a Brahmin should not visit, and includes the land of the Gāndhāras in the north-west. This may be in agreement with the *Mahābhārata* (12.65.12ff) which describes Gandhāra as being beyond the system of *varṇas*. Patañjali describes the lands to the west of the Thar Desert as non-Brahmanical territory,

[10] *Vyākaraṇa-Mahābhāṣya* 1, p. 475 l. 3 (on Pāṇini 2.4.109; III p. 174 l. 7-8 (on Pāṇini 6.3.109), ed. F. Kielhorn, Bombay 1880-85; cf. Bronkhorst 2007: 1.

[11] *Jaiminīya Brāhmaṇa* 1.337-38; transl. Bodewitz 1990: 191, 'Now this Brahmadatta Caikitāneya was appointed Purohita by the king of the Kosalas Brahmadatta Prāsenajita. His (i.e. the king's) son talked like the Easterner. He (Caikitāneya) spoke: "This man (i.e. the son of the king) is not to be understood. Yoke my chariot. I shall come back." He went away.' Cf. Bronkhorst 2007: 8.

[12] Cf. Zin 2010, in Buddhist narrative reliefs from the first century BC until the third century AD there are several representations of Brahmanical *āśramas* characterized as such by representations of sepulchral monuments, apparently graves of the deceased teachers. In representations in Mathurā, the objects are square and similar to the 'pyramids' build till modern times in Nepal (De Marco 1987), while in other parts of India (preserved are representations in Sanchi and Andhra), the graves are round.

which he confirms by naming the Śakas and Yavanas as people living beyond this limit. According to the definition provided by Patañjali, Bronkhorst believes that Gandhāra does not belong to the *āryavarta*.

It appears, however, that the 'territory belonging to the *āryavarta*' and the region which was home to the extraordinary Vedic culture were not one and the same, as there is a great deal of evidence for a strong continued Brahmanical culture in this territory, as we can see, for example, in the narrative literature in which, particularly in the *jātakas*, Taxila is delineated as a centre of Vedic education.[13] As Witzel (2006: §2.1) has shown, Gandhāra played an outstanding role in the formation of the Vedic canonical tradition. Vedic texts, such as the *Kauṣītaki Brāhmaṇa* (7.7.36-39), present a picture of Gandhāra, or more generally, *udīcya/udīca*, 'northern', as a traditionally conservative area, where the 'best speech' could be found, and where one would send one's sons for study – a conviction which goes back to the *Upaniṣad* era (*Bṛhadāraṇyaka-Upaniṣad* 3.3, 7; cf. Witzel 2011: 493). Pānini, who, in his *Aṣṭādhyāyī,* formulated the Sanskrit grammar which remains normative today, came from this area, specifically, from the village of Śalātura at the convergence of the Kabul and Indus rivers (*ibid.* 494).

The seeming contradictions about Gandhāra in the records as both a 'non-Brahmanical territory' and as the area with 'best speech', where the *Aṣṭādhyāyī* was formulated and where 'one should send one's sons for study' seems to indicate a region dominated by isolation – not to say 'apartheid' – in which the extremely conservative authorities of Sanskrit and the Vedic culture held firm to their tradition notwithstanding the foreign surroundings.

Witzel (2011: 494) underlines the fact that Pāṇini knew the words for script, *lipi* or *libi*, and even for book, *grantha*, 'bound together', and yet composed his *Aṣṭādhyāyī*, consisting of extremely short formulas, for the oral tradition, meant to be learnt by heart. He states: 'Pāṇini composed his grammar right *inside* the Persian province of *Gandāra*. He lived in a culture that was aware of and used writing and books' (Witzel 2011: 494). One might suggest that such a conservative attitude towards scripts could also be indicative of a general approach which included the prohibition of visual illustrations. This would explain the lack of representations, an absence which appears to have existed beyond the timeframe of the Brahmanic religion when we call to mind the nonexistence of *yakṣa* and *nāga* statues as well as the late beginnings of the visual representations in Buddhism. The question of whether Butkara was early, or instead, the product of a local style, should perhaps be reformulated: was Butkara early because it was remote from Brahmanical centres?

The immediate reasons for the sudden and dramatic appearance of Gandhāran art are not known, but it appears that they were somehow related to the religious polity of the Kushan empire. One begins to feel as if the sculpture workshops were simply ready and waiting to produce art *en masse*. In fact, the objects themselves can be understood as testimony for the lack of an earlier Indian pictorial tradition in the area. The artists, whose aesthetic was that of the Mediterranean, were illustrating Buddhist or Hindu material. The art of Andhra under the Sātavāhanas also had a strong influence from the Mediterranean world;[14] let us therefore discuss western 'influences' in Gandhāra. The visual world of the Mediterranean was part of the area. It was not foreign. The question presented earlier could be simply repeated: why did the art of the region appear so late and not before Bharhut?

As we know, the art of Gandhāra used Mediterranean models to represent narrative content. The models are well-chosen, but interpreting the meaning of the depictions is not always a straightforward task as the representations are often based on associations with represented items which are not self-explanatory. As an example, we can examine the scene showing the approaching Buddha crossing the

[13] Cf. s.v. Takkasilā in Malalasekera 1937-38: vol. 1, 982-983.

[14] Cf. Stoye 2006; Zin 2015a-b; and works of Elisabeth Rosen Stone: e.g. 2006 and 2008, with references to the earlier research.

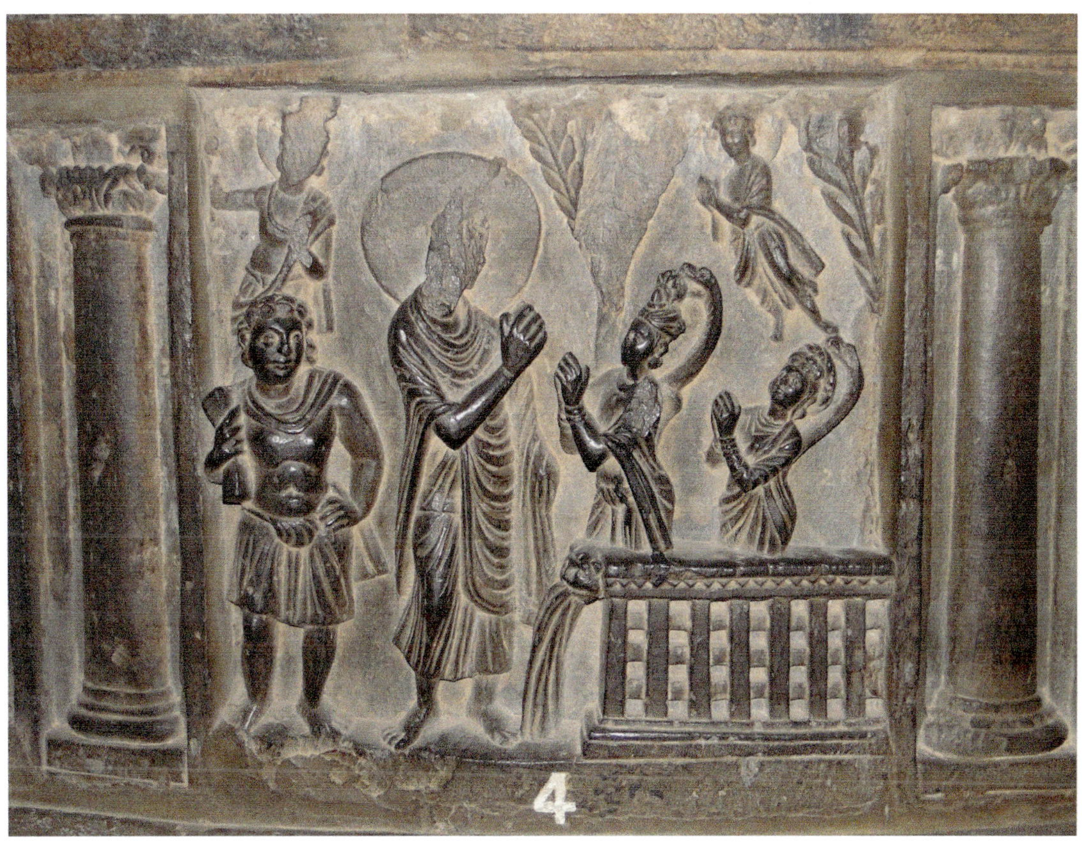

Figure 2. The Buddha crossing the river Nairañjanā. From Sikri. Lahore Museum, no. 1277, G-6. (Photograph by Muhammad Hameed.)

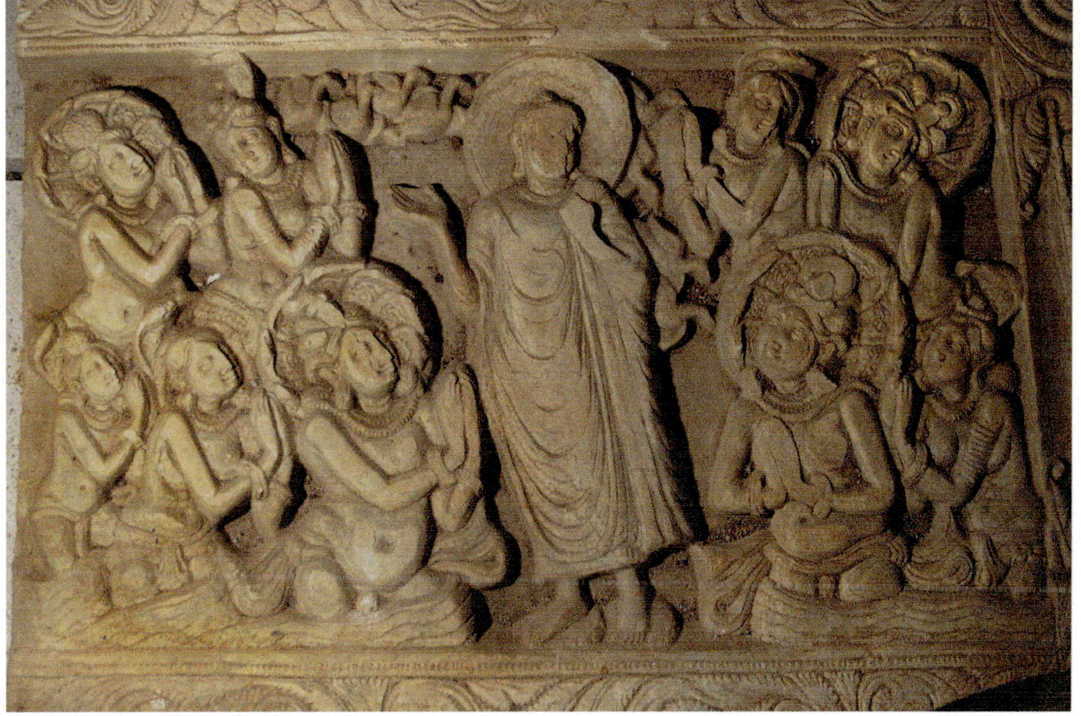

Figure 3. The Buddha crossing the river Nairañjanā. Nagarjunakonda, Archaeological Site Museum, no. 614 (depot). (Photo: Wojtek Oczkowski.)

river Nairañjanā on his way to the tree of enlightenment.[15] The story tells us that Kālika, the *nāgarāja*, emerged from the river and praised the Buddha with a song. What we see (Figure 2)[16] is the Buddha standing on dry ground in front of a fenced-in enclosure, inside which we see a couple of *nāgas* standing and a tree (it is possible that the tree is behind the enclosure). The *nāgas* emerge here from a well, which stands a substitute for the river. The identification of the enclosure as a well is suggested by means of the Graeco-Roman fountain placed on the fence, which has the form of a lion's head with water flowing from the lion's open mouth. The crossing of the river is not depicted at all, and only the western pictorial element indicating water makes it possible for us to recognize the episode. A comparison with a depiction of the same occurrence from Nagarjunakonda (Figure 3)[17] underscores the skills of the Andhran artists: the well or other adaptations from the West were not necessary here. The future Buddha stands surrounded by the *nāgas* who are emerging from floods of water. For the artists in Andhra, the representation of the episode was unquestionably less problematic than for their colleagues from Gandhāra. It should not surprise us, as the iconography of *nāgas* emerging from water had already been used in an early relief in Kanaganahalli.[18]

It is a generally known fact that Gandhāra was adopting pictorial motifs from the West, but Gandhāra was, of course, also adopting elements from the art of the subcontinent. One should be aware of the fact that even fundamental elements, such as the preaching gesture of the Buddha, the so-called *dharmacakrapravartanamudrā*, were used in Andhra generations earlier than they were in Gandhāra (cf. Zin forthcoming a; Zin forthcoming b), however, this particular gesture was never used there in representations of the Buddha. This gesture, clearly denoting teaching, was used in representations of monks, or for Vidhura, preaching to the *nāgas*.[19] The representation can be found as early as Kanaganahalli.[20]

Often, Gandhāran artisans were not inventing but rather incorporating pictorial elements to create their own sophisticated visual language. We can, however, also find examples documenting experimentation with new forms once the iconography was already established. One peculiar late example - apparently one of a kind - was discovered in the Hyderabad area (Figure 4).[21] The relief, showing the birth of the Buddha, is unquestionably an adaptation from Andhra (Figure 5),[22] but it is modified for the Gandhāran viewer. Queen Māyā is standing in the 'Gandhāran way', with the right side of the body exposed towards the gods; she is holding the branch of a tree with her right hand (in Andhra, the gods always stand on the side where her arm is held akimbo). The gods, carrying a long fabric, are - as is always the case in Andhra - four in number. However, the first of the gods is Indra (wearing his characteristic crown), as it is Indra in Gandhāran reliefs who receives the new-born Bodhisatva. The biggest alteration is the new-born himself, who was never depicted in Andhra in person. It is an astonishing object of art, providing, once again, a testimony to Gandhāra's ability to generate its own formula from adopted forms.

As we can observe in Figure 4, the legacy of early Gandhāran artists adopting the forms and re-using them to represent specific narrative contexts continues in later examples. This also seems to be the case

[15] For the literary sources cf. Vogel 1926: 97-102; Zin forthcoming a.

[16] Sikri, Lahore Museum, no. 1277, G-6; illustrated e.g. in: Kurita 2003, I: fig. 202.

[17] Nagarjunakonda, Archaeological Site Museum, no. 614 (depot); illustrated in Yaldiz 1992: no. 16; Rama 1995: pl. 18.

[18] Kanaganahalli, slab no. 10, *in situ*. Illustration: Aramaki, Dayalan & Nakanishi 2011: 67; Poonacha 2011: pl. 40; Zin forthcoming c: no. 7(7), pl. 5 (drawing).

[19] For comparison of Gandhāra and Andhra cf. Zin forthcoming a.

[20] Kanaganahalli, slab no. 57, *in situ*. Illustration: Aramaki, Dayalan & Nakanishi 2011: 90; Poonacha 2011: pl. 80; Zin forthcoming c: no. 2(2), pl. 2 (drawing).

[21] The image here is taken from the database of the Leiden University Libraries, 1034, P-036683, where it is labelled 'Birth of the Buddha, Tul Mir Rukhan', apparently meaning Thul-Mir-Rukhan, Hyderabad District in Sindh. I would like to thank Dr Gudrun Melzer (Munich) for bringing this relief to my attention.

[22] Amaravati, Archaeological Site Museum, no. 19; illustrated by Rosen Stone 1994: fig. 72.

in the group of reliefs whose narrative content has been a matter of scientific controversy for generations.[23] The most beautiful example is the famous stela of Mohammed Nari (Figure 6).[24] The traditional explanation for such reliefs, provided by Foucher (1909), and enduring in further research (e.g. Schlingloff 1991; 2015: 50-68), sees in them representations of the miracle of Śrāvastī in which the Buddha - to defend the heretics and for the salvation of hundreds of people - performed a miracle in which he multiplied himself. The explanation is convincing if one sees the reliefs as a continuation of the earlier models depicting the Buddha surrounded by radially ordered emanations, as such representations are found on the stelae in Mohammed Nari in both upper corners. Several other details in the stela correspond precisely with descriptions of the Śrāvastī miracle in the texts,[25] for example, that the Buddha was performing the miracle while sitting on a lotus with a stem made of precious stones which was being held by the *nāgas*.

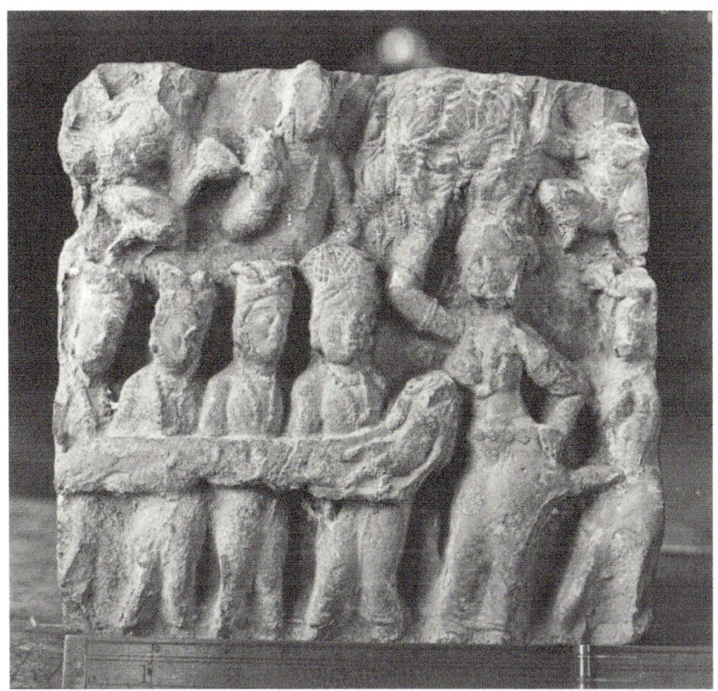

Figure 4. Relief of the birth of the Buddha from Thul-Mir-Rukhan, Hyderabad District, Sindh. (Photo: Leiden University Libraries, 1034, Kern Collection, P-036683, with kind permission of the Friends of the Kern Institute.)

Both the stela from Mohammed Nari as well as similar reliefs contain, however, several details which do not correspond with descriptions of the Miracle of Śrāvastī nor in general with the literary tradition of the Śrāvakayāna Buddhism: there, we see preaching bodhisatvas and bodhisatvas holding a book that is displaying the iconography of the Bodhisatva Mañjuśrī. Explanations of the stela using the textual tradition of the Mahāyāna or of the Mahāyāna imagery (i.e. not connected with any

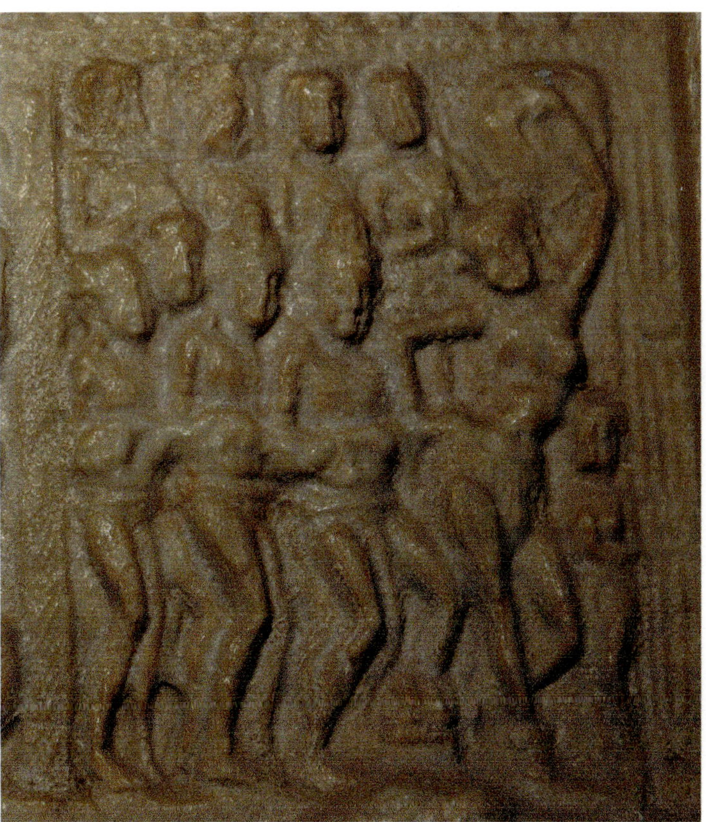

Figure 5. Birth of the Buddha. Amaravati, Archaeological Site Museum, no. 19. (Photo: Wojtek Oczkowski.)

[23] Summary of the previous research in Rosenfield 2006: 20-21; Harrison & Luczanits 2011: 71-72.

[24] Lahore Museum, no. 1135, G-155; illustrated e.g. in Kurita 2003, I: fig. 395; Harrison & Luczanits 2011: figs. 1-4.

[25] Cf. e.g. *Divyāvadāna* XII: 143-166; transl. Rotman 2008: 253-287.

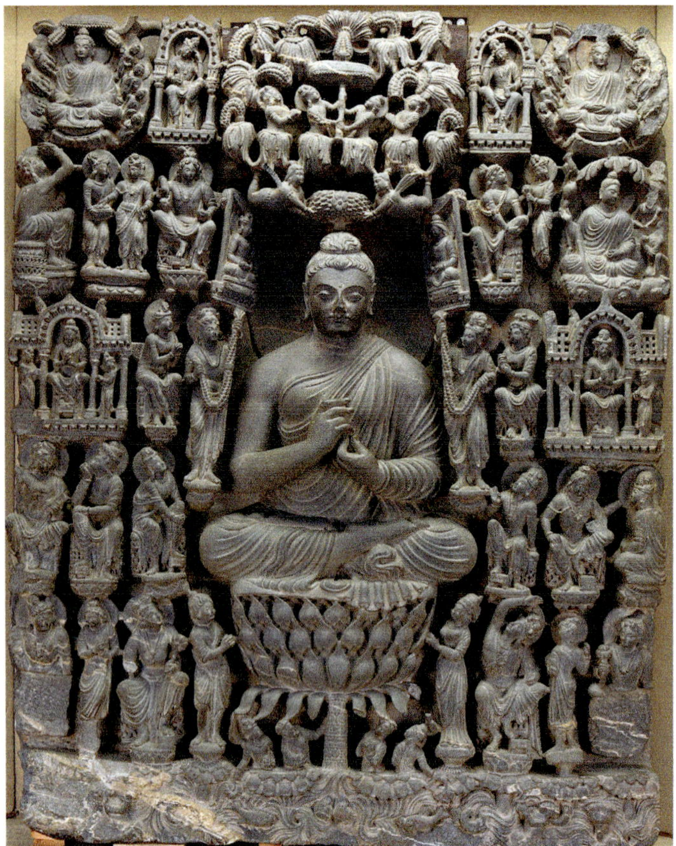

Figure 6. Relief Mohammed Nari. Lahore Museum, no. 1135, G-155. (Photo: Muhammad Hameed.)

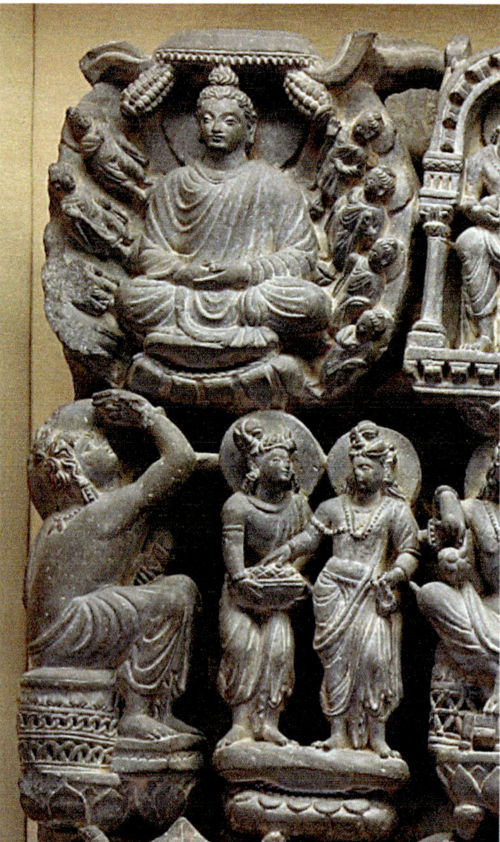

Figure 6a. Detail of Figure 6.

particular text) fit very well with the representations.[26] One gets a feeling that it is not possible to come up with generalizing explanations of such representations, or of representations of triads of a Buddha and two accompanying bodhisatvas. There are cases (Figure 7)[27] in which the difficult conversions represented on the pedestal – the subjugation of Apalāla and the conversion of Aṅgulimāla – provide a clear link to suggest that the teaching Buddha in the middle is Śākyamuni performing the great miracle through which he will convert hundreds of people (Zin 2006: 7-8). On the other hand, other representations give us nothing which could constitute a barrier to identifying them as depictions of Amitābha flanked by Avalokiteśvara and Mahāsthāmaprāpta – giving them the meaning such representations have in Tibet or China. It appears that the connotation of the reliefs has been changed, even if the form remains that of the tried-and-tested visualisation of the Śrāvastī miracle. The Mohammed Nari stela incorporates an element which seems to point a finger for us. The upper left corner (Figure 6a) shows the miracle with emanations around the central Buddha and a person with their right arm held above their head. The same gesture is repeated by a male person sitting to the right of the lotus (from the viewer's perspective) of the main Buddha.

The gesture – which is in fact self-explanatory – is documented in Indian culture as a sign of desperation,[28] and it is repeated many times in exactly the same context by defeated heretics watching

[26] Huntington 1980; Miyaji 2002; Rhi 2008a-b; Harrison & Luczanits 2011.

[27] From Sahrī Bahlol; Peshawar Museum, no. 02770 (158); illustrated e.g. in Kurita 2003, I: fig. 403; Rosenfield 2006: fig. 1.3; *Gandhara. Das buddhistische Erbe Pakistans* 2008: 275; Zin 2006: 7, figs. 1-2.

[28] Cf. Schlingloff's 'Index of Pictorial Elements' of the Ajanta paintings, in Schlingloff 2000 and 2013, II: no. 135, 'Being horrified'.

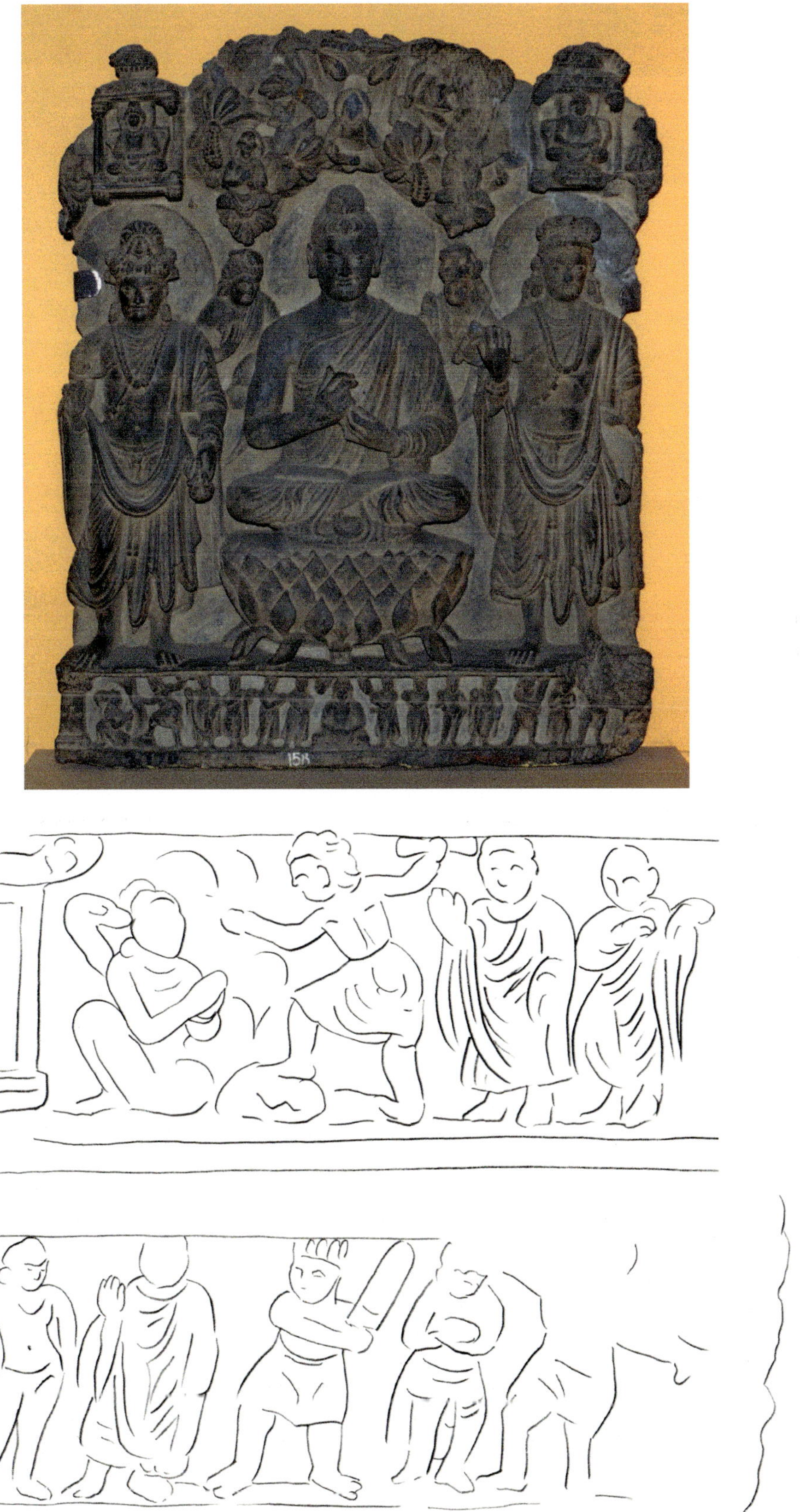

Figure 7. Buddha triad stela from Sahri Bahlol. Peshawar Museum, no. 02770 (158). (Photo: Muhammad Hameed.)

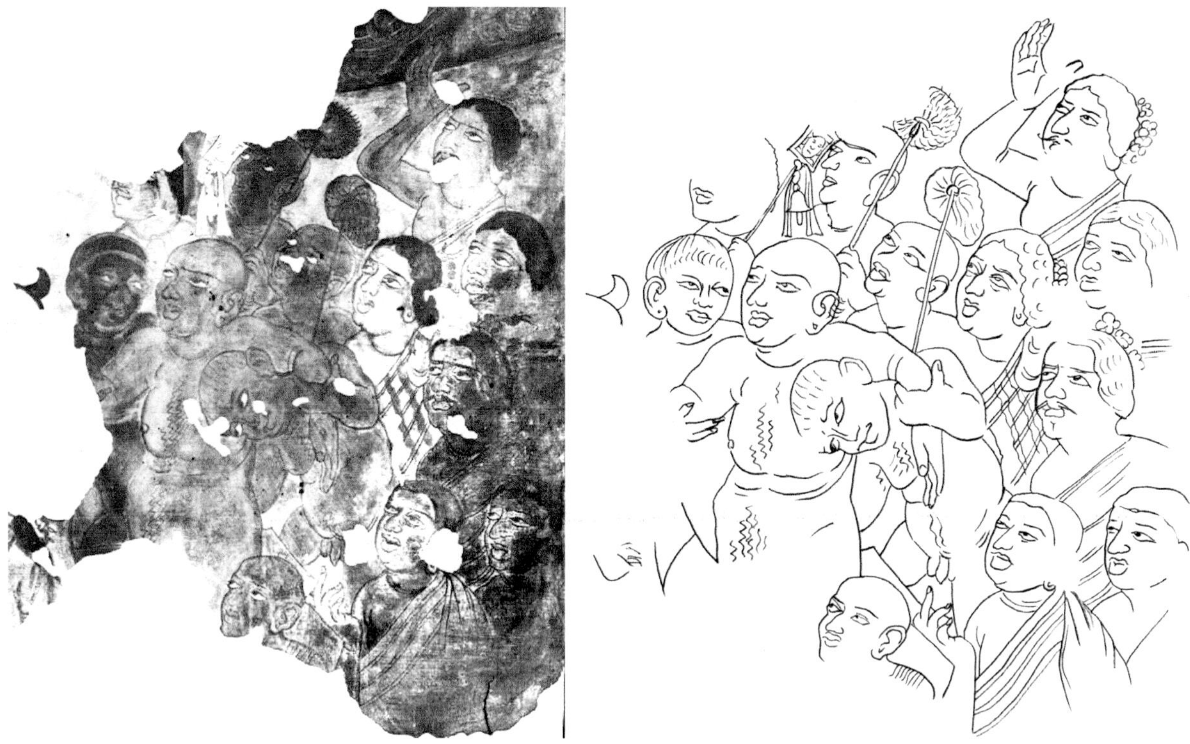

Figure 8. Miracle of Śrāvastī. Ajanta, cave XVII, antechamber, right side wall. (Griffiths copy no. 17 M, photograph in India Office, vol. 70, no. 5972, 5977.)

Figure 8a. Drawing of Figure 8 by Monika Zin.

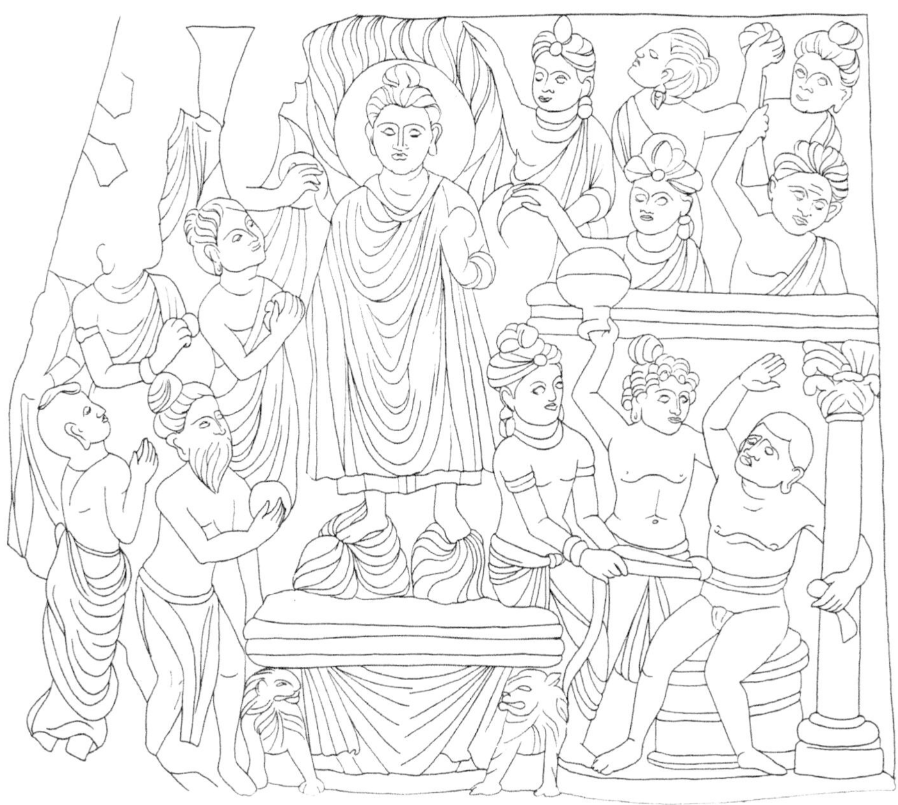

Figure 9. Relief in private collection in Japan. Drawing after Schlingloff 2000/2013, II: p. 101 [47].

the Great Miracle (Figure 8),[29] including examples from Gandhāra (Figure 9).[30] The only difference is that the two persons in the Mohammed Nari stela are not heretics, but instead bodhisatvas adoring the Buddha. They are represented as richly ornamented with heads surrounded by nimbi. Their gesture is apparently a remnant of the older iconography of the Śrāvastī miracle, while the Buddha in the middle or the representation of the emanations might now have a different meaning, and illustrate the Buddha Amitābha or Akṣobhya.[31] We should probably stop searching for a textual tradition that directly and entirely corresponds with the representations. Just as we will never find a source describing the Nāgarāja Kālika emerging from a well with a fountain in the form of a lion face, the literary sources for stelae, like the one from Mohammed Nari, most likely never existed. The representations are probably utilizing the visual phenomena and not the literary descriptions, giving them new meanings. Sometimes, one has the impression that the literary works – such as the 'Appearing of the Tathāgata' quoted by Rhi[32] which recounts the appearance of the great lotus ornamented with jewels which the Buddha, surrounded by adoring gods, is sitting on – are themselves secondary, and describe the art objects. If we were to go back to the beginnings of such pictorial representations we might, generations earlier, find depictions of the miracle of Śrāvastī.

Even in its form and composition, the stela from Mohammed Nari has a different character than the narrative reliefs. What it shows is, first and foremost, the Buddha, even if he is surrounded by scenes. The form is shifting the general function of the object from the narrative to the devotional. Furthermore, the physical form of the relief is not that of the familiar bearers of narrative scenes (such as 'false niche') which were located on the domes of *stūpas*; the relief was probably standing inside a shrine – this is all the more likely when considering the excellent state of preservation (Rhi 2011). The art of Gandhāra produced earlier specimens – which might perhaps be understood as preliminary stages of this manner of representation – standing somewhere between an illustration of a narrative and an image meant for worship. Taddei (1993) makes a distinction between 'narrative representation' and 'icon'. We can think, for example, about the Buddha with the converted Kāśyapa ascetic who can be depicted so small that he only reaches to the Buddha's knees,[33] so that the sculpture primarily features the Buddha; the narrative subjects are reduced to a less important addition. One might risk making a general statement, and surmising that the character of the Gandhāran reliefs was developing from narrative to devotional. This seems to be true for later representations as well, which still carry narrative content, such as in the case of the *parinirvāṇas* which turn into massive implementations – the form which will be adopted by other art centres, including in Central Asia (cf. Behrendt 2016).

While reading Gandhāra as a source of iconography for other areas, it is of greatest importance to establish which forms or – as in the case of the Miracle of Śrāvastī vs. Sukhāvatī – which meanings had already been established in Gandhāra. It seems that many of the pictorial patterns are creations of Gandhāra, although this cannot always be demonstrated. I once presented the hypothesis that there must have been later Gandhāran art which is no longer extant. It might be useful briefly to repeat the thesis from my paper on the 'lost Gandhāran School of Paintings' (Zin 2013), written as a contribution to Central Asian studies, as it is relevant to the aim of the paper at hand – analysing Gandhāra in the context of other schools of Buddhist art.

[29] Ajanta, cave XVII, antechamber, right side wall; cf. Schlingloff 2000 and 2013, I: 514, no. 92; illustrated in Yazdani 1930-55, IV: pls. 42-44.

[30] Private Collection in Japan; illustrated in Brancaccio 1991: fig. 1.

[31] Cf. Harrison & Luczanits 2011: 112-13, for possibilities of different explanations.

[32] Rhi 2008b: 258; T 278, vol. 9, 613b-614a.

[33] Cf. Karachi, National Museum, no. P 1865, illustrated e.g. in Ingholt 1957: fig. 437; Kurita 2003, I: fig. 312; Peshawar Museum, nos. 1373 and 1378, illus.: Ingholt 1957: figs. 87-88; Kurita 2003: fig. 310.

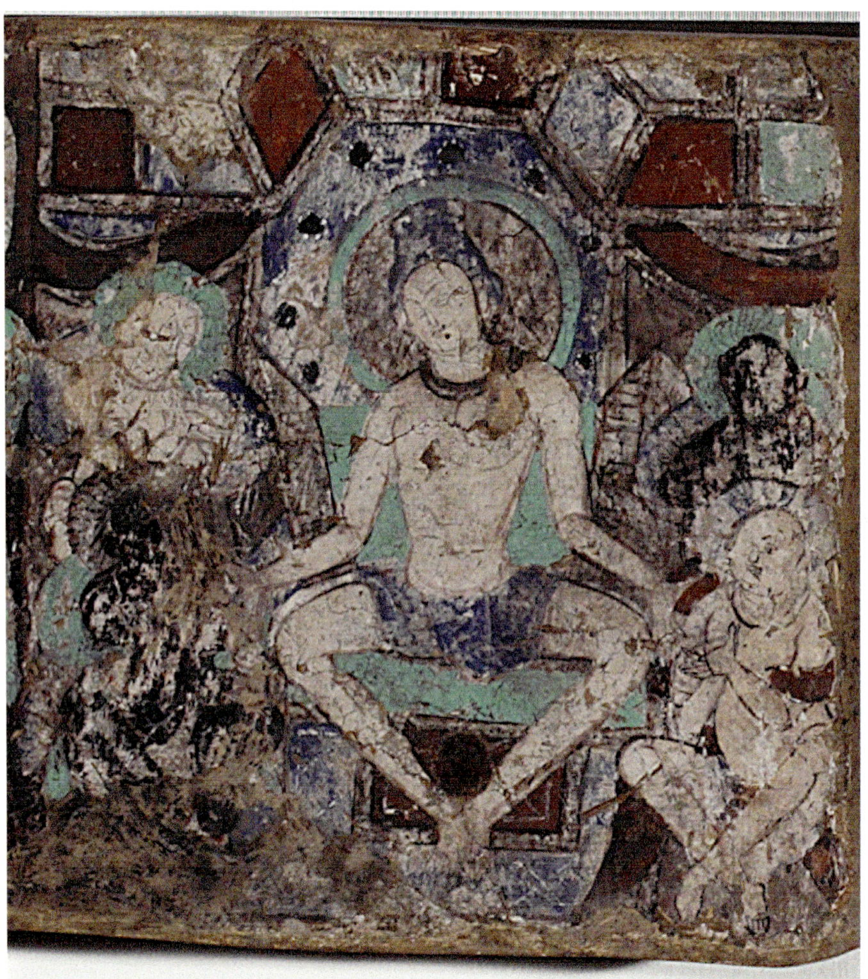

Figure 10. Painting from Kizil, cave 184(?): Maitrībalajātaka. (Photo: copyright Staatliche Museen zu Berlin, Museum für Asiatische Kunst, no. III 8888; by Jürgen Liepe.)

To state that the art of Central Asia comes from that of Gandhāra is to state an oft-repeated truism. When making more precise comparisons between Gandhāra and the paintings of Kucha and trying to adjust for Kucha as continuation of Gandhāra, the issue is, however, far from being simple. What we know today does not make it possible for us to date the earliest Kuchean paintings (in what is known as the first Indo-Iranian style) any earlier than the second half of the fifth century. At this time, Gandhāra was still active, but no longer producing representations of *jātakas*, or scenes from the Buddha's life; such pictures were absolutely typical of Kucha. We can not only conclude that a gap of some hundred years lies between similar representations in both regions, but also observe that development took place during that time. This development is most observable in representations of the *jātakas*. In Kucha, the (human) Bodhisatvas in *jātaka* stories are, as a rule, depicted with nimbi. In the Gandhāran reliefs, we encounter a nimbus in a late representation of Viśvantara.[34] The biggest difference between representations of the *jātakas* in Gandhāra and in Kucha manifests itself in the composition of the scenes. While in Gandhāran reliefs, the Buddha in his former existence was never placed in the middle of the composition (even when the *jātaka* was only represented in one scene), in Kucha the Bodhisatva is most often placed in the centre. The representations of the *jātakas* in Kucha often use a composition which is reserved for

[34] Cf. Viśvantara in the British Museum, acc. no. 1913,1108.21, illustrated e.g. in Zwalf 1996: fig. 139; Kurita 2003, II: pl. 846.

the Buddha only in Gandhāra (Figure 10).[35] There, the Bodhisatva of a *jātaka* is placed in centre of the composition; he is shown with a nimbus, and is also larger than the other figures. These figures are arranged around him, frequently revealing different episodes from the narrative in the conflated mode of representation, in the same manner as, for example, the *Māravijaya* is depicted.

Because such compositions of the *jātaka* representations do not appear in the Gandhāra reliefs (which is true of all of Indian art) one might think that they are an invention of Kuchean artists. However, in all probability this is not the case. One surviving painting from Gandhāra (Figure 11)[36] displays all the characteristics of a 'Bodhisatva-centric' composition; the longish eyes of the central person signal the Gupta period. The painting represents the *Śibijātaka*. King Śibi, with his head surrounded by a large nimbus, is placed in the centre of the composition. The dove is represented at least twice: sitting on the king's lap and sitting on the scale-pan. It is possible that the dove was represented once more while escaping from the falcon (there are still some lines visible in front of the bird of prey). To the (viewer's) right we see the scene depicting the cutting of the king's flesh and the man with the scales. The figure of an old man with long hair standing in a sort of entryway(?) on the left side is striking. The man is stretching his right hand towards the king in a demanding gesture. Such a personage does not belong in the story of King Śibi giving his flesh to the falcon to save the dove. It is evident that the person, apparently a begging Brahmin, illustrates an additional line of the narrative. One might conceive that it is a representation of the general generosity of the king towards all those in need. Might it also, perhaps, be a particular Brahmin? Perhaps the Brahmin who claimed King Śibi's eyes?[37] The idea seems odd as it is a story from another *jātaka*, i.e. another incarnation of the future Buddha Śākyamuni. The idea appears less illogical once we are familiar with the paintings of Kucha which often work with highly complex visual conventions and can represent, for example, not only the preaching Buddha but also the context of his sermon in the very same pictorial unit. The paintings occasionally show individuals in two different incarnations in the same picture – such as in the story of the *nāga* Elapatra (Figure 12).[38] In the story, as a punishment for destroying leaves of the *ela* plant during his existence as monk during the lifetime of the Buddha Kāśyapa (upper right corner), the *nāga* Elapatra was reborn with the *ela* plant on his head, which caused severe pain (lower left corner, the *nāga* is represented twice here, in his animal form with a tree growing on his head and in his human-like form with cobra hoods).

Such sophisticated pictorial language was only partially an invention of Kuchean painters; most of the methods already existed in Gandhāra. It is only possible to understand these methods when comparing them with Kucha. The comparative analysis, for example, of the representations of the *Parinirvāṇa* (Zin forthcoming d) demonstrates that, in Gandhāra, the scenes around the dying Buddha show different time periods and different places from the narrative in one pictorial unit; individual figures might even be substituted for one another.

If we are aware of the use of such refined and highly conventionalized methods, it appears conceivable that the painting of King Śibi from Gandhāra could be a combination of two narratives into one depiction.

The Gandhāran model for painting King Śibi was repeated in Kucha (Figure 13)[39] and in Dunhuang (Figure 14).[40] The Brahmin, stretching the hand towards the king, also appears in the last representation (lower right side), demonstrating that the genius of Gandhāra is responsible not only for the composition of the pictures but also for the manner of representation which intertwines different re-births as well as different stories.

[35] *Maitribalajātaka*, Kizil, cave 184(?). Staatliche Museen zu Berlin, Museum für Asiatische Kunst, no. III 8888; illustrated in: Le Coq & Waldschmidt 1928: pl. 2.14; *Kizil Grottoes* 1983-85, III: fig. 207.

[36] Kyoto, Ryukoku Museum (depot); illustrated in Kurita 2003, II: fig. 868 (without right part); Zin 2013: fig. 3.

[37] For the representation of the story in Ajanta XVII cf. Schlingloff 2000 and 2013, II: 233-237, no. 49; comparative material in the paintings in Kucha, II: 46.

[38] Kizil, cave 206 (Foot-Washing Cave); Berlin, Asian Art Museum, no. III / IB 8649/2.

[39] Kizilgaha, cave 13; illustrated in *Mural Paintings in Xinjiang of China: Kucha* 2008: fig. 327; Zin 2013: fig. 2.

[40] Dunhuang, cave 254; illustrated e.g. in *Mogao Grottoes of Dunhuang* 1980-82, I: fig. 32; Zin 2013: fig. 1.

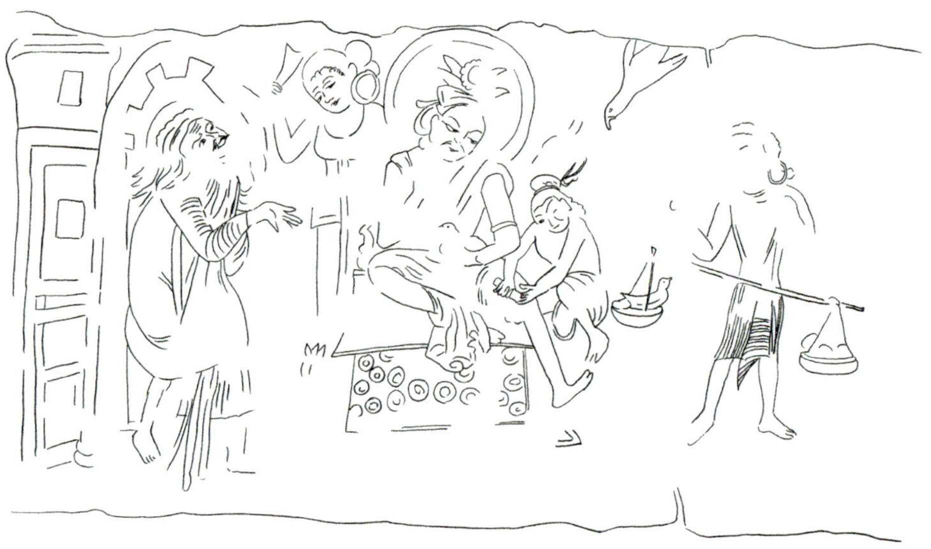

Figure 11. Painting of the Śibijātaka from Haḍḍa? Kyoto, Ryukoku Museum (depot). (Drawing by Monika Zin.)

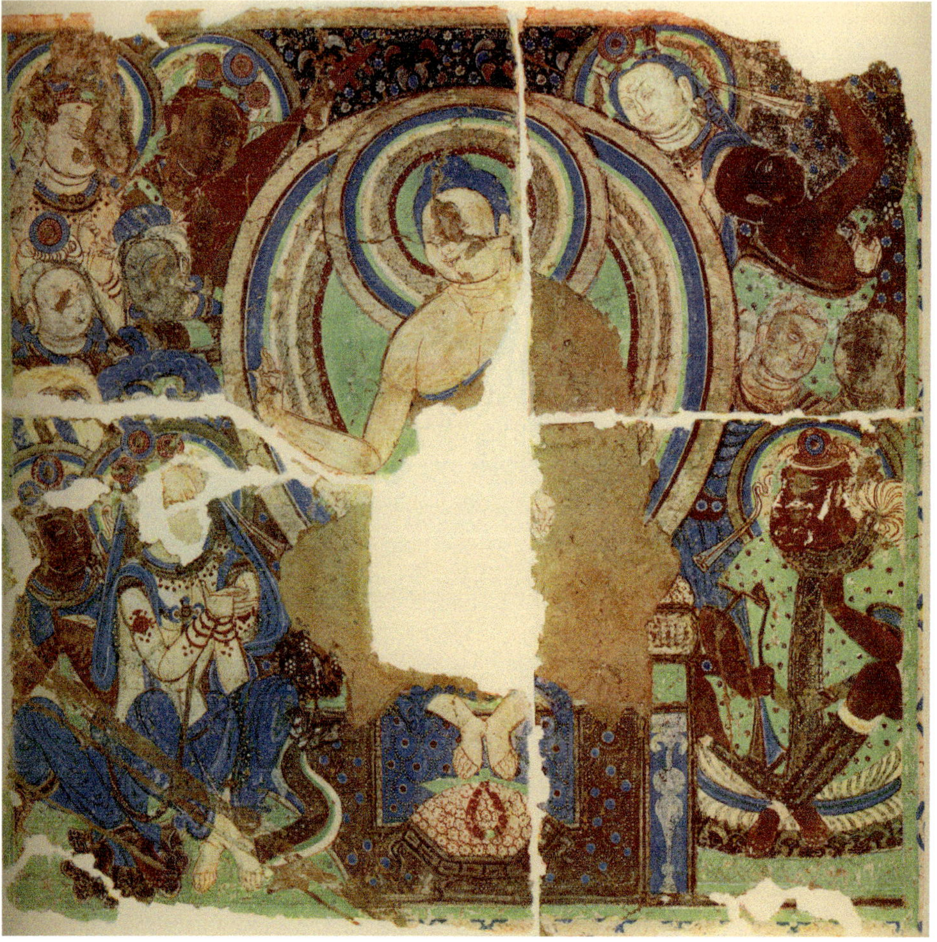

Figure 12. Painting from Kizil, cave 206 (Foot-Washing Cave) showing the story of the nāga Elapatra. Staatliche Museen zu Berlin, Museum für Asiatische Kunst, no. III / IB 8649/2 (partially lost in World War II. (After Grünwedel 1920, pl. 28-29.)

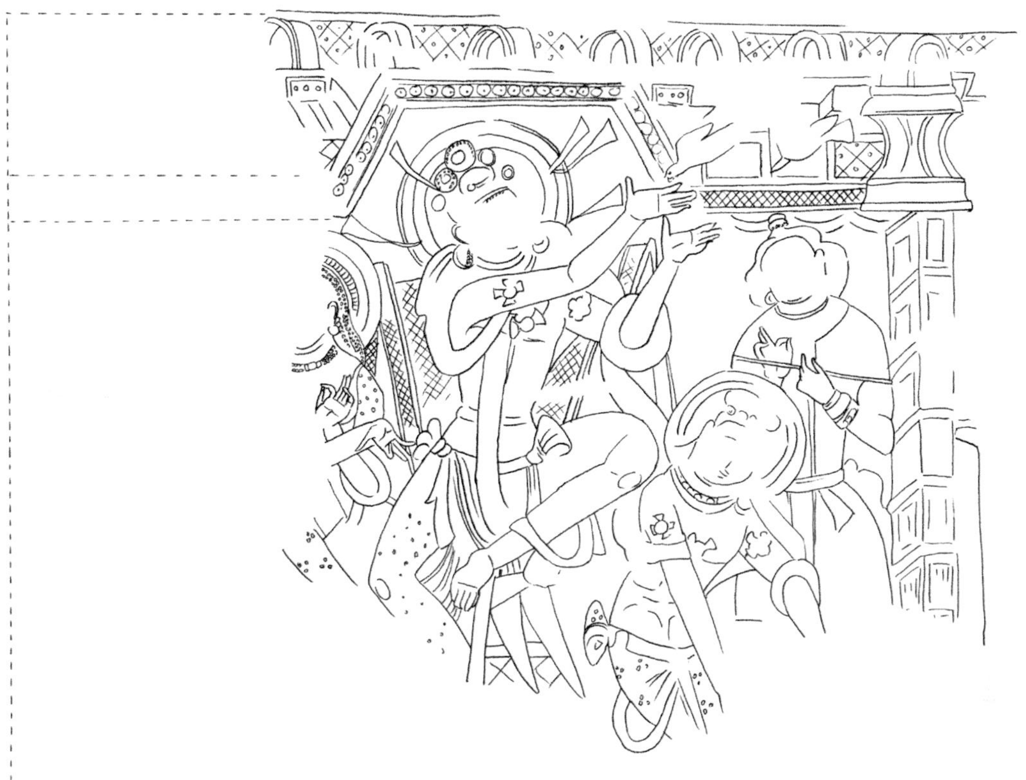

Figure 13. Painting of the Śibijātaka at Kizilgaha, cave 13. (Drawing by Monika Zin.)

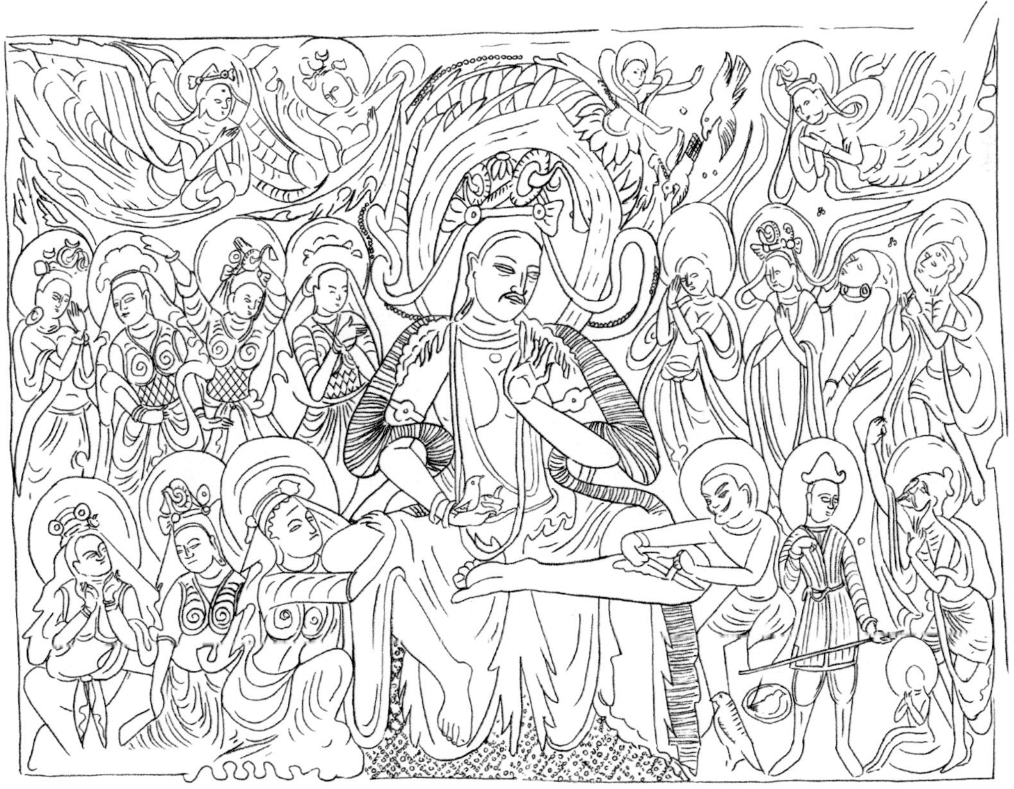

Figure 14. Painting of the Śibijātaka at Dunhuang, cave 254. (Drawing by Monika Zin.)

References

Aramaki N., Dayalan D. and Nakanishi M. 2011. *A New Approach to the Origin of Mahāyānasūtra Movement on the Basis of Art Historical and Archaeological Evidence. A Preliminary Report on the Research*, Grant-in-Aid for Scientific Research, The Japan Society for Promotion of Science, Project (C) no. 20520050.

Arlt R. 2016. Kunsthistorisch-philologische Untersuchung des Bildprogramms am Satavahana-zeitlichen Stupa von Chandavaram. MA thesis, LMU Munich.

Behrendt K. 2016. Evidence for the Diffusion of Gandharan Forms after the late 5th Century. Pages 407-416 in V. Lefèvre, A. Didier and B. Mutin (eds), *South Asian Religions and Visual Forms in their Archaeological Context. South Asian Archaeology and Art 2012. Proceedings of the 21st International Conference of the European Association for South Asian Archaeology and Art, Paris, 2-6 July 2012.* Vol. 2. Turnhout: Brepolis.

Bodewitz H.W. 1990. *The Jyotiṣṭoma Ritual, Jaiminīya Brāhmaṇa 1, 66-364, Introduction, Translation and Commentary.* (Orientalia Rheno-Traiectina). Leiden: Brill

Brancaccio P. 1991. The Buddha and the Naked Ascetics in Gandharan Art, A New Interpretation. *East & West* 41: 121-31.

Bronkhorst J. 2007. *Greater Magadha: Studies in the Culture of Early India.* (Handbook of Oriental Studies Series 19). Leiden: Brill.

Carter M.L. 1993. Petroglyphs at Chilas II: Evidence for a Pre-Iconic Phase of Buddhist Art in Gandhara. Pages 349-366 in A.J. Gail & G.J.R. Mevissen (eds), *South Asian Archaeology 1991. Proceedings of the 11th International Conference of the Association of South Asian Archaeologists in Western Europe, Berlin, 1-5 July 1991.* Stuttgart: Franz Steiner.

De Marco G. 1987. The Stūpa as a Funerary Monument: New Iconographical Evidence. *East & West* 37: 191-246.

Faccenna D. 1962-64. *Sculptures from the Sacred Area of Butkara*, = Is.M.E.O., Reports and Memoirs, 2.2-3, Photographs: F.Bonardi; Descriptive Catalogue: M. Taddei, Rep. Mem. (Series Maior II.2-3). Rome: Istituto Poligrafico dello Stato, Libreria dello Stato.

Faccenna D. 2007. The Artistic Center of Butkara I and Saidu Sharif I in the Pre-Kuṣāṇa Period. Pages 165-199 in D.M. Srinivasan (ed), *On the Cusp of an Era, Art in the Pre-Kuṣāṇa World.* Leiden: Brill.

Foucher A. 1909. Le 'grand miracle' du Buddha à Śrāvasti. *Journal Asiatique* 2:1-78. English version: The Great Miracle at Çrâvastî. Pages 147-184 in A. Foucher, *The Beginnings of Buddhist Art.* Paris: Paul Geuthner and London: Humphrey Milford, 1917 (repr. Varanasi, 1972).

Gandhara. Das buddhistische Erbe Pakistans. Legenden, Klöster und Paradiese, 2008. Bonn & Mainz: Kunst- und Ausstellungshalle der Bundesrepublik Deutschland & Philipp von Zabern.

Griffiths J. 1896-97. *The Paintings in the Buddhist Cave-Temples of Ajanta, Khandesh, India* (2 volumes).London: W. Griggs (repr. New Delhi, 1983).

Harrison P. & Luczanits C. 2011. New Light on (and from) the Muhammad Nari Stele. Pages 69-127 and plates 197-207 in *Nendo dai ikkai, kokusai shinpojiumu puroshīdingusu: Jōdokyō ni kansuru tokubetsu kokusai shinpojiumu.* (BARC International Symposium Series 1: Special International Symposium on Pure Land Buddhism). Kyoto: Ryukoku University Research Center for Buddhist Cultures in Asia.

Hinüber O. von 2003. *Beiträge zur Erklärung der Senavarma-Inschrift = Abhandlungen der Akademie der Wissenschaften und der Literatur, Geistes und sozial wissenschaftliche Klasse.* Mainz: Akademie der Wissenschaften und der Literatur.

Huntington J.C. 1980. A Gandharan Image of Amitāyus' Sukhāvatī. *Annali dell' Istituto Universitario Orientale* 40: 652-672.

Ingholt H. 1957, *Gandhāran Art in Pakistan.* (With 577 illustrations photographed by Islay Lyons and 77 pictures from other sources. Introduction and Descriptive Catalogue by Harald Ingholt). New York: Pantheon Books (repr. 1971).

The Kizil Grottoes, 1983-85, vols. 1-3, *The Grotto Art of China*, Tokyo: Heibonsha.

Kurita I. 2003. *Gandhāran Art (An revised and enlarged edition)*. (Ancient Buddhist Art Series 1-2). Tokyo: Nigensha.

Le Coq von A. & Waldschmidt E. 1928. *Die buddhistische Spätantike in Mittelasien = Ergebnisse der Kgl. Preussischen Turfan Expeditionen, VI, Neue Bildwerke II*. Berlin: Dietrich Reimer Verlag (repr. Graz, 1975).

Lohuizen-de Leeuw J.E. van 1981. New Evidence with Regard to the Origin of the Buddha Image. Pages 377-400 in H. Härtel (ed), *South Asian Archaeology 1979. Papers from the 5th International Conference of the Association of South Asian Archaeologists in Western Europe*. Berlin: Dietrich Reimer Verlag.

Malalasekera G.P. 1937-38. *Dictionary of Pali Proper Names*, 1-2. London: Pali Text Society.

Marshall J. 1960. *The Buddhist Art of Gandhāra: The Story of the Early School, Its Birth, Growth and Decline*. (Memoirs of the Department of Archaeology in Pakistan 1). Cambridge: Cambridge University Press (repr. 1980).

Miyaji A. 2002. Syaeijo no Jinpen to Daijo Bukkyo Bijutsu no Kigen [The Miracle of Srāvastī" and the origin of Mahāyāna Buddhist Art]. *Bigaku Bijutsushi Ronshu* 20: 1-27.

Miyaji A. 2008. Aspects of the Earliest Buddha Image in Gandhāra. Pages 25-42 in C. Bautze-Picron (ed), *Miscellanies about the Buddha Image, South Asian Archaeology 2007. Proceedings of the 19th International Conference of the European Association of South Asian Archaeology* (BAR International Series 1888). Oxford: Archaeopress.

Mogao Grottoes of Dunhuang, 1980-82, vol. 1-5, *The Grotto Art of China*. Tokyo.

Mural Paintings in Xinjiang of China: Kucha, Zhongguo Xinjiang Bihua: Qiuci, 2008, Urumchi: Xinjiang Meishu Sheying Chubanshe.

Neelis J. 2008. Review of Johannes Bronkhorst. Greater Magadha: Studies in the Culture of Early India (2007). *Journal of the Royal Asiatic Society*, 18/3: 381-383.

Poonacha K.P. 2011. *Excavations at Kanaganahalli (Sannati, Dist. Gulbarga, Karnataka).* (Memoirs of the Archaeological Survey of India 106). Delhi: Archaeological Survey of India.

Rama K. 1995. *Buddhist Art of Nāgārjunakoṇḍa*. Delhi: Delhi Sundeep Prakashan.

Rhi J. 2008. Komplexe Stellen. Großes Wunder, Paradies oder göttliche Erscheinung?. Pages 254-259 in: *Gandhara. Das buddhistische Erbe* Pakistans. *Legenden, Klöster und Paradiese*. Bonn & Mainz: Kunst- und Ausstellungshalle der Bundesrepublik Deutschland & Philipp von Zabern.

Rhi J. 2008a. Changing Buddhism. Pages 242-248 in *Gandhara - the Buddhist Heritage of Pakistan: Legends, Monasteries, and Paradise*. Mainz: Philipp von Zabern.

Rhi J. 2008b. Complex Steles: Great Miracle, Paradise, or Theophany. Pages 254-259 in *Gandhara - the Buddhist Heritage of Pakistan: Legends, Monasteries, and Paradise*. Mainz: Philipp von Zabern.

Rhi J. 2011. Wondrous Vision: the Muhammad-Nari Stele from Gandhara. *Orientations* 42/2: 112-115.

Rosenfield J.M. 2006. Prologue: Some Debating Points on Gandhāran Buddhism and Kuṣāṇa History. Pages 9-37 in P. Brancaccio & K. Behrendt (eds), *Gandhāran Buddhism, Archaeology, Art, Texts*. Vancouver and Toronto: UBC Press.

Rosen Stone E. 1994. *The Buddhist Art of Nāgārjunakoṇḍa.* (Buddhist Tradition Series 25). Delhi: Motilal Banarsidass.

Rosen Stone E. 2006. The Amarāvatī Master: Spatial Conventions in the Art of Amarāvatī. Pages 51-60 in A. Banerji (ed) *Hari Smriti: Studies in Art, Archaeology and Indology: Papers Presented in Memory of Dr. Haribishnu Sarkar*. ii. New Delhi: Kaveri Books.

Rosen Stone E. 2008. The Sculpture of Andhra Pradesh and Roman Imperial Imagery. Pages 100-106 in P. Chenna Reddy (ed), *Krishnabhinandana: Archaeological, Historical and Cultural Studies, Festschrift to Dr. V. V. Krishna Sastry*. New Delhi: Research India Press.

Rotman A. 2008. *The Divine Stories, Divyāvadāna Part I*. (Classics of Indian Buddhism). Boston: Wisdom Publications.

Schlingloff D. 1991. Yamakaprātihārya und Buddhapiṇḍī in der altbuddhistischen Kunst. *Berliner Indologische Studien* 6-7: 109-51.

Schlingloff D. 2000. *Ajanta - Handbuch der Malereien / Handbook of the Paintings 1. Erzählende Wandmalereien / Narrative Wall-paintings*. Wiesbaden: Harrassowitz Verlag.

Schlingloff D. 2013. *Ajanta - Handbook of the Paintings 1. Narrative Wall-paintings*. New Delhi: IGNCA.

Schlingloff D. 2015. *Die Übermenschlichen Phänomene. Visuelle Meditation und Wundererscheinung in buddhistischer Literatur und Kunst. Ein religionsgeschichtlicher Versuch.* (Buddhismus-Studien 7). Düsseldorf: EKO-Haus der Japanischen Kultur e.V.

Srinivasan D.M. (ed) 2007. *On the Cusp of an Era, Art in the Pre-Kuṣāṇa World.* Leiden: Brill.

Stoye M. 2006. Māyā Anadyomene' – die schöne Śākya-Fürstin beim Bade. Zum Import einer etablierten Bildformel in ein erzählendes Relief aus Amarāvatī. Pages 224-34 in K. Bruhn & G.J.R. Mevissen (eds), *Vanamālā, Festschrift Adalbert Gail.* Berlin: Weidler.

Taddei M. 1993. *Arte narrativa tra India e mondo* ellenistico. (Conferenze IsMEO Series, 5). Rome: ISIAO.

Taddei M. 2006. Recent Archaeological Research in Gandhāra: the New Evidence. Pages 41-59 in P. Brancaccio & K. Behrendt (eds) *Gandhāran Buddhism, Archaeology, Art, Texts.* Vancouver and Toronto: UBC Press.

Thapar R. 2012. Aśoka: A Retrospective. Pages 17-37 in P. Olivelle, J. Leoshko and H.P. Ray (eds), *Reimagining Aśoka, Memory and History.* Delhi: Oxford University Press.

Vogel J.P. 1926. *Indian Serpent-Lore or the Nāgas in Hindu Legend and Art.* London: A. Probsthain.

Witzel M. 2006. Brahmanical Reactions to Foreign Influences and to Social and Religious Change. Pages 457-499 in P. Olivelle (ed), *Between the Empires: Society in India between 300 BCE and 400 CE.* Oxford: Oxford University Press.

Witzel, M. 2011. Gandhāra and the Formation of the Vedic and Zoroastrian Canons. Pages 490-532 in J. Rotaru (ed), *Traveaux de symposium international. Le Livre. La Roumanie. L'Europe. Troisième edition, 20-24 Septembre 2010. Tome III. Etudes euro- et afro-asiatiques.* Bucharest: Bibliothèque de Bucarest.

Yaldiz M. (ed) 1992. *Palast der Götter, 1500 Jahre Kunst aus Indien.* Berlin: Reimer.

Yazdani G. 1930-55. *Ajanta, The Colour and Monochrome Reproductions of the Ajanta Frescoes Based on Photography* (4 volumes). London: Oxford University Press [repr. New Delhi, 1983].

Mural Paintings in Xinjiang of China: Kucha, Zhongguo Xinjiang Bihua: Qiuci, 2008, Urumchi: Xinjiang Meishu Sheying Chubanshe.

Zin M. 2006. *Mitleid und Wunderkraft. Schwierige Bekehrungen und ihre Ikonographie im indischen Buddhismus.* Wiesbaden: Harrassowitz.

Zin M. 2009. The Water Tank from Gandhara. Pages 7-21 in G. Bhattacharya, G.J.R. Mevissen and A. Banerji (eds), *Prajñādhara - Essays on Asian Art, History, Epigraphy and Culture in Honour of Gouriswar Bhattacharya.* New Delhi: Kaveri Books.

Zin M. 2010. Brahmanische Asketengräber. Pages 1075-1098 in S. Dieter, E. Franco & M. Zin (eds), *From Turfan to Ajanta, Festschrift for Dieter Schlingloff on the Occasion of his Eightieth Birthday.* Rupandehi: Lumbini International Research

Zin M. 2011. The Identification of Kizil Paintings V (9. The Painted Dome from Simsim and its Narrative Programme; 10. Elapatra). *Indo-Asiatische Zeitschrift* 15: 57-69. Repr. as pages 253-270 in Shashibala (ed), *Sanskrit on the Silk Route.* Delhi: Bharatiya Vidya Bhavan, 2016.

Zin M. 2013. Buddhist Narrative Depictions in Andhra, Gandhara and Kucha – Similarities and Differences that Favour a Theory about a Lost 'Gandharan School of Paintings'. Pages 35-66 in A. Miyaji (ed), *Gandhara, Kucha no Bukkyo to Bijutsu, i, [Kokusai Symposium "Silk Road no Bukkyo Bunka - Gandhara, Kucha, Turfan" 2012. 11.3-5, Ryukoku Daigaku, Seika Houkokusho I].* Kyoto: Ryukoku Daigaku.

Zin M. 2015a. Buddhas Löwenstimme und das römische Wagenrad, Buddhistische Kunst im Reich der Satavahanas. *Antike Welt* 5: 51-56.

Zin M. 2015b. Nur Gandhara? Zu Motiven der klassischen Antike in Andhra (incl. Kanaganahalli). *Tribus, Jahrbuch des Linden-Museums, Stuttgart* 64: 178-205.

Zin M. Forthcoming a. Gandhara and Andhra: Varying Traditions of Narrative Representations (Some Observations on the Arrangement of Scenes Citing the Example of the Bodhisatva crossing the River Nairañjanā). *Indo-Asiatische Zeitschrift.*

Zin M. Forthcoming b. Gandhara Iconography: Dissemination and Impact. In J. Pons (ed), *Gandhara: De l'Oxus au Ganges. Etudes en l'honneur de Francine Tissot Actes du colloque en l'honneur de Francine Tissot organisé par Jessie Pons et Osmund Bopearachchi, à l'Ecole Normale Supérieur, Paris, le 8 juin 2013*. Paris: Brepols.

Zin M. Forthcoming c. *The Kanaganahalli Stupa: An Analysis of the 60 Massive Slabs Covering the Dome.*

Zin M. Forthcoming d. Some Details from the Representations of the Parinirvāṇa Cycle in the Art of Gandhara and Kucha: The Iconography of the Wandering Ascetics (Parivrājika, Nirgrantha and Ājīvika), in *Art and Religions in Pre-Islamic Central Asia, Proceedings of the Conference, Polish Institute of World Art Studies*. Torun: Tako.

Zwalf V. 1996. *A Catalogue of the Gandhāra Sculptures in the British Museum*. London: British Museum Press.

Zysk K. G. 1991. *Asceticism and Healing in Ancient India, Medicine in the Buddhist monastery*. New York and Oxford: Oxford University Press.

On the relationship between Gandhāran toilet-trays and the early Buddhist art of northern India

Ciro Lo Muzio

Although there are reasons to suspect that they might have had nothing to do with cosmetics, an alternative and unanimously accepted denomination for Gandhāran 'toilet-trays' is still lacking. For this reason, in this paper I will refer to them using the traditional, though unsatisfactory name.

What we are certain of is that they are a class of artefacts peculiar to Gandhāra, and that their chronology is far from being settled. They are commonly understood as dating from before, perhaps not long before, the inception of Gandhāran Buddhist art, but there are reasons to think that part of this production might have been coeval with Gandhāran sculpture.

Their formal layout and the thematic repertoire of the subjects worked in relief on their inner face has been described and classified in a number of studies.[1] The patently classical inspiration of the themes and motifs depicted in a fairly good number of specimens has made 'toilet-trays' particularly appealing to Western scholars. Along with mythological scenes, sometimes linked with or hinting at Dionysism, there are ritual ceremonies, banquets, and single symbolic figures or motifs, above all the Nereid mounted on a sea-monster. A significant number of trays, however, do not show any straightforward relationship with classical imagery, thus inviting us to search for suitable parallels elsewhere, a stimulus which has so far received a much weaker response. It seems that the search for Alexander's legacy is still a polarizing factor.

Another debated question, as anticipated in the first lines of this paper, is the very function of these artefacts: the assumption that they are to be understood as cosmetic trays goes back to John Marshall (1951, I: 190; II: 493), after whom they have been labelled 'toilet-trays', or equivalent formulas in other languages, by the majority of authors. Marshall's hypothesis gained further support from Henri-Paul Francfort, author of one of the first comprehensive studies on the topic (Francfort 1979), who restated their cosmetic function, dismissing any direct link with religion.

Since then other authors, including myself, have dealt with toilet-trays pointing out iconographic elements, which seem to refer to the eschatological realm or to marriage, or both. More recently, the scope of the discussion has been enriched by Harry Falk, who offers interesting arguments for linking Gandhāran 'libation trays', as he proposes to name them, with the ritual sphere (Falk 2010). Falk's hypothesis is perhaps more in keeping with the general orientation of the subjects, but leaves room for further elaboration with regard to the specific context – funerary rites or marriage or otherwise – in which they might have been used.

In an article of a few years ago (Lo Muzio 2011), I argued that the evaluation of the classical component in the iconography, in the style, and in the workmanship of Gandhāran toilet-trays is perhaps not the best method to reach safe results in chronology, especially when one keeps to the assumption that the classical component basically (or exclusively) stems from the Indo-Greek cultural layer, as seems to be the case with the majority of scholars who have dealt with toilet-trays.

[1] Marshall 1951, II: 493-498; Francfort 1979; Dar 1979; Tanabe 2002; Lo Muzio 2002; 2011; Falk 2010; Pons 2011.

Based on George Erdosy's reassessment of the chronology of Taxila (as formulated by John Marshall) (Erdosy 1990), I made some remarks on the chronology of the toilet-trays unearthed in Sirkap, a significant sample of the whole evidence at our disposal, that I will summarize as follows:

1. No toilet-tray can be dated with certainty before the end of the Indo-Greek period; we are therefore left to wonder if it still makes sense to situate the beginning of this 'minor art' during Greek rule (Lo Muzio 2011: 338).

2. The bulk of Sirkap toilet-trays were found in layers IV to I, a chronological span extending from the reign of Azes I (mid-first century BC) to the epoch of the Great Kushans. A point which is worth being stressed is that the highest concentration of finds (nineteen toilet-trays) was recorded in layer II, which covers the first century AD and the first two or three decades of the second; if our understanding of the chronology of Gandhāran art is correct, then these toilet-trays are coeval with Gandhāran Buddhist sculpture; furthermore, a Roman component in their classical repertoire should not therefore be ruled out (Lo Muzio 2011: 338-339).

One may question the accuracy of John Marshall's digging method and stratigraphies, as of any other excavation carried out in the early twentieth century, yet the Sirkap specimens are the source of the few objective data – an ascertained place of provenance and a chronological span, however approximate it may be – that we have at our disposal for Gandhāran toilet-trays altogether.

As announced in the title, the aim of this paper is to highlight elements of a so far unnoticed or underrated iconographic relationship, along with their possible chronological implications, between Gandhāran toilet-trays and the art of Bharhut, Bodhgayā, Sanchi (more specifically, Stūpa 2), and Mathurā. All these sites are traditionally held as emblematic examples of Buddhist architecture and art of the second – early first centuries BC, and historically related with the Śunga dynasty. Both assumptions, however, are now disputed: the historical relationship with the Śungas is no longer taken for granted, and, broadly speaking, the chronological framework in which the sites have been distributed is being reconsidered on epigraphic and art-historical grounds (see further below).

I will focus on a selection of toilet-trays unearthed at Sirkap (Taxila), plus a few cognate specimens from other Gandhāran sites, which share style, workmanship, and a rather limited range of thematic choices – drinking couples or animals – most often set on the background of a lotus blossom (or a half-lotus). They form a coherent group, which is probably to be attributed to a single workshop (or to related workshops) and is the expression of a specific social and/or ethnic group, possibly – as I guess – of Śaka origin. An important point to underscore is that the *origin* of the motifs I will deal with is not at issue: most of them (especially the zoomorphic repertoire, except for the elephant) were part of a remote Greek or Western Asian legacy, which, through the Achaemenians, had some impact on South Asian architecture and sculpture well before Alexander the Great's heirs established their power in the Gandhāran area. What matters most to me is to point out the occurrence of certain motifs in Gandhāran toilet-trays and in the art of northern Indian Buddhist sites, to highlight their iconographic and formal similarities as well as the peculiar combinations in which they can appear. The following overview will hopefully bring evidence of a closer relationship between early Gandhāran art and the traditions of the Gangetic plain, also from a chronological viewpoint.

I will start with one of the leading motifs, the full-blown lotus flower, which often appears on the backside of the trays and, in a significant part of the specimens we know, on the inner surface as well. Being meant for containing something, even if we do not know what exactly, toilet-trays never show the lotus in its complete shape, as there are usually one or more lintels splitting the tray into discrete decorated and undecorated portions. There are a number of combinations, one of the most frequent

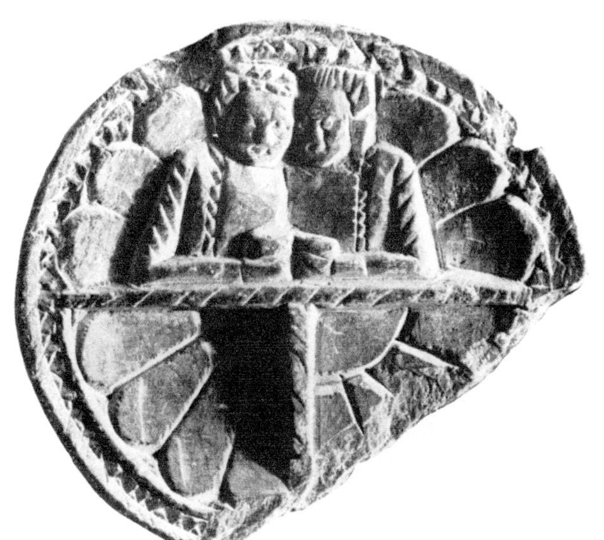

Figure 1. Toilet-tray: drinking couple, Sirkap. Taxila Museum. (After Francfort 1979: pl. XXXI, no. 62, courtesy of DAFA)

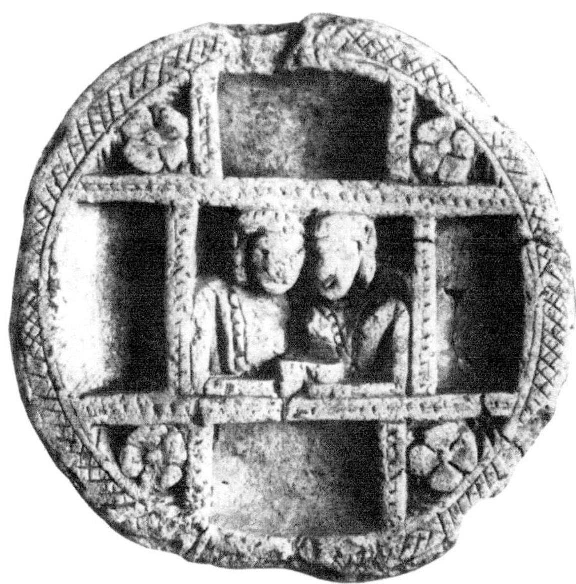

Figure 2. Toilet-tray: drinking couple. Location unknown. (After Francfort 1979: pl. XLI, no. 82, courtesy of DAFA)

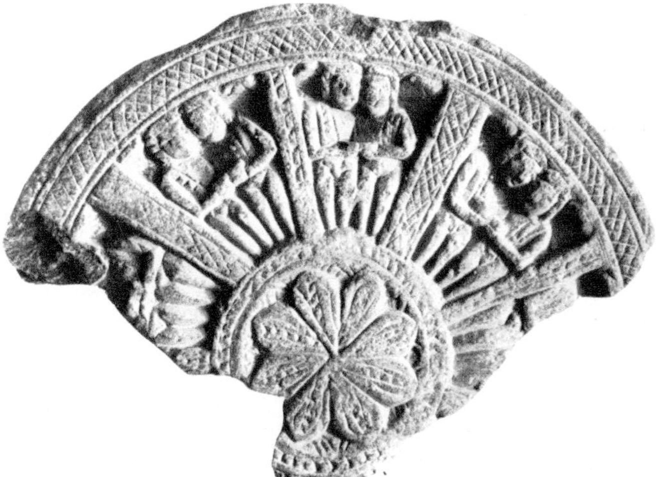

Figure 3. Toilet-tray: drinking couple. Taxila Museum. (After Francfort 1979: pl. XXXVIII, no. 77, courtesy of DAFA)

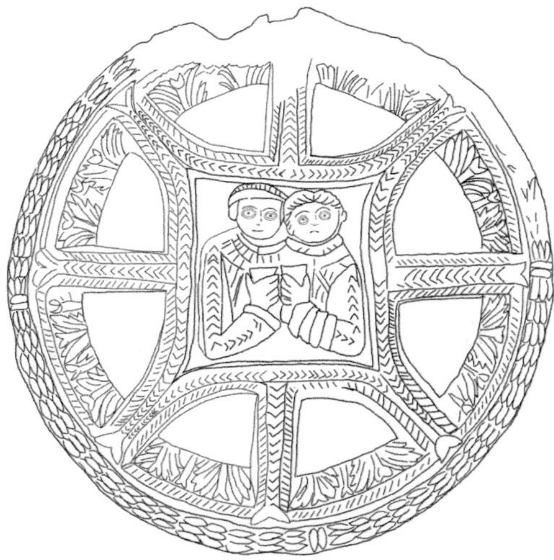

Figure 4. Toilet-tray: drinking couple. Unknown provenance. London, British Museum. (Drawing by Ciro Lo Muzio.)

shows a couple (or one or more animals) represented in the upper half of the tray (Figure 1); a more elaborated layout consists of a grid based on a cruciform pattern, with the couple (or animal) appearing in the central square (Figure 2).[2] An interesting variant is provided by a few specimens in which the lotus takes the shape of a solar symbol with a row of drinking couples, either as full standing figures or as busts, arranged in the spaces between the rays (Figure 3); a more emphatic solar twist is shown by the layout of a specimen of unknown provenance, now in the British Museum, which for iconography and workmanship seems to fit in the Sirkap group (Figure 4).

[2] See also Francfort 1979, XLI: no. 83, from the Taxila area. To the same typology belongs a toilet-tray from Uḍegrām (Swat), showing three human busts (Taddei 1966; Francfort 1979: pl. XL, no. 83).

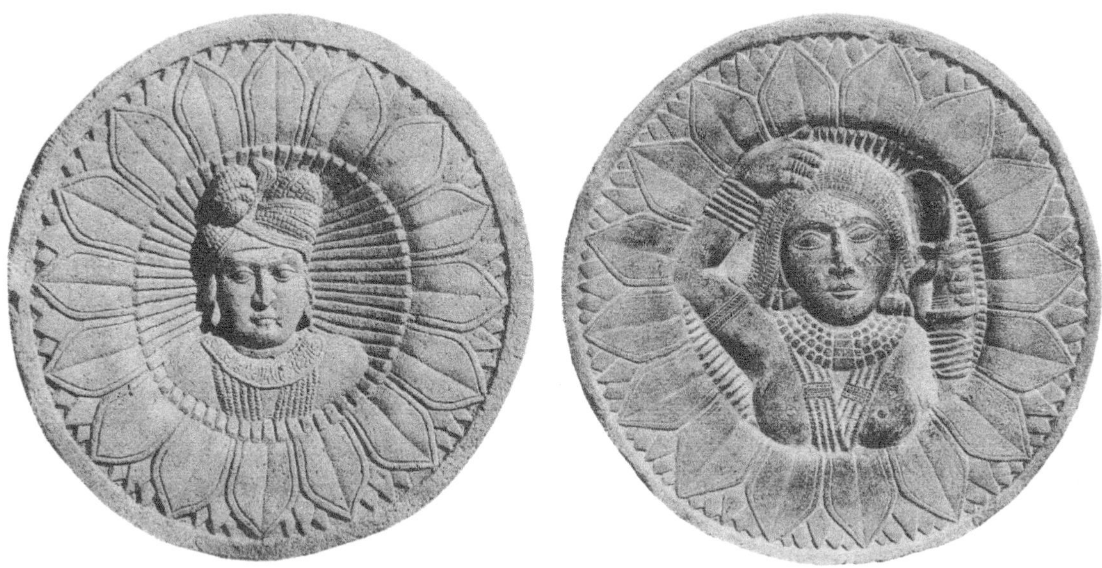

Figure 5. Two medallions of the Bharhut stūpa railing with a human bust on the background of a lotus flower: a man (left) and a woman holding a mirror (right). Kolkata, Indian Museum. (After Coomaraswamy 1956: pl. 38, 112 and 114.)

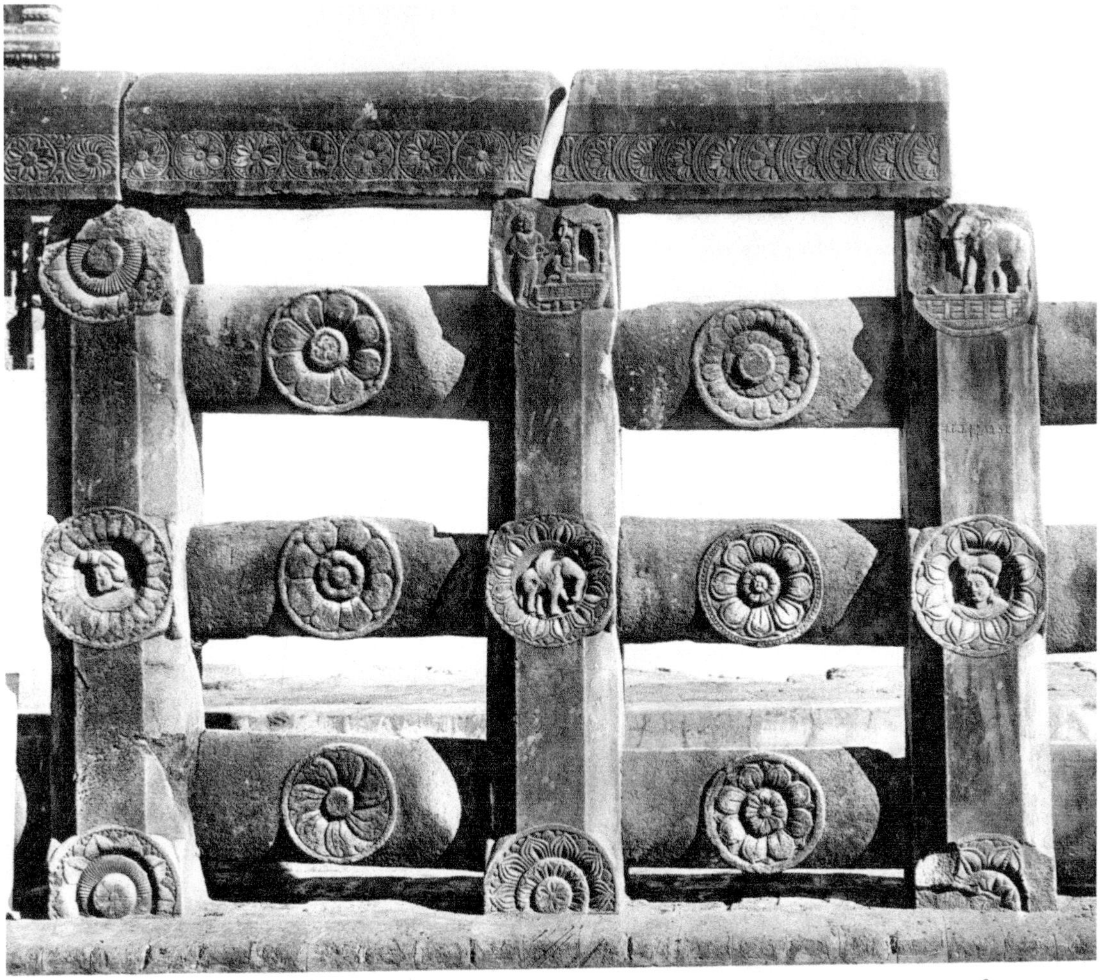

4 3 2

Figure 6. Part of the Bodhgayā railing. After Coomaraswamy 1935: pl. II.)

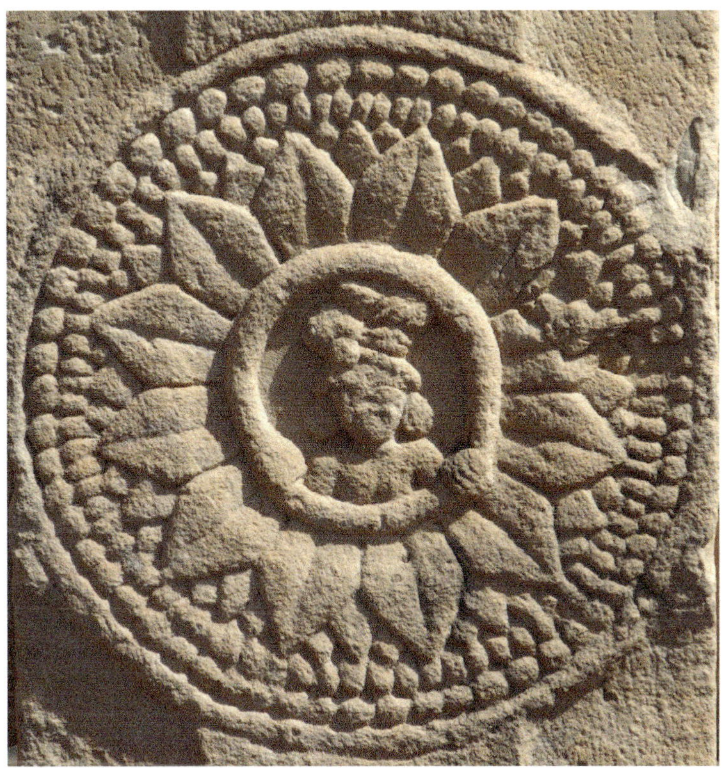

Figure 7. Sanchi, Stūpa 2, vedikā: medallion showing a male bust on the background of a lotus flower. (Photo: courtesy of Flavia Zaghet.)

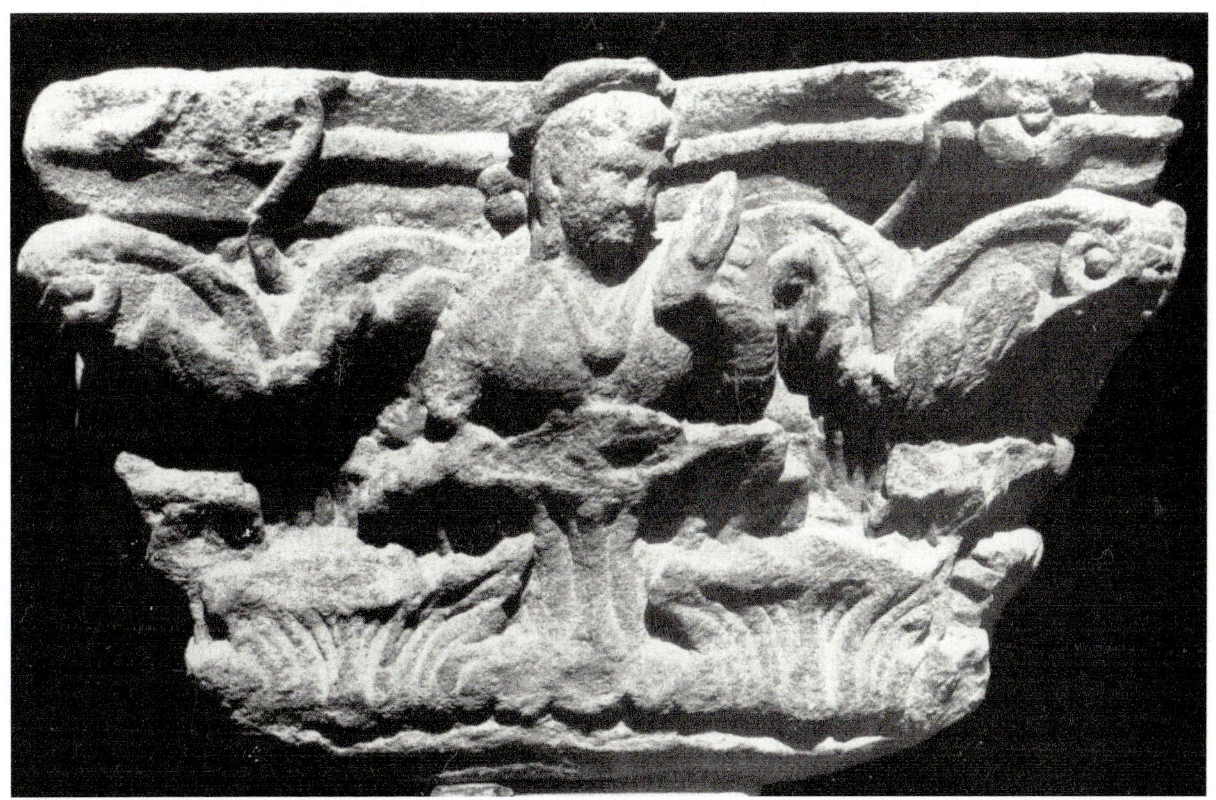

Figure 8. Butkara, Indo-Corinthian capital with human bust: a woman holding a mirror. (After Faccenna 1962-64: II/3, pl. DXLIX.)

The lotus is largely employed in the Gandhāran ornamental repertoire too, most often in scrolls or in combination with garlands, whereas, if used as an isolated pattern, it mostly appears in diminutive scale, if compared with the Indian practice. What matters most, however, is that all the subjects we have listed above can be found in Gandhāran sculpture as well, but *not* on the background of an open lotus blossom. On the contrary, this combination was much in favour at Bharhut (Figure 5), Bodhgayā (Figure 6), and, although to a lesser extent, at Sanchi 2 (Figure 7) and Mathurā (Quintanilla 2007: 71, figs. 66, 67). It seems as if, in Gandhāran sculpture, the pattern of the human bust emerging from a lotus flower was transferred into a different setting, i.e. the pseudo-Corinthian capitals, with busts emerging from the acanthus leaves (Figure 8).[3]

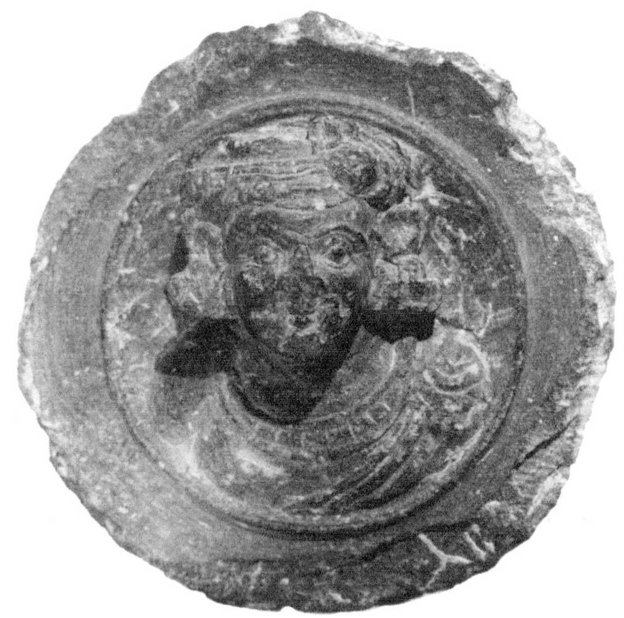

Figure 9. Toilet-tray(?) from Bārāma (Swat). (Photo: Courtesy Italian Archaeological Mission in Pakistan.)

As I anticipated, the toilet-trays belonging to this group regularly show a couple, whereas in northern India we typically find the bust of a single personage, either male or female. Nonetheless, there is at least one artefact of ascertained provenance, a toilet-tray or, more likely, a sort of medallion (diam. 7 cm.), from Domenico Faccenna's excavations at Bārāma, in the Swat valley (Figure 9)[4], showing a single turbaned male bust in a lotus blossom; the rim is damaged, but traces of the petals outline as well as stamens can still be discerned in some spots. The similarity with the Indian model of lotus medallion framing a human figure is, in this case, very close.

The acknowledgment of iconographic parallels between a group of toilet-trays, on one side, and the reliefs on the *vedikā*s of Bharhut and related sites, on the other, is all the more interesting because, apart from very few exceptions[5], toilet-trays are or, at least, seem to be largely unrelated to Buddhism, unless we give credit to Katsumi Tanabe, who claims that the funerary orientation we infer in a large part of toilet-trays is nothing but an allusion to *nirvāṇa* or to the Buddhist paradise (Tanabe 2002). In other words, Tanabe thinks of a Buddhist repertoire disguised in Hellenistic or Western garments, an explanation which is not easy to agree with.

Yet, in the semantic frame of Gandhāran toilet-trays, the lotus, a symbol of transcendence, otherworldliness, might have taken a more specific funerary or eschatological meaning, which is implicit in the Buddhist context as well. After all, the lotus was thought to be a most appropriate pattern to be carved on the lids of Buddhist reliquaries.

We can point out analogies in the animal repertoire as well. Unlike the elephant - a ubiquitous subject in northern Indian sites, but, to my knowledge, still unrecorded in toilet-trays - horses and lions, either winged or not, and sea-monsters are found both in toilet-trays and on the *vedikā*s of Bharhut, Bodhgayā

[3] For more specimens from Butkara (Swat), see Faccenna 1962-64, II/3: pls. DXLVII ff.

[4] The item is unpublished. On the Bārāma excavations, see Faccenna 1964-65.

[5] Cf. Francfort 1979: 70-71 (nos. 96 and 97), pl. XLVII.

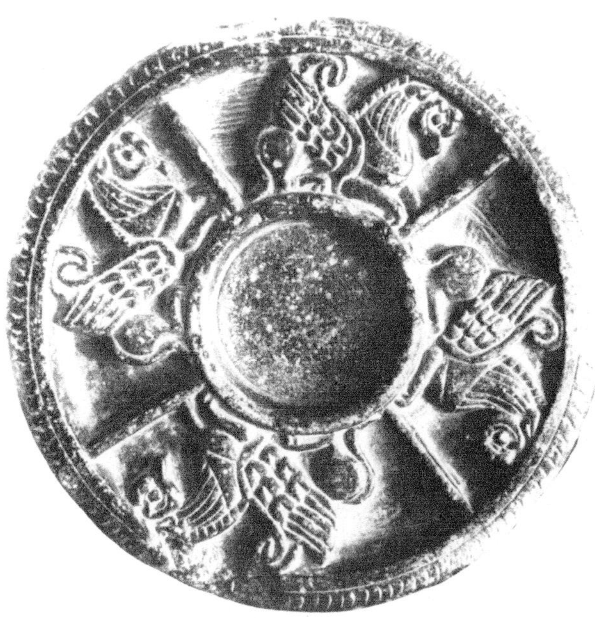

Figure 10. Toilet-tray with winged lions. From Sirkap. (After Francfort 1979: pl. XX, no. 40, courtesy of DAFA)

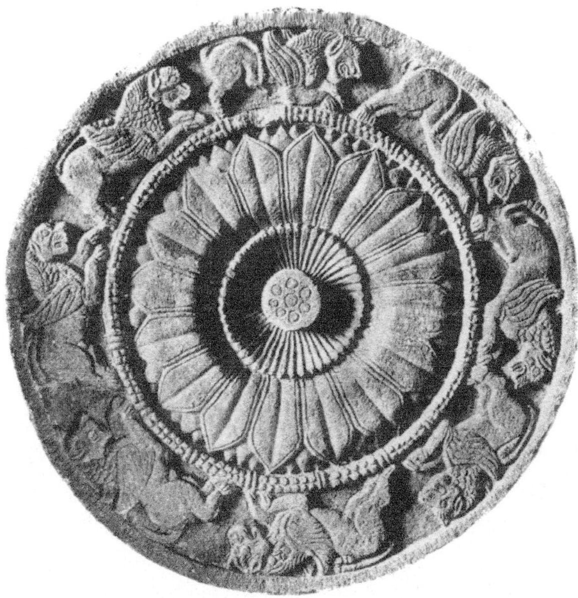

Figure 11. Medallion from the Bharhut vedikā. Kolkata, Indian Museum. (After Coomaraswamy 1956: pl. XXXIX, fig. 118.)

and cognate sites.[6] We are not just dealing with the co-occurrence of similar motifs: there is little doubt that the Sirkap toilet-tray with winged lions running in circle (Figure 10) (as well as the replica found at Charsadda, in the Peshawar Museum, possibly from the same workshop, Francfort 1979: pl. XX, no. 39) is closely related in concept, style, and, we may guess, semantic associations with a medallion of the Bharhut *vedikā* (Figure 11).

Going back to humans, a few more intriguing concomitances can be pointed out. Two toilet-trays from Sirkap are thought to depict a drunken Dionysus supported by two female figures, possibly maenads (Figure 12).[7] Given the classical orientation of so many toilet-trays, this has always been assumed to be the most obvious explanation, although in classical imagery a drunken Dionysus is generally supported by a satyr or Silenus.[8] Curiously enough, the only representations of a drunken Dionysus supported by two Maenads I could find in the *Lexicon Iconographicum Mythologiae Classicae* are those listed in the section dedicated to Gandhāran art, namely the two toilet-trays for which such an interpretation has been assumed in Gandhāran studies (Augé 1986: 521, nos. 78-80; cf. respectively, Francfort 1979: nos. 13, 19, 25).

I wonder if we should rather guess a relationship with a very close iconographic scheme – a central male figure (who does not seem to be drunk) flanked by two females, and often with his arms around their shoulders – recorded at Sanchi (railing of Sanchi 2,[9] Figure 13, and southern *toraṇa* at Sanchi 1,[10] where it is thought to illustrate Mara's despair for having being defeated,[11] or Aśoka's grief for the decay of the

[6] As for toilet-trays (from Sirkap or other sites, or of unknown provenance), see Francfort 1979: pls. XIX (no. 38), XX (nos. 39, 40), XXIII (no. 45), XXV (no. 50), XXVI (nos. 51, 52), XXVIII (no. 55), XXXIII (no. 67), XXXIV (nos. 68, 69), XXXV (nos. 70, 71), XXXVI (no. 72), XXXVII (nos. 74, 75), XXXVIII (no. 76), XLII (nos. 84, 85), XLIII (no. 86), XLV (no. 90). At Bharhut: Coomaraswamy 1956: pls. 34 (figs. 95, 97), 39 (118, 119, 121); at Bodhgayā: Coomaraswamy 1935: pls. II-V, VI, IX-XIII, XV, XVI, XIX, XXXVII.

[7] For the second specimen, from Barikot (Swat), in the Victoria and Albert Museum, see Francfort 1979: no. 25, pl. XIII.

[8] Cf. Gasparri 1986: 453 (nos. 320-324), 448-450 (nos. 262-264, 267).

[9] The scene illustrated here belongs to the latest phase of Stūpa 2, which is probably related with the Stūpa 1 *toraṇas*.

[10] Marshall–Foucher 1940, III: pl. 79.

[11] Schlingloff 1988: 7, figs. 6 and 7.

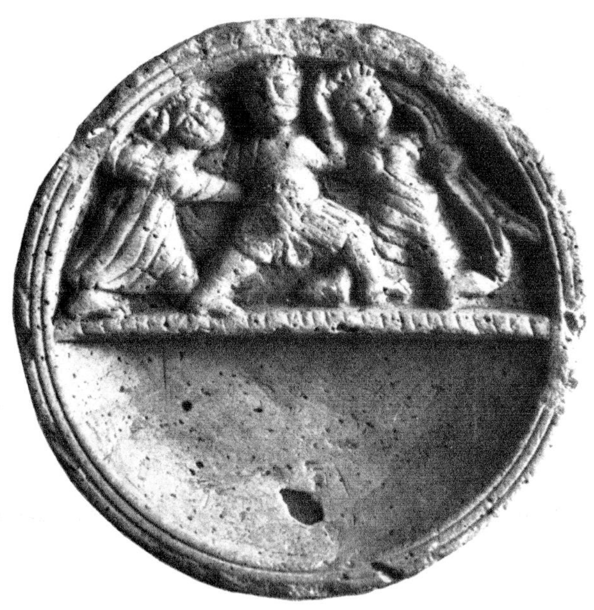

Figure 12. Toilet-tray from Sirkap.
(After Francfort 1979: pl. VII, no. 13, courtesy of DAFA)

bodhi tree[12]), Bodhgayā (Coomaraswamy 1935: pl. XXXIII, right), Mathurā (on a railing post from Kankālī Ṭīlā, cf. Quintanilla 2007: 71, figs. 66, 67, who assimilates the relief to the category of 'amorous scenes'), as well as, although much later, in a huge number of *virakals* (or 'hero-stones'), in Medieval Deccan and southern India (Figure 14).[13] The most common layout of such funerary *stelae* consists of three (sometimes four) panels in a vertical row. Each panel shows a scene according to a well-established sequence, which, starting from the bottom, illustrates the circumstances of the hero's death, the dead hero ascending into Heaven accompanied by two (sometimes more) *apsarases*, and, in the uppermost panel, the hero in Heaven (*śivaloka*) worshipping a Śiva *linga*. The 'hero accompanied by the *apsarases*' is an overtly eschatological motif illustrating a most sought-after reward for Indian warriors,[14] and, in its iconographic layout, bears a strong resemblance with the scenes claimed to represent a 'drunken Dionysus', on toilet-trays, and Aśoka's (or Mara's) grief or an amorous trio at Sanchi, Bodhgayā, and Mathurā. A curious detail is worth mentioning: the posture of the male figure in one of the Sirkap trays (Figure 12), with his legs slightly bent and turned aside, as if stepping towards the right, seems to anticipate the standardized manner in which the hero ascending into Heaven (who is not supposed to be drunk) is portrayed in *virakals*.

Whether we are dealing with one and the same iconographic pattern, charged with different meanings depending on the contexts it occurs in, or with an iconographic archetype implying an eschatological association, whatever the cultural, religious and chronological contexts of its depictions, is a question which requires further research. It seems undeniable, however, that we deal with a *longue durée* iconographic pattern, which can be listed among the links between Gandhāran toilet-trays and the South-Asian artistic and symbolic *lexicon*.

I will close this overview with a piece of evidence provided by the Stūpa 2 *vedikā* at Sanchi (Figure 15): a relief showing a male figure of north-western or Central Asian origins, as revealed by his attire: a tight sleeved tunic with folds rendered with parallel lines forming a chevron-like motif along the arms. But for a few details, the figure, possibly depicting a Śaka, strongly recalls the members of a drinking couple in a toilet-tray in the British Museum (Figure 4): same tunic, same chevron pattern on the sleeves (and, in the toilet-tray, also on the 'solar' motif framing the couple), a very similar hair treatment, and eyelids in strong relief, a detail which is not found in other human figures on the same *vedikā*.

Some final remarks on the chronological implications of this sketchy overview. If the bulk of the subjects and motifs discussed in this paper appear in toilet-trays roughly dating from the first century AD, we should infer a rather long chronological distance from their Indian parallels, i.e. 100 to 200 years, depending on the specific site and on the subjective views held by scholars for each of them.

[12] Lahiri 2015: 296, fig. Epilogue 1.

[13] The main reference work on these artefacts is still Settar-Sontheimer 1982. For a recent research on memorial stones in Maharashtra, see Trinco 2015.

[14] For the literary background of this theme, including the *Mahābhārata*, Kālidāsa's plays and other sources, see Hara 2001.

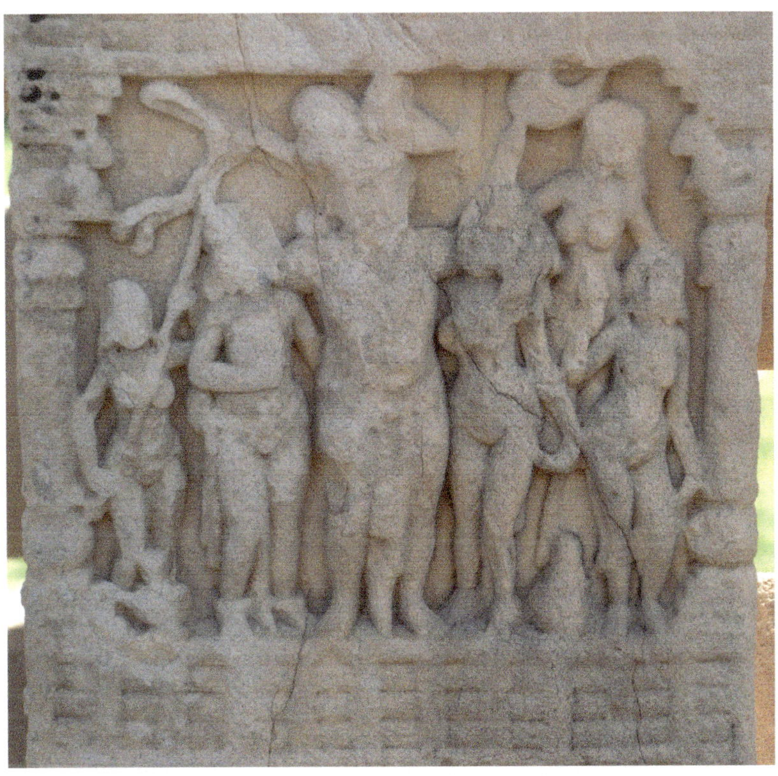

Figure 13. Sanchi, Stūpa 2, vedikā*: a man resting his arms on the shoulders of two women. (Photo: courtesy of Flavia Zaghet.)*

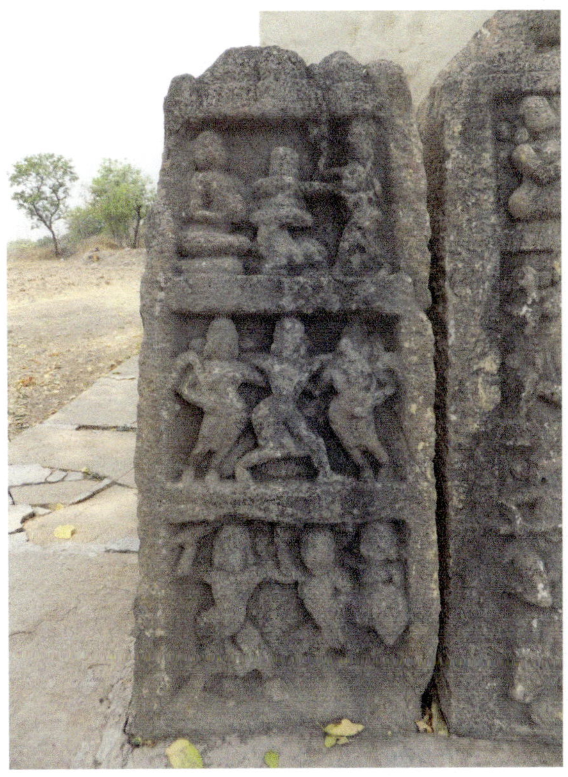

Figure 14. 'Hero-stone', Kumbharvalan (Pune District, Maharashtra, India). (Photo: courtesy Letizia Trinco.)

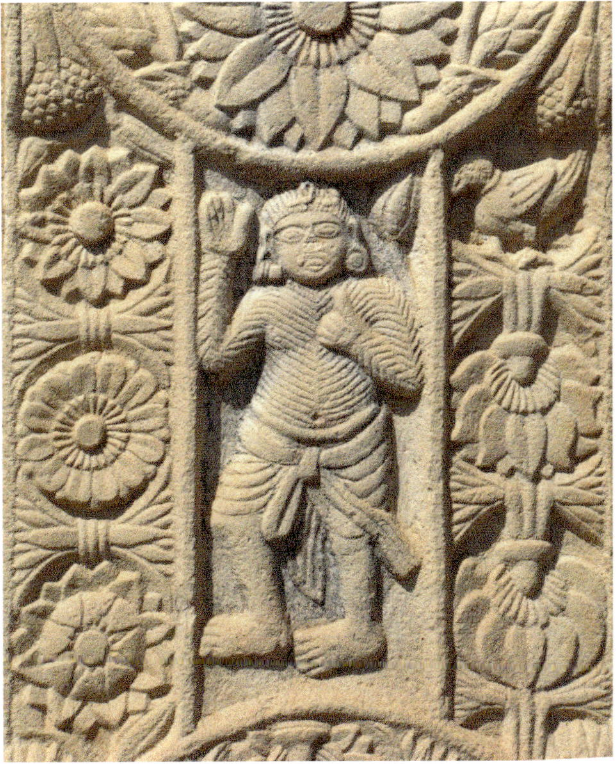

Figure 15. Sanchi, Stūpa 2, vedikā*: male figure in Central Asian or north-western attire. (Photo: courtesy Flavia Zaghet.)*

As I anticipated, the relationship between the Indian Buddhist sites I have referred to above and the Śunga period is now a debated issue. The assumption of their Śunga association derives almost exclusively by the reading of an inscription on the sole preserved *toraṇa* of the Bharhut *stūpa*. It records the name of one Dhanabhūti, who is reputed to be a Śunga feudatory or a chief coeval with the Śunga rule on account of the words '*Suganam raje*', in which 'Suga', at first identified by A. Cunningham as 'Srughna', in the upper course of the Yamuna (Cunningham 1879: 128-129), has been later assumed to mean 'Śunga' (Barua 1934-37, I: 29-36). Based on this assumption, Bharhut is dated to the Śunga epoch (184-82 BC), preferably to *c.* 150 BC or, at the latest, before the end of the same century. The chronology of the other sites, Sanchi (Stūpa 2), Bodhgayā, and the earliest sculptures from Mathurā, mostly depends on this *terminus post quem*; the periods of their respective flourishing are distributed during a period of fifty to one hundred years (with Bharhut's peculiar style as a starting point) in a linear sequence based upon stylistic analysis (in the case of Bodhgayā and Mathurā also on controversial epigraphic evidence[15]). The analysis is mainly ruled by a criterion that we may summarize in the formula 'the flatter, the earlier'; in other words, the more in the round the figures are worked, the later their date. The flatness of the reliefs is therefore taken as a primary diagnostic tool, and one of the main reasons for asserting that between Bharhut and Sanchi 2 we cannot guess a significant chronological distance; one may wonder why the substantial differences between the two *stūpas* in the richness and complexity of the repertoire as well as in the narrative modes, iconographic choices, and technical refinement seem, on the contrary, to have no bearing in the chronological analysis. As a matter of fact, a chronological sequence may not be the only possible approach to explain the diverse artistic orientations witnessed in the ancient Buddhist sites of northern India, or, at least, not the most appropriate.

In fact, there are good reasons to suspect that the attribution of Bharhut to the Śunga epoch, with all its consequent effects, rests on shaky grounds. The refreshing overview of the numismatic and epigraphic evidence of the post-Maurya period offered by Shailendra Bhandare (2006) – including a re-assessment of the data concerning the Śunga dynasty – reveals the weakness of the historical reconstruction we have taken for granted for a long time. On the art-historical side, Frederick Asher declares all his scepticism about the evolutionary pattern of the traditional reconstruction we have summarized above (Asher 2006). He rightly argues that what we commonly interpret as differences in style, iconography and narrative mode due to a gradual transformation, occurred during a certain time span, should be rather explained on a regional base, that is as results of local idiosyncrasies of distinct workshops, rather than distinct phases of a linear artistic development (Asher 2006: 61-63).

A further step on this issue has been more recently taken by Ajit Kumar (2014), who reconsiders all evidence, epigraphic and art-historical, and redraws the historical scenario to which Bharhut and cognate sites more plausibly belong. Kumar rejects the current interpretation of the Bharhut Dhanabhūti inscription and revives Cunningham's reading (*Suga-* stands for Srughna/Sug; therefore, no relationships with the Śungas is to be inferred). Kumar argues that the earliest Buddhist sites of the Gangetic plain – which, in spite of the differences, show a significant range of stylistic and iconographic consistencies – belong to a political landscape made of a series of small principalities, ruled by chieftains who referred to themselves as *rāja*, had names ending in *-mitra*, *-datta* and *-bhūti*, as we know from inscriptions and coins, and established a confederacy among themselves and with the Śaka/Kṣatrapa; a scenario which, according to Kumar, corresponds with a period starting no earlier than the beginning of the Common Era, and covering the first two to three decades of the first century AD (Kumar 2014: 237-239).

[15] On the Bodhgayā inscriptions supposedly bearing evidence of a link with the Śunga kingdom, see Asher 2006: 59-59, note 9. On the Dhanabhūti recorded at Mathurā, and on whether he should be considered identical with the Bharhut's donor bearing the same name, see Asher 2006: 58; Bhandare 2006: 58, 76-77: Quintanilla 2007: 10-13; Kumar 2014: 224-226, 237, 238; Milligan 2015: 7.

Finally comes the new evidence provided by Milligan (2015) on the relative chronology of Sanchi Stūpas 2 and 1. The author points out a number of cases in which the name of one and the same donor (identified also by its profession and place of origin) occurs in inscriptions in both *stūpas*. This demonstrates that we should not postulate a chronological distance between the two monuments longer than a reasonable human life span (in ancient India). If we add the epigraphic evidence which seems to link Sanchi Stūpa 2 with the Bharhut *vedikā* (Milligan 2015: 20-21), the periods of architectural and artistic activities of the three *stūpas* 'could have been closer together than previously thought' (Milligan 2015: 21). The chronological span within which we should distribute the *stūpas* of Bharhut, Sanchi 2 and 1 may therefore start around the mid-first century BC and end in the early first century AD (which is the date assumed for the completion of Sanchi 1).

It is evident that a healthy revision of the history of early Buddhist art and architecture in the Gangetic plain has started. The issue clearly asks for further research based on a multidisciplinary approach but, should this historical and chronological reassessment of early Buddhist art in northern Indian sites prove right, the iconographic similarities with Gandhāran toilet-trays I have been highlighting in this preliminary overview would make sense also from a chronological viewpoint.

References

Asher F. 2006. Early Indian Art Reconsidered. Pages 51-66 in P. Olivelle (ed), *Between the Empires*. Oxford and New York: Oxford University Press.

Augé Ch. 1986. Dionysos (in peripheria orientali). *Lexicon Iconographicum Mythologiae Classicae* III: 540-566.

Barua B. 1934-37. *Barhut* (3 volumes). Calcutta: The Indian Research Institute.

Bhandare Sh. 2006. Numismatics and History: The Maurya-Gupta Interlude in the Gangetic Plain. Pages 67-112 in P. Olivelle (ed), *Between the Empires*. Oxford and New York: Oxford University Press.

Colledge M.A.R. 1981. Review of Francfort 1979. *Bulletin of the School of Oriental and African Studies* 44/1: 174-175.

Coomaraswamy A. K. 1935. *La sculpture de Bodhgaya* (Ars Asiatica, XVIII). Paris: Les éditions d'art et d'histoire.

Coomaraswamy A. K. 1956. *La sculpture de Bharhut.* (Annales du Musée Guimet, VI). Paris: Vanoest, Éditions d'art et d'histoire

Cunningham A. 1879. *The Stûpa of Bharhut: A Buddhist Monument Ornamented with Numerous Sculptures Illustratitive of Buddhist Legend and History in the Third Century B.C.*, London, W.H. Allen and Co, Trübner and Co., Edward Stanford, W. S. Whittingham and Co., Thacker and Co.

Dar S. R. 1979. Toilet Trays from Gandhara and Beginning of Hellenism in Pakistan. *Journal of Central Asia* 2/2: 141-184.

Erdosy G. 1990. Taxila: Political History and Urban Structure. Pages 657-674 in M. Taddei (ed. with the assistance of P. Callieri), *South Asian Archaeology 1987* (*Serie Orientale Roma*, 66). Rome: Istituto Italiano per il Medio ed Estremo Oriente.

Faccenna D. 1962-64. *Sculptures from the Sacred Area of Butkara I (Swat, W. Pakistan)* (with a descriptive catalogue by Maurizio Taddei) (2 volumes). Rome: Istituto Poligrafico dello Stato.

Faccenna D. 1964-65. Results of the 1963 Excavation Campaign at Barama I (Swat - Pakistan): Preliminary Report. *East and West* 15: 7-23.

Falk H. 2010. Libation Trays in Gandhara. *Bulletin of the Asia Institute* 24: 89-113.

Francfort H.P. 1979. *Les palettes du Gandhāra.* (Mémoires de la Délégation archéologique française en Afghanistan, 23). Paris: Diffusion De Boccard.

Gasparri C. 1986. Dionysos. *Lexicon Iconographicum Mythologiae Classicae* III: 414-514.

Hara M. 2001. Apsaras and Hero. *Journal of Indian Philosophy* 29/1-2 (Special Issue: Ingalls Festschrift): 135-153.

Kumar A. 2014. Bharhut Sculptures and Their Untenable Sunga Association. *Heritage: Journal of Multidisciplinary Studies in Archaeology* 2: 223-241.

Lahiri, N. 2015. *Ashoka in Ancient India*. Cambridge: Harvard University Press.

Lo Muzio C. 2002. L'artigianato di lusso nel Nord-Ovest di epoca indo-greca, saka e partica: i "piattelli per cosmetici". Pages 77-83 in P. Callieri and A. Filigenzi (eds), *Il Maestro di Saidu Sharif. Alle origini dell'arte del Gandhara*. Rome: Istituto italiano per l'Africa e l'Oriente.

Lo Muzio C. 2011. Gandharan Toilet-Trays: Some Reflections on Chronology. *Ancient Civilizations from Scythia to Siberia* 17: 331-340.

Marshall J. 1951. *Taxila* (3 volumes). Cambridge: Cambridge University Press.

Marshall J. & Foucher A. 1940. *The Monuments of Sāñchī (with the texts of inscriptions edited, translted and annotated by N.G. Majumdar)* (3 volumes). Calcutta, Government of India Press.

Milligan M.D. 2015. Five Unnoticed Donative Inscriptions and the Relative Chronology of Sanchi Stūpa II for the Evaluation of Buddhist Historical Traditions. *Annual Report of The International Research Institute for Advanced Buddhology at Soka University for the Academic Year 2014* 18: 11-22.

Olivelle P. (ed) 2006. *Between the Empires: Society in India 300 B.C.E. to 400 C.E.*. Oxford and New York: Oxford University Press.

Pons J. 2011. From Gandhāran Trays to Gandhāran Buddhist Art: The Persistence of Hellenistic Motifs from the Second Century and Beyond. Pages 153-175 in A. Kouremenos, S. Chandrasekaran and R. Rossi (eds), *From Pella to Gandhara. Hybridisation and Identity in the Art and Architecture of the Hellenistic East* (BAR International Series 2221). Oxford: Archaeopress.

Quintanilla S. 2007. *History of Early Stone Sculpture at Mathura, ca. 150 BCE-100 CE*. Leiden and Boston: Brill.

Schlingloff D. 1988. *Studies in the Ajanta Paintings. Identifications and Interpretations*. Delhi: Ajanta Publications.

Settar S. & Sontheimer, G.H. (eds) 1982. *Memorial Stones: A Study of their Origin, Significance and Variety*. Dharwad: Institute of Indian Art History, Karnatak University; New Delhi: South Asia Institute, University of Heidelberg.

Taddei M. 1966. A Problematic Toilet-Tray from Uḍegrām. *East and West* 16/1-2: 89-93.

Tanabe K. 2002. Greek, Roman and Parthian Influences on the Pre-Kushana Gandharan 'Toilet-Trays' and Forerunners of Buddhist Paradise (Pâramitâ). *Silk Road Art and Archaeology* 8: 73-100.

Trinco, L. 2015. Hindu Funerary Stones: A Study of their Iconography, function and variety as from the Context of South-Eastern Maharashtra (PhD Dissertation, Sapienza Università di Roma).

Is it appropriate to ask a celestial lady's age?

Robert Bracey[1]

This short piece is adapted from the text of the presentation I gave at the Gandhāra Connections workshop on 24th March 2017 so it is somewhat informal in style. I have in some cases expanded the references and argument, but it remains an exploration of a theme based on a single piece rather than an attempt at a comprehensive study.

I wished to explore two central and related questions. The first is how pieces can be dated when they are deprived of either firm archaeological context[2] or dated inscriptions?[3] And the second question is whether this is the right question to be asking. These questions are important for almost all Gandhāran work, and also for the class of Mathurān pieces I have chosen here.

The choice of a Mathurān piece reflects both my own interests and also my belief that viewing Gandhāra in isolation from its southern neighbour has been harmful to the study of both.[4] I also want to make clear that this is not really a paper about the Cleveland Dancers. Though the central question is when the Cleveland Dancers were made, the purpose is to explore whether dating is the right question to pursue.

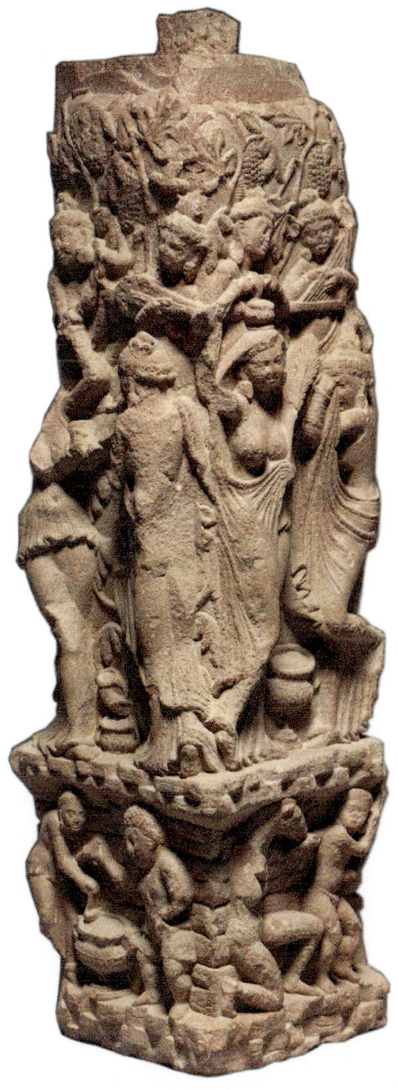

Figure 1. The Cleveland Dancers, described by the Museum as follows: 'Railing Pillar, 100s. India, Mathura, Kushan Period (1st century-320). Red sandstone; overall: h. 80 cm (31 7/16 in). The Cleveland Museum of Art, John L. Severance Fund 1977.34'.

[1] Several colleagues, including Peter Stewart, Christian Luczanits, and Joe Cribb, have discussed aspects of the paper with me, and I am grateful to the audience at the Gandhāra Connections event for similar engagement. Sushma Jansari was kind enough to read an early draft and comment on the content, and Ysa Frehse carefully read my final draft.

[2] Gandhāra is generally much better off for well excavated sites than Mathurā but the relatively long life and potential of re-use for sculpture applies in both cases (for Gandhāra, see Behrendt 2009) complicating the use of archaeological context in both cases.

[3] To the best of my knowledge there is only one inscribed railing pillar of the type being discussed here from Mathurā (Quintanilla 2007: fig.189). This pillar is in a private collection but is reported as inscribed by a donor, Kathika, who also donated a fragmentary railing pillar not featuring a nymph (fig.185-188) in the Mathurā museum. The inscription on the Mathurā example does not have a date but two of the characters are diagnostic. The tripartite form of the conjunct *ya* ceases to be used early in the reign of Huviṣka, *c.* 150 AD, while the curved base of *na* probably rules out a very early date (Bracey 2011). This still leaves a broad range of possible dates in the first century BC or the first or early second century AD. A fragmentary free-standing nymph from Kankali Tila (Smith 1901: pl.XCIX) is also inscribed but the inscription has not been satisfactorily read.

[4] The northwest of India through Central Asia is a patchwork of different artistic centres, containing various transient and long lived workshops which must have responded to each other through changes in clients' taste, transmission of prototypes, and transfer of personnel. That these coalesced at times into relatively distinct regional styles, such as Mathurān art, is an interesting phenomenon but the historical entities that produce it (and Gandhāran art, whatever is meant by that) remain only very poorly understood.

The Cleveland Dancers

This piece (Figure 1), acquired (with no archaeological provenance) by the Cleveland Museum of Art in 1977 (acquisition no. 77.34), was first reported in the review of 1977 in the Museum's bulletin and described as 'late second century' (Lee 1977). It was subsequently exhibited in the early 1980s and ascribed then by Stanislaw Czuma (1985) to the 'second century'.[5] The piece has also been used in several papers over the years as an example of 'Dionysiac' or 'bacchanalian' imagery in Mathurān art.[6]

The Cleveland Dancers are the corner-post of a railing pillar. There are slots for crossbars on two adjacent sides (for a total of six crossbars) and a tenon survives on the top to allow a coping stone to be mounted in place. The piece is about 80 cm high and when mounted would have been part of a stone railing about chest height used to surround a sacred space. The use of such pillars was common to many traditions and different sorts of spaces had railings but it is often assumed the piece belonged to a Buddhist *stūpa*. Like most Mathurān railing pillars it has a design arranged in several registers. The highest register consists of grapes amongst foliage, the next of onlookers playing instruments. The third register is the largest with four dancing female figures, and the final register is separated by a stone pattern and consists of two distinct narrative scenes on the two decorated sides of the pillar.

The piece is unusual in several respects. Though it is of a railing pillar type made in Mathurā, and carved in the 'red', 'red-mottled', or 'sikri' stone normal for that city's workshops in the first to fifth centuries AD, the depictions themselves seem to employ 'classical' or 'Hellenistic' elements not normally seen in artistic pieces at Mathurā.

Think horse, not zebra

The subtitle to this section refers to a common aphorism in medical diagnosis. The heuristic suggests that when you consider a symptom (the sound of hooves, for example) you should, unless you live in Africa, think first of common causes (horse) before uncommon ones (zebra). Sometimes, of course, the sound will be a zebra but that is not where your investigation should *start*.

The same general principle should apply when looking for artistic prototypes. Mathurā was a major urban centre, whose products are found across South Asia. So it was connected to trade routes that covered the whole of Eurasia. In principle an artist could have drawn on prototypes from Rome, the classical world, or even China, but they are much more likely to have drawn on closer traditions: in Andhra, western India, the Gangetic valley, or Gandhāra.

On seeing elements that appear 'classical' in the Cleveland pillars, therefore, we should think first of nearby Gandhāra, where such elements occur frequently, not further afield in Greece or Rome. However, in an article published in 2011, Seungjung Kim began his examination by comparing the piece with a Classical Greek vase, and then with a Roman sarcophagus. Kim is quite dismissive (Kim 2011: 25) of the Gandhāran parallels but is equivocal about the precise prototype so it is unclear if he is arguing that the piece drew directly on a Greek or Roman design.

However, in terms of imagery, there are quite obvious Gandhāran parallels. The Edinburgh University Art Collection contains a schist piece (EU1325) depicting a group of dancers and musicians (Figure 2).

[5] It is not mentioned by Czuma in his 1977 article on the Mathurān art in the Cleveland collection published two issues later so was presumably acquired subsequent to that article being prepared.

[6] The lengthiest treatment of the piece is in Carter (1982), with a substantial response in Kim (2011: 21ff) but it is also treated in Peterson (2011-12: 16-17). Carter (1992; 2015: 29, 355-356) subsequently treats the association with Dionysiac imagery at length but these add nothing significant on the Cleveland pillar.

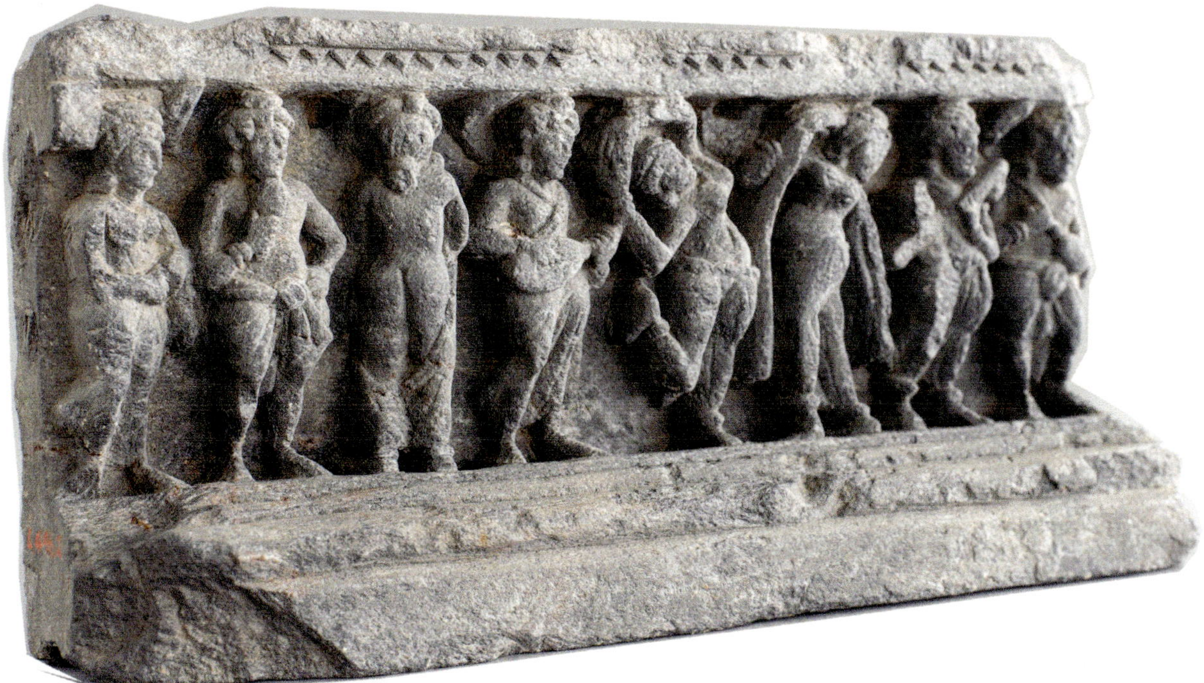

Figure 2. Gandhāran frieze. (Photo: copyright the University of Edinburgh/Thomas Morgan.)

Though the piece is much smaller in scale the women have similar hair styles and the third figure from the right is turned away from the audience with her robe draped in a similar fashion. The figures seem much more comparable to the Cleveland piece than any of Kim's examples[7].

Nudity, nymphs, and women

Kim makes a further remark on the figures in the Cleveland pillar that requires particular correction. In all publications it has been assumed, incorrectly, that the pillar was made by a workshop which normally produced Mathurān style pillars, but on this occasion used Gandhāran (or in Kim's view Western) prototypes. Following this line of argument, Kim connects the nudity on the pillars with the local practice in Mathurā, before again returning to classical Roman types:

> As for the partial nudity on the Cleveland pillar, precedents can be found locally in voluptuous Yakshi figures that have adorned other Buddhist stūpas. Other parallels from the West, and visually striking ones at that, can be found in contemporary Roman visual tradition ... (Kim 2011: 24)

In fact the 'nudity' of the Cleveland figures bears no resemblance to treatments of the female form in Mathurā. First, though this is not at all obvious[8] the female images that appear on railing pillars at Mathurā are not technically nude. Though very little is left to the viewer's imagination, a careful examination of images shows they wear skin tight, diaphanous, and for practical purposes, invisible garments. In some cases a prominent hem-line is shown without apparently connecting to anything

[7] It is possible that Kim intends to draw attention not to the figures themselves but to their interaction. The Gandhāran figures are arranged independently in a flat plane, while those on the Cleveland pillar seem more unified in their composition. While true, this ignores the very different frames a railing pillar and a panel from a *stūpa* provide. I am grateful to attendees at the talk for this suggestion.

[8] For example Coomaraswamy (1926: 60) refers to the figures as 'often nude or semi-nude', and both Trivedi (2004: 57) and Wangu (2003: 55) refer to them as nude without qualification. Though I think most specialists recognize the existence of a diaphanous garment.

else.[9] Though something akin to nudity is suggested by the visible girdle, itself an undergarment, this is very different to the disrobing figures on the Cleveland pillar. And of course we should remember that we perceive the figures in monochrome, with the possibility that paint could have radically transformed perception of their 'nudity'.

Kim refers to the female figures at Mathurā as 'Yakshi', one of a wide range of terms used for them. To simplify discussion I will from here on refer to independent female figures in architectural contexts (railing pillars or columns) as 'nymphs'.[10] Such nymphs can be further sub-divided based on their iconography but there are clues, especially in the treatment of their 'nudity' that contemporaries thought of them as a class, distinct from other female images.

They are obviously not 'real' women – not even courtesans. Female donors (who certainly did include courtesans[11]) are depicted on the pedestals of a number of Buddhist and Jain images.[12] These women generally wear a long, heavy dress with high collar, which reaches to their ankles, and unlike the nymph's diaphanous drapery, obscures the girdle. Presumably well-to-do Mathurān women wore girdles, just not visibly in public. The nymphs are probably also not 'divine' figures. There are two relatively common iconographies at Mathurā: one is a squatting female figure usually holding a child; the other is a standing female flanked by two male figures. Both of these types seem to represent deities, or at least the objects of religious worship. The squatting figures are usually referred to as *mātrikās* (mothers), while the female figure in the triad is variously identified as Ekanamsa, the sister of Krishna (Couture & Schmid 2011), or the folk goddess Shashthī (Agrawala 1971; Joshi 1986). These divine figures do wear girdles, but they are arranged differently with material draped in the centre, rather than at the side (see the right-most drawing in Figure 3).[13]

This is a marker for the difference between a feminine idealization that represents fertility, plenty, or (possibly dangerous) sexuality,[14] and the girdle-less donor figures with whom female viewers were expected to identify.[15]

[9] For example, all of the railing pillars recovered at Sanghol were made at a workshop that followed this last convention.

[10] The range of terminology that has been used is vast and largely unsupported by any contemporary literature. For a list of terms and some references see Trivedi (2004).

[11] Courtesans were amongst the donors at religious establishments, and donors are consistently depicted as indicated in the next note. An inscription from Kankali Tila was dedicated by a courtesan, and other similar dedications are known from a variety of later sites in India. For an overview see Mokashi (2015), and on the term *gaṇikā* see Srinivasan 2005. On a related note it has become fashionable to identify the image of a kneeling woman on several plaques as a particular courtesan, Vasantasena, the principle female character in a much later play. This identification and the relevant pieces are discussed at length in Rossi (1995: 7-8) and Czuma (1985: cat. no. 41). The treatment of the female figure is very similar to that of the nymphs and this identification remains open to dispute.

[12] An image of a nun wearing a chequered robe in the National Museum Delhi (acc. no. 49.13/3; Asthana 1999: no. 89) is also worth noting in this context; again no girdle is visible, as is the case for an old woman buying fruit in a narrative panel from a pillar in Mathurā (Quintanilla 2007: fig. 243). The Aryavati Ayagapata from Kankali Tila (Smith 1901: xiv; Quintanilla 2007: fig. 148) has a figure on the viewer's left who appears to be a donor insert (head-scarf, long dress, no sign of a girdle) in a scene with mythological figures (they wear girdles but the treatment is different to the majority of nymphs).

[13] A figure that may be Durga in Berlin (inv. no. MIK I 5894; Luczanits 2008: cat. 113), has the same arrangement. While a column identified as Lakshmi does not and has probably been mis-identified (acc. no. B.89; Czuma 1985: fig. 26.3). Early, probably Kushan period, depictions of Mahishasurmardini slaying a buffalo also seem to show a similar depiction of the goddess' dhoti; see for example Viennot 1956: fig.1. These differences suggest that the apparent nudity formed part of visual coding contemporaries were expected to recognise and which would be an interesting topic for a more in-depth analysis.

[14] Though also note the provocative article by Sunil (2001/2002) which suggests these figures enjoyed an unusual level of 'semiotic openness' allowing meaning to be imposed by the viewer, including nineteenth and twentieth century scholars.

[15] With regard to the donor figures on pedestals DeCaroli (2015: 80-90) makes the point that very few depictions match the details of donors given in the inscription. He stops short of suggesting that the workshops produced generic images in advance rather than taking commissions, though this would be very interesting and is what the evidence implies. At the least though it suggests that while female donor images represent 'real' women not all represent 'actual' women.

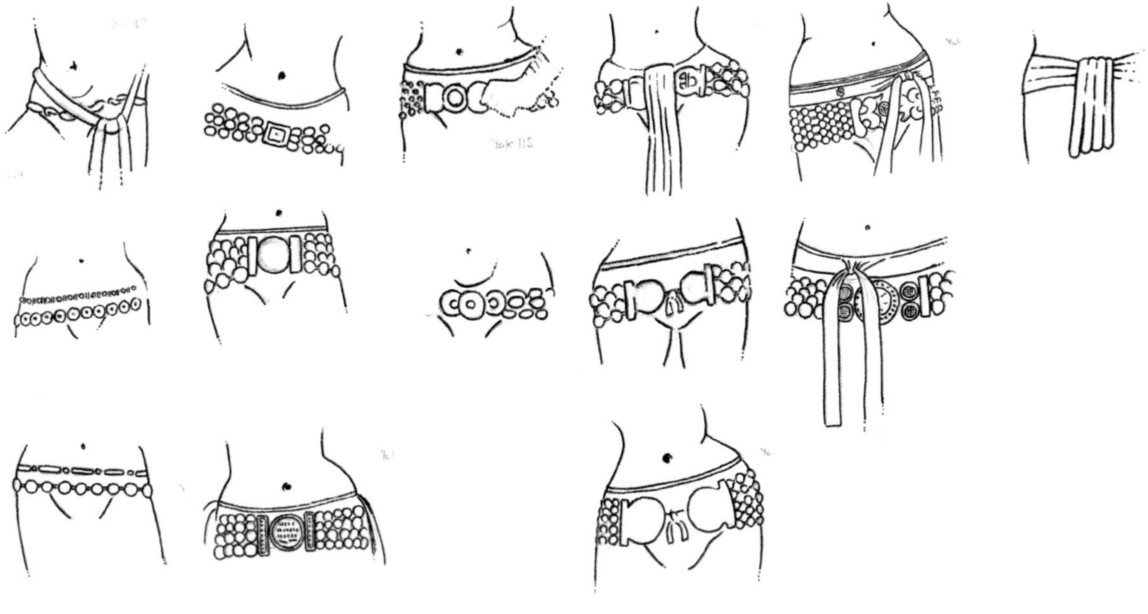

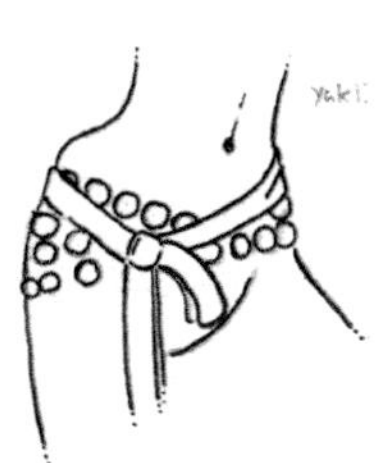

Figure 3. Variety of girdles in Mathurān art (from author's notes).[16]

While the girdle is common in Mathurā it is almost entirely absent in Gandhāra. Railing pillars, which seem to have been relatively common in Mathurā, are rare in Gandhāra, but there is an iconographically equivalent depiction. Gandhāran narrative reliefs are often broken up with spacing images. Some of these are architectural elements like columns, and others show male or female figures contained within a frame, often standing on a pot. Female figures of this type may stand cross-legged with one hand reaching into foliage above their head, an arrangement which is very like the type of nymph known as a śālabhañjikā.[17] There is, for our purposes, an important difference. The Gandhāran female figures are wearing obvious full-length dresses, with no girdle visible.[18] In fact when nudity, actual or apparent, does appear in this context it is those spacer figures, which are male, that are usually shown nude.[19] This gendering of the figures in decorative contexts is important. Male figures are known on railing pillars from Mathurā but they are rare, and so is nudity. So the two contexts reverse not only the dominant gender of the figures but also the visual treatment of the body, in terms of perceived or actual nudity.

[16] This is only a partial representation of what is the most variable aspect of the nymph's costume. The girdles can be classified in a variety of ways and it is tempting to see a chronological progression from those consisting only of discs (the fashion at Sanchi and Bharhut) to the more complex types with a central plate or plates. However different types seem to co-exist at both Sanghol and Kankali Tila, and it is likely that as well as changing fashion the design could vary with iconography or other factors. For example, the more complex pieces with five part clasps, the fifth column of Figure 3, seem to be more common on large free-standing pieces, which probably reflects the greater space the artist had for elaboration.

[17] Examples showing various of these characteristics include Dar 2016: pls. XXVII.f, XLIV.c, LIV; Khan 2005: nos. 203, 220; Zwalf 1996: nos. 187, 232, 349, 350, 351, 352, 353, 501.

[18] The only example of a girdle I am aware of is Khan: 2005, no. 399 from a narrative depiction at Taxila.

[19] Khan (2005: no. 278 and 279) and Zwalf (1996: nos. 180, 216, 228). Zwalf (1996: no. 493) shows an example of a clothed male figure. I am aware of only one 'female' nude figure in this context. The piece (Pal 2003: no. 34) in the Norton Simon Museum (acq. no. 1979.14.1.S) is odd in a number of respects, and unfortunately also lacking provenance so conclusions should be cautious. The naked male is holding grapes but apparently with female sexual characteristics. My, uninformed, inclination is that if genuine the piece has been modified, possibly unintentionally.

It would be interesting to pursue this issue further. Such a stubborn difference in the way the female form is depicted, despite extensive cross-contamination in the artistic traditions, must point to some profound cultural differences in the perception of gender. In fact, though the nymph type figures have attracted much attention, it has generally been taken as unproblematic that they function as 'paradise' imagery of some sort. It has not been recognised that if the railing pillars are a paradise imagery, it is firmly a male, heterosexual, paradise, even if they were not read as overtly erotic. So, how did the many female patrons and monastics at these sites experience this imagery? Or for that matter the prevalence of male rather than female nudity at Gandhāran sites? It was precisely this point that I raised at the beginning: that there might be more interesting questions to ask about these objects than when they were made. For the moment, the important point to take away is a stubborn difference in cultural attitudes to gender and nudity between Gandhāran and Mathurān artists, despite extensive cultural exchange in other artistic elements.

Not a Mathurān artist

The treatment of 'nudity' alone is not sufficient to doubt that this piece was made by a Mathurān trained artist.[20] Much more problematic is the disregard of proportional systems. Artists operating in long-term workshop traditions, where apprenticeships in the craft would be normal, develop proportional systems as a way of reliably scaling their subject matter. The use of proportional systems at Mathurā has received only one detailed study: that by Mosteller (1991). Mosteller's study focuses on standing male images, such as *yakṣas* (the pot-bellied male counterparts to *yakṣīs*), Buddhas, *tīrthankaras*, or Vishnu. Reproducing a similar study here is impossible as it requires identifying the component parts that an artist worked with and careful measurements of where those parts intersected with the original plane on which the master roughed out the figure.

Instead, to illustrate the problem, a proxy for the proportional system will be used. This is the ratio of the height to the width of a series of intact frontally facing nymphs (from pillars, brackets, or columns). The height is measured from the centre point between the eyes to the approximate position of the heel. The width is considered to be bound by the outer-most points indicated by hips and breasts. Of the Cleveland Dancers, only the figure carrying a palm branch is facing frontally, and is photographed straight on in Carter 1982 (fig. 2). That figure has a ratio of 4.27.

For comparison I was able to find twenty-four nymphs of definite Mathurān origin for which there were good photographs taken from the front and which were intact enough to take measurements. None of the twenty-four produced a ratio over 4.[21] To put it bluntly, the Cleveland Dancers are too tall and thin to be a Mathurān product (Figure 4).

It is true that the stone, the general framing (in multiple registers), and the purpose (a railing pillar), speak to Mathurā, but these are superficial elements that an artist could easily adapt. It is much more difficult to believe that an artist would create an independent and original piece based on mixing Gandhāran and Mathurān elements but disregard not only the conventional coding of 'nudity' in the local aesthetic repertoire but also their[22] basic training in proportional systems.

[20] Note that in addition to the treatment of the dancers the horse-headed ogress in the bottom panel is depicted nude but without any girdle. Her pose resembles a famous narrative scene from Mathurā (see footnote 10) but is not used for other images of the horse-headed ogress at Mathurā or elsewhere (see Rowland 1953: pl.15.B; Gill 2000: 75-77).

[21] The actual results were 2.83, 2.88, 3.07, 3.24, 3.27, 3.37, 3.40, 3.41, 3.42, 3.43, 3.45, 3.46, 3.47, 3.49, 3.50, 3.50, 3.52, 3.58, 3.58, 3.64, 3.64, 3.80, 3.82, 3.90.

[22] It remains the case that we know frighteningly little about the artists who made either Gandhāran or Mathurān work, or in fact about South Asian work more generally. A recent attempt to correct this (Dehejia & Rockwell 2016) unfortunately does not cover Mathurā. For example, it is unclear if artists themselves were gendered. Though it is assumed that they were male the medieval Nadlai stone inscription apparently refers to a woman working in a team of artist (Misra 2011: 49).

So on this point I will break company with all of the previous commentators who took the piece as a Mathurān work. If the piece does not look like a Mathurān piece it probably isn't – think horse not zebra.

The Punjab, itinerant workman, or 1970

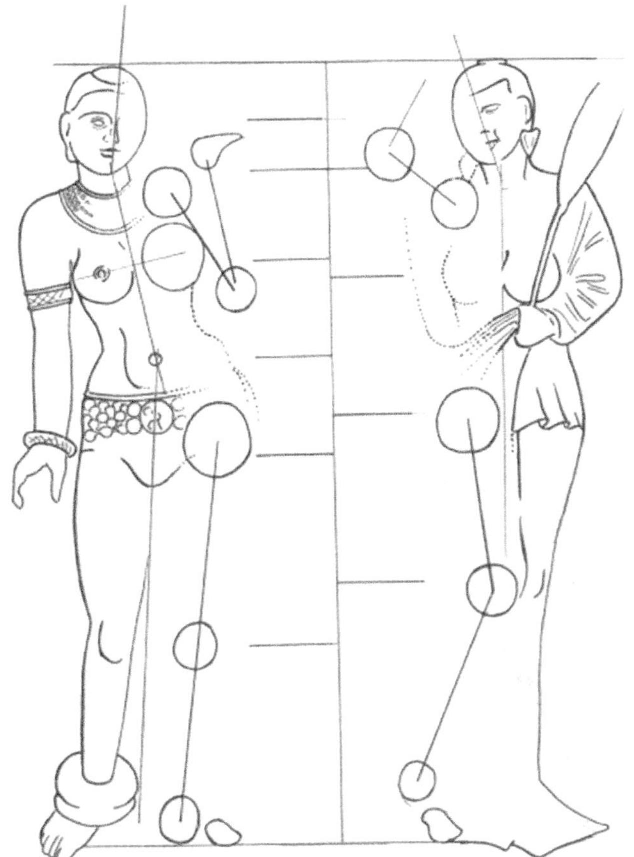

Figure 4. Speculative construction schemes for a Mathurān nymph (left) and a Cleveland dancer (right) showing the marked differences in proportions. (Drawing: author.)

There are three realistic possibilities for who made the piece, all of which have a bearing on the date – which was the nominal question this paper began with. The first is that it was not made in Mathurā but simply from Mathurān stone, in which case a location between the two centres in the Punjab, such as Sanghol, would be logical. Information about Sanghol's sculptural tradition is limited but both Mathurān and Gandhāran objects were imported to the site. If Sanghol did not have its own sculptural tradition, it is possible that other unexcavated sites in the Punjab did and might have produced pieces borrowing from the major centres to the north or south. This would imply a date later than both the Mathurān and Gandhāran prototypes. The second possibility is that a non-Mathurān artist (perhaps one from Gandhāra) was employed in Mathurā to make a piece for a local purpose but in non-local style. This second possibility raises interesting questions about who determines an image's appearance. Do artists make work 'on spec' and sell it to patrons? Or do patrons commission works? And, in the latter case, how and in what detail do they specify the appearance of a sculpture? One of the issues with railing pillars is precisely that they are parts of large sets so one usually expects to find stylistically similar examples, unless this piece was a repair or replacement stylistically at odds with its neighbours, or never formed part of an actual railing.The third possibility is that this is a modern concoction, a fantasy piece, made by a skilled modern forger in the 1970s. We need seriously to entertain this possibility with all pieces that have no archaeological provenance, and so far no one has done so publicly in this case. It would be an elaborate and very skilled forgery, but that would also explain the way it closely parallels superficial elements of Mathurān or Gandhāran art while apparently deviating from underlying technical practices. It might also explain why Kim sees direct classical borrowings rather than the more logical intermediary of Gandhāra.

After I raised this possibility at the Gandhāra Connections workshop, and following the discussion of details (below), several participants were convinced that the piece is indeed a modern forgery.[23] It is important to point out that although I think this is the most likely explanation for its incongruities

[23] The original presentation and questions are available online at <http://podcasts.ox.ac.uk/problems-chronology-Gandhāran-art-session-4b-24th-march-2017-0> (last accessed 21st February 2018), though a small section is missing in the middle part of the recording.

(think horse, not zebra) there is no 'smoking gun' and more importantly authenticity is not the purpose of this paper. Genuine or not the Cleveland Dancers have clearly motivated Carter to make interesting observations about Gandhāran art (1992) and they have already posed interesting questions about cultural exchange through their incongruities.

Some details

The following points cover some, but not all, of the details of the pillar. They are supplementary to rather than a replacement for the lengthy discussion in Carter (1982).

Grapevines

Usually Mathurān pillars feature a single upper register, with either onlookers or foliage.[24] The Cleveland pillar has both, with the top register composed of foliage, and overlapping with the onlookers below. The foliage in this case is composed of a grape vine, which has drawn comment from a number of contributors. Carter places most weight on its presence, connecting it to Dionysiac influence:

> ... it appears most probable that the Mathurān sculptor who executed this work allowed himself to be strongly influenced by Gandharan imagery in order to depict more authentically the exotic Yakṣa paradise far away among the snowy peaks of the northwest where grapevines flourished to provide their amrita substance, the wine of the grape. (Carter 1982: 255)

I have already explained, contra Carter, why this is not a Mathurān sculptor (and we have no idea if it is a 'he') but what about the grapevine? Grapevine motifs are not uncommon motifs at Mathurā. There are a number of door-jambs and Jain decorated tablets (known as *āyāgapaṭas*) which use grapes as a decorative technique. The detail here (Figure 5) is from the Mora door-jamb (Smith 1901: pl. XXVI; see also Quintanilla 2007: figs. 264-266). Sharma (1995: figs. 34 and 37) features two more comparable door-jambs, and Quintanilla (2007: figs. 150-153 and 162-164) identifies three *āyāgapaṭas* which also show the motif.

The grapevine motif is the element most suggestive of a date. All of the doorjambs and *āyāgapaṭas* I have mentioned are similar in style and might date to the mid-first century AD. This is Quintanilla's comment (2007: 125):

> The stylistic characteristics noted in the ornamental carvings of the Pārśvanātha and Nāṃdighoṣa āyāgapatas are like those on the Vasu doorjamb which is dated by an inscription to the reign of svāmi mahākṣatrapa Śoḍāsa and the Morā doorjamb which was found at the same place as a stone slab carved with an inscription also dated to the time of Śoḍāsa.[25] Joanna Williams has suggested that the Vasu doorjamb dates to the third century AD, and that its ornamental reliefs were carved later than the inscription, for the relief carvings seem to her to presage those of the Gupta period in their elegance. However, they do not concur with the dry, schematized styles of the third century AD.

[24] There are certainly exceptions. A Sanghol pillar (Gupta 2003: no. 10) features a building; a piece in the National Museum (Delhi J278; Agrawala 1966: no. 15) depicts a bather below a rocky outcrop, a feature seen on a few other pillars; and there is a Mathurā Museum piece (J2; Quintanilla 2007: fig. 52) in which the upper register is a medallion with a narrative scene. At least two pillars (Czuma 1985: no. 29; Pal 2003: fig. 2) have both onlookers above and foliage below. Another Cleveland Museum piece (1943.71) also has both but this is a complete railing carved in one piece and the onlookers are a part of the architrave rather than the pillar.

[25] Joe Cribb spoke at the event about chronology in general (see his paper in the present volume). Positioning Sodasa beyond a vague 'first century' bracket is not straightforward.

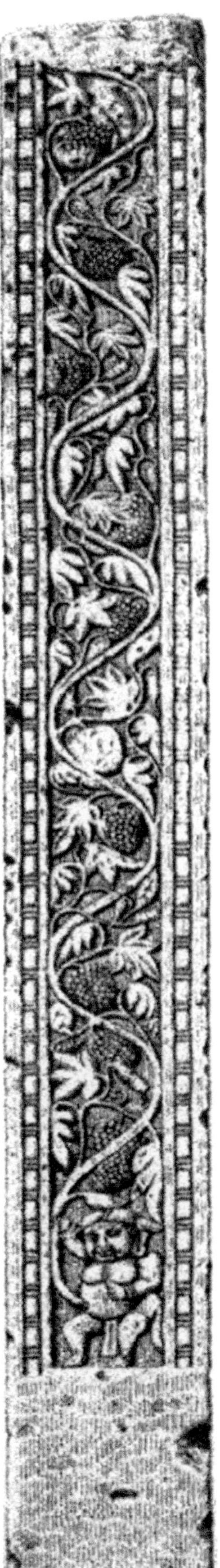

Figure 5. Drawing of the Mora door-jamb. (After Smith 1901: pl. XXVI.)

Quintanilla generally has far too much confidence in the accuracy of stylistic dating deriving from connoisseurship. However, tentatively, on the basis of find spot, similarity of style, and palaeography, it is plausible all these pieces date to the first century. Perhaps the use of the grapevine as a motif flourished at a particular workshop in this period and reflects the northern tastes associated with the Satrap rulers? If we wish to imagine the import of a northern artist this seems like a sensible moment.[26] At least one of the door-jambs features a standing figure with a spear in the armour of a heavy cavalryman (Sharma 1995: fig. 34). If the maker of the Cleveland pillar is not simply using these pieces as prototypes at a much later date then the pillar might date to the mid-first century and be the work of a northern workman associated with the wider Śaka community.[27]

If this were true, it makes the date much less interesting than the implications. It would suggest, given the workshop hypothesis, that this was intended for a non-Buddhist site (none of the doorjambs show any evidence of coming from a Buddhist site and the *āyāgapaṭas* are all Jain), and that there was an influx of northern artists in the first century AD, very early in the development of Gandhāran art.

Musicians

Below the grapevines are four female musicians. They employ cymbals, two lyres, and a lute-like stringed instrument. Their hair is tied up and braided in the same manner as the dancers below, they wear similar leaf-shaped ear-rings, and two have folds of material visible at their shoulders which suggest similar dresses. None of these features are typical for Mathurā.

Onlookers are not unusual on Mathurān railing pillars though they are usually set in an architectural frame of some sort, such as a window or a railing. When depicted they almost always conform to the same fashions of hair style and ear-rings as the nymphs. Even where drapery is show in such a way as to give the impression of a non-diaphanous dress (Vogel 1929: fig. 47) the individuals still wear the same heavy disc-shaped ear-rings commonly found in other depictions.

Musical instruments are not commonly depicted in Mathurān art. An image of a male flute player on a railing pillar whose costume suggests a north-western ethnicity[28] is one example. I am unaware of any showing similar instruments to those used by the onlookers though similar depictions seem to be relatively common in Gandhāran art.

[26] Though several railing pillars from Mathurā, one featuring a figure in northern nomadic dress, have names of artists and these seem to be local rather than Śaka (Lüders 1961: #145-148). However there has been no systematic study of artists' names recorded on Mathurān pieces.

[27] The famous lion capital inscription is engraved in Kharoṣṭhī and so testifies to the presence of skilled foreign workers in the period.

[28] See *British Museum Quarterly* 1965: 64, fig. 15.

Stone ground

Beneath the lower dancers the lower register has a stone background. The use of a stone pattern in the lowest register eventually becomes a standard element of this iconography in Nepal in the sixth and seventh centuries. Amongst Mathurān railing pillars a stone pattern is not unknown,[29] being most common under figures who hold a tree and stand on a dwarf (the śālabhañjikā pose).

A nymph on a corner bracket which has a stone ground beneath the figure can be dated archaeologically.[30] It was found at Sonkh with a variety of other pieces which undoubtedly belonged to a railing pillar. One of the crossbars has an inscription on the end, which would have been hidden from view in the final construction (Hartel 1993: 308). The crossbar was subsequently re-used for another carving which has damaged the part of the inscription in which the date was recorded but enough of the king's name (Kaniṣka) survives that combined with diagnostic characters it can be firmly placed in the reign of Kaniṣka I (*c.* AD 127-150).[31]

However, the Cleveland stone pattern does not compare particularly well with either Mathurān or later Nepalese or Kashmiri uses of the design. One element is particularly odd. The stone design projects outwards beyond the body pillar, in such a way that it would obscure the join between crossbar and pillar. I am unaware of this feature on any other Mathurān pillar, though the frequent lack of photographs from different angles makes it difficult to confirm.[32]

Some thoughts on a date

In summary, the piece draws heavily on non-Mathurān prototypes. Those elements in common with other Mathurān pieces, particularly the grapevine, suggest a date in the first century AD (earlier than that usually given in publications). However if it draws heavily on Gandhāran imagery (itself hard to date) this might suggest a later date. However, the most likely explanation for the juxtapositions and incongruities in the piece remains that it is made much later based upon existing pieces – most likely as a modern fantasy.

How wrong could we be?

Let us for a moment take the possibility of a late Kṣatrap or early Kushan date seriously. Czuma (1985) applies such a dating for all of the pieces which were exhibited alongside it, and Trivedi (2004: 58) takes it to be the case for almost all nymphs. Pal (2003) and Quintanilla (2007) give a broader range of dates for Mathurān art in general but, on the basis of stylistic similarity, both place the overwhelming bulk of nymphs in the second century AD.

---

[29] Stone patterns on railing pillars and brackets include: Smith 1901: pl. 29, fig. 1; Lee 1949: figs. 1-2; Czuma 1985: no. 34a; Sharma 1995: fig. 23; Gupta 2004: nos. 4 and 13; Agrawala 1966: no. 15.

[30] Some non-architectural pieces with related iconography also have a bearing. A bronze figurine published by Goetz (1963) from South Arabia offers no immediate help as Goetz appears to depend on the Indian evidence to date the piece. A more useful example is the well-known ivory figurine recovered at Pompeii as the eruption in AD 79 provides a terminus ante quem. The ivories from Begram also depict many female figures of similar iconography, though their date is contested (attractive images and a list of important treatments are given in the short pamphlet by Simpson 2011). However these are problematic comparanda as it is not always clear where they were made, what role such portable pieces played in transmitting artistic ideas, or whether contemporaries thought of such domestic figures as equivalent to the public images on railing architecture.

[31] Sharma (1995) gives *c.* AD 100 but this is mostly a function of his early dating. Unfortunately though the Sanghol railing also has an archaeological context there is nothing to establish the date of that.

[32] Projection over the edge is not itself unique to this piece. In a piece from the Indian Museum in Kolkata the arm of the figure projects beyond the column (see Auboyer 1948: no. 1). In my original talk I suggested that since the stone ground is not a ubiquitous feature of Mathurān art it would be an odd thing for a forger to pick up and then misinterpret, so this might be evidence for a contemporary artist.

How wrong could this be? An analogy suggests we could be very wrong indeed. Mary Shepherd Slusser published a major study of a set of wooden struts from Nepal in 2010 (Slusser 2010). Not only do these struts inherit elements of one of the nymph iconographies (the śālabhañjikā), they are also conceptually similar. Based solely on stylistic assumptions (and relative similarity) these struts were broadly dated to the mid-second millennium AD. In fact, as Slusser demonstrates, by combining very careful study of the objects with radiocarbon dates, the tradition can be shown to begin six hundred years earlier in the late first millennium AD. Could our dating of Mathurān sculpture, or for the purposes of the event at which this paper was presented, Gandhāran sculpture, be as badly wrong?

The problem is in part one of assessing the degree of conservatism/diversity in Mathurān workshops. Are so many figures on railing pillars so similar because the bulk of our surviving examples belong to a single period of relatively intense construction (in the late first or early second century?) or because Mathurān artists were very conservative. Are stylistically odd pieces, such as the nymphs on gateway brackets from Kankali Tila (Quintanilla 2007: figs. 39-41), chronologically distinct from the bulk of the pieces, or simply experimental (as the Cleveland piece would need to be if genuine)? The answers to those questions would take us some way to understanding the mind-set of patrons and artists, and it might answer some interesting questions about why railing pillars around the sacred sites of different traditions are indistinguishable, or how viewers understood and interpreted 'nudity'.[33] And they might, incidentally, date the individual pieces of sculpture.

Conclusion

As I have tried to sketch out in this paper, the Cleveland pillar raises a lot of interesting questions about our understanding of the relationship between workshops in Gandhāra and those in the city of Mathurā. How experimental were the artists? Which elements did they adopt, and why? That the Cleveland pillar has been consistently misidentified as a product of a Mathurān artist or workshop shows that the criteria for identifying workshops are not adequate to the task. The female figures at Mathurā, which are difficult to date for most of the same reasons as Gandhāran pieces (i.e. they lack inscribed dates or secure archaeological contexts), also offer a host of interesting questions about the way they were understood by contemporary audiences, and the differences between Gandhāran and Mathurān audiences.

Answers to almost all of the questions sketched out here either depend upon dates or impinge on our dating of objects. However, I would like to suggest that pursuing the question of dating is probably the least profitable way of approaching this. In the first chapter of this book, Joe Cribb gives a very detailed presentation of our current understanding of the political chronology of the north-west in the early centuries AD, something that for a long time was synonymous with the 'date of Kaniṣka'. I recently gave a lengthy account (Bracey 2017) of the historiography of this problem from 1960 until its resolution in the last decade. Most of the advances that were made actually came from studies of sources (text, epigraphy, or coins) which were not directed at the problem itself but at answering some other question.

[33] I have previously suggested that there is a correlation between the prominence of the order of Buddhist nuns, textual evidence of antipathy/discomfort towards women's independence, and the portrayal of 'nudity' in Kushan art. Art does reflect in complex ways social anxieties (at least amongst that section wealthy enough to patronise it). However, some of the ideas I have sketched out in this article might suggest, contrary to my earlier thoughts, that the apparently more revealing depictions at Mathurā might reflect the sort of female images which are made ('nymphs' rather than goddesses), rather than a general change in the practice of depicting the female form.

The same is likely to apply to these nymphs in particular, and both Mathurān and Gandhāran art in general. Dates matter for our understanding of relationships between the centres, for workshop practices, and social responses to art. For example, it is a genuinely interesting question as to why both Mathurā and Gandhāra have their own consistent śālabhañjikā type of nymph but neither seems to have influenced the other. If either art were insular that would be explicable, but both borrow heavily in other features, such as the grapevine discussed above or representations of the Buddha. Addressing this sort of question means developing a better understanding of workshop practices and patronage (far more complex in the region of Gandhāra than the city of Mathurā) and will likely lead to a better understanding of dating. However, focusing on dating is not the route to arrive at that solution. So, no, to answer the question of the title, it is not appropriate to ask a celestial lady's age.

References

Agrawala P.K. 1966. *Mathura Railing Pillars.* Varanasi: Prithvi Prakashan.

Agrawala P.K. 1971. Mātṛkā Reliefs in Early Indian Art. *East and West* 21/1-2: 79-89.

Asthana S.P. 1999. *Mathurà Kalà (A Catalogue of Mathura Sculptures in the National Museum)*, New Delhi: National Museum.

Auboyer J. 1948. Indian Sculpture at Burlington House. *The Burlington Magazine* 90/539: 32-42.

Bauze-Picron C. 2002. 'Nidhis' and Other Images of Richness and Fertility in Ajaṇṭā. *East and West* 52/1-4: 225-284.

Behrendt K.A. 2009. The Ancient Reuse and Recontextualisation of Gandharan Images: Second to Seventh Centuries CE. *South Asian Studies* 25: 11-27.

Bracey R. 2011. Kankali Tila and Kushan Chronology. Pages 65-79 in S. Garg & S. Bhandare (eds), *Felicitas: Essays in Numismatics, Epigraphy & History in Honour of Joe Cribb.* Mumbai: Reesha Books.

Bracey R. 2017. The Date of Kanishka since 1960. *Indian Historical Review* 44/1: 1-41.

Carter M. 1982. The Bacchants of Mathura: New Evidence of Dionysiac Yaksha Imagery from Kushan Mathura. *The Bulletin of the Cleveland Museum of Art* 69/8: 247-257.

Carter M. 1992. Dionysiac Festival and Gandhāran Imagery. Pages 51-60 in R. Gyselen (ed), *Banquets d'Orient.* (Res Orientalis 4). (Res Orientales IV), Bures-sur-Yvette: Groupe pour l'Étude de la Civilisation du Moyen-Orient.

Carter M. 2015. *Arts of the Hellenized East, Pecious Metalwork and Gems of the Pre-Islamic era.* New York: Thames & Hudson.

Couture A. & Schmid C. 2001. The Harivaṃśa, the Goddess Ekānaṃśā, and the Iconography of the Vṛṣṇi Triads. *Journal of the American Oriental Society* 121/2: 173-192.

Coomaraswamy A.K. 1926. *Yakṣas.* Washington, DC: Smithsonian Institution. (Reprinted New Delhi, Munshiram Manoharlal, 1971.)

Czuma S. 1977. Mathura Sculpture in the Cleveland Museum Collection. *The Bulletin of the Cleveland Museum of Art* 64/3: 83-114.

Czuma S. 1985. *Kushan Sculpture: Images from Early India.* Cleveland and Ohio: Cleveland Museum of Art.

Dar S.R. 2016. *Dusting Off Doubts: A Story of Waxing and Waning Fortune of Gandharan Collection in Lahore Museum 1867 -2007.* Lahore Museum.

DeCaroli R. 2015. *Image Problems: The Origin and Development of the Buddha's Image in Early South Asia.* Seattle: University of Washington Press.

Dehejia V. & Rockwell P. 2016. *The Unfinished: The Stone Carvers at Work in the Indian Subcontinent.* New Delhi: Roli Books.

Gill S. 2000. *Phantasmic Anatomy of the Statues of Mathurā.* New Delhi: Munshiram Manoharlal.

Gill S. 2010. Celestial women in a ring around the Buddhist stupa, the case of Sanghol. Pages 143-165 In H.P. Ray (ed), *Sanghol and the Archaeology of the Punjab.* New Delhi: Aryan Books.

Goetz H. 1963. An Indian Bronze from South Arabia. *Archaeology* 16/3: 187-189.

Gupta S.P. (ed) 2003. *Kushāṇa sculptures from Sanghol (1st-2nd century A. D.)*. New Delhi: National Museum.
Hartel H. 1993. *Excavations at Sonkh: 2500 Years of a Town in Mathura District*. Berlin: Reimer.
Joshi N.P. 1986. *Mātrkās: Mothers in Kuṣāṇa Art*. New Delhi: Kanak Publications.
Khan M.A. 2005. *Gandharan Stone Sculpture in the Taxila Museum*. Taxila: Department of Archaeology and Museums.
Kim S. 2011. The Beginnings of the East-West Dialogue: An Examination of Dionysiac Representations in Gandharan and Kushan-Mathuran Art. Pages 16-35 in M.Y.L. Huang (ed), *Beyond Boundaries: East and West Cross Cultural Encounters*. New Castle upon Tyne: Cambridge Scholars.
Lee S.E.1949. A Kushan Yakshi Bracket. *Artibus Asiae* 12/3: 184-88.
Lee S.E. 1977. The Year in Review for 1977. *The Bulletin of the Cleveland Museum of Art* 65/1: 2-42.
Luczanits C. 2008. *Gandhara: The Buddhist Heritage of Pakistan*. New York: Asia Society.
Lüders H. 1961. *Mathura Inscriptions* (unpublished papers edited by Klaus L. Janert). Göttingen: Vandenhoeck & Ruprecht.
Misra R.N. 2011. Silpis in Ancient India: Beyond their Ascribed Locus in Ancient Society. *Social Scientist* 39/7-8: 43-54.
Mokashi R. 2015. Expressions of Faith: Courtesans as Gleaned through Ancient India Donative Inscriptions. *International Journal of Social Science and Humanities Research* 3/2: 491-497.
Mosteller J.F. 1991. *The Measure of Form: A New Approach for the Study of Indian Sculpture*. New Delhi: Shakti Malik.
Pal P. 2003. *Asian Art at the Norton Simon Museum. Vol.1: Art from the Indian Subcontinent*. New Haven: New University Press.
Peterson S. 2011-12. An Account of the Dionysiac Presence in Indian Art and Culture. Unpublished paper available online: <https://www.academia.edu/1503231/An_account_of_the_Dionysiac_p resen ce_in_Indi an_art_and_culture> (accessed April 2017).
Quintanilla S.R. 2007. *History of Early Stone Sculpture at Mathura, ca. 150 BCE - 100 CE*. Leiden: Brill.
Rangarajan H. 2004. Feminine Beauty in Divine Figures in Indian Art. Pages 103-108 in M.N. Tiwari and K. Giri (eds), *Indian Art and Aesthetics: Endeavours in Interpretation*. New Delhi: Aryan Books.
Rossi A.M. & Rossi F. 1995. *Sculpture from a Sacred Realm*. London: Rossi & Rossi.
Rowland B. 1953. *The Art and Architecture of India*. Harmondsworth: Penguin Books.
Sharma R.C. 1995. *Buddhist Art: Mathura School*. New Delhi: Wiley Eastern Limited.
Simpson S. 2011. *Indian Ivories from Afghanistan: The Begram Hoard*. London: British Museum Press
Slusser M.S. 2010. *The Antiquity of Nepalese Wood Carving*. Seattle: University of Washington Press.
Smith V.A. 1901. *The Jain Stupa and Other Antiquities*. Allahabad: Government Press.
Srinivasan D.M. 2005. The Mauryan Gaṇikā from Didārgañj (Pāṭaliputra). *East and West* 55/1-4: 345-362.
Sunil, G. 2001/2002. Torana Salabhanjika: The Transformations of a Motif. *The Sri Lanka Journal of the Humanities*, 27-28/1-2: 126-145
Trivedi S.D. 2004. Apsaras Figurines from Kaṅkālī Mound, Mathura. Pages 57-66 in M.N. Tiwari and K. Giri (eds), *Indian Art and Aesthetics: Endeavours in Interpretation*. New Delhi: Aryan Books.
Viennot O. 1956. The Goddess Mahishâsuramardini in Kushâna Art. *Artibus Asiae* 19/3-4: 368-373.
Vogel J. Ph. 1929. The woman and tree or Śālabhañjikā in Indian literature and art. *Acta Orientalia* 7: 201-31.
Wangu M.B. 2003. Images of Indian Goddesses: Myths, Meanings and Models. New Delhi: Abhinav.
Zwalf W. 1996. *A Catalogue of the Gandhāra Sculpture in the British Museum*. London: British Museum Press.

Architectural evidence for the Gandhāran tradition after the third century

Kurt Behrendt

This study attempts to characterize the late horizon of Gandhāra's sacred architectural tradition in an effort to address larger questions of chronology. In particular, I examine the issue of earthquakes and the consequent repair or replacement of existing structures and imagery. In this light, the sudden or punctuated reconceptualization of the sacred precincts following the collapse of old structures is particularly telling as it reveals the changing interests of patrons. Focusing on the micro-chronologies of a series of small sites, this paper traces modifications to the sacred area. Changing structural typologies will be considered in conjunction with categories of recovered sculpture and numismatic evidence. After starting with the Taxila sites of Kālawān and Jauliāñ, where evolving masonry techniques allow chronologically distinct construction phases to be distinguished (Figure 1) (Behrendt 2004: 255ff.), developments in the Peshawar Basin are considered, focusing on the sites of Mekhasanda and Ranigat. Drawing on these micro-chronologies some broad observations can be made regarding the development of the massive sacred precincts of Takht-i-Bāhī, Butkara I, and the Dharmarājikā complex. Together I hope this evidence offers a foundation for better understanding the changing Gandhāran architectural and sculptural tradition.

The early seventh-century Chinese pilgrim Xuanzang describes Gandhāra as '1000 *sangharamas*, which are deserted and in ruins. They are filled with wild shrubs and are solitary to the last degree.' (Beal 1884: 98). Although seemingly categorical, clearly all the Buddhist sites were not abandoned as Xuanzang goes on to tell us of an inhabited monastery outside of the city of Pushkalāvatī (Beal 1884: 110) and of the restoration of Kaniṣka's *stūpa*, which had been damaged by fire (Beal 1884: 103), that is probably the cruciform *stūpa* at Shāh-jī-kī-ḍherī (Kuwayama 1997). He notes other activity in the city of Po-lu-sha, likely Sahrī-Bahlol (Errington 1993), where he encountered a monastery with fifty priests (Beal 1884: 112). The decline of the Gandhāran tradition is attributed by Xuanzang and Sun Yun to the Hephthalites, and Marshall goes a step further to suggest iconoclasm and the burning of monasteries (Marshall 1951: 76-77). A more recent suggestion that trade routes shifted in favor of the Kabul Valley in Afghanistan seems reasonable as there was a clear economic decline in Gandhāra in the mid-sixth century (Kuwayama 2006: 124-127). In all of these scenarios it is possible that earthquakes could have played a key role in the rising and falling fortunes of the Gandhāran tradition and may well have caused the widespread destruction Xuanzang observed.

Understanding the Gandhāran sacred area in relation to earthquakes is important given the seismic instability of the region. Faccenna and Marshall both suggested that earthquakes created early phase I and II horizons of destruction at Taxila and Butkara I respectively (Marshall 1951: 118; Faccenna 1980 (1): 134-135). More recent excavations at the urban site of Barikot in Swat have uncovered levels of destruction that can be dated using C-14 analysis; here Olivieri notes earthquakes occurring circa AD 50, AD 120, AD 230, and AD 260 (Olivieri 2014: 140-41; cf. the paper by Olivieri and Filigenzi in the present volume). The periodic destruction of sacred areas also explains why so many damaged schist images were recovered in reuse contexts at sites like the Dharmarājikā complex, Kālawān, Sahrī-Bahlol and Takht-i-Bāhī (Behrendt 2009). Earthquakes may also account for the fact that essentially no narrative sculpture has been found in situ and why so many 'early' *stūpas* were rebuilt and adorned with stucco imagery. The pattern of destruction and rebuilding at sites across Taxila, the Peshawar Basin, and Swat suggests that much of what has survived in the archaeological record likely dates to the later stages of the Gandhāran Buddhist tradition.

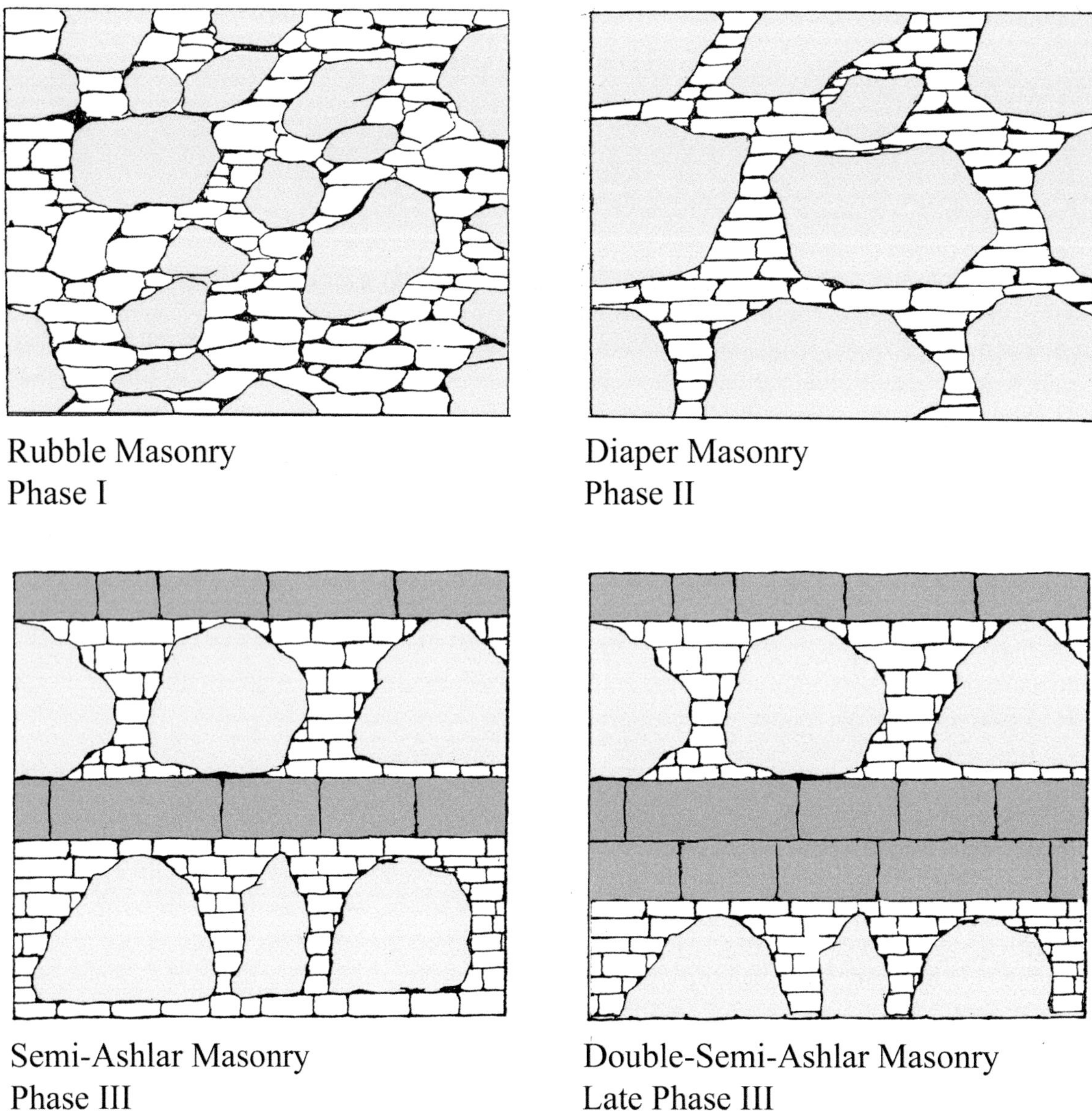

Figure 1. Sketch showing main Taxila masonry types: phase I rubble masonry, phase II diaper masonry, phase III semi-ashlar masonry, and late phase III double-course semi-ashlar masonry (Kurt Behrendt, modified from Marshall 1916: fig. 1).

Over the last hundred years the seismic activity in and around the region of Gandhāra has been systematically documented, evidence that shows this region is subjected to numerous and sometimes massive earthquakes (Figure 2). Given Gandhāra's five-hundred-year tradition, major earthquakes must have periodically occurred and there would have been constant smaller quakes mirroring today's seismic activity.

Kālawān

The Taxila sacred area of Kālawān is a good place to begin as the founding structures were all constructed in diaper masonry during my phase II period (Behrendt 2004: 255-265). Subsequently, some of these structures were refurbished and the site was expanded using phase III semi-ashlar masonry (Figure 3). The early central monument at Kālawān is the A4 *stūpa*, with its oversized relic chamber (Behrendt 2006:

Recent Earthquakes in Pakistan and Afghanistan

Place	Date	Magnitude
Hindu Kush	2015	6.3
Hindu Kush	2015	7.5
Jarm Afghanistan	2015	7.5
Jalalabad	2013	5.5
Hindu Kush	2009	6.2
Ziarat	2008	6.4
Kashmir/NWFP	2005	7.6
Hindu Kush	2002	7.4
Dashkin	2002	6.3
Peshawar	1992	6.0
Hindu Kush	1991	6.4
Quetta	1990	6.1
Hindu Kush	1984	6.1
Hunza, Swat/NWFP	1974	6.2
Peshawar	1972	6.2
Gwadar	1947	7.6
Quetta	1935	7.5
NWFP	1909	7.2

Figure 2. Recent earthquakes in and around the area of Gandhāra (National Geophysical Data Center/World Data, NOAA).

92). Adjacent are the large conventional A12 *stūpa* and the A14 *stūpa* shrine. These three relic structures align with monastery C suggesting that they all might have been constructed together when the site was initially founded. Subsequently, additional *stūpa* shrines were added to the east (A1 and A13) and probably more *stūpa* shrines stood along the western edge of the sacred area, though these structures are too damaged for certain identification.

At some stage structures started to be made in phase III semi-ashlar masonry at all of the sites in Taxila, including Kālawān. The late modifications to the Kālawān sacred area include the construction of the sizable multi-storied monastery B along with image shrines and a *stūpa* shrine in the sacred area. Perhaps most interesting from the perspective of rebuilding are the A2 and A5 shrines that stand on the northern edge of the sacred area. These phase III shrines rest on multiple phase II diaper remains (Marshall 1936: 166). While we do not know the form of these earlier structures, the fact that the rest of this sacred area to the east and west is enclosed by two-celled shrines done in diaper masonry suggests that similar structures originally stood in the north. The appearance of an early shrine format in phase III semi-

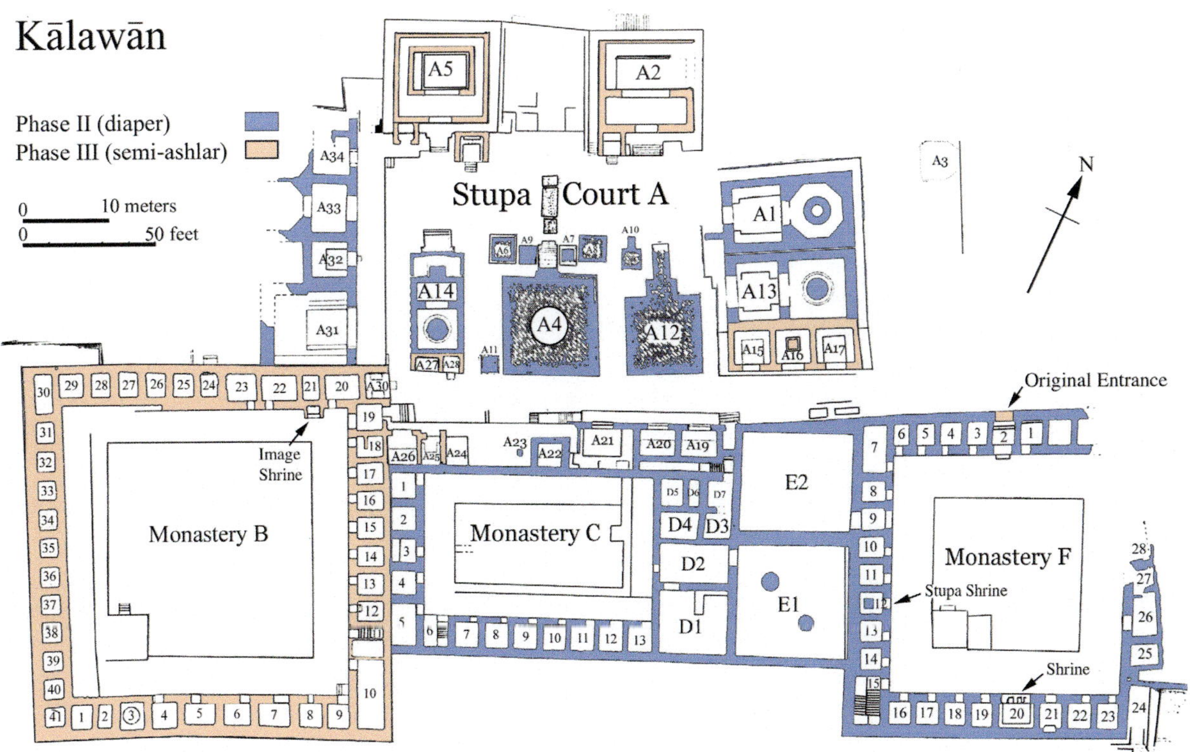

Figure 3. Plan of sacred area and monasteries at Kālawān, Taxila, with phase II and phase III construction indicated (Kurt Behrendt, modified from Marshall 1951: pl. 72).

ashlar masonry seems to indicate that these monuments were rebuilt because they were crucial to the devotional function of this sacred area. While not conclusive evidence of an earthquake it is noteworthy that no other two-celled shrines in semi-ashlar masonry are known from Taxila.

The inscriptional and numismatic evidence from this site indicates a first-century foundation and an occupation period well into the fourth century (Table 1). Next to a reliquary in *stūpa* shrine A1, a long donative inscription on a copper plate was found that mentions the 134th year of Azes – according to Marshall (1951: 53, 257) AD 86 or Cribb AD 88 (cf. his paper in the present volume). The 203 coins found at Kālawān comprise one Azes (57-10 BC), one Hermaeus imitation, five Wima Takto (c. AD 90-113), four Wima Kadphises (c. AD 113-127), seventeen Kaniṣka (c. AD 127-150), two Huviṣka (c. AD 150-190), 164 Vāsudeva (c. AD 190-227, mostly from a single hoard), three later Kushan, one Ardashir, four Kushano-Sasanian, two Hormazd (AD 285-300) (Marshall 1951: 322-341; Errington 1999: 216). These numismatic finds indicate a period of activity that is in accord with the kinds of sculpture recovered. They include twenty-three narrative fragments and related images that roughly can be placed in the time of the Great Kushans. From phase III or approximately the time of Vāsudeva and later are four large schist devotional images (some fragmentary) as well as sixty-three stucco heads and major fragments (Marshall 1951: 322-341). I have argued elsewhere (Behrendt 2009) that the narrative imagery and related fragments, which largely survive as heterogeneous broken pieces, belong to the early part of the site's life and were redeposited after being damaged (perhaps as the result of an earthquake). The later part of Kālawān's occupation, when the semi-ashlar phase III structures built, corresponds to the time when significant quantities of stucco imagery were added. This modification and repair of the site may correspond to an earthquake that damaged much of the schist imagery. Taken together this evidence suggests an early phase II foundation and an occupation that went to the middle of phase III. Kālawān is an important site as there is notably no late phase III evidence of monumental images or related massive shrines.

Jauliāñ

While the Taxila site of Jauliāñ was founded during phase II – founding structures include a main *stūpa* and monastery fabricated in phase II diaper masonry – most of the sacred area and corresponding surviving imagery dates to phase III (Table 1). In this later period the site was expanded with the addition of many semi-ashlar masonry shrines and small *stūpas* (Figure 4). Patronage continued late into the Gandhāran period as indicated by several monumental image shrines constructed in double-semi-ashlar masonry (C14-C16). This dating appears to be generally confirmed by the numismatic evidence. Of the 119 coins recovered at the site thirty-one were minted under the Great Kushans or before (four local Taxilan, one Apollodotus II (80-65 BC), one Gondophares (AD 20-45), one Kujūla Kadphises (AD 30-78), seven Kaniṣka I (AD 127-150), six Huviṣka (AD 151-189), and eleven unidentified Kushan). A late Kushan horizon is attested by thirty-seven coins of Vāsudeva (AD 190-226), but this group also includes later imitations (Vāsudeva II is AD 268-308 and later copies). There are at least fifty-one coins from the late Gandhāran period, which comprise one Varaharan II (AD 276-293), three Hormazd II (AD 300-303), four Shapur II (AD 309-79), two Shapur III (AD 383-388), twenty-four Indo-Sasanian and Sasanian, and seventeen late Indo-Sasanian (Marshall 1951:385-386; Errington 1999: 212). Taking into consideration the fact that some of these coins would have remained in circulation for a considerable time, this evidence supports a late occupation for the site in a period that largely postdates the Kushans.

The surviving sculptural evidence at Jauliāñ is consistent with this late dating as a huge amount of stucco imagery survives at this site – some of it at a very large scale. *In situ* stucco imagery survives on the main *stūpa* and embellishing many of the small *stūpas* (Figure 5) and one thousand small heads and many other fragments were found in the sacred area (Marshall 1951: 384). Stucco assemblages of figures with particularly late iconography occur in seven small shrines that were added to the monastery (Behrendt 2004: 171-174). In contrast, no phase II schist narrative reliefs were found. Of the five schist sculptures recovered from Jauliāñ three are large devotional icons and two are small fragments (Marshall 1951: 384).

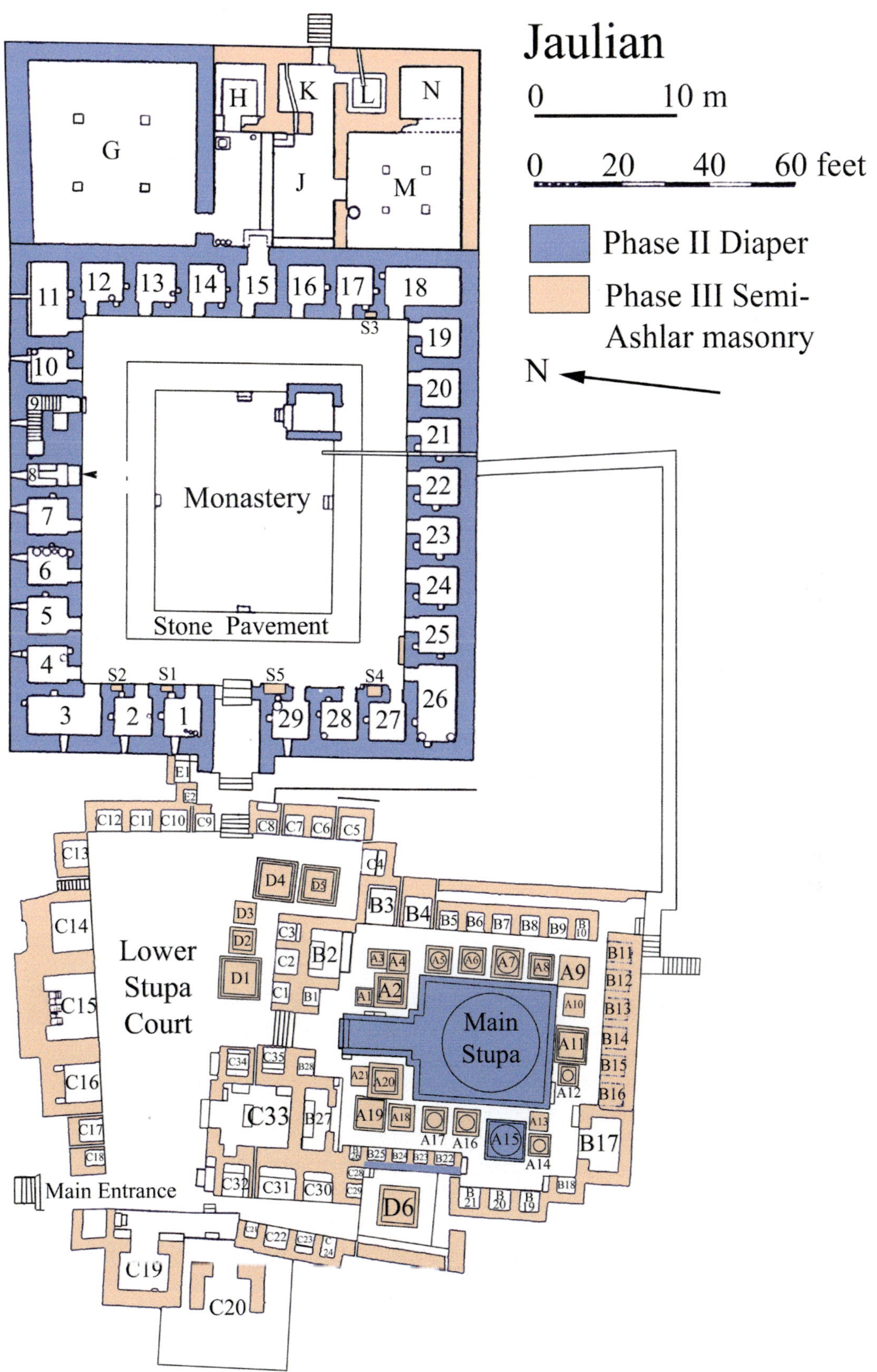

Figure 4. Plan of sacred area and monastery at Jauliāñ, Taxila, with phase II and phase III construction indicated (Kurt Behrendt, modified from Marshall 1951: pl. 101).

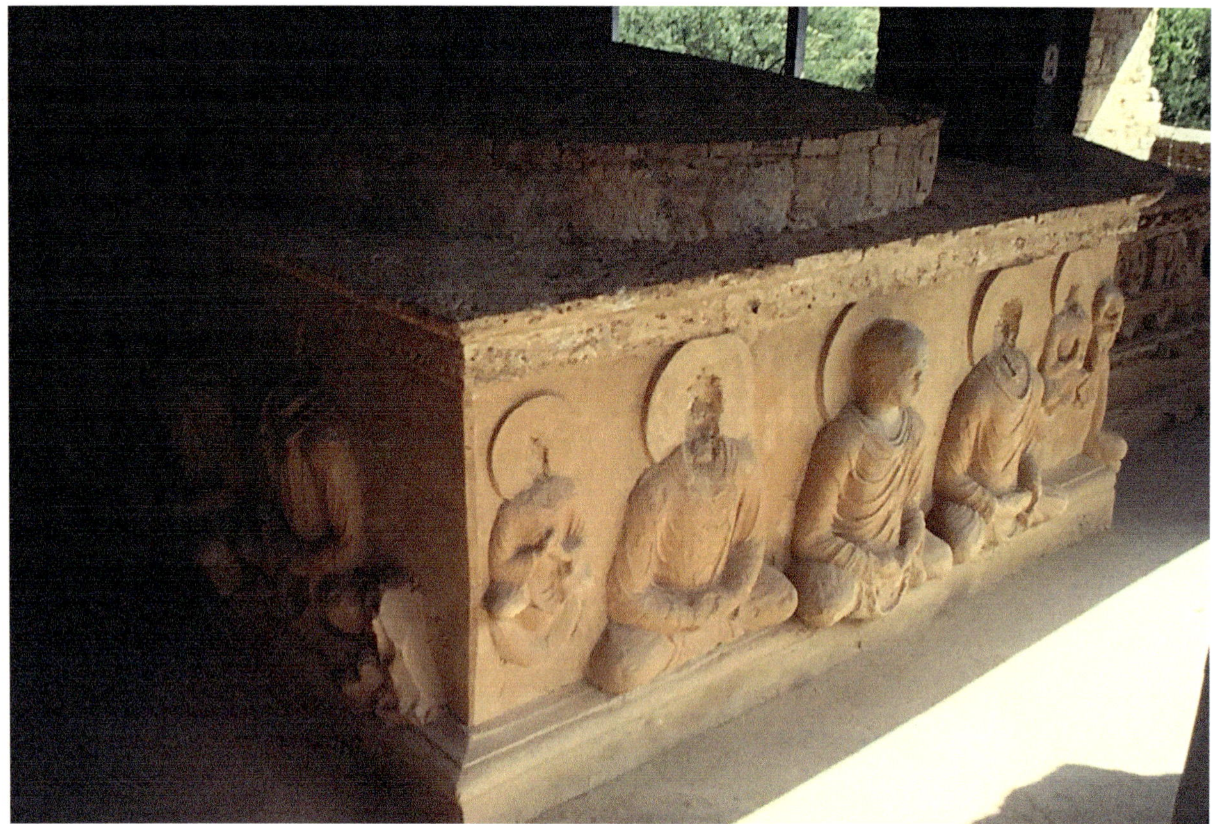

Figure 5. Jauliāñ small stūpa *A15, south face; diaper masonry* stūpa *with later stucco Buddha images. (Photo: Kurt Behrendt, 1992).*

At Jauliāñ the compact placement of small *stūpas* around the main *stūpa* follows a consistent pattern that can be observed at many sites across Gandhāra, good examples being the lower *stūpa* court at Takht-i-Bāhī (Figure 11), Mekhasanda (Figure 7) and the early *stūpa* court around the main *stūpa* at Ranigat (Figure 8). A clear pattern emerges suggesting that the most desirable location for a patron to build a small *stūpa* is adjacent to the stairway of the main *stūpa*. However, at Jauliāñ the small *stūpas* in this location (A2 and A20) are fabricated in kanjur masonry sitting on bases done in semi-ashlar masonry, their surfaces being embellished in stucco imagery. Their location suggests they are likely replacements for earlier structures built in conjunction with the main *stūpa*. The only diaper masonry *stūpa* to survive in this court (A15) (Marshall 1921: 4) sits off to the side in a rather undesirable location indicating that it was added at a point when all the space bracketing the front of the *stūpa* had been filled with other *stūpas*; it too is embellished with fairly large stucco Buddha images, suggesting refurbishment (Figure 5).

In the later part of the site's history, patrons enclosed this *stūpa* court with banks of image shrines executed in semi-ashlar phase III masonry. These image shrines neatly fit around the small *stūpas* indicating that they must postdate their construction. These image shrines are fairly small. The fact that they could have housed images that are generally smaller than life-size suggests they were fabricated in the early or middle part of phase III. The presence of *in situ* stucco remains of sculptures in some of these image shrines supports this conclusion. The placement of the image shrines around the upper court at Jauliāñ indicates that they must postdate the small *stūpas* as they neatly fit around these relic monuments. Based on these observations it would seem that all of the image shrines belong to the later part of Jauliāñ's history, which on the basis of the numismatic evidence places them in the third century or later. Consistently, the micro-chronologies of Gandhāran sites indicate that the earliest shrines are relatively small, as can be observed at Takht-i-Bāhī, Jamāl Garhī, Mekhasanda, and Thareli. In contrast, shrines large enough to house monumental images are the latest additions to a given sacred area, as is the case at Jauliāñ with shrines C14-C16 that were done in double course semi-ashlar masonry (Figure 1). Further, the vast majority of standing schist images recovered in excavations from Taxila and the Peshawar Basin range from about 1 m to nearly life-size, which seems in perfect agreement with the smaller image shrines that enclose the upper *stūpa* court at Jauliāñ (Figure 4).

Eventually when all the space in the upper *stūpa* court was exhausted, small *stūpas* and image shrines started to be constructed in the lower court, an area that was only fully enclosed at the end of the site's occupation with the construction of monumental image shrines along the north edge (C14-C16). An early foundation for at least part of the lower court is indicated by the fact that it provides access to an auxiliary small sacred area around *stūpa* D6. The eastern wall of the D6 court is done in diaper masonry. Although all of the other structures are in semi-ashlar this remnant may point to a phase II foundation for the D6 *stūpa*, which was ultimately refurbished. It is interesting that this small D6 *stūpa* must have had independent significance as no fewer than nine image shrines were added to the walkway leading into its enclosure, which were all done in semi-ashlar masonry.

Jauliāñ is crucially important because the form of its sacred area can be linked to complex architectural developments in the Peshawar Basin. The Jauliāñ phase III semi-ashlar image shrines can be directly compared to those found at the Peshawar Basin sites of Mekhasanda, Takht-i-Bāhī, Jamāl Garhī, Thareli, Ranigat, and Sikri. This is important because at Taxila the masonry development from rubble, to diaper to semi-ashlar and ultimately to double semi-ashlar provides a relative chronology (Figure 1). In the Peshawar Basin, limestone blocks were not available, resulting in a developed masonry construction technique that used interlocking irregular pieces of schist. While this technique was effective and allowed for the construction of monumental structures, it differs from site to site depending on available schist building materials and cannot be readily sequenced. Fortunately, structural typologies that appear in datable contexts in Taxila give us a broad relative chronology.

Mekhasanda

A key Peshawar Basin site that can be productively compared to the sacred precincts in Taxila is the small, relatively simple complex of Mekhasanda in the hills above the town of Shābāz Garhī (Figure 6). The site appears to have a phase II foundation and an occupation that continued into the late period of Gandhāran activity (Table 1). While only nine coins were recovered, they do support this dating. Relating to phase II are coins that include one of Kaniṣka I (AD 127-150) and one of Huviṣka (AD 151-189), with phase III corresponding to one of Vāsudeva (AD 190-226), five Vāsudeva imitations (AD 268-308 or later), and one Kushan-Sasanian coin (Mizuno 1969: 94-95). Fortunately, a considerable amount of sculpture was found that also helps in establishing the relative chronology. Phase II occupation is evidenced by three small *stūpa* domes, five narrative panels, fifteen fragments of narrative panels, four sections of schist false gables and 210 related schist architectural fragments (atlantes, lions, garland-bearers, rows of small seated Buddhas in niches and various decorative motifs) (Mizuno 1969: 90, pls. 39-49). Four of the narrative fragments were found in the debris of a looter's hole dug into the core of the main *stūpa*, damaged sculptures that appear to have been deposited at the time of the main *stūpa*'s encasement. Although the form of the original phase II main *stūpa* is obscure, the plinth of the core structure extends under the bases of small *stūpas* 2 and 4, suggesting that they were likely built in phase II soon after the original main *stūpa* was established (Mizuno 1969: 83). Small *stūpas* 3 and 5 may also have an early date though this is less certain. Here the evidence of refurbishment possibly following an earthquake is clear as no early *stūpas* are extant at the site, but considerable quantities of early broken sculpture are present. It seems that at some point all of the early monuments were refurbished.

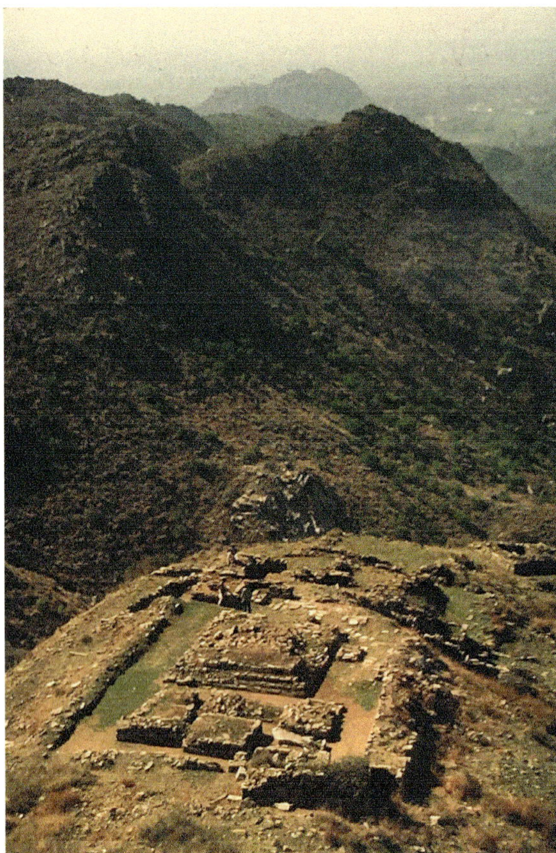

Figure 6. General view of Mekhasanda, Peshawar Basin (Photo: Kurt Behrendt, 1993).

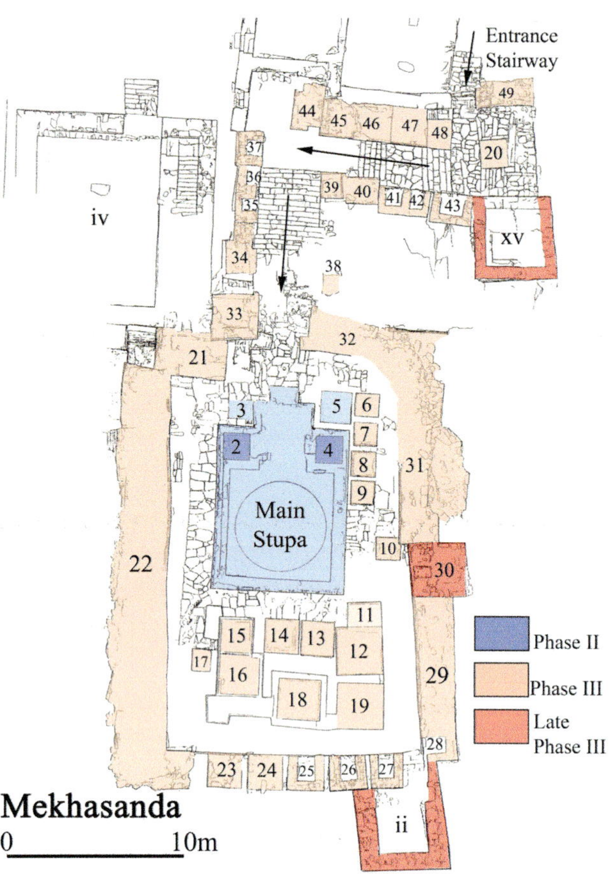

Figure 7. Plan of sacred area at Mekhasanda, Peshawar Basin, with phase II and III construction indicated (Kurt Behrendt, modified from Mizuno 1969: plan 2).

The late additions to Mekhasanda include many small *stūpas* embellished with *in situ* stucco imagery as well as image shrines enclosing the sacred area (Figure 7). This is a pattern which mirrors Jauliāñ (Figure 4) or the lower *stūpa* court at Takht-i-Bāhī (Figure 11). At all of these sites, a relatively small main *stūpa* was surrounded by a tightly packed group of small *stūpas* that in turn were enclosed in a court bounded by small to medium image shrines. Some of the small *stūpas* within the sacred area at Mekhasanda have stepped bases, which are generally comparable to semi-ashlar phase III *stūpas* at Jauliāñ (Behrendt 2004: 165-166). Although only a handful of image shrines survive along the edge of the sacred area (shrines 23-28), the sacred area is bounded by plinths for such structures (bases 21-22, 28, 30, 31). This is confirmed by the presence of a significant number of *in situ* schist and stucco sculptures found in association with these shrines that include a schist Buddha torso in shrine 21, a sculpture base in shrine 33, a schist bodhisattva image recovered to the left of shrine 33, an image socket in shrine 36, the base and feet of a schist Buddha in shrine 43, a schist bodhisattva head in shrine 45, and a large stucco head in front of shrine 45 (Mizuno 1969: 15, 85-89). The total sculptural production at Mekhasanda may help us to understand the relative proportion of schist to stucco devotional icons produced during phase III that once stood in these shrines. About twenty-two devotional icons executed in schist can be estimated (counting heads and bases as full images), while more than 180 stucco heads and body fragments survive. Even given the fragmentary nature of this stucco evidence and the looting that occurred, it seems likely that the majority of image shrines at this site originally housed stucco figures. In other words, there is strong evidence to suggest that the widespread construction of image shrines must have occurred in conjunction with sculptural production in stucco. Thinking in terms of earthquakes it would have been expedient to repair a sites using stucco, which could be moulded or fashioned more rapidly than schist.

Still this could equally reflect a change in sculptural media that occurred over time and not actually be tied to issues of refurbishment.

Late construction at Mekhasanda is limited to two monumental image shrines (shrines ii, xv), although shrine 30 probably can also be so identified. The recovery of a monumental Buddha head and fragments of a second monumental head show that massive images were part of Mekhasanda's sculptural program (Mizuno 1969: 91, fig. 17). Regardless of the placement of these monumental images, their presence demonstrates that Mekhasanda was still receiving patronage in the late part of phase III, at a time when construction of monumental images at other sites was common.

Ranigat

Ranigat is another site that fortunately has a very clear phase II, phase III and late phase III structures and imagery (Table 1). This extensive complex is located at the north-eastern most edge of the Peshawar Basin (Figure 8). As one of the first Buddhist sites to be discovered in Gandhāra (Cole 1883: 2), it suffered

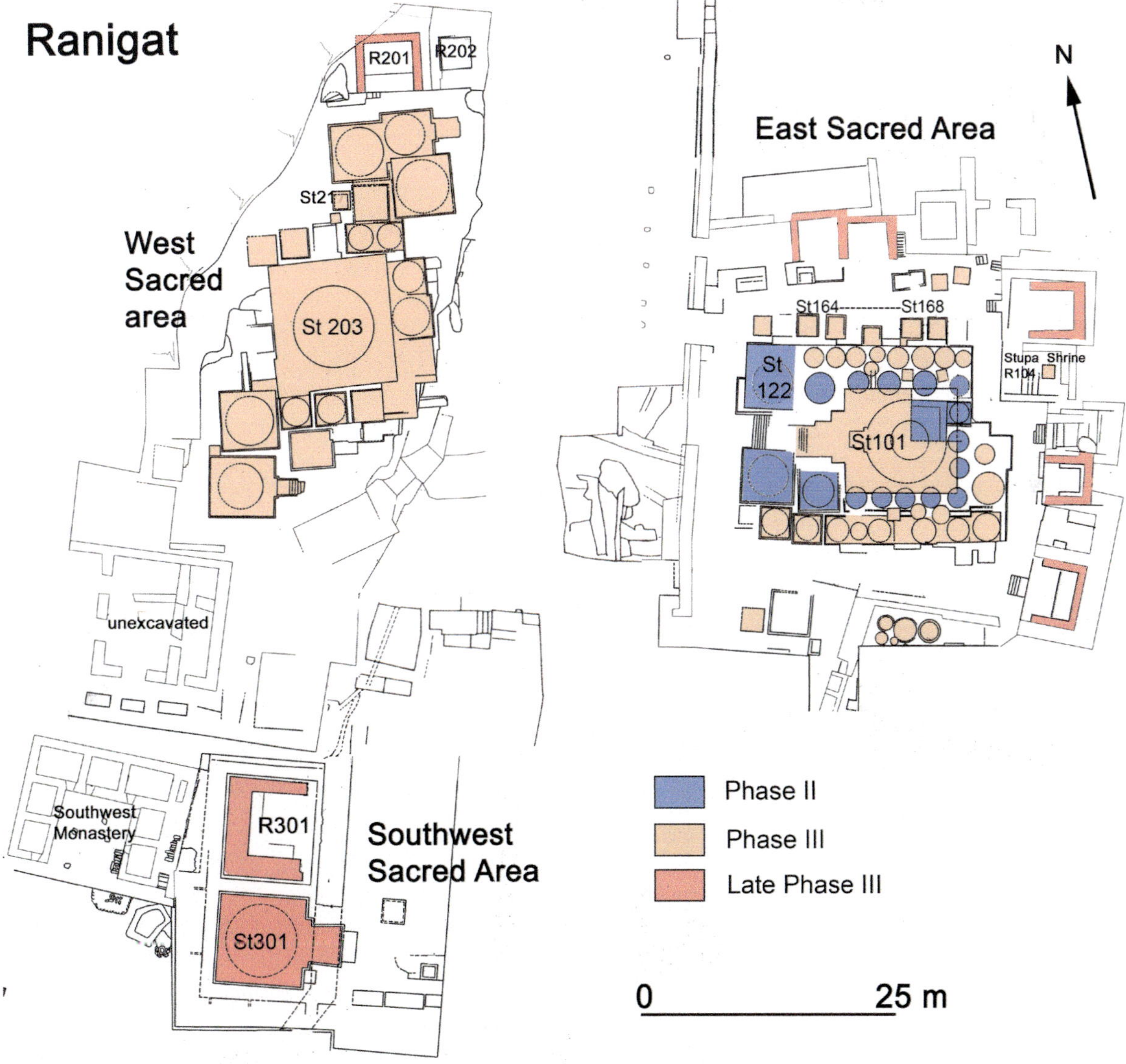

Figure 8. Plan of sacred areas at Ranigat, Peshawar Basin, with phase II and III construction indicated (Kurt Behrendt, modified from Nishikawa 1994: plans 1, 5, 6).

from early undocumented excavation and looting before ultimately being excavated late in the twentieth century. This complex helps to shed light on the chronological development of the Gandhāran sacred area because of the large body of sculpture that was recovered and photographed. The considerable early phase II sculptural record includes nearly eighty damaged narrative reliefs and more than 1600 schist elements including many fragmentary figures and architectural moldings plus 131 pieces of an early *vedikā* fence. Later sculptural finds include the remains of fifty-eight large schist devotional images. The sculpture done in stucco includes 136 heads, 230 fragments of figures, and a handful of *in situ* sculptures (Nishikawa 1994: plates; Behrendt 2004: 303-304). The excavators point out that some of the stucco *stūpas* must have originally been embellished with schist reliefs, which is consistent with patterns of refurbishment observed at the other sites discussed above (Nishikawa, Odani & Namba 1986: 85).

The early founding of the sites is borne out by the numismatic evidence, as eight coins of Wima Kadphises (AD 125-135) were found in conjunction with the core of the main *stūpa*, suggesting it was established during or not long after his reign (Nishikawa et al. 1988: 85, 89; Odani 2000: 838). The site may have had even an earlier foundation as two loose coins of Azes (57-10 BC) were found a short distance from the eastern sacred area in trench II (Errington 1999: 154; Nishikawa et al. 1988: 52, 109). During this early period, twelve phase II small *stūpas* were constructed surrounding the main *stūpa*. Much of the early narrative schist sculpture found at this site originally may have embellished these monuments. Since a later datable phase III encasement of the main *stūpa* engulfed this group of small *stūpas*, the relative time of their establishment is clear.

At the base of the encased main *stūpa's* stairway *in situ* pavement stones were found that had holes bored in them for the donation of coins. Of the more than 180 holes, fourteen still contained coins that included an Azes II coin (AD 6-17), a single Kujūla Kadphises issue (AD 30-78), three of Huviṣka (AD 151), and eight of Vāsudeva (AD 190-226) (Nishikawa, Odani & Namba 1986: 92-93; Odani 2000:834-39). Errington has suggested that the pavement stone coins of Huviṣka and Vāsudeva date to a period of rebuilding (Errington 1999: 197). This group of coins shows that this slab was in place very early in phase III. Overlaying and hence postdating this datable paving stone is a stucco bodhisattva image affixed to the base of small *stūpa* 22 (Nishikawa, Odani & Namba 1986: 92-94). Although only the sandalled feet and traces of the robe remain, the fact that this sculpture can be so securely dated is quite remarkable and helps us to corroborate phase III as the main period of stucco production.

Following the phase III encasement of the main *stūpa*, many small *stūpas* were added to this part of the sacred area. The last of these was a group of eight small *stūpas* (St161-St168), which all have characteristic stepped bases and relatively intact stucco embellishment (Nishikawa 1994: pls. 26-31). These stepped based *stūpas* are directly comparable to similar small *stūpas* at Jauliāñ that were fabricated in semi-ashlar masonry (Behrendt 2004: 165-166) and this is a *stūpa* type also found in the phase III sacred area of Mekhasanda. At all of these sites the stepped *stūpas* were embellished with stucco imagery replacing the phase II *stūpa* type embellished with its schist narrative imagery. The latest structures to be added to this sacred area are a group of monumental shrines along the northern and eastern edges of this sacred area.

Although no excavation report was produced for the west area, photographs provide some information (Nishikawa 1994: pls. 53-87). The west area consists of a main *stūpa* (St203) and more than twenty tightly-packed small *stūpas* that fit well with phase III models. The extant structures appear to be built upon earlier monuments and one wonders if many of these monuments are refurbished earlier structures, especially since so many early schist phase II architectural fragments have been found at Ranigat. The configuration of the west sacred area is unique as the small *stūpas* in this area are so tightly packed around the major *stūpa* St203 that it would have been impossible to circumambulate or otherwise move through this area. While a monumental image shrine stands on the northern edge (R201), no other bounding shrines are extant, but structures have been lost due to erosion along the western edge of this area.

The last period of construction at Ranigat took place in the southwest sacred area at the very end of activity in Gandhāra. Of the ten coins found in this part of the complex, six were minted in the fourth and fifth centuries AD; it is worth noting that four late Alchon Hun coins were found in other parts of the site (Nishikawa et al. 1988: 101-102). This part of the site is composed of two structures, a fairly large *stūpa* (St301), and a massive image shrine (R301), the biggest image shrine thus far uncovered in all of the Peshawar Basin, Taxila or Swat. The shrine is 10.3 m wide and 9.1 m deep, with 2.1-m-thick walls; while there is no way to gauge how high it originally stood, remains of walls in the southwest corner stand 5.8 m high (Nishikawa et al. 1988: 98-99). Massive image shrines like this one have only been found at the Abba Sahib China site in Swat where there is a huge shrine sitting on an 8.2 m square base with extant walls 9.5 m high (Barger & Wright 1941: 25). The presence of this massive image shrine at Ranigat can also be loosely compared to the late colossal Buddha images being fabricated in Afghanistan at sites like Bamiyan. However, the Afghan examples would seem to be part of an even later phenomenon. In any case, evidence from Ranigat, Abba Sahib China, and probably even the Dharmarājikā complex provides us with a clue as to how images were being used at the end of the period of active patronage in the Peshawar Basin, Swat, and Taxila.

Late construction at the major sites of Takht-i-Bāhī, Butkara I and the Dharmarājikā complex

The above micro-chronologies offer some clear patterns regarding the expansion and transformation of the sacred area in Gandhāra. Based on these relative construction chronologies it is worth turning our attention to the major sacred areas of the Dharmarājikā complex in Taxila, Takht-i-Bāhī in the Peshawar Basin and Butkara I in Swat. While these huge, complex sites are less readily discussed, some broad construction patterns are evident. Let us start with the Dharmarājikā complex, as the changing masonry allows for early and late structures to be readily distinguished (Figure 9). The rubble and diaper masonry structures of phase I and II immediately give us a sense for the organization of this site from the time of its foundation through that of the great Kushans. While this is a topic beyond the scope of this paper (see Marshall, 1951), it is worth noting that even among these early structures there is clear evidence of repair and rebuilding; this is especially evident in the northeastern part of the circumambulatory path. When semi-ashlar masonry came to be used, and marking the phase III boundary, again there are many instances of earlier structures being repaired, reinforced, or simply replaced. During phase III the organization of the site changed with image shrines blocking the northern and western entrances into the circumambulatory path of the main *stūpa*. As this cut off major parts of the sacred area, one wonders if many of the earliest structures had been abandoned at this point in the site's history. It seems that the Dharmarājikā complex continued to receive ample patronage during the phase III period. Roughly speaking as many early monuments survive as do late ones and the *stūpa* was encased using semi-ashlar masonry. Monumental image shrines of truly massive proportions were added to the site, indicating patronage continued till the end of the Gandhāran tradition.

The massive complex of Butkara I in Swat roughly follows the same pattern that is observed in Taxila with the Dharmarājikā complex. While we lack the masonry evidence of Taxila, this is a site that was painstakingly excavated giving us a clear sense of its relative chronology (Faccenna 1980) (Figure 10). There is a clear early core of the site that can roughly be attributed to the time of the great Kushans and before (phase I and II). Again there is considerable evidence that these early structures were repaired and modified in phase III. In terms of patronage in the early and late periods there is clear evidence to show that about as many structures were built during phases I and II as were during phase III and later (Butkara has a very late occupation). This follows what was observed at the Dharmarājikā. It is worth noting that in phase III the organization of the site was considerably modified and that a majority of the later structures were clustered together, suggesting different parts of the site were important for the early and late communities.

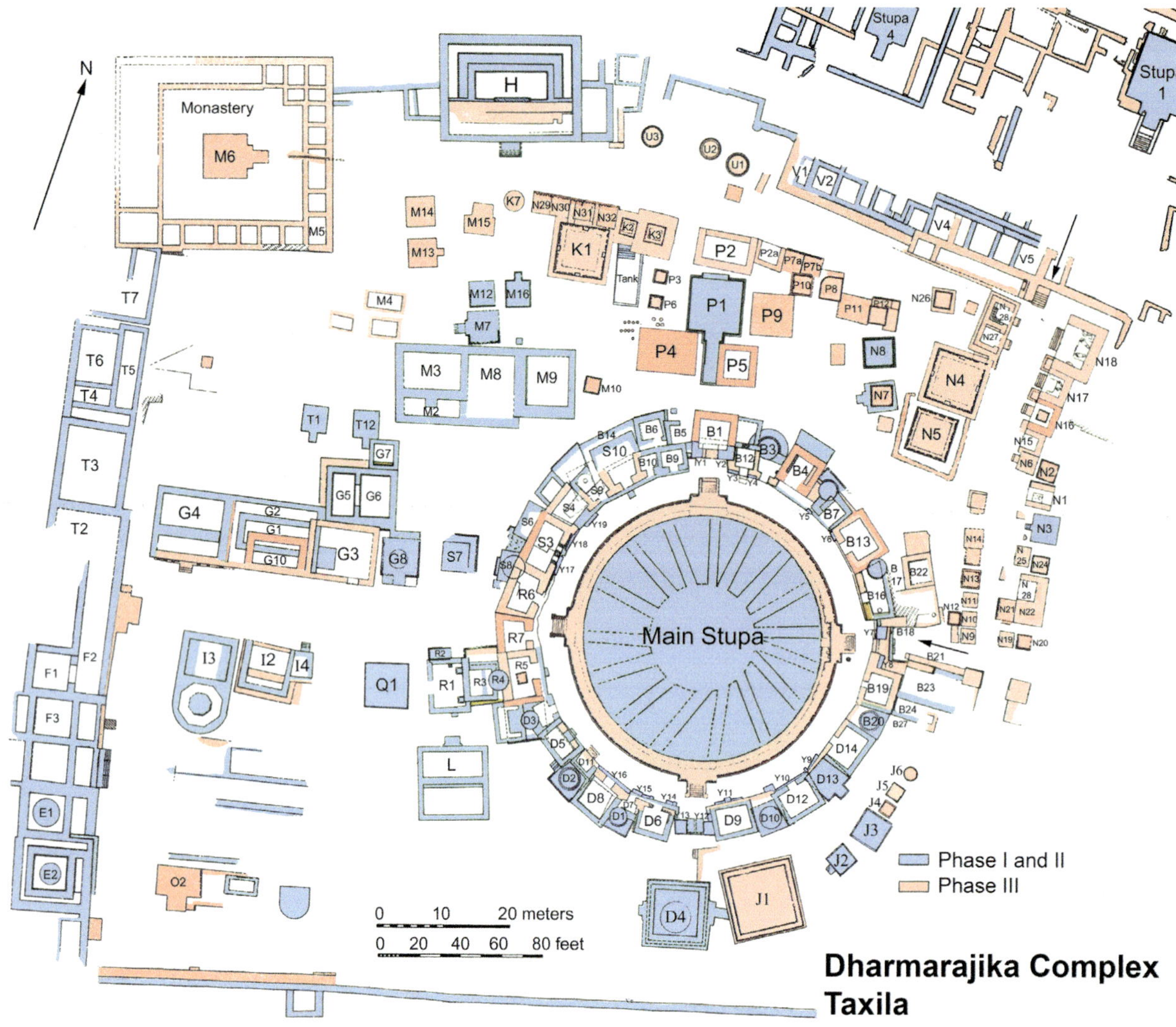

Figure 9. Plan of sacred area at the Dharmarājikā complex, Taxila, showing phase II and III construction (Kurt Behrendt, modified from Marshall 1951: pl. 45).

The Peshawar Basin site of Takht-i-Bāhī (Figure 11; Table 1) would appear to be somewhat later than the Dhārmarājika complex and Butkara I. The earliest part of the sacred area in the lower court is defined by the P1 main *stūpa* and a tight cluster of small *stūpas*, which in turn are enclosed by banks of image shrines built during phase III. There are also late phase III monumental image shrines in this area. The lower court at Takht-i-Bāhī is most comparable to the late sacred areas of Mekhasanda (Figure 7) or Jauliāñ (Figure 4). While large numbers of schist narrative relief panels were recovered at this site, nearly all of the small *stūpas* were embellished in stucco imagery. Considerable refurbishment is evident around the P1 main *stūpa*; at the time of the initial excavation early photos indicate that many of these small *stūpas* have stucco imagery (indicated with cross-hatching). While the excavations at this site took place in the late nineteenth and early twentieth century, a rough sculptural count can be established. From phase II there are forty-seven narrative panels, forty-two fragments, and twenty-one false gable panels (some of these must date to phase III). From the phase III and later there are 110 un-photographed standing and squatting figures along with forty-six heads from an 1871 excavation (Wilcher 1871: 434-437). Photographed sculptures include twenty-four Buddhas and bodhisattvas, twenty-four heads, two bases, nine composite or 'Śrāvastī' panels, fourteen life-sized stucco heads, and one monumental head (for breakdown see Behrendt 2004: 297-300). The evidence suggests significant, but still limited, phase II

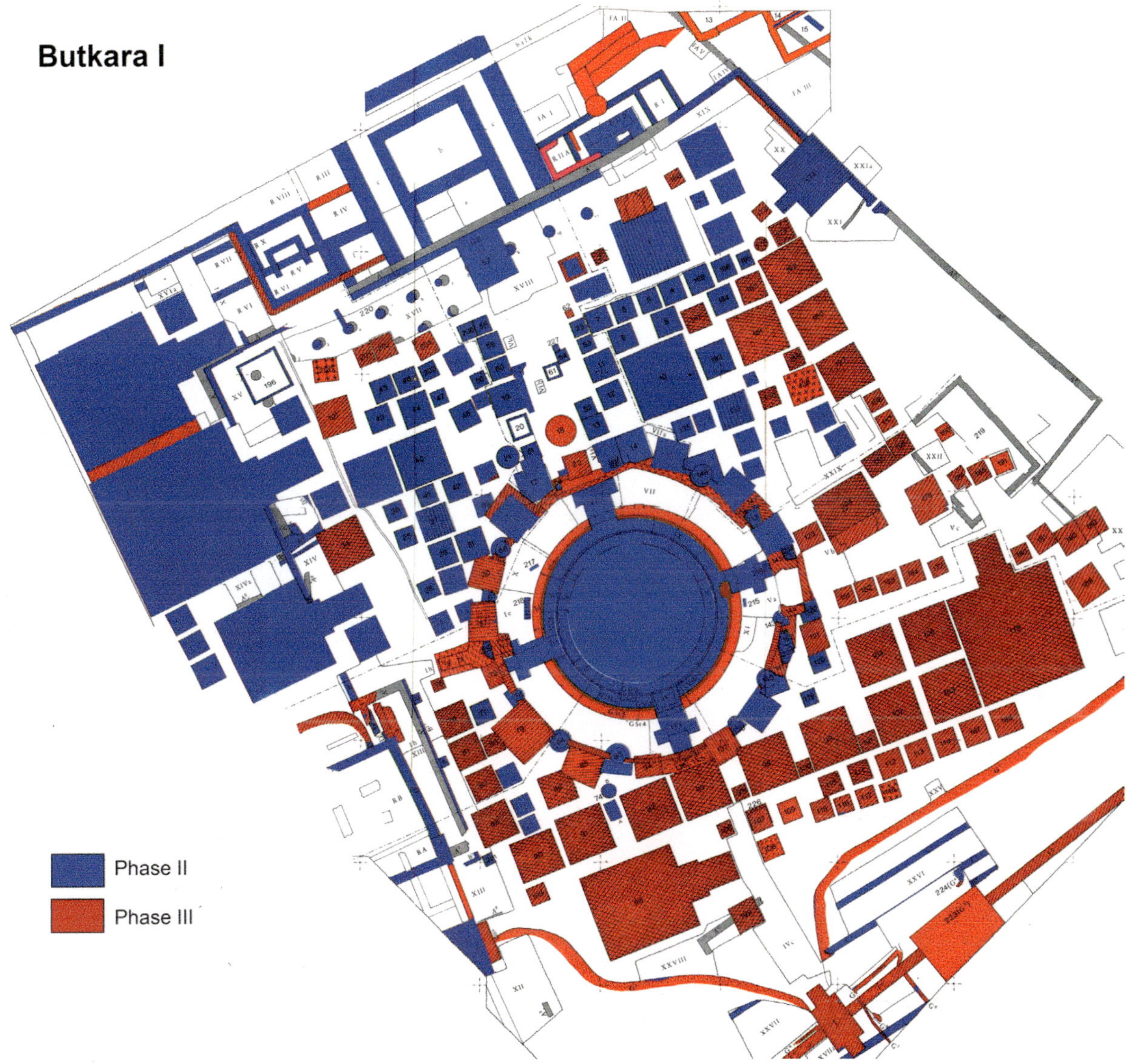

Figure 10. The sacred areas of Butkara I, Swat, grouping phase I and II construction and phase III and later construction (Kurt Behrendt, modified from Faccenna 1980, III: no. 1, pl. VI).

activity and then major patronage in phase III and late phase III. While only a single monumental stucco head was recovered, no fewer than fourteen monumental image shrines stand at this site marking it as one of the latest active Gandhāran centres that are known.

Conclusion

Hopefully this brief survey of some key Gandhāran sites helps to broadly clarify patterns of foundation, expansion, and repair that occurred between the first century, or centuries when sites were being founded, and the fifth to early sixth centuries when major patronage in this region came to an end. Damage from use and an ongoing series of earthquakes necessitated the refurbishment of key devotional early monuments. Often the imagery of early monuments was replaced with sculpture done in stucco, which helps to explain the systematic deposition of broken re-used stone sculptures. Stucco seems to have been a popular medium for refurbished monuments as well as for embellishing new structures. It would seem that schist devotional images were also reused or recontextualized, as so much of this category of

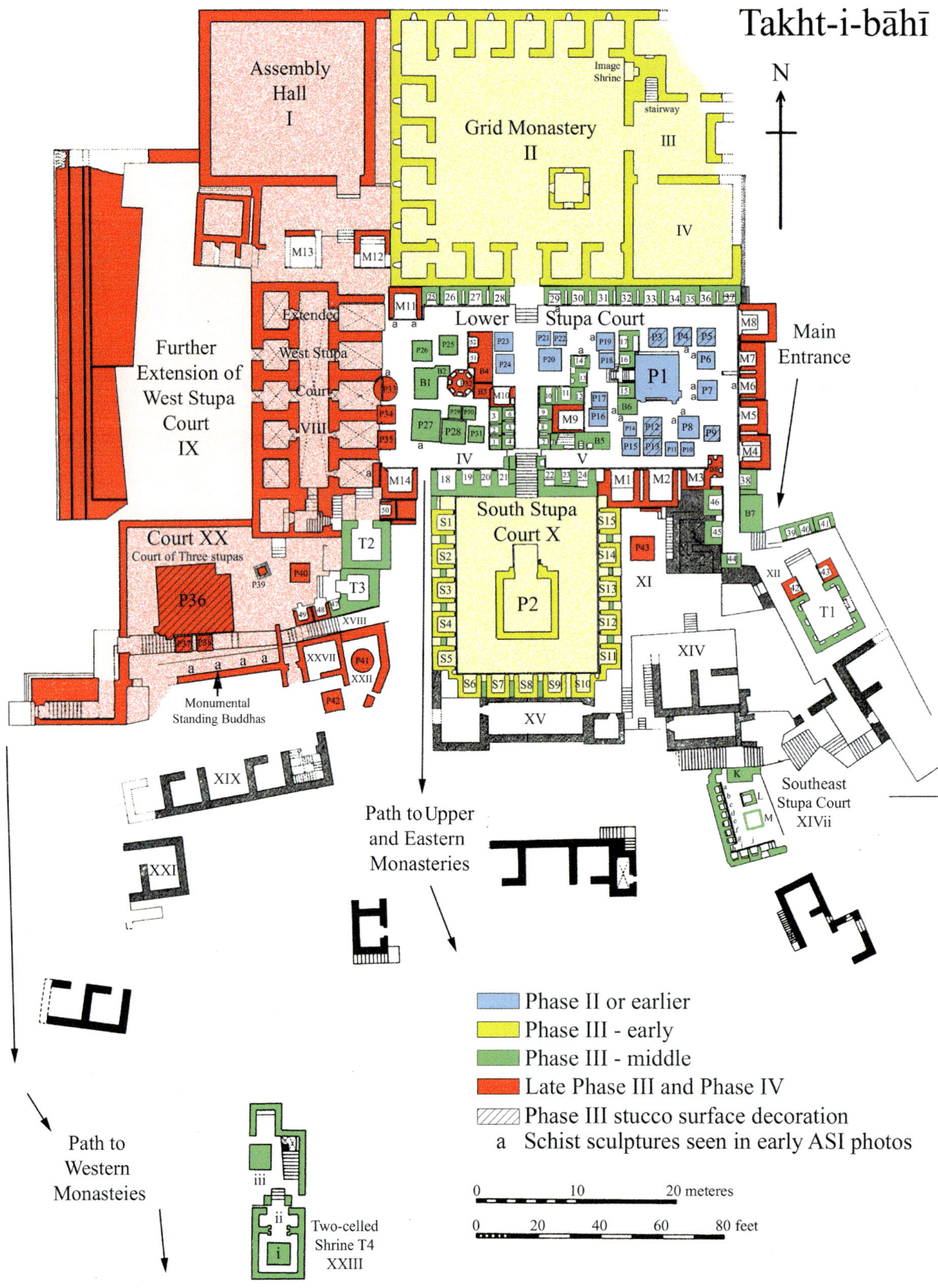

Figure 11. Sacred area and monastery at Takht-i-Bāhī, Peshawar Basin, showing phase II and III construction (Kurt Behrendt, modified from Hargreaves 1914: pl. XVII).

		Kālawān	Jauliāñ	Mekhasanda	Ranigat	Takht-i-Bāhī
Phase II and earlier		Diaper masonry	Diaper masonry	Irregular diaper masonry	Irregular diaper masonry	Irregular diaper masonry
	Coins: pre-Kushan to Kujūla Kadphises	2	6		4	x
	Coins: Wima Takto to Huviṣka	28	14 +11 unidentified	2	11	x
	Early *stūpas* and fragments			210 fragments 3 *stūpa* domes	1730 fragments	x
	Narrative and false gable panels	23		27	80	109
Phase III and later		Semi-ashlar masonry	Semi-ashlar masonry	Irregular diaper masonry	Irregular diaper masonry	Irregular diaper masonry
	Coins: Vāsudeva and late Kushans	167	37	6	8	x
	Coins: post-Kushan	6	51	1	10	x
	Large schist devotional images	4	3 + 2 fragments	22	58	45 + 110 with no photos
	Small to medium image shrines	5	49	9 + long bases originally ~50		58
	Stucco heads and major fragments	63	1000+ heads and many fragments	180 heads many fragments	180 heads, 230 fragments	14 heads
	In situ stucco imagery	some	great many	many	some	some
	Stepped *stūpas* stucco		x	x	x	x
	Monumental images		multiple large stucco images	2 heads		1 head
	Monumental image shrines		3	2 + 1 base	7	14

Table 1. Summary of finds at selected sites.

sculpture survives at sites like Mekhasanda or Takht-i-Bāhī in conjunction with suitable image shrines. Considering these sites as a whole it appears that there was extensive construction during phase II which corresponds to the time of the Great Kushans. Perhaps surprisingly, the architectural evidence reveals as much if not more construction in the post-Kushan period, my phase III. Assuming earthquakes necessitated ongoing repair and given the wealth of these Gandhāran Buddhist establishments, it should not surprise us that so much late construction is extant in the sacred areas. Moreover in the late period, the sites continued to expand with the construction of many new image shrines, *stūpas*, and monasteries. When we consider the much debated issue of sculptural chronology it would seem that the latter half of the Gandhāran tradition witnessed the greatest construction of shrines suited to housing large devotional icons and that correspondingly much of this imagery must date between the third and fifth century, not to the time of the Great Kushans as is so often suggested.

References

Barger E. & Wright P. 1941. Excavations in Swat and Explorations in the Oxus Territories of Afghanistan: A Detailed Report of the 1938 Expedition. *Memoirs of the Archaeological Survey of India*. Delhi: Manager of Publications.

Beal S. 1884. *Si-Yu-Ki, Buddhist Records of the Western World Translated from the Chinese of Hiuen Tsiang A.D. 629*. London: Trubner and Co. (reprinted 1983, Delhi: Oriental Book Reprint Corporation).

Behrendt K. 2004. *The Buddhist Architecture of Gandhāra*. Leiden: Brill.

Behrendt K. 2006. Relic Shrines of Gandhara: A Reinterpretation of the Archaeological Evidence. Pages 83-103 in P. Brancaccio and K. Behrendt (eds), *Gandharan Buddhism: Archaeology, Art, Texts*. Vancouver: UBC Press.

Behrendt K. 2009. The Ancient Reuse and Recontextualization of Gandharan Images: Second through Seventh Centuries CE. *Journal of South Asian Studies* 25: 11-27.

Cole H. H. 1883. *Memorandum on Ancient Monuments in Eusofzai, with a Description of the Explorations Undertaken from the 4th February to the 16th April 1883: Curator of Ancient Monuments in India, Illustrated by a Map, 8 Plans of Buildings and 17 Plates of Rough Sketches, June 1882*. Simla: Government Central Branch Press.

Errington E. 1993. In Search of Palusha, a City of the Central Gandhara Plain. *Bulletin of the Asia Institute* 7: 55-66.

Errington E. 1999. Numismatic Evidence for Dating the Buddhist Remains of Gandhara. *Silk Road Art and Archaeology* 6: 191-216.

Faccenna D. 1980. *Butkara I (Swāt, Pakistan) 1956-1962*. 5 Vols. Rome: IsMEO.

Hargreaves H. 1914. Excavations at Takht-i-Bāhī. *Annual Report of the Archaeological Survey of India 1910-11*. Calcutta: Superintendent of Government Printing.

Kuwayama S. 1997. *The Main Stupa at Shāh-jī-kī-dherī: A Chronological Outlook*. Kyoto: Kyoto University Institute for Research in Humanities.

Kuwayama S. 2006. Pilgrimage Route Changes and the Decline of Gandhara. Pages 107-134 in P. Brancaccio and K. Behrendt (eds) *Gandharan Buddhism: Archaeology, Art, Texts*. Vancouver: UBC Press.

Marshall J. 1916. Excavations at Taxila. *Annual Report of the Archaeological Survey of India 1912—13*. Calcutta: Superintendent of Government Printing.

Marshall J. 1921. Excavations at Taxila: The Stupas and Monasteries at Jauliāñ. *Memoires of the Archaeological Society of India*. 7. Calcutta: Superintendent of Government Printing.

Marshall J. 1936. Exploration at Taxila 1930-34. *Annual Report of the Archaeological Survey of India for the Years 1930-31, 1931-32, 1932-33 & 1933-34*. Delhi: Manager of Publications.

Marshall J. 1951. *Taxila: An Illustrated Account of Archaeological Excavations Carried out at Taxila under the Orders of the Government of India between the Years 1913 and 1934* (3 volumes). Cambridge: Cambridge University Press.

Mizuno S. (ed) 1969. *Mekhasanda: Buddhist Monastery in Pakistan Surveyed in 1962-67*. Kyoto: Kyoto University Press.

National Geophysical Data Center/World Data Service, *Significant Earthquake Database, National Geophysical Data Center*. NOAA. Doi:10.7289/V5TD9V7K.

Nishikawa K. 1994. *Ranigat: A Buddhist Site in Gandhara Pakistan Surveyed 1983-92*. Kyoto: Kyoto University Press.

Nishikawa K. et al. 1988. *Gandhara 2: Preliminary Report on the Comprehensive Survey of Gandhara Buddhist Sites*. Kyoto: Kyoto University Press.

Nishikawa K., Odani N., & Namba, Y. 1986. *Preliminary Report on the Comprehensive Survey of Gandhara Buddhist Sites, 1983, 1984*. Kyoto: Kyoto University Press.

Odani N. 2000. New Discoveries from Ranigat. Pages 831-841 in M. Taddei and G. De Marco (eds), *South Asian Archaeology 1997*. Rome: IsIAO.

Olivieri L.M. et. al. 2014. *The Last Phases of the Urban Site of Bir-Kot-Ghwandai (Barikot): The Buddhist Sites of Gumbat and Amluk-Dara (Barikot)*. Lahore: Sang-e Meel Publications.

Wilcher F. 1871. Report on the Exploration of the Buddhist Ruins at Takht-i-bai, January to April 1871. *Punjab Government Gazette, Supplement 6th August 1874*. 528-32. Reproduced pages 434-437 in E. Errington, The Western Discovery of the Art of Gandhara and the Finds of Jamalgarhi. (Ph.D. thesis, University of London, 1987.)